Yovhannēs Tʿlkurancʿi
and
The Mediaeval Armenian Lyric Tradition

University of Pennsylvania
Armenian Texts and Studies

Supported by the Sarkes Tarzian Fund

SERIES EDITOR
Michael E. Stone

YOVHANNĒS TʿLKURANCʿI and THE MEDIAEVAL ARMENIAN LYRIC TRADITION

by
James R. Russell

Scholars Press
Atlanta, Georgia

Yovhannēs Tʿlkurancʿi
and
The Mediaeval Armenian
Lyric Tradition

by
James R. Russell

© 1987
University of Pennsylvania
Armenian Texts and Studies

Library of Congress Cataloging in Publication Data

Russell, James R.
  Yovhannes Tʿlkurants ʿi and the Mediaeval Armenian
lyric tradition.

  (University of Pennsylvania Armenian texts and studies ;
no. 7)
  Includes translations of poems by Tʿlkurants ʿi
Hovhannes.
  Thesis—Oxford University.
  Bibliography: p.
  I. Yovhannes Tʿlkurants ʿi, 14th/15th cent.
II. Title. III. Series.
PK8547.H58A27   1987   891'.99213   85-22066
ISBN 0-89130-929-2 (alk. paper)
ISBN 0-89130-930-6 (pbk. : alk. paper)

Printed in the United States of America
on acid free paper

TABLE OF CONTENTS

LIST OF ABBREVIATIONS

AH - <u>Azgagrakan Handēs</u>, Šuši, Tiflis.

Ačařean - H. Ačařean, <u>Hayerēn armatakan bařaran</u>, Erevan, 1926.

Aḷayan - Ē. B. Aḷayan, <u>Aknarkner miǰin grakan hayereni patmut^cyan</u>, Vol. I, Erevan, 1972.

Ar. - Arabic.

Arm. - Armenian

Bedrossian - M. Bedrossian, <u>New Dictionary: Armenian-English</u>, Venice, 1879.

BSOAS - <u>Bulletin of the School of Oriental and African Studies</u>.

C - Bishop N. (orayr Poḷarean) Covakan, (Xew) Yovhannēs T^clkuranc^ci: Taḷagirk^c, Jerusalem, 1958. Poems are given by page number.

Frik - Abp. Tirayr, <u>Frik Diwan</u>, New York, 1952. Roman numerals refer to poems.

Hübschmann - H. Hübschmann, <u>Armenische Grammatik</u>, Leipzig, 1897.

JAOS - <u>Journal of American Oriental Studies</u>.

KE - H. M. Poturean, <u>Kostandin Erznkac^ci, XIV daru žoḷovrdakan banasteḷc</u>, Venice, 1905. Roman numerals refer to poems.

Maten. - Mesrop Maštoc^c Institute of Ancient Manuscripts (Matendaran), Erevan.

MN - Ed. Xondkaryan, <u>Mkrtič^c Naḷaš</u>, Erevan, 1965. Roman numerals refer to poems.

Mnac^cakanyan - A. Mnac^cakanyan, <u>Haykakan miǰnadaryan žoḷovrdakan erger</u>, Erevan, 1956.

MS - Manuscript.

NK - Nahapet K^cuč^cak, <u>Hayreni Kargav</u>, Erevan, 1957. Roman numerals refer to poems.

NP - New Persian.

P - Ēm. Pivazyan, <u>Hovhannes T^clkuranc^ci: Taḷer</u>, Erevan, 1960. Roman numerals refer to poems.

Phl - Pahlavi.

RDEA, REArm - <u>Rēvue des études arméniennes</u> (and New Series).

Sayat^c-Nova - M. S. Hasrat^cyan, <u>Sayat^c-Nova</u>, Erevan, 1959. Roman numerals refer to poems.

Tk. - Turkish.

YE - A. Srapyan, <u>Hovhannes Erznkac^ci</u>, Erevan, 1958. Roman numberals refer to poems.

ŽHLBB - A. S. Ḷaribyan, ed. <u>Žamanakakic^c Hayoc^c lezvi bac^catrakan bařaran</u>, Vols. I-IV, Erevan, 1969-1980.

To my parents, Joseph and Charlotte Russell

ACKNOWLEDGEMENTS

This book began as a thesis presented in Trinity Term, 1977, for the degree of B.Litt. in Armenian Studies at Oxford University under the supervision of Prof. C. Dowsett; his insights are acknowledged in the text, although in many cases I have revised previous interpretations. I thank Prof. Leo Hamalian for permission to publish here 'Spring passes into yet another spring' (P XIV), which appeared with prefatory notes as 'Yovhannēs T^{c}lkuranc^{c}i, Master Minstrel,' <u>Ararat Quarterly</u>, Vol. 20, No. 3, Summer 1979, 61-62.

It is a pleasure here to record my gratitude to the Executive Committee of the Armenian General Benevolent Union, Alex Manoogian Cultural Fund, for their very generous support towards the publication of this book; I thank also Prof. Michael Stone and the Armenian Texts and Studies Series of the University of Pennsylvania.

I owe the profoundest debt of gratitude, however, to Alma Mater, Columbia College, for the Kellett Fellowship that enabled me to read at Oxford, and for continuing inspiration, no less to the teacher today than to the student of fifteen years ago.

Columbia University,
New York
June 1986

INTRODUCTION

The work of Yovhannēs T^{c}lkuranc^{c}i, a lyric poet of Mediaeval Armenia, is little known in the West. I offer here a translation into English of T^{c}lkuranc^{c}i's poems, the first comprehensive rendering of the poet's work into a foreign language. Points of theme (including development of the given theme in mediaeval Armenian lyrics), vocabulary, grammar and syntax are discussed in the commentary to each translated poem. In this Introduction will be summarized the early roots of Armenian lyric poetry in a country intimately linked to the culture of pre-Islamic Iran, in particular the Parthian gōsān ('minstrel') tradition, and the transmission of Armenian literature in the fifth to tenth centuries A.D. A gradual shift westwards of centres of Armenian culture and population with the growth of Cilician Armenia is noted later, with the influence of Western Armenian dialects on the development of the mediaeval Armenian vernacular in Cilicia and other regions. Mediaeval Armenian poetry was profoundly influenced in this period by the poetic traditions of the surrounding Muslim cultures. In order to place Yovhannēs T^{c}lkuranc^{c}i within this Armenian poetic tradition, one must consider the probable dates of his life, the character of his time, his birthplace, and the themes of his poems. A model of his thought is proposed on the basis of the latter, with reference to Armenian and some Muslim poetry. The poet's patron saint, and the tools of his craft: rhyme, metre, prosody and vocabulary--are to be discussed, as well. Detailed consideration of many of these subjects is left, however, to the notes on each poem.

In ancient days, particularly during the reign of the Armenian Arsacids (A.D. 66-428),[1] Armenia was strongly influenced by the culture of neighbouring Zoroastrian Iran. The Classical Armenian historians: Agathangelos, Mošēs Xorenac^{c}i and others--relate that the Armenian king sat at the right hand of the Iranian šahǎnšah at feasts; before the overthrow of the Iranian Arsacid house circa A.D. 226 by the Persian Ardašīr, son of Pāpak and the founder of the Sasanian dynasty, the Iranian (Parthian) and Armenian kings exchanged their sons and daughters in marriage. Innumerable details, from the stylised headdress of the Parthian horseman with its protective earflaps that was worn as a crown by the Armenian monarch, to the wealth of Parthian and Pahlavi loan words in the Armenian language, attest to the country's long and intimate association with Iran. The conversion of the Armenians to Christianity by St. Gregory the Illuminator in the reign of Tiridates III early in the fourth century marks a decisive break with the Mazdā-worshipping Sasanians, and in the razm ud bazm (Phl. 'war and feasting') of the Sasanian kings Armenia began

1

to figure more in the former than in the latter. Yet Armenia was still probably to be counted as Ērān 'of the Aryans' amongst the haft kišwarān (Phl. 'seven climes') of the world. For although Iran rarely proselytised its faith amongst the indigenous peoples of anērān 'the non-Aryans', even in the kišwār of Iran, which it ruled, or Rūm (the Eastern Christian empire), which it fought, the Sasanians thought it as politic to make war on Armenian Christianity and to re-establish the Zoroastrian church in Armenia. The Armenian historian Eliše tells us that the Magi sought to make Armenia i mi awrēns 'of one law' with the rest of Iran.[2] Persian persecution of the Armenian Church and the noble faction faithful to it culminated in the Battle of Avarayr, A.D. 451, which was a military disaster but a spiritual triumph for the Christians, who were allowed to preserve their faith intact.

But if the awrēnk^c of the Prophet Zarathushtra had failed ultimately to establish themselves in Armenia, other Iranian mores remained, notably in language and literature. The Armenian language is richer in Middle Iranian loans than perhaps any other non-Iranian tongue. Armenian poetry was as strongly influenced. Most pre-Islamic Iranian secular literature, according to M. Boyce, was in the form of minstrel poetry, and was not committed to writing: 'The Sasanian minstrel was entertainer of king and commoner . . . present at the graveside and at the feast; eulogist, satirist, story-teller, musician; recorder of past achievements and commentator of his own times.'[3] The Parthian word gōsān 'minstrel' survives as the Armenian loan word gusan. The Armenian king Aršak died in captivity in Persia while being entertained by his former minister Drastamat in the Fortress of Oblivion, who urax arnēr zna gusanawk^c 'delighted him with gusans' (P^cawstos Buzand, Hist. Arm. 5.7), and King Pap was murdered while nayēr ēnd pēs pēs ambox gusanac^cn 'he looked upon the motley crowd of gusans.' In a sermon attributed to the fifth-century Catholicos Yovhannēs Mandakuni, who was alarmed at the popularity of this secular art, we find a bitter attack on the gusank^c, 'On the Heathen Theatres of the Demonic' (Vasn anawrēn t^caterac^c diwakanac^c). If any 'plays' in these 'theatres' were written down, none has survived. Still, the eleventh-century scholar and cleric Gregory Magistros in his Letters (XXXIII) provides this fragment of an ancient lyrical lament spoken by the dying Armenian king Artašēs I:

> O tayr inj zcux cxani
> Ew zarawawtn Nawasardi,
> ZVazeln ełanc^c ew zvargeln ełjeruac^c:
> Mek^c p^cox haruak^c ew t^cmbki harkaneak^c,
> Orpēs awrēn ēr t^cagaworac^c.

'Who would give me the chimney smoke / And the morning in the New Year month[4] / The running of the hinds and the skipping of the stags? / We blew the trumpet

and struck the drum / As is the way of kings.'[5] A similar recollection of
solemn, regal music is found in a Pahlavi text, probably a translation of a
Parthian original, Ayādgār Ī Zarērān 'The Memorial of Zarēr', which describes
a scene at the court of Vistasp: . . . tumbag zad ud nāy pazdēnd ud gāwdumb
wāng kardēnd '. . . They struck the drum and played the reed-flute and made
the trumpet call.'[6]

Unfortunately, there survive only occasional fragments of the Armenian
lyric poetry of ancient days. But it seems certain that minstrel poetry, recited or sung to musical accompaniment, flourished in Arsacid Armenia, and
bore many resemblances to the art as practised in Iran. Moses Xorenac^{c}i, for
instance, records a song on the birth of the god Vahagn (the Iranian
Verethraghna) and adds (Hist. Arm., 1.31): zAys ergelov omanc^c bambr̄mamb luak^c
isk akanjawk^c merovk^c 'We heard with our own ears how some sang this with the
bambir̄n (a musical instrument, probably a drum or cymbals).' Pre-Islamic
Iranian documents of a secular character are also meagre though, as in Armenia,
perhaps because of the oral tradition in Zoroastrian culture that did not en-
courage the development of written literature.[7]

Christianity changed decisively the character of Armenian literature in
this regard at least. In Armenia, the alphabet created by St. Mesrop Maštoc^c
and his disciples circa A.D. 406-407[8] was used at first by the clergy in
translation of theological, historical and philosophical literature from the
Greek and Syriac, and in the composition of similar works in the fifth-century
dialect of the province of Ayrarat. But classical Armenian literature pos-
sesses numerous hymns (Arm. šarakank^c), some of which are attributed to
Maštoc^c himself. Traces of the ancient poetic images and forms are seen in
these. Dawt^{c}ak the Poet (7th cent.) wrote a lament for Jewanšēr, great prince
of the Alans, which contains many fine, poetic passages: 'He sat like a lion
in its lair / And his enemies trembled before him, even when he was still
. . .' Music, never absent from secular life, was also cultivated at Armenian monasteries, and Samuēl of Kamrjajor (10th cent.) was particularly renowned for his musical talents; many manuscripts were marked with xazk^c, or
supralineal neumes.[9] It seems that minstrelsy in Armenia, however altered by
subsequent influences, had ancient origins, and T^{c}lkuranc^{c}i still used the
ancient Parthian word gusan to describe himself.

The Muslim Arabs sacked the capital of the Armenia marzbanate, Duin, in
A.D. 640,[10] and the Sasanian army of Yazdagird III was routed eleven years
later at Nehāvand. Armenia remained under the dominion of the Caliphate until
a prince of the Armenian Bagratuni family, Ašot I (A.D. 885-890), led a successful rebellion against the ^{c}Abbāsids and was crowned by them. The new
Bagratid kingdom, with its capital Ani on the banks of the Araxes, enjoyed
relative independence, and a second Armenian kingdom was founded by the

Arcruni prince Gagik in the province of Vaspurakan with its capital at Van.
There is ample evidence to indicate that Armenian artistic and literary cre-
ativity burgeoned in this period, under the patronage of princes and merchants.

Wealthy men commissioned illuminated manuscripts, built palaces, and
subscribed to the construction of churches. But Armenia's prosperity suffered
from the onslaught of the Seljuk Turks under their chieftain Alp Arslan, before whom the Byzantine army of Emperor Romanos Diogenēs scattered in igno-
minious defeat at Manazkert in 1071. Many Armenians fled from their devastated
ancestral highlands, west into Cappadocia, or wouthwest across the Taurus
mountains into Cilicia. There, the Armenian prince R̊uben founded a state in
1080; the state became a kingdom with the coronation of Levon I in 1198. The
Rubenid kingdom in Cilicia remained an important centre of Armenian culture
until the fall of its capital, Sis, to the Mamluks in A.D. 1375; the last
Armenian king, Levon V Lusignan, died in exile in Paris in 1393.[11]

It has been suggested that the fall of the Arsacid state weakened the
position of the Classical Armenian dialect, which lost its status as a state
language, although its importance as a literary and sacerdotal medium remained
undiminished; Karst has also noted Armenian migrations westwards and away from
the 'central' province of Ayrarat as a factor in the weakening of Classical
Armenian, which had been the language of that region.[12] (It seems unlikely to
this writer, however, that Armenian was written in Arsacid times, whether or
not it was employed officially at court: all epigraphic evidence for the
period was Greek, Aramaic, and, after 428, Middle Iranian.) Yovhannēs
Erznkac^{c}i, writing in A.D. 1293, cited Step^{c}annos Siwnec^{c}i (8th cent.), who,
in his Interpretation of Grammar, divided the Armenian language into eight
dialects: ostanik 'court' or miǰerkreay 'central' Armenian, i.e., the dialect
of Ayrarat; and seven ezerakan 'peripheral' dialects. Texts of the seventh
century appear to exhibit the influence of these ezerakan dialects; indeed,
dialect forms may be detected in the fifth-century Armenian writings themselves.[13] In the sixth and seventh centuries, too, the Hellenophilic school
introduced complex syntactical structures and abstruse, highly synthetic gram-
matical forms and compound words into Armenian; many a reader must have needed
some knowledge of Greek before he could unravel the text in the strange version of his native language that lay before him. This factor may have con-
tributed to the gradual relegation of grabar to the status of a purely
literary language.[14]

In the twelfth century, Mxit^{c}ar Goš and Mxit^{c}ar Herac^{c}i wrote texts in
vernacular Armenian on law and medicine that practical men of affairs could
readily understand and use. In his book Therapy for Fevers, Mxit^{c}ar Herac^{c}i
wrote Ew arari zsa gełǰuk ew arjak barbaṙov, zi diwrahas lic^{c}i amenayn
ĕnt^{c}erc^{c}ołac^c 'And I made this in a rustic and prosaic dialect, that it might

be easily accessible to all readers.'[15] Amirdovlat[c] Amasiac[c]i wrote in what
he called ašxarhabar 'the vernacular', and St. Nersēs Šnorhali wrote several
works in the ašxarhakan xōsk[c] 'vernacular speech.'[16] This vernacular tongue
was an aggregate of mainly Western Armenian dialects, differing considerably
from Classical Armenian grabar, in phonetics, syntax, and grammar.[17] It ab-
sorbed many loan-words from Arabic, New Persian and Turkish; H. Ačařean counted
4702 in Mediaeval Armenian, of which he reckoned only 73 are in common use in
modern literary Armenian.[18] But in fact most spoken Armenian dialects still
contain a large proportion of loan-words from Turkish and from Arabic or
Persian via Turkish. Only where the standard literary language has been im-
posed on everyday speech have such loan-words greatly decreased--often to be
replaced, however, only by new loans from Russian or French. Much of the
vocabulary is still, as in grabar, Parthian. Classical Armenian did not dis-
appear; it continued to play an important part in ecclesiastical life and
learning, and experienced a revival amongst the Armenian Catholic Mxit[c]arist
monks of Venice and Vienna in the eighteenth century. It remained a model of
style, but its use in secular writings declined steadily, and a literary vernacular, also shaped by the Mxit[c]arists, came into wide use. The uses of
Mediaeval Armenian were varied, indeed; there was a wide demand for entertaining and edifying literature, which was collected in manuscript miscel-
lanies. Prose works, long popular throughout the Near East such as the
Wisdom of Ahikar, the Alexander Romance, and the History of the City of Bronze,
appear in Armenian translation in these manuscripts, together with works on
astrology, illustrated reference books on the identification and use of medi-
cinal herbs, treatises on mathematics, demonologies and angelologies,[19] and
poetry.

Mediaeval Armenian lyric poetry is a descendant of the ancient minstrel
tradition, with links to the Parthian gōsāns. And it was durable. For it
should perhaps be considered that, for all the vicissitudes of Armenian history, the gusan did not really rely on a reigning prince unless he was a rare
talent. Most minstrels probably lived off village weddings and the like.
Some were monks, supported in their orders (often in more than holy poverty,
if we are to believe the poets' own bitter attacks on hypocritical contemporaries). And this leads one to observe that, in the centuries after the
coming of Christianity, the imagery of the Song of Songs and the hymns of
Christian poets such as Ephrem Syrus (whose works were translated into Classical Armenian) on minstrel poetry had great effect. Subsequently, Armenians
acquired the use of rhyme from the Arabs, as well as the vast store of extravagant and elaborate imagery familiar to any reader of Persian or Ottoman
Turkish verse. These images are of love and the beloved, mainly, and Manuk
Abełyan has summarised their use in Mediaeval Armenian lyric poetry, as

follows:[20] The beloved's hair is a cloud. Her body is a slender tree. She minces like a partridge. (The kak^{c}aw 'partridge' dance is a feature of pagan Armenia also, though, so the image where it appears may sometimes be native.) Her eyes are the sun and moon (but they outshine both these celestial bodies), or bottomless seas teeming with fish. Her mouth is a treasure house of sweet wine (often pomegranate, the ambrosia of Armenian poets), and her lips are rubies, or strands of pearls. Her tongue is a parrot's, delicate and eloquent. The brows of the beloved are pen-traced, and her face is compared to a great city (or several; even the most sympathetic reader may often suspect that the poet is more eager to display his knowledge of geography than to praise the lady,[21] nor would a villager or trader hearing such a poem think little of this achievement). The swaying of the beloved's hips destroys cities and fortresses, and mountains melt before her gaze. Her beauty corrupts and ensnares even the pious, and afflicts the lover with a malady that only her love can cure. Armenian lyric poetry in the Middle Ages came out of the pre-Islamic Iranian tradition of minstrelsy that Arsacid Armenia shared. But to these very archaic origins were added the innovations of a Christian culture, and, often, an 'Islamic' aesthetic (itself again largely Iranian and drawing upon images of gardens, wine, and lovers which antedated and frequently opposed Islam).

The most important poets in this lyric genre are Yovhannēs T^{c}lkuranc^{c}i, Nahapet K^{c}uc̆^{c}ak,[22] Kostandin Erznkac^{c}i,[23] and Grigor Al̵t^{c}amarc^{c}i. Nal̵aš Yovnat^{c}an and Sayat^c Nova in later centuries continued many of the traditions of these poets. All are quoted in the notes to illustrate the treatment of lyric themes used by T^{c}lkuranc^{c}i, as they are altered or developed.

Wisdom poetry is an ancient and popular genre in the Near East, and most lyric poets wrote didactic verses, too; these extolled the virtues of the spiritual life and lamented the vanity of earthly pursuits and the helplessness of men in a world of cruelty and death. Frik,[24] Mkrtic̆^{c} Nal̵as,[25] and T^{c}lkuranc^{c}i wrote many poems of this type (see chapter 3, infra). Rhymed hagiographies and narratives of Creation and Adam and Eve were composed by Yovhannēs T^{c}lkuranc^{c}i and Yovhannēs Erznkac^{c}i Pluz (flourished circa A.D. 1250-1330, see chapter 7, 'Songs of Creation and Adam').[26] The latter also wrote a Discourse on Celestial Movements--in the vernacular 'so the reader will understand it easily.'[27] Not all Mediaeval Armenian writers shared his purpose; Amirdovlat^c Amasiac^{c}i wrote a text for his fellow savants, arrogantly titled Angitac^c anpēt ('Useless to the Ignorant').

An interesting feature of Mediaeval Armenian poetry is the Christian content of poems whose metre or imagery are familiar to most Western readers only in an Islamic context. Some Armenian poets, for instance, were familiar with Ferdowsī's epic Šāh-nāme, and used its metre in their own compositions.[28]

Kostandin Erznkac^{c}i wrote, <u>Ayr mi kayr ew Šahnamay asēr jaynov; nay e⅃bark^c</u>
<u>xndrec^{c}in t^{c}ē i Šahnamayi jaynn mez otanawor asay. Es šinec^{c}i zbank^{c}s ays, i</u>
<u>Šahnamayi jaynn kardac^{c}ēk^c</u> 'There was a man and he recited the Šāh-nāme aloud,
and the brothers asked, "Recite a poem for us in the voice of the Šāh-nāme."
I composed these words. Read them in the voice of the Šāh-nāme.' Jayn 'voice'
probably refers not only to metre, but also to the chant traditionally employed
by Persians in reciting their national epic. The beginning of Erznkac^{c}i's
poem reads <u>Yanun ane⅃in Astucoy ew mecin, / Yanun Hōr, ew Ordwoyn or ē</u>
<u>miacin, / Yanun c̆ĕšmarit Surb Hogwoyn yawitean / Or mi tērut^{c}iwn ē hzōr i</u>
<u>yatean</u> 'In the name of the uncreate, great God, / In the name of the Father
and the Son sole-begotten, / In the name of the true Holy Spirit eternal, /
Who are one dominion, mighty in judgement,'[29] preserving all the magnificence
of Ferdowsī's very similar invocation: <u>Ba-nām-e Xodāvend-e J̌ān ō xerad, /</u>
<u>K-az-īn bartar andīše bar na-gozarad; // Xodāvend-e nām o Xodāvend-e J̌āy, /</u>
<u>Xodāvend-e rūzīde rahnamāy</u> 'In the name of the God of soul and of counsel /
Whom the highest wisdom shall never exceed, // God of name and God of place, /
God, giver of daily bread and shower of the Way.'[30] Erznkac^{c}i's line may be
scanned very similarly to Ferdowsī's if one properly stresses the ultima in the
Armenian, and the Armenian poet's invocation of the Trinity turns the Persian
form to Christian use. In another poem, <u>Yovanēs T^{c}urguranc^{c}oy asac^{c}eal vasn</u>
<u>yarut^{c}ean K^{c}ristosi</u> ('Spoken by Yovhannes T^{c}lkuranc^{c}i on the Resurrection of
Christ'), the familiar rose and nightingale of Persian lyric poetry go through
their customary love duet with one difference: they are Christ and St. John
the Baptist.[31]

Little is known of the life of Yovhannēs T^{c}lkuranc^{c}i, and there is no
certainty about basic facts. The poet T^{c}lkuranc^{c}i has been identified with
the Yovhannēs T^{c}lkuranc^{c}i who was ordained Catholicos of Sis in Cilicia on
Wednesday, 26th January 1489 and died on Monday, 1 May 1525, at the age of
80-85,[32] and who is mentioned in two manuscript colophons, dated A.D. 1511 and
1523.[33] Yovhannēs Catholicos spent a good deal of his time in Jerusalem try-
ing to remedy the financial problems of the Armenian Monastery of St. James',
which was heavily in debt, and an Arabic document of the time mentions a law-
suit involving one 'Bishop John, son of Luke.'[34] A chapel to St. Karapet in
the Church of St. T^{c}oros at St. James', Jerusalem, contains a white marble
xac̆^{c}k^{c}ar 'Cross-stone' affixed to the north wall, a memorial to Yovhannēs
Catholicos T^{c}lkuranc^{c}i and to his parents, including his father ⅃ukas.[35] But
Fr. A. Akinean argues that this Catholicos had no literary aspirations, and
that a manuscript of A.D. 1371--long before the birth of Yovhannēs Catholicos--
contains poems by Yovhannēs T^{c}lkuranc^{c}i;[36] this poet lived through the fall
of Sis to the Mamluks in A.D. 1375, which he chronicles in his heroic poem
'The Lay of Brave Liparit',[37] and he died past the age of seventy.[38] Conse-
quently, two different people are involved and the spare facts recorded by

Akinean--derived mostly from the internal evidence of his lyric poems and a ballad--are all we know of the poet T^{c}lkuranc^{c}i's life.

E. G. Browne has observed that Persia produced its finest poetry in times of general woe.[39] This is probably not true; Ferdowsī and other early poets flourished in small, fairly prosperous kingdoms where native Iranian culture had been revived, and later poets benefited from the economic and cultural expansion that followed the initial devastation of the Mongol conquest. The great flourishing of Armenian mediaeval culture, too, came in times of relative sovereignty and of extensive trade. T^{c}lkuranc^{c}i's century, though, is characterized by material hardship and the erosion of Armenian power: the gradual subjugation of the Armenians had begun, and the process was not to be reversed until our times. Since the poet probably never inhabited a royal court--his lines in 'Liparit' sound more wistful than descriptive of real experience--the country's fortunes probably affected him but slightly. Still one may gain a sense of his time by noting that a colophon written at Alt^{c}amar in A.D. 1355 laments the fall of the spiritual and temporal authority of the Armenian nation under the sway of the Antichrist, while a priest writing in Jerusalem, A.D. 1366, tells us many Armenians converted to Islam because of their bitter suffering. Yet another colophon, written at the Monastery of St. Karapet, Muš in A.D. 1368, records the sale of many of the monastery's manuscripts to infidels to alleviate the poverty of the monks.[40] And St. Karapet must have been one of the richest of Armenian monasteries at the time. Only eleven years after the fall of Sis, Tamerlane captured Tabriz and Nakhichevan; the invader erected six minarets of human skulls at Baghdad in 1387,[41] and Van was devastated in 1389.[42] Timur captured Sivas in August 1400 and buried 4,000 Armenians and other Christian defenders alive.[43]

T^{c}lkuranc^{c}i wrote only one ballad on the events of his time,[44] preferring to escape into precincts of pleasure; he devoted most of his talent to singing of love and of the soul. In a time of enmity between Christian and Muslim, T^{c}lkuranc^{c}i wrote a poem based on the folk tale of an Armenian boy's love for a Turkish girl.[45] The minstrel practises his trade in all weathers, and none tire of hearing songs of love and spring. In a time when great kingdoms fell and strong-built cities vanished from the face of the earth, the lyric poet provided respite and even delight. And when this was impossible, he could at least give voice to people's sufferings: the songs of the wanderer (łarib, panduxt) forced from home by want or strife, are amongst the most heartbreakingly moving of the poems of K^{c}uč^{c}ak and his contemporaries. One song of those times, Krunk 'The Crane', is still very popular. Grigor Xlat^{c}ec^{c}i (Cerenc^c), who lived in the fifteenth century, wrote a 'Memorial and Eulogy of Priests', which was copied in A.D. 1490. Together with praises of Grigor Narekac^{c}i,[46] Aṙak^{c}el Bałišec^{c}i, Xač^{c}atur Keč^{c}arec^{c}i and others, we find this brief notice: <u>Ew Yovannēs T^{c}ĕlguranc^{c}in / Bolor lusin mēǰ giserin</u> 'Also Yovhannēs T^{c}lkuranc^{c}i, / A full moon in the night.'[47] It seems likely that the poet, not the Catholicos, is meant. A century later, Yovasap^c Sebastac^{c}i wrote eight love poems for his friend Andreas with this dedication: <u>Ov ełbayr Antrēas, sakaw siru bans vasn srti k^{c}o grec^{c}i uraxut^{c}ean, xew Yovanēs T^{c}ilkur goyn 'Arek, arek'</u> 'Brother Andreas, I have written these few words of love for your heart's delight, in the manner of <u>xew</u> Yovhannēs T^{c}lkuranc^{c}i's "Come, come."'[48] <u>Xew</u> 'crazy' is T^{c}lkuranc^{c}i's perennial epithet, his <u>takhallus</u>, and deserves examination.

Every bird, say the Armenians of Musa Dagh, eats figs, but the <u>xew</u> is renowned for it.[49] Given the common erotic symbolism of the fruit in the Near East, one might interpret the proverb to imply that all men are lovers, but the <u>xew</u> man is love-crazed. Archag Tchobanian, in a French translation of one of T^{c}lkuranc^{c}i's poems, renders <u>xew</u> as <u>pauvre fou</u>,[50] and Valerii Briusov follows Tchobanian's translation in a Russian version of the same poem.[51] Nahapet K^{c}uc^{c}ak wrote (XLV):

> Stars, descend together in your hundreds of thousands.
> Where wise Xikar[52] is, make a remedy, a cure for my wound.
> I have become a crazy (<u>xew</u>) lover, helpless and unpitied.[53]
> I cannot give my soul rest; it keeps me under siege.

Kostandin Erznkac^{c}i wrote 'For your love / I have become crazy and stupid', 'I am crazy and bewildered for you',[54] and 'I have become stupid and crazy and melancholy, wandering about.'[55] 'You made me crazy with sweet wine, I who was a prisoner of your breast', T^{c}lkuranc^{c}i declares to his beloved,[56] and confesses 'I was crazy for her',[57] recalling Virgil's exclamation (<u>Ecloga</u> II:69) 'Ah, Corydon, Corydon, quae te dementia cepit!' Vrt^{c}anēs P^{c}ap^{c}azean interpreted the epithet <u>xew</u> as 'free-thinking, mocking established norms.'[58] Kiwlēsērean--who identified poet with Catholicos--suggested '<u>xew</u> is a term of self-endearment for a poet and writer of philosophical verses.'[59] But Archag Tchobanian states flatly 'A cleric would not call himself <u>xew</u>',[60] and T^{c}lkuranc^{c}i's admission that he became spellbound (<u>xew kapelu</u>)[61] indicates a level of emotion more powerful than a term of self-endearment might describe, unless it is an utterly insincere literary flourish, and T^{c}lkuranc^{c}i's poems are too impassioned for this to be at all likely. The madness of one who is <u>xew</u> comes from his love, and perhaps also from the insights into the vanities of men that the experience affords him. It comes, too, from his intoxication (see n. 56 above): the poet drinks. An Armenian poet of our own century, Ełisē Č^{c}arenc^c, wrote 'Desperate with the pain of my heart, I drank a glass of vodka. / Č^{c}arenc^c is a dissipated alcoholic, a foolish (<u>himar</u>) drunkard--they said.'[62] Ultimately, the <u>xew</u> is a man apart, an alien--indeed the word is sometimes used for certain non-Armenians[63]--one whose experiences and feelings separate him from other men. Love-crazed, intoxicated, alienated: not, perhaps, the epithets a Catholicos would want associated with his name.

What we know of the birthplace of xew Yovhannēs sheds little light on his life. The Armenian town of T^{c}lkuran[64] lay between the cities of Diyarbekir (Arm. Tigranakert) and Mardin; the modern Tel Kavran is a small hamlet near Viran Shehir with 20-25 houses inhabited by Arabic-speaking Kurds;[65] a recent visitor was unable to locate the Armenian Church of the Holy Mother of God (Arm. Surb Astuacacin) that had once stood there, where the scribe Step^{c}anos the Elder had worked circa A.D. 1388.[66] The Mediaeval Armenian historian Matthew of Edessa described T^{c}lkuran as a berd 'fortress';[67] forty Frankish troops of the County of Edessa defended it unsuccessfully against Emir Mamdud of Mosul, who conquered it in A.D. 1111-1112.[68] The latter delegated the administration of T^{c}lkuran to a certain Armenian named Ar̊iwc ('Lion'), at whose request the famed theologian and poet St. Nersēs Šnorhali wrote a lengthy epistle.[69] A 'notable householder' from T^{c}lkuran, Šahrman by name, is mentioned in an inscription of A.D. 1447 as a contributor towards the construction of the Kat^{c}oɫikē Church at Diyarbekir.[70] There is also a list of Classical Armenian toponyms and their sixteenth-century (?) equivalents in Columbia University Smith Collection Armenian MS. 5, fol. 117a. Following the entry for Ani-Kamax and preceding that for Aleppo is Awsit or e t^{c}ulkurwn 'Awsit, which is T^{c}ulkur(a)n.' I do not know Awsit from the Classical Armenian books. Other Armenians of T^{c}lkuran distinguished themselves in public service as clerics at Lwów and Constantinople in the seventeenth century.[71]

Insights into Yovhannēs T^{c}lkuranc^{c}i's character came from his lyric poems, and these reveal much passion, and, sometimes, subtlety of thought and construction. In the poem Yovasap^c Sebastac^{c}i admired, one may discern a fine symmetry (cf. n. 48 above):[72] the first quatrain praises a triad: the face of the beloved, its creator and its portrayer. The face alone is viewed as an object, a patker(k^c) 'image'[73] such as an artist might create. But to worship it, as the lover does, is idolatry, and in the last quatrain it crumbles to dust, as idols must, and a more Christian triad--the Father, the Son, and the poet himself (in an envoi)--is invoked. Self-knowledge and harmony with God,[74] the freedom of the soul that T^{c}lkuranc^{c}i seeks and expresses through such phrases as srti mitk^c 'thoughts of the heart, contemplation' and bann ēakan 'the Existent Word' in the final lines of his poems,[75] are gained only after experience and travail. The poet doubts his ability to come through the fire, and feels bitter and humiliated, xew 'crazy' among men. He rebukes himself (perhaps with reference to the triad of P I:25-28 cited above):

> Is there anyone so adept in counsel,
> Counselling the world threefold,
> Himself outside all advice,
> Every man's laughter and scorn.[76]

It is hard to withstand the xub surat 'lovely visage' of the beloved, and the poet confesses his impotence against the force of passion and kamk^c 'desire'[77] that has subjugated him.[78] He regards his passion as a light which he at once desires[79] and fears: it is a light which does not spiritually enlighten, but darkens counsel and banishes learning.[80] The poet sees himself as a fragile piece of gold leaf, a mere mirror of the beloved. Without her light, he cannot shine, but the fire of that light melts him.[81] He fears the light of the beloved,[82] and, much as he desires his love, deprivation of her fire is salvation from the Inferno.[83] T^{c}lkuranc^{c}i is ever aware of death, which defeats all carnal love, against which the ardour of youth has no power:

> I saw brides and bridegrooms
> With their beauty gone
> And the spider plundering in his web
> Above the grave.[84]

The heart of the xew poet is still 'excited without measure'[85] by womankind, although the wisdom of mortality and sin transforms the swaying willow of his passion into a twisting serpent;[86] whatever repose he finds in a woman's embrace only inflames his passion and leaves him with less repose than before.[87] Image, passion, and renunciation: the progress from patker(k^c) 'image', the inanimate, through kamk^c, the loss of the poet's reason and identity in the anima of the beloved, to srti mitk^c, the liberated soul--as a recurring theme in T^{c}lkuranc^{c}i's verse, has been considered by some as the moral voice of the poet, the minstrel's troubled conscience asserting itself at the song's end. Thus, M. Y. Ananikian wrote of T^{c}lkuranc^{c}i: 'This poet sings of love and celebrates beauty with all a lover's ardour and splendour. But his inescapable obligation to his Christian faith obliges him to demolish the secular impulse of his poetry in the final lines. Is this man a fiendish hypocrite or a pious minstrel tortured by the insurmountable contradiction of the spiritual and carnal loves?'[88] The contradiction exists only if one fails to distinguish between purely carnal desire and a more spiritual love. T^{c}lkuranc^{c}i, as a pious Christian, records the frailty of his heart and its sinful desires, which he sometimes surmounts. There is nothing inherently evil in nature's beauty or in the emotion of love. It is lust, which sets an impediment between the poet and God, that T^{c}lkuranc^{c}i laments. Love between man and woman need not be profane: Gregory of Narek, the great Armenian mystic and theologian of the tenth century, wrote: 'Now there is nothing finer and more honourable on this earth than the love of a man and woman.'[89] T^{c}lkuranc^{c}i does not speak as a married man, though, and conjugal love is surely what Narekac^{c}i had in mind. Instead, he is obsessed with the power of woman's beauty to distract celibate monks. This theme appears over and over. Was the poet a love-crazed monk, torn between the joys of the world and the discipline of the order, like one of the mediaeval Latin lyricists brought to life by Helen Waddell? It seems likely he was, but there is not evidence for a conclusive answer.

In much mediaeval Persian poetry, the beloved to whom a poem is addressed--
frequently a beautiful young man, like the Šamsu 'd-Dīn of Jalālu 'd-Dīn Rūmī--
is the vehicle of the poet's fervour towards the divine, and the poet desires
complete submission (Arm. taslīm) to him and complete self-abnegation in him.
He wishes to be consumed by the flame of his passion for the beloved, and
equates this state with the annihiliation (Arm. fanā') whereby the mystic seeks
to achieve unity with the One. St. John of the Cross addresses such intensely
erotic poetry, at once sensual and utterly transcendent, to his own Beloved,
the incarnate Christ. T^{c}lkuranc^{c}i does not choose this mystic path. Resolution can be found, not in submission of one's own being before the earthly beloved, nor, as it seems, in Sufi-like dedication to a lover in whom one sees
divinity reflected, but in a love which is founded in an equal exchange of
sacred vows.[90] Such a love is truly motivated by srti mitk^c 'thoughts of the
heart',[91] rather than by unreasoning passion: a new triad, that of lover and
beloved bound to God, is formed.

Such loves are, however, scarce in T^{c}lkuranc^{c}i's poetry. His songs have
an undercurrent of bitter scepticism towards human nature. Spring comes and
goes, and love comes and goes with it;[92] the passion of Adam and Eve overcomes
one generation after another.[93] T^{c}lkuranc^{c}i is weary, frustrated as a lover
yet contemptuous of lust, condemning the avarice and corruption he beholds in
himself and in those around him.[94] If the way of grace and of a love sanctified
by mutual vows is always open to him, he seems never to find it. Omar Khayyam
wrote of the čarx ke be-kasī namīgūyad rāz 'the Wheel (of Fate) that tells its
secrets to none', that destroyed Mahmud of Ghazna and his beloved slave Āyāz;
for many Muslim poets, submission to Fate, as to passion, was part of man's
lot. Yet however grim and cynical T^{c}lkuranc^{c}i may become, he cannot be called
a fatalist; his Christian faith is paramount. Fate itself, Frik argued circa
A.D. 1286 in his poem 'Against the Wheel', is subject to the will of God, and
must yield to God's grace.[95]

In one poem, T^{c}lkuranc^{c}i declares himself the servant of St. Karapet
(St. John the Baptist), and asks that the saint 'save my reciters and listeners
from evil.'[96] St. Karapet has been the patron of Armenian minstrels down to
recent times. The eighteenth century bard Sayat^c Nova attributed his mastery
of the kemancha, chonguri and tambur to the saint's power.[97] Like
T^{c}lkuranc^{c}i,[98] Sayat^c Nova wrote a poem on the martyrdom of the Forerunner of
Christ, in which he declares 'St. Karapet, Sultan of Muš, your praise has
reached the skies!' In memory of the saint and of the wicked Herodias, women
were barred from the Monastery of St. Karapet at Muš of which Sayat^c Nova
speaks.[99] The monastery, also known as Mšoy Sult^{c}an Muratatur ('The Sultan of
Muš, Bestower of Desire') and to local Kurds as Čankli Divan Šerp Garabed,
stood about 25 miles from the city of Muš, in the province of Tarōn, west of

Lake Van. Down to its destruction during the Turkish genocide of the Armenians
in 1915, it was the chief place of pilgrimage in Western Armenia. It was built
over the ruins of the pre-Christian Armenian temple of Innaknean on K^{c}eark^c
mountain, overlooking the river Aracani; pilgrims once worshipped a statue of
the god Gisanē there.

Legend has it that St. Gregory the Illuminator brought the bones of
St. John the Baptist on a mule to the spot, intending to inter them. The
caretaker-priest of Gisanē's sanctuary was wounded in the leg in his attempt to
drive off the Christian intruders. He limped to a well in the temple dungeon
and hid in it. The priest, Kaɫ Dew ('Lame Demon'), is still there, or so some
Armenians believe; when he lowers his arms, a terrible wind sweeps over the
high Armenian plateau. When he raises them, he keeps Armenia separated into
two parts: Eastern and Western. On Christian festival days, Armenian minstrels at the monastery sang the praises of St. Karapet for love-stricken
young men.[100] St. Karapet, himself a victim of a woman's passion, was the
patron saint of the love-crazed, the xewk^c, and, by extension, of the minstrels who sang of passion. One Armenian folk song relates:

> I parted with my tawny beloved on the road
> And--Alas!--said nothing to him.
> He has no helper on the road,
> No St. Karapet to guard him.[101]

A wedding song of Tarōn province asks God to bless the young couple 'by the
power of St. Karapet'. Armenian minstrels of the late nineteenth century still
came to the monastery to ask the Muratatur to increase their skill, as we
learn from the modern Western Armenian writer, Minas Č^{c}eraz: 'The Armenian
. . . expects the power of the mind, too, from St. Karapet, whom boxer and
poet turn to alike, who represents for us what Heracles and Apollo did for the
ancient Hellene.'[102] The practice of invoking a saint against the power of
passion and frustration in love seems very much in keeping with the thought
that informs T^{c}lkuranc^{c}i's poetry; perhaps T^{c}lkuranc^{c}i and his reciters sang
at the gates of Muratatur.

For there can be little doubt that these poems were not merely recited,
but chanted, like the ancient poems of the gusans, to the accompaniment of
musical instruments. Manuscripts of Sayat^c Nova's poems contain explicit instructions on the mode in which each is to be sung. Sayat^c Nova composed his
music, and performed it. Taimuraz, one of the sons of the last Georgian king,
Irakli II, wrote that Sayat^c Nova 'as he played the saz very well' was often
commanded to perform before the king.[103] The tunes have not been recorded,
but we can examine T^{c}lkuranc^{c}i's metre. L. H. Gray wrote of Classical Arme-
menian verse, '. . . le système se calculait simplement sur le nombre des
syllabes, sans aucun compte des longues ni des brèves . . . son accent
n'était pas de hauteur, mais d'intensité, de sort que l'on peut le comparer

par exemple, à des vers de l'Avesta et du néo-grec.'[104] The same, with the
addition of rhyme (An Arab contribution), equally describes Mediaeval Armenian
verse, and it is largely on the basis of syllable count that one may distinguish three main metres used by T^{c}lkuranc^{c}i. The first, and predominant,
form is the couplet of two 16-syllable lines, in monorhyme.[105] Each line is
divided into two hemistichs of eight syllables each, with caesura following
the fourth syllable, thus:

SYLLABLES   4+4/4+4/4+4/4+4   (Armenian full stop, :)

RHYME   x   A   y   A

In one of the first Armenian printed books, the Taɫaran ('Song Book') of Yakob
Meɫapart, printed at Venice in 1513, T^{c}lkuranc^{c}i's poems are divided into
quatrains of hemistichs, each quatrain marked by a red capital at the beginning
and a full stop (:) at the end. Pivazyan's edition follows this scheme, while
Covakan (Abp. Poɫarean) prints the lyric poems in couplets. I have generally
followed Pivazyan. Exceptions are to be noted in which a full stop follows
2(4+4) or 6(4+4) syllables,[106] and in one poem (which has been sometimes attributed to Nahapet K^{c}uč^{c}ak) a full stop occurs only after four 16-syllable
lines.[107] In a form whose basic unit is the octosyllabic hemistich, these
exceptions do not present great difficulty to the reciter. Internal rhymes
(the rhyming of the first hemistich with the second or third) are common: in
addition to the prevailing rhyme scheme xAyA, one finds BBAA,[108] BBxA,[109]
AAAA[110] and BABA.[111] But P XIV:85-88, with the scheme xyzA, is likely to be
a corrupt reading, and one prefers Erevan MS 5668, which restores the form
xAyA (cf. Note to P XIV:86).

The second pattern, employed by the poet less frequently than the
first,[112] consists of a quatrain of four hendekasyllabic lines, with caesura
following the sixth syllable of each line, in monorhyme:

SYLLABLES   6+5//6+5//6+5//6+5

RHYME   A   A   A   A

The third pattern embraces the first two in terms of syllable count, but is
distinguished by the addition of a refrain. This form is employed in two
poems: P XXIII:1-48 'The Lay of Brave Liparit'

SYLLABLES   4+4/4+4/4+4/Refrain of 4+4

RHYME   A   A   A   A

P XIII
SYLLABLES   x(6+5)   Refrain of 6+5

RHYME   A   B

The 16-syllable line of two octosyllabic hemistichs is fairly common in Armenian poetry; we find it in the works of Grigor Magistros, Kostandin Erznkac^{c}i

and Mkrtič^c Nałaš in the mediaeval period, in the songs of Sayat^c Nova in the eighteenth century, and in the verses of twentieth-century poets such as Awetik^c Isahakean, Ełiše Č^{c}arenc^c and Vahan Terean.[113] The 11-syllable line with caesura following the sixth syllable is found in works of Grigor Narakac^{c}i, Grigor Ałt^{c}amarc^{c}i and Nersēs Šnorhali.[114]

T^{c}lkuranc^{c}i's rhymes reflect the peculiarities of Middle Armenian pronunciation: verses are made to rhyme in -an, -ayn and -aw,[115] in -in and -iwn,[116] in -ac and -ac^c,[117] in -ac, -aj and -anc^c,[118] and in -er, -el.[119] Two of T^{c}lkuranc^{c}i's poems, PX and P Appendix IV, are abecedarian, with 36 lines for the 36 letters (a-k^c) of the ancient Armenian alphabet.

The problem of stress is complex. In proto-Armenian, accent fell regularly on the penultimate syllable of a word;[120] with the loss of the proto-Armenian ultima, accent coincided with the ultima in Classical Armenian, and generally in later forms of the language, except notably in words with the definite article postposition -ĕ(n), which is not stressed. But the stress on many words is in fact variable (e.g., Karapét, Karápet, Kárapet; erkrórd, érkrord 'second', etc.).[121] Unlike the Modern Greek to which Gray refers above, Armenian stresses are not marked in writing. P XIV:1-2 may be scanned as an iambic tetrameter:

Genáy bahár aylw'í bahár

Aylw'í ku'tán siróy xabár

This same form is found in most poems in which the octosyllabic hemistich is the primary unit. A variant of the Armenian hayren metre studied by M. Abełyan,[122] consisting of iamb + anapest repeated after caesura, is found in certain of T^{c}lkuranc^{c}i's verses;[123] another poem contains an amphibrach at the end of each line.[124]

Yovhannēs T^{c}lkuranc^{c}i's vocabulary is rich in Arabic, Turkish and New Persian loan-words, most of which are examined in the notes to the translations. Here, however, mention will be made of three particularly interesting problems. Addressing the beloved, the poet exclaims IP VI:5-8):

> The hundred year old monk
> Whose white has turned yellow
> Cuts the sacred girdle of the Mass (Ktrē zk^{c}ustik pataragin)
> And desires you before the Cross.

Pivazyan's interpretation of the k^{c}ustik word, as Arm. k^{c}usitay 'sacredotal hood', Gk. koukoullion via Syriac kōsitā, is wrong. Without considering the obvious problems that Pivazyan's explanation presents (how does one cut a hood?), one may suggest with certainty that Arm. k^{c}ustik is a loan from Phl. kustīg (NP kustī), the Zoroastrian sacred girdle.[125] The Iranian term comes from kōs(t) 'side', and k^{c}ustik is found in the Armenian Ašxarhac^{c}oyc^c in the sense of 'side, region.'[125] Binding the girdle (NP kustī bastan[126]) symbolizes obedience to Ahura Mazda, closing the door against sin, and breaking the power

of destruction; it is tied around the waist in order to prevent the passions
of the lower part of the body from rising to gain control over the higher regions.[127] The latter symbolism is singularly appropriate to T^{c}lkuranc^{c}i's
poem. The ceremony at which a child is invested with the sacred girdle and
admitted thereby into the Zoroastrian community dates back to Indo-Iranian
times and its essential elements, and the believer must untie and re-tie the
girdle thrice daily thereafter as part of his regular religious observances.
It is the sole external badge of the Zoroastrian, charged with symbolism.[128]
Just as binding the kustī was an act of piety and devotion, so breaking it
became a metaphor for impiety and desecration; Arm. ktrem zk^{c}ustik 'I cut the
k^{c}ustik' is most likely an ancient idiom meaning 'I desecrate, violate'. The
Brahmin sacred thread goes back to the same ancestor as the Zoroastrian
kusti. In Rabindranath Tagore's play 'Sacrifice', tearing the thread is a
sign of madness; the South Indian Śaivite poet Basavaṇṇa is said to have freed
himself from home and caste by tearing off his sacred thread. The symbolism
in India is the same as in Armenia and Iran. The emendation of zk^{c}ustik by
Tewkanc^c (Hayerg, pp. 45-46) to zkōrtik, acc. sing., 'a priest's coat' is
unnecessary.

In another poem, T^{c}lkuranc^{c}i addresses his beloved (P XII:5): Du spitak u
karmir xatič^c xncor es 'You are white and red, colocynth and apple.' Arm.
xatič < Ar. hadaǰ, T. hadec 'colocynth, citrullus colocynthis, bitter apple,
wild gourd, fresh melon.'[129] Pivazyan explains the word as 'odoriferous,
fragrant' (hotel, hotavet), but the colocynth is renowned for its bitterness,
not its fragrance.[130] T^{c}lkuranc^{c}i possibly means to describe the contradictory emotions of love, its bitterness and sweetness.

A favourite conceit of Mediaeval Armenian lyricists, as we have noted
above, is immersion in the pelagic depths of the beloved's eyes; the image
occurs frequently in T^{c}lhuranc^{c}i's verses.[131] In P XIV:19-20, the beloved is
said to sway Ayd anatak covud nman, / Or zis i k^{c}ez arir larar 'Like the bottomless sea / Where you made me my rest in you.' Arm. larar < Ar. qarār,
which means both 'rest' and 'sea bottom'. The contradiction of love is again
presented in this subtle pun: the lover's only resting place is at the bottom
of the beloved's bottomless sea.

T^{c}lkuranc^{c}i wrote of himself:

> Yovhannēs! Young in years,
> Young in years but weighty in thought,
> You have not betrayed your God,
> Nor have you been at a loss for words.[132]

He was not at a loss for words; the poet wrote some twenty poems on love and
the joys of spring, seven poems of wisdom and counsel, three rhymed hagiographies, one heroic lay on Liparit, defender of Sis, three lengthy hymns (ganǰ)

on religious subjects,[133] and a 360-line poem on the creation of the world.
He seems also to have left his own version of at least one popular song (see
Note to P XIV:19). The young T^clkuranc^ci was an assiduous student of
^cešqbāzī (N.P., 'the game of love'); his pessimistic thoughts on the affliction
of love were profound, and he expressed them finely, yet he followed the biblical injunction to 'remember thy God in the days of thy youth' in nearly every
envoi. But the dates of his life are disputed, the course of it unknown, and
his birthplace now a tiny Kurdish hamlet where the Armenian church no longer
stands.

Note on the Text

The present translation is based principally upon two critical editions
by E. Pirazyan and Abp. Norayr Pōłarean (Lovakan); MSS. are not cited except
where a reading is in doubt. The Armenian texts from these editions are reproduced at the end of the book. It was not possible to consult K. Kostanean,
Yovhannēs T^clkuranc^ci ew iwr tałerě, Tiflis, 1892. Several ecclesiastical
hymns (Arm. ganj) attributed to T^clkuranc^ci are appended; their subject matter
and language, so different from the lyric poems, illustrate the presumed
breadth of T^clkuranc^ci's intellectual concerns and literary talent. Such
variety in style and theme makes it difficult to decide the true provenance of
a poem, where it is attributed to T^clkuranc^ci in one MS., but to another, contemporary poet elsewhere. In such cases previous editors have generally been
followed, where they have accepted a poem as T^clkuranc^ci's by antiquity and
frequency of attribution. I have sought also to define characteristic words
or expressions (like anyatak) in identifying doubtful poems. This is not a
foolproof method of course. In recent months, debate has raged over the attribution to Shakespeare of a newly-discovered love poem, and Shakespeare's
style has been more minutely studied, his texts more carefully established,
than T^clkuranc^ci. It seems to me that most of the poems P I-XIV are the
poet's (but see n. 31). It is less likely that the poems which closely re-
semble those of Nahapet K^cuč^cak are T^clkuranc^ci's, particularly when the element of misogynist pessimism is absent. The theological poems may demonstrate
the poet's versatility and learning, but it is also possible that they were
attributed to the Catholicos T^clkuranc^ci: we simply cannot tell from the
available evidence.

Notes to Introduction

1. H. Manandyan, K^cnnakan tesut^cyun Hay žoɫovrdi patmut^cyan, Vol. II, Part 1, Erevan, 1957, p. 6.

2. Ž. Elč^cibekyan, 'Hay miǰnadaryan skzbnaɫbyurnerě K^cušanneri masin,' Lraber, No. 8 (404), Erevan, 1976, pp. 90-91. Andreas and Meillet derive Arm. awrēn(k^c) from Phl. *awdhēn (cf. H. Ačarean, Hayerēn armatakan bararan, Vol. VI, Erevan, 1932, pp. 1609-1613; this word is read as ēwēn, ēwēnag by D. N. MacKenzie, A Concise Pahlavi Dictionary, London, 1971, p. 31). The Classical Armenian has the sense of custom, a way of life, rather than only the letter of the law.

3. M. Boyce, 'Middle Persian Literature,' Handbuch der Orientalistik, Leiden, 1968, p. 55.

4. Arm. Nawasard < Pth. naw 'new' + sard 'year', cf. M. Boyce, 'On the Calendar of Zoroastrian Feasts,' BSOAS, XXXIII, 3, 1970, p. 523 and L. H. Gray, 'On certain Persian and Armenian month names as influenced by the Avesta calendar,' JAOS, XXVIII, 2, 1907, pp. 331-344.

5. Cf. Note 2 above.

6. H. S. Nyberg, A Manual of Pahlavi, Vol. I, Wiesbaden, 1964, p. 20. Line 10 (= J. M. Jamasp - Asana, Pahlavi Texts, Bombay, 1913, p. 3, lines 26-27). The Aškane, i.e., 'Arsacid' mode is listed amongst the 30 lahn of Barbadh, cf. A. Christensen, 'Some notes on Persian melody-names of the Sassanian period' in Dastur Hosang Memorial Volume, Bombay, 1918, p. 377.

7. Cf. the Chapter 'Patvand' in H. W. Bailey, Zoroastrian Problems in the Ninth-Century Books, Oxford, 1971.

8. A. G. Abrahamyan, Hayoc^c gir ew grč^cut^cyun, Erevan, 1973, p. 46.

9. Frédéric Macler, La Musique en Armenie, Paris, 1917.

10. V. H. Vardanyan, Hay grakanut^cyunē VII darum, Erevan, 1970, p. 19.

11. Frédéric Macler, 'Armenia', The Cambridge Mediaeval History, Vol. IV, Ch. VI, Cambridge, 1923, p. 167; H. Thorossian, Histoire de la Littérature Arménienne, Paris, 1951, p. 22.

12. E. B. Aɫayan, Aknarkner miǰin grakan hayereni patmut^cyan, Vol. I, Erevan, 1972, p. 14; A. Ł. Ʌazaryan, Hayoc^c lezvi hamarot patmut^cyun, Erevan, 1954, p. 193.

13. For the fifth-century texts, see W. Winter, 'Traces of early dialectical diversity in Old Armenian', in H. Birnbaum, G. Puhvel, eds., Ancient Indo-European Dialects, Berkeley, 1966, p. 201; and E. B. Aɫayan, Hay lezva-banut^cyan patmut^cyun, Vol. I, Erevan, 1958, p. 291. Seventh-century dialectical influences on Classical Armenian include changes in the meaning of words (e.g., harust fifth-century 'powerful' > seventh-century 'rich'), changes in the declension of personal pronouns, the use of the auxiliary verb in forming the present indicative (e.g., duk^c ztačarn ayl yayrel ēk i tal 'you are consigning the cathedral to fire') and the use of the present indicative active as a subjunctive (e.g., ek or tesanemk^c 'come that we may see'). The latter two phenomena in particular distinguish most mediaeval and modern Armenian dialects from fifth-century grabar. Cf. Ʌazaryan, pp. 217-219.

14. Thorossian, p. 192; Lazaryan, pp. 199-215; H. Manandean, Yunaban dproc͑ē
    ew nra zargac͗man srǰannerĕ, Vienna, 1928.

15. Lazaryan, p. 251.

16. Artasches Abeghian, Neuarmenische Grammatik, Berlin, 1936, pp. 5a, 8.

17. The mediaeval Armenian vernacular has often been called Cilician Armenian
    because of its use in affairs of state in the Cilician kingdom (cf. A. L.
    Lazaryan, p. 334), and perhaps also because its flowering as an artistic
    medium in the fourteen-fifteenth centuries (cf. F. Macler, La Musique en
    Arménie), p. 16) began when the kingdom still existed. For a description
    of the phonetic and grammatical features of the language, cf. A. Abeghian;
    Alayan; J. Karst, Historische Grammatik des Kilikisch-Armenischen, Stras-
    bourg, 1901; and G. Jahukyan, Hayoc͑ lezvi zargac͗umĕ ev karuc͑vack͗ē,
    Erevan, 1969. The modern Western Armenian literary language, a grammar of
    which was first published by Mxit͑ar Sebastac͑i in 1727, is considered a
    descendant of the mediaeval Armenian dialects of Cilicia and Asia Minor
    (cf. V. L. Ačemyan, Grakan arevmtahayereni jevarorumĕ, Erevan, 1971).
    Various Eastern Armenian dialects, particularly those of Tiflis (the di-
    alect of the eighteenth-century Armenian bard Sayat͑ Nova, cf. H. H. Peter-
    mann, Über den Dialect der Armenier von Tiflis, Berlin, 1886) and Erevan
    (the dialect of the writer Xac͑atur Abovean, who published his novel Verk͑
    Hayastani 'The Wounds of Armenia', considered the first modern Eastern
    Armenian novel, in 1840), are considered the basis of the modern Eastern
    Armenian literary language. Down to the eighteenth century, however, many
    vernacular works contained elements of both Western and Eastern Armenian
    dialects (cf. Ṙ. A. Isxanyan, '17 dari miasnakan ašxarhabarĕ, Lraber,
    Erevan, 9 (369), 1973, p. 92. In spoken Armenian, the distinction between
    Western and Eastern dialects today is not rigid, and there was never a
    real boundary-line between the two groups. H. Ačaṙean, in Hay
    barbaṙagitut͑yun, Moscow, 1911, distinguished on the basis of the verb
    seven Eastern Armenian dialects (forming the indicative with verbal present
    stem + -um + the verb 'to be'), 21 Western Armenian dialects (forming the
    indicative with kĕ--pronounced gĕ--and verbal present stem + personal end-
    ings) and three -el group dialects. More recently, A. Laribyan has dis-
    tinguished, also on the basis of verbal formation, seven types and a
    grabar-type (i.e., forming the verb as in Classical Armenian), cf. H. D.
    Muradyan, 'Hay barbaragitut͑yun anc͑ac ulin ew zargac͑man herankarnerĕ,'
    Lraber, Erevan, 4 (376), 1974, p. 15.

18. H. Ačaṙean, Hayoc͑ lezvi patmut͑yun, cited by A. L. Lazaryan, op. cit.,
    p. 321. Armenian scholars of the fifteenth century were capable of dis-
    tinguishing Iranian words from Arabic loan-words in New Persian, cf.
    B. L. Č͑ugaszyan, 'Parskerenum araberenic͑ p͑oxaṙyal bareri hayataṙ
    mijnadaryan mi baṙaran,' Patma-banasirakan handes, Erevan, 3 (50), 1970,
    p. 149.

19. On the Armenian version of the City of Bronze, see J. R. Russell, 'The
    Tale of the City of Bronze in Armenian', in M. E. Stone and T. Samuelian,
    eds., Mediaeval Armenian Culture, Philadelphia, 1983; on the Armenian ver-
    sion of the Alexander Romance, see J. R. Russell, review of M. S. Southgate,
    tr., Iskandarnameh, in JAOS 103.3, 1983, pp. 634-636; on Armenian magical
    texts, see J. R. Russell, 'Magic and Folklore, Armenian', in Dictionary
    of the Middle Ages (in publication).

20. M. Abelyan, Erker, Vol. II, Erevan, 1967, pp. 135-157; see also
    V. Nersisyan, 'Makdirĕ XIII-XVI dareri hay talergut͑yan mej', Banber
    Erevani Hamalsarani, Erevan, 3 (12), 1970, p. 190. It should be noted,
    however, that the kak͗aw 'partridge' is a pagan Armenian lewd dance, so
    the image may be very old. The lady as a cypress, too, is an ancient

image, most likely; the Zoroastrians of Parthian days accounted the tree sacred.

21. Cf. Note to P XIII:24

22. Av. Łukasyan, <u>Nahapet Kᶜučᶜak: Hayreni kargav</u>, Erevan, 1957, p. 3. A bilingual Armenian-Russian edition of Kᶜučᶜak's quatrains has been published: L. Mkrtčᶜyan, <u>Nahapet Kᶜučᶜak: Haryur u mek hayren</u>, Erevan, 1976. Another edition of Kᶜučᶜak, <u>A Hundred and One Hayrens</u>, Armenian title, <u>Haruyr u mek hayren</u>, Armenian text with English translation by E. Osers and critical introduction by L. Mkrtčᶜyan, was published in Erevan, 1979, with an idiosyncratic preface by the late William Saroyan. The English edition was edited by Arline Abdalian. Osers' versions are, if free, melodious, accurate in spirit, and highly to be recommended. Kᶜučᶜak, according to a much-disputed tradition, died over a hundred years of age in 1592 and was buried at Xarakonis on the shores of Lake Arčak.

23. H. M. Poturean, <u>Kostandin Erznkacᶜi, XIV daru žołovrdakan banastełc</u>, Venice, 1908, pp. 10-14. A bilingual Armenian-Russian edition of the lyric poems has been published: L. Mkrtčᶜyan, <u>Kostandin Erznkacᶜi, Loysn aŕawōtun</u>, Erevan, 1981. Kostandin was born at Erzincan <u>ca.</u> 1250-60, and died after 1336.

24. Born <u>ca.</u> 1236; see M. Abełyan, <u>Erker</u>, Vol. IV, Erevan, 1970, p. 290.

25. Born 1393-4, died <u>ca.</u> 1470; see Ēd. Xondkaryan, <u>Mkrtičᶜ Nałaš</u>, Erevan, 1965, pp. 27, 40.

26. Armenuhi Srapyan, <u>Hovhannes Erznkacᶜi</u>, Erevan, 1958, pp. 27 ff.; Thorossian, p. 172. The main sources of the Adam poems, aside from the biblical story itself, are the Apocrypha and Aŕakᶜel Siwnecᶜi's 'Adambook', cf. A. Madoyan, 'Aŕakᶜel Sewnecᶜu "Adamgirkᶜē" ev anvaverakanneŕe,' <u>Banber Erevani Hamalsarani</u>, Erevan, 3 (13), 1970, p. 198.

27. Thorassian, p. 172.

28. Cf. M. Abełyan, 'Šahnamayi otanavori čᶜapᶜē Hay banastełcutᶜyan meǰ,' <u>Firdusi</u>, Erevan, 1935, pp. 117-128.

29. KE XIV:1-4.

30. E. E. Bertel's, ed., <u>Šāh-nāme</u>, Vol. I, Moscow, 1960, p. 12.

31. This poem was published by Poturean (XI) and is probably Kostandin Erznkacᶜi's, as it is attributed to him in a closely contemporary MS of A.D. 1336, and to Tᶜlkurancᶜi only in a much later MS. I have translated it in full in the note to P VIII:1 Aha ełew paycaŕ garun 'Behold it was a glowing spring' as it begins Aysor ełew paycaŕ garun 'Today . . .' The rose of P XV:35 represents Christ as well. The use of rose and nightingale in Persian poetry to represent the seeker of unity with God and his Beloved is notable in Farīdu d-Dīn ᶜAṭṭār Nīsābūrī's 'Conversation of the Birds'; the development of this allegorical treatment in Iran has been seen as a parallel to a similar process in Armenia, rather than the source of the Armenian usage, cf. V. Nersisyan, 'Vardi u soxaki aylabanutᶜyan hay-parskakan msakumneri aŕncᶜutᶜyan harcᶜi masin,' <u>Banber Erevani Hamalsarani</u>, Erevan, 3 (9), 1969, p. 226.

32. V. A. Hakobyan, ed., <u>Manr žamanakagrutᶜyunner XIII-XVIII dd.</u>, Vol. I, Erevan, 1951, p. 394. Tᶜlkurancᶜi's name is here spelled in Armenian as Tᶜulkuracᶜanlnyi, perhaps betraying the scribe's uncertainty between Turkish and Armenian suffixes of place and origin -li and -cᶜi. See also

B. Kiwlēsērean, Patmut^ciwn Katołikosac^c Kilikioy (1441-ēn minč^cew mer ōrerē), Antelias, 1939, p. 87.

33. Ibid., p. 102.

34. Bishop Astuacatur Tēr-Yovhannēseanc^c, Žamanakagrakan patmut^ciwn surb Erusałemi, Vol. I, Jerusalem, 1890, pp. 251-254.

35. Kiwlēsērean, pp. 80-81.

36. P. N. Akinean, Areg, No. 18, 15th April 1924, pp. 470-473.

37. P XXIII.

38. P XVI:49-52: 'Yovhannēs T^clkuranc^ci, / You speak in vain, you preach in vain! / At the fullness of seventy years / You have reached death's door.'

39. E. G. Browne, A Literary History of Persia, Vol. III, Cambridge, 1928, p. 207.

40. A. K. Sanjian, Colophons of Armenian Manuscripts, 1301-1480, Cambridge, Mass., 1965, pp. 90, 94, 96.

41. A. G. Galstian, ed., Armianskie istochniki o Mongolakh, Moscow, 1962, p. 89.

42. Sanjian, p. 106.

43. Browne, III, p. 196.

44. P XXIII:147-148.

45. P Appendix V, the Chapter 'Yovhannēs and Aša'.

46. T^clkuranc^ci wrote a hagiographical poem on Grigor Narekac^ci (Chapter 5).

47. L. S. Xač^cikyan, XV dari hayeren jeṙagreri hišatakaranner, Part III (A.D. 1481-1500), Erevan, 1967, p. 150.

48. H. Sahakyan, Uš mijnadari Hay bạnastełcut^cyun, Erevan, 1975, p. 175; V. Gevorgyan, Hovasap^c Sebastac^ci, Erevan, 1964, pp. 65-84. The poem is P I, the first line of which reads Arek, arek im xup surat^c.

49. C. J. F. Dowsett, 'Some Gypsy-Armenian Correspondences', REArm, 10, 1973-74, p. 64 n. 17.

50. A Tchobanian, Les Trouvères Arméniens, Paris, 1906, p. 189.

51. L. M. Mkrtchian, ed., Armianskaia srednevekovaia lirika, Leningrad, 1972, p. 248.

52. Cf. Note to P X:31.

53. Ełer em xew siru tēr, anmatat^c u anzenehar. Siru tēr, lit. 'master of love'. The expression can also be translated simply as 'in love', and it is applied to men and women alike. In the Epic of Sasun, for instance, the golden-haired heroine Dełjun Cam Šat siru tēr ēłav ver enor 'fell in love with him [the hero Sanasar] greatly': H. Ōrbeli, ed., Sasunc^ci Davit^c, 2nd ed., Erevan, 1961, p. 56.

54. KE, p. 176, line 19: Es vanc^c k^{c}o sir̥ut hamar / Es xew em eɫer 'w yimar; p. 177, line 24: Es xew u hayran em k̄ez. Arm. hayran < A hāirān 'astontonished, confounded'.

55. Ibid., p. 91, line 1: Em yimar dar̩jel u xew u sawdayi i šur̃j galov. Arm. sawdayi <Ar. saudā' 'black bile'. In an unpublished poem of T^{c}lkuranc^{c}i's cited by A. A. Mnac^{c}akanyan, 'Mi̩jnadaryan siro ergeri nor̥ahayt andranik žoɫovacun̬ev hayrenneri harc^{c}ě', Ējer hay zoɫovrdi patmut^{c}yan ev banasirut^{c}yan, Erevan, 1971, p. 97, the poet declares, Xew Yovannēs anpēt hogis 'Crazy Yovhannēs, my useless soul!' (Erevan Matenadaran MS 10208 fol. 145-146a).

56. P Appendix I:12: Anuš ginov zis xew arir, or i coc^{c}ěd zntanec^{c}ay.

57. P Appendix II:7: Xew eɫay noray hamar.

58. Vrt^{c}anēs P^{c}ap^{c}azean, Patmut^{c}iwn Hayoc^c grakanut^{c}ean, Tiflis, 1919.

59. Sion, Jerusalem, 1928, p. 219.

60. Cf. Hayastani koč̌^{c}nak, 1929, p. 76.

61. P II:19, VII:8.

62. Eɫišě Č^{c}arenc^c, Erkeri žoɫovacu, Vol. I, Erevan, 1962, Taɫaran XV (1920-21), p. 240, lines 7-8: Ev srti c^{c}avic^c es me t^{c}as ōɫi xmec^{c}i- / Č^{c}arenc^{c}ě c^{c}ndac-ginemol, harbec^{c}oɫ-himar ē, asin.

63. Dowsett, p. 64, n. 17.

64. Also spelled T^{c}urkuran, T^{c}ulkuran, T^{c}ulguran, etc.

65. Bishop N. Covakan, (Xew) Yovhannēs T^{c}lkuranc^{c}i: Taɫagirk^c, Jerusalem, 1958, p. 5; A. Tchobanian, La Roseraie d'Arménie, Vol. II, Paris, 1923, p. 153.

66. Fr. Abraham Arewean, Diwc^{c}aznakan Urfan, Beirut, 1955, p. 116; L. S. Xač̌^{c}ikyan, XIV dari hayeren jer̥agreri hišatakaranner, Erevan, 1950, p. 574.

67. Matt^{c}eos Ur̥hayec^{c}i, Žamanakagrut^{c}yun, Erevan, 1973, p. 211.

68. E. Rey, Les Colonies Franques de Syrie aux XII-me et XIII-me siècles, Paris, 1883, p. 321.

69. St. Nersēs Šnorhali, Ēndhanrakan t^{c}uɫt^{c}k^c, Jerusalem, 1971, p. 240.

70. Xač̌^{c}ikyan, XV dari . . ., Part I, p. 629.

71. Dr. V. Y. T^{c}orgomean, ed., Eremia Č^{c}elēpi K^{c--}miwrčean, Stampōlay patmut^{c}iwn, Vol. I, Vienna, 1913, p. 51, and Vol. II, 1932, p. 813.

72. P I

73. Arm. patker < Pth. patkar 'image', NP paikar; paikar parast 'an idolater'.

74. P III:19.

75. P IV:22, II:32

76. P XXII:9-12.

77. P V:20; Arm. kamk^c 'will, desire' carries also the sense of love or passion, cf. Indic kāma-.

78. P V:11-12.

79. P VI:1, II:15.

80. P XII:20, II:11-12.

81. P V:13-14, XIII:40.

82. P XII:21, Appendix V:1.

83. P II:26-28.

84. P XVIII:29-32.

85. P XX:55.

86. P XIV:18, 70.

87. P XII:13,

88. Koč^cnak, 1923, pp. 969-970.

89. Grigor Narakac^ci, Matenagrut^ciwnk^c, Venice, 1840, p. 275: Ard č^cik^c yerkri patuagoyn ew arawel, k^can zsēr arn ew knoj.

90. P X:13-16.

91. P IV:22

92. P XIV:1-4.

93. See I:3, XIII:12-13, XIV:53, 78, XV:67-68, XVI:26, XVII:5, XX:6, and Chapter 7, 'Songs of Creation and Adam'.

94. See Chapter 3, 'Wisdom Poems of Yovhannēs T^clkuranc^ci'; T^clkuranc^ci reserves particular scorn for immoral priests and monks, see Note to P II:11-12.

95. Abp. Tirayr, Frik diwan, New York, 1952, XXVII:47-55.

96. P XII:35-36: Surb Karapet šat ku xndrem zk^cez / zAsōłk^cs ew zlsōłk^cs i č^carēn p^crkes.

97. M. S. Hasrat^cyan, Sayat^c-Nova, Erevan, 1959, p. 10.

98. Vasn surb Yovhannu glxatman 'On the decapitation of St. John' (C III, translated in the Note to P XIV:61-64).

99. Hasrat^cyan, p. 80: Mšu sult^can surp^c Karapit, erkink^c ē hasyal govk^cen k^co; S. M. Coc^cikean, Arewmtahay ašxarh, New York, 1947, p. 445.

100. Dr. Armenak Alixanean, in K. Sasuni, Patmut^ciwn Tarōni ašxarhi, Beirut, 1957, pp. 58-60, 93, 95; A. G. Perikhanian, Khramovye ob'edineniia Maloi Azii i Armenii, Moscow, 1959, p. 9; A. Łanalanyan, Avandapatum, Erevan 1969, p. 253; the cult of St. John the Baptist at Muš replaced that of the Zoroastrian yazata Verethraghna, Arm. Vahagn (see J. R. Russell, 'Zoroastrian Problems in Armenia: Mihr and Vahagn', in T. Samuelian, ed., Classical Armenian Culture, Philadelphia, 1982, and Russell, Zoroastrianism in Armenia, Cambridge, Mass. [in publication], Ch. 6).

101. Komitas Vardapet and M. Abełyan, Hazar u mi xał, Erevan, 1969, p. 22.

102. Sěb Karapetu zōrutenov: Sasuni, p. 179; Minas Č^{c}eraz, 'Ea, Surb Karapet', Arewelean vipakner, Paris, 1927, p. 199.

103. Hasrat^{c}yan, p. 302.

104. L. H. Gray, 'Les Mètres Païens de l'Armenie,' RDEA, 1926, p. 164.

105. P I-IX, XI, XIV-XXII, XXIV, Appendix I-III, V, C II, III, Tałě vasn stełcman ašxarhi 'Song on the Creation of the World'.

106. P XV:63-64, Appendix V:71-76, 89-94, 95-100.

107. P Appendix III:v.

108. P IX:5-8.

109. P XI:9-12, XX:1-4.

110. P III:5-8, XIV:1-4, XV:1-14, Appendix III, V.

111. P II:13-16, III:17-20, etc.

112. P X, XII; Appendix IV.

113. M. Abełyan, Erker, Vol. V, Erevan, 1971, pp. 177-179; Hasrat^{c}yan, p. 7.

114. Abełyan, V, pp. 194-195.

115. P XV.

116. P XXIV:102, 104.

117. P XVII.

118. P XIII.

119. P XVIII:64, cf. Note to VII:3.

120. A. Meillet, Esquisse d'une Grammaire Comparée de l'Arménien Classique, Vienna, 1936, p. 19.

121. Abełyan, V, p. 20.

122. Ibid., II, p. 38.

123. Cf. P XIII:2: Ač^{c}erd ē cover, xumar u mēstan. In this case, the deka-syllabic line is anomalous; the rest of the poem is written in lines of 6 + 5 syllables.

124. P XII.

125. MacKenzie, p. 177; Arm. k^{c}ustik 'region' is found in the Geography, cited by N. Garsoian and N. Adentz, Armenia in the Period of Justinian, 126, xxxv.

126. Ferdowsī describes the conversion of the Iranians to Zoroastrianism at the court of Vīštāspa (N.P. Goštāsp)(apud S. D. Bharucha, Dastur Hošang Mem. Vol., Bombay, 1918, p. 253): Hame sū-ye šāh-e zamīn āmadand be-bastand kustī be dīn āmadand 'All came to the king of the land, / Tied the sacred girdle, and entered the Religion'.

127. Cf. The Phl. Dādistān i Dēnīg, XXXIX:19 and Gizistag Abāliš (cited in Dastur Hošang Mem. Vol., p. 164); the Pazand Čim ī Kustīg ('Reason for the Sacred Girdle') in T. D. Anklesaria, ed., Dānāg-i Mainyō-i Khard, Bombay, 1913, and J. J. Modi, The Religious Ceremonies and Customs of the Parsees, 2nd ed., Bombay, 1937, p. 179.

128. M. Boyce, A History of Zoroastrianism, Vol. I, Leiden, 1975, pp. 13, 257; see also J. R. Russell, 'The Word kᶜustik in Armenian', in J. Greppin, ed., First International Conference on Armenian Linguistics, Proceedings, Caravan Books, Delmar, N.Y., 1980. To our remarks there the following points may now be added. J. Sampson, The Dialect of the Gypsies of Wales, Oxford, 1926, 151, cites a form kiustȳk 'girdle' among the gypsies of Turkey. S. Runciman, The Mediaeval Manichee, New York, 1961, 160, notes that the thirteenth-century Cathars wore 'a distinctive girdle', and in R. Tagore's play 'Sacrifice', the tearing of the Hindu sacred thread is a sign of madness (xew Yovhannēs Tᶜlkurancᶜi!).

129. Armenak Petewean, Illustrated Polyglottic Dictionary of Plant Names, Cairo, 1936, No. 1059.

130. An Iranian king berates the minstresl Sarkaš (R. Levy, trans., The Epic of the Kings, Chicago, 1967, p. 388): 'You feeble performer, you are as bitter as colocynth, whereas Barbādh is as sweet as sugar'. A pagan Arab poem on vengeance describes a man's kindness and harshness in the following terms (Browne, I, p. 192): 'And he had two tastes, honey and colocynth, of which two tastes everyone had tasted'. On Ar.-N.P. kabast, ḥanẓal 'colocynth' in Persian poetry, see C. H. de Fouchecour, La description de la nature dans la poésie lyrique Persane du XI-e siècle, Paris, 1969, p. 91.

131. Cf. Notes to P I:11, XV:19, 20.

132. P Appendix V:117-120.

133. C pp. 67-74; see also A. Mnacᶜakanyan in Grakan Ṭᶜertᶜ, No. 23, 1940, cited by A. G. Aṙakᶜelyan, Hay žaɫovrdi mtavor mšakuytᶜi zargacᶜman patmutᶜyun, Vol. 3, Erevan, 1975, pp. 260-270.

CHAPTER ONE

SONGS OF LOVE AND SPRING

This poem (P I), which was used by Yovasap^C Sebastac^{C}i as a model of his
own lyrics (cf. Introduction), is published in quatrains of eight-syllable
lines; the caesura falls after the fourth syllable in each line. The second
and fourth lines of every quatrain rhyme in -in. The same poem was published
by Covakan (p. 12) in couplets of sixteen-syllable lines.

It is characteristic of T^{C}lkuranc^{C}i's lyrics. The images it contains are
found often in his other poems, and in the works of other contemporary Armenian
poets. The pleasure of the poem is its graceful construction, whereby familiar
yet exquisite pictures of love are presented in elegant sequence, and a subtle
symmetry pervades the whole. The opening quatrain invokes the beloved, her
creator and her portrayer, while the final quatrain addresses the poet, the
Father and the Son. The first quatrain introduces the beloved's beautiful
face; in the last, that face crumbles to dust. In the second stanza, the beloved's face is compared to the heavenly spheres, and the poet declares that
its sight alone is sufficient to him; in the next quatrain T^{C}lkuranc^{C}i suggests
that it is a doctor to the lover's ills. If sight is physician, then the beloved's eyes are medicine itself, and her mouth exudes sweetness, which must be
imbibed for a cure to be effected. In the next quatrain, the poet praises
still lower regions of the body of his beloved, until in the sixth quatrain we
at last behold her supple waist.

It is with the lover, xew ('crazy') Yovhannēs himself, that the poem will
end. He appears in Line 17, first meeting his beloved in joy, then kissing her
face in rejoicing, then embracing her, and, like an eternally green tree, ob-
taining the immortality first mentioned in Line 13. The motions of the lover
follow the progress of the first four stanzas; it is as though the passages of
description had created a form which would determine the later shape of experience. Sight leads to touching the face and drinking its sweetness, exploring
its sea. Finally, the lover wanders through the verdant garden of the Beloved,
and is himself transformed into a green tree of her unending spring.

But the last stanza of the poem describes the final, albeit unexpected,
curve of its symmetry. The poem begins with an idyllic vision of the beloved;
it ends with the poet's self-knowledge and experience. The bright dream passes
through the test of experience and the examination of the heart.

TRANSLATION

1 Come, my lovely visage, come;
    Glory and honour to your creator!
    It is from Eden's Paradise you come;
    Blessed is the name of your portrayer!

5 Come, sun of spring;
    Come, brilliant autumn moon.
    Sit, that I may behold your face.
    Your sight is sufficient lot for me.

10 Your sight is doctor to the sick
    And health to the fevered.
    Your eyes are a sea to the thirsty,
    And to the famished one your mouth is sweet.

13 Your breast is a paradise of immortality
    Alluring to the risen soul.
    Then it does not die or age,
    Nor does its face turn jaundiced.

17 He whom you meet in the morning
    Begins the day in joy.
    He who kisses your face
    Rejoices all year long.

21 He whom you call in love within
    Flowers more than the frankincense tree.
    He who embraces your supple waist
    Remains greener than the hornbeam.

25 Crazy Yovhannēs T^clkuranc^ci,
    Glorify the Father and the Son.
    The fine face turns to earth;
    One's beloved, to the unquenchable fire.

Notes

Line 1. Ar'ek, ar'ek im xup surat^c. Ar'ek (cf. P XIV:37) is a contraction of the imperatives ari 'rise' and ek 'come'; xup < NP xūb 'good'; surat^c < Ar. sūrat 'face'. Cf. NK XIII:

> Whose face [surat^c] is like yours? That of Joseph, who ruled Egypt.
> You are like that Persian face [p^carsi surat^c] that was in the city
>   of Baghdad.
> The Creator is an interceder before you, he who gave you your
>   face [surat^cd].
> Do not deceive the youth who loves you with his heart.

Cf. also NK LXIX:

> This is your image [patkerk^cd]; cf. P II:1] and your face [surat^cd],
>   of the red roses.

The Armenian word eres 'face' is used in Lines 8 and 16, while surat^c is re-peated in Line 19; it is hard to detect any difference in meaning between the two words in Armenian usage. Xub surat as a compound means 'beautiful' in

NP and as a loan in modern Aryan Indian tongues, and should probably be read
as such in Armenian (cf. P IV:2, xup surat^C).

Line 2. T^{C}lkuranc^{C}i merely praises the creator of his beloved, but Nahapet
K^{C}uč^{C}ak (XIII) invokes the creator of the beautiful surat^C as an intercessor on
his behalf.

Line 4. Ōrhneal anun k^{C}o naxšoɫin. Naxšoɫ is pres. part. act. of Arm. naxšem
'I portray' < Ar. naqqaš 'painter'. NP compounds employing the word which have
entered Mediaeval Armenian include: naxsideuar < NP naqš-i divar 'wall paint-
ing', hence the sense of 'foolish, superficial'. (KE IV:9, Surat^C en bēsifat^C
ew yandiman naxšidēar 'They are unlovely of face and shallow to behold'); and
Arm. naxšnigar or naxš u nigar < NP naqš-i nigār 'picture-painting', hence
'adorned, adorned with paintings' (KE XIV:15, Šinac amēnn oskwov u naxš i nigar
'All fashioned of gold and adorned with paintings'; IIV:23-24, Ē! geɫec^{C}ik
kerpiw surat^C / Or ē steɫcac naxš u nigar 'O face beautiful in form / Which
painter and artist have created'--here the sense is clearly of the man who made
the thing rather than the thing itself). On the naqš of his beloved, Nahapet
K^{C}uč^{C}ak wrote (NK LXXIV):

> They took the face [surat^{C}n] of my love and brought it as a gift to
> Č^{C}in-mač^{C}in ['China and Mahā China'; see P VI:2].
> They took it and went about with it, but they found none like that
> face.
> Five hundred and six thousand painters [naxšararn] came together
> And not one could depict the likeness of my beloved's face.

The portrayer of T^{C}lkuranc^{C}i's beloved was to be praised, but Nahapet K^{C}uč^{C}ak's
is beyond the skill of a myriad of artists to depict. In Modern Armenian, the
word naxšun has the generalised meaning of 'nice' or 'fair', as in this poem by
Eɫisē Č^{C}arenc^C (Erkeri žoɫovacu, Vol. I, Erevan, 1962, p. 222):

> You are the sweet summer's scorching fire, my love;
> The fragrance of pomegranate, you are fair my love
>   (Naxsun: nran hot es, jan).
> When you glare at me suddenly with visage severe,
> You are as the bitter tidings of my heart's death, my love.

Lines 5-6. In P XIV:6, T^{C}lkuranc^{C}i addresses the beloved as both sun and moon,
šams u ɫamar (<Ar. šams 'sun', qamar 'moon'); here, the same idea is drawn out
into two lines. In P XII:8, K' t^{C}ui bdri lusin, zēt aregakn es 'It seems a
full moon; you are like the sun', the comparison takes one line. Nahapet
K^{C}uč^{C}ak's beloved outshines both celestial orbs with her own radiance
(NK LXVIII):

> Sun and bright moon, that rise over the same hill's crest;
> My love come outdoors confounds their combined light.
> You are like that star which rises every morning.
> It rises slowly, slowly, and brings with it its good light.

T^{c}lkuranc^{c}i's beloved is light and fire. Like Nahapet K^{c}uč^{c}ak above, the poet
compares his beloved to Venus (P XIII:50 Eresd ē arew, čakatd ē Zōhran 'Your
face is the sun, your brow is Venus') and to the dawn (P VII:5-6 Es zk^{c}ez tesay
nman lusoy, / Zēt zaregakn or nor k'elnu 'I saw you as the light, / Like the
sun that that rises anew'). He desires her light (P VI:1 Loys eresac^{c}d em k^{c}o
p^{c}ap^{c}ak^c 'I thirst for the light of your face'), but fears it as well, acknowledg-
ing its power over him (P XII:21 Es em ap^c mi hołē, dun hrelēn es 'I am a handful of earth; you are fiery'; P XIII:7 Hrelēn es, hołelēn, t^{c}ē mardadēm k^{c}aǰ
'Are you fiery or earthborn, or a k^{c}aǰ [the k^{c}aǰk^c in Armenian folklore are
supernatural beings inhabiting Mount Ararat, cf. P X:36] with human face?').
The radiance of the beloved calls up images of the pre-Christian past, not only
in the form of k^{c}aǰk^c, but of Vahagn. Of his hrelēn 'fiery' beloved,
T^{c}lkuranc^{c}i writes (P IX:1-2), Es jez tesay sirov nstac, / Arewnman aregakunk^c
'With love I saw you seated, / Sunlike little suns'; the Song of Gołt^{c}n on the
birth of Vahagn in Movsēs Xorenac^{c}i I:XXXI reads Na hur her unēr. / (Apa t^{c}e)
boc^c unēr morus. / Ew ač^{c}kunk^c ein aregakunk^c. 'He had fiery hair. / (Then) he
had a flaming beard / And his little eyes were little suns.' The beloved's
eyes scatter beams of light (P III:1-2): Arewnēman sołsol kē'tan / K^{c}ani sirov
zač^{c}erd aces. 'They shed sunlike rays / When you turn your eyes with love'.
Zenob Glak, Narekac^{c}i, and others also use the image of sunlike eyes, and the
typology of sun and eye(s) is of Indo-European origin. The fire of love is not
the true light of the redeemed soul; it is passion without illumination. The
lover Yovhannēs, possessed by desire for the infidel girl Aša, cries (P Appendix V:1-2) Ays inč^c krak ēr zis ayrec^c, / Kam inč^c xawar or zis patec^c 'What
fire is this that burned me, / Or what shade has hemmed me in?'

Line 9. The beloved as doctor, cure and malady is a frequent image in Eastern
poetry. Cf. NK XCVIII:

> I saw a little partridge yesterday--her master is most blessed.
> Her little breast was carded cotton, and her face was a nightingale
>   of the roses.
> Her mouth sifted sugar, and her breath was medicine to the sick.

The potion is sweet as well as powerful, cf. P I:12 and X:2 (Berand šak^{c}rov i
li 'Your mouth is full of sugar'); indeed, it is the potion of happiness
(P VI:9 Ayl du deł es uraxut^{c}ean 'But you are the potion of happiness').
T^{c}lkuranc^{c}i declares in P XIII:8 Hiwand em: olǰanam, erb inǰ nēstis yaǰ 'I am
sick, but will recover when you sit at my right'.

The lover's recovery at the sight of the beloved is like the final Resurrection, cf. NK CVIII:

> Come, a thousand greetings! I rejoice at your coming.
> As the trumpet of Gabriel cries to the dead 'Arise!'
> So when I heard your voice, then did I become alive.

The resurrection of the lover at the sight of the beloved is followed by the state of blissful immortality at the beloved's breast, thus P I:13 Coc^{C}d ē draxt anmahut^{C}ean 'Your breast is a paradise of immortality' and NK CV:

> The reed nods from the middle of its stalk; that is your person.
> Your waist is long and slender; your stature is the swaying cypress.
> They say it is the water of immortality which gushes from your
> breast.
> Would I could give it to him who has learned of your water.
> He would come and sit before you and drink a drop from you.

Fruits of marvellous nature abound in that well-watered region, as we learn from P IV:13-14: Coc^{C}d ē děraxt anmahut^{C}ean / Anmahakan pĕtłov děraxt 'Your breast is a paradise of immortality, / A paradise with immortal fruit'. The fruit is either apple or melon. The Moslem girl Aša, inviting Yovhannēs to make love to her, throws apples to him as she rides past on her Arab steed (P Appendix V:21-25). The most famous apple is the malum of the knowledge of good and evil (Malum) in Eden (in the Near East, a fig), from which came the evil of lust. But apples are erotic in ancient Greek poetry. In P XIII:51, the jaw of the beloved is an apple, while her breasts are melons, cf. NK XCII:

> The apple on the branch of the tree, beneath the branch's leaf,
> Is like my beloved's breasts on her bosom beneath her chemise.
> The sun has gone down into the water: moonlight, and the
> frustration of hope.
> She walked: her waist swayed, only the melon at her breast rose.

In our day, Ełišē Č^{C}arenc^C wrote (Erkeri žołovacu Vol. I, Erevan, 1962, p. 331, Trioletner Arp^{C}ikin [1921], III):

> You have two red pomegranates at your breast,
> Two ripe red melons.
> Give me that I may drink of them and marvel;
> You have two red pomegranates at your breast.
> Give me those limpid, precious fruits
> That I may drink of them and marvel.
> You have two red pomegranates at your breast,
> Two ripe red melons.

T^{C}lkuranc^{C}i uses the same imagery in describing a real garden (P VIII:13-16):

> And beyond all price is this rose bush
> Where one might meet such joy.
> Were it the Paradise of immortality
> [K^{C}awel draxtn anmahut^{C}ean]
> In which the first man was placed!

Paradise recalls the story of Adam to Nahapet K^{C}uč^{C}ak as well (LV):

> I needed wine of your colour to drink and be drunk.
> Your breast is Adam's Paradise; I would enter and pick apples
> [K^{C}o coc^{C}d Adamoy draxt, mtnēi xnjor k^{C}ałēi].
> Between your breasts I would lie and sleep;
> In that hour would I consign my soul to the groł ['writer', i.e.,
> 'recorder of souls', an Armenian psychopompos, cf. P XII:16]
> would he but come and take it away.

It is somewhat surprising that NK found apples, not figs, in Eden. On the power of the beloved to bestow life on the lover, Rūmī (R. A. Nicholson, trans., The Mathnawī of Jalālu'ddīn Rūmī, Vol. II, London, 1926, I:30) states succinctly:

> The Beloved is all and the lover [but] a veil;
> The Beloved is living and the lover a dead thing.

But this same love that cures and revivifies also smites the lover; its torment casts him into hell-fire (P I:28, II:17-24). The glance of the beloved (cf. Note to Lines 5-6) has terrifying power: 'Him you regard with love / Do you ignite with undwindling flame' (P III:7-8). And the lover wanders about, bereft of breath and sense (P V:4-6). In our century, C̆c̆arenc̆ has written (Vol. I, p. 230, line 8): C̆c̆i lawanay ĕs̆xid ĕrac̆ĕ, gozal 'The one burned by your love does not recover, my beauty!' Of this mystery of the disease which is balm and the death which is resurrection, Rūmī (Mathnawī I:110) said 'The lover's ailment is separate from all other ailments: love is the astrolabe of the mysteries of God'. Kostandin Erznkac̆i wrote (p. 177, line 25):

> Kc̆o sirut hiwand em es,
> Hēkc̆im ew carah du es,
> Del̄ kc̆o tesn yac̆c̆erus ōc̆tes: C̆c̆gites.

> I am sick for your love;
> You are doctor and physician.
> You know not! Give the balm of your gaze to my eyes!

Line 11. A favourite conceit of Mediaeval Armenian poets is immersion in the seas of the beloved's eyes, which sometimes are swarming with fish (NK LXXXII):

> I die a sacrifice to your chin whiter than ghee.
> Your face is red, like a rose; your lips are a place for kissing.
> You have arched your brows tauter than a bow;
> Your eyes are a sea where a thousand fish are swimming.

One imagines the morning light playing on the coruscating surface of the sea where the flecks of the fish breaking water are brilliant, instantaneous flashes, like the speckled, fiery dance of the beloved's eyes. The sea, mesmerizing the onlooker with its brilliance, is a trap for the unwary (NK XLII):

> I was one of those birds who do not eat the earth's bounty;
> I flew and went up to heaven, lest I fall into love's trap.
> The trap was set in the midst of the sea and I knew it not.
> Every bird fell to its feet; I fell both feet and wings.

But the beloved's sea-like eyes (P II:3, IX:5, XIV:3), shaded by the dark clouds of her brows (P XI:5 Ac̆c̆ern ē cov, unkc̆n tc̆ux amp 'Your eyes are a sea; your brows, a dark cloud') and filled with love-potions (P XII:25 Zayd kc̆o cov ac̆c̆erd del̄ov lcc̆er es 'You have filled the two seas of your eyes with a potion') to intoxicate the swimmer (P XIII:2 Ac̆c̆erd ē cover, xumar u mēstan 'Your eyes are seas, potent and intoxicating'). The two seas are found also in a description by Narekac̆i of the eyes of the Virgin Mary (see Russell, trans. of Mel̄edi cnndean, REArm [in publication]).

Line 12. Cf. also P X:2 Berand šak^c rov i li t^c ut^c ak lezu es 'You are parrot-
tongued, your mouth full of sugar' and XII:30 Atamunk^c d margarit, šak^c arberan
es 'Your teeth are pearls; you are sugar-mouthed'. The poet (Note to Line 9,
p. 9) ascribes therapeutic powers to this sweetness. Muhammad is said to have
advised the faithful to marry virgins with sweet mouths and capable of bearing
many children (B. A. Donaldson, The Wild Rue, A Study of Muhammadan Magic and
Folklore in Iran, London, 1938, p. 48).

Lines 15-16. Oč^c merani, oč^c ceranay, / Oč^c eresvin darnay delin. These lines
are repeated almost exactly in P VI:13-14: Ov zk^c ez sirē onc^c merani / Kam
eresvin darnay delin 'How will the one who loves you die / Or become yellow of
face'? Maten. MS 7708 reads Oč^c eresin gunēn erday 'Nor does the colour depart
[from] his face'. The ašuł Zarkâr (19th century) wrote: 'If, when you speak but
a moment with a hundred-year-old man, / You re-acquaint him with the love of his
youthful days, / Who would not prefer your company in hell / To heaven with the
saints and their sermons on love?' (cited in Hay nor grakanut^c yan patmut^c yun,
I, Erevan, 1962, p. 264).

Lines 23-24. Ov kuř mijac^c ēd girk acē / Kananč^c mēnay k^c an znšdarin. On the
greenness of the lover, Nahapet K^c uč^c ak wrote (II):

> I came down from your mountain and cried out 'Where is the green?'
> And another answered me: 'All mountain and valley are green.
> 'Green are his heart's veins, who has love in his heart.
> 'Black is the heart of him who does not, and his face is green.'

Rabī^c ī of Bušanj wrote (cited by E. G. Browne, A Lit. Hist. of Persia,
Cambridge, 1928, Vol. III, p. 150):

> Whenever I grow merry from the green,
> I must mount the green steed of the spheres;
> On the grass would I eat the green with the ones on whose cheeks
>   the down is green,
> Before I become green under ground.

Cf. also NK LXXI:

> Behold my love: all she wears is green.
> She has put on a multicolored robe with rows of ribbons; the
>   buttonhole is green.
> She has arisen and entered the garden. She goes to the water: the
>   shore is green.
> Below the trees: the tree has flowered, and its leaf is green.

The hornbeam (Arm. nšdari, nšdareni) is frequently used as a simile or metaphor
of the beloved (cf. P XIV:25 Nšdareni car es całkeal 'You are a hornbeam tree
in flower'). Mkrtič^c Nałaš, in a poem on the flower which is Christ, speaks of
that flower's effects on the evil and the good (II:9-12):

> Some from that flower's love
> Turned dry and yellow [cf. P I:15-16].
> Many in that flower's love
> Flowered more than the hornbeam [Całkec^c an k^c an znšdarenin].

In another poem, a rose addresses a nightingale (MN III:56): <u>Erak kanac̆^{c} kenas k^{c}an znšdarenin</u> 'You stand, eternal, greener than the hornbeam.' The hornbeam, which looks like a beech, flourishes in Armenia. It can grow to 60-70 feet, and every two years it gives a harvest of nuts. Its wood is hard, heavy, and good for tools. In America is found the <u>carpinus carolina</u>, whose wood was used on the ship "Old Ironsides". But it is in southeastern Europe and the Caucasus that the hornbeam is most common (see P. Friedrich, <u>Proto-Indo-European Trees</u>, Chicago, 1970, pp. 99-106).

* * *

This poem of love (P II, C, p. 13) is of the same form and metre as P I, and its structure closely resembles that of P I, as well: the sunlike face appears, the sealike eyes, and the cloudlike brows. The image is vast, perfect in its isolation and unapproachability. After the overpowering initial quatrain, the description of the rest of the beloved's body in the next four lines seems swift, although every part is adorned with some choice epithet, as in P I.

But here, a profound change occurs. Rather than embracing the waist of his beloved and tasting the fruits of love, the poet remains riveted to the subject of the first stanza, wishing only to gaze upwards, towards her eyes (Line 15). The beloved chooses to avert her eyes from the lover, who is already aflame and might well be reduced to cinders by their terrifying power, which can banish even sacred learning from the mind (Lines 11-12). The mention of the eyes of the beloved in P I:5-6 occasioned comment; in P II, T^{c}lkuranc^{c}i is (Line 17) denied their light, through a rejection in love which saves him from hellfire--the poem ends on a positive note of blessing and immortality: again, the typical clash of love and religion which obsesses T^{c}lkuranc^{c}i. But the beloved face does not crumble to earth, finally bereft of its power to harm (P I:27), and one is left with the uneasy afterthought of that trap, unsprung in the depths of the sea (cf. Note to P I:11, NK XLII), awaiting the unresolved soul.

TRANSLATION

1   I saw a lovely image
    Like the light-giving sun.
    I saw eyes like seas
    And brows heavier than cloud and sea.

5   A pale brow and splendid mouth;
Her locks and tresses drew out the soul.
Her breast was full of white roses;
Her loins and back swayed more than the willow.

9   She filled me with fire and flame
So that I burn all day long.
I forgot the learning which I had
And have remained but a layman.

13   I said, 'Love me, eyes like the sea.'
She said, 'I keep my eyes to myself.'
Sit, that I may gaze upwards at your face;
Come, arise before me.

17   God pitied me, brothers,
That she answered me thus.
Else were I spellbound,
Wandering about more than the ferocious wolf.

21   Whether I draw back more or less
Will this fire come to an end?
Such love penetrates my heart
And I remain in the trap of sin.

25   Wherever I go, I carry my fear
And the eternal fire of Hell.
Will I be freed of this fire
With which I was ignited unawares?

29   Crazy Yovhannēs T^{c}lkuranc^{c}i,
Cast away your demoniac counsel.
Draw love of this world out of your heart;
Bless the uncreate, existing Word.

Notes

Lines 2-3. These images recall P I and the other lyric poems. Nahapet K^{c}uč^{c}ak
is distinguished by overstatement of such themes (XC):

> I saw my beloved seated, like a thousand full moons,
> Inflamed like the sun, adorned like a brilliant star . . .

Maten. MS 2566 has <u>nor k'elnu</u> 'which rises anew' instead of <u>loys ku tay</u> 'light
giving'.

Line 4. <u>Uner k^{c}an zamp u ztariay</u>. The word used for 'sea' (Arm. <u>cov</u>, cf.
Line 3, <u>ēzcover</u>) is NP <u>daryā</u>, for the sake of metre; the brows of the beloved
are described as a 'dark cloud' (t^{c}ux amp) in P XI:5. In NK LXXXI, another
image is used to describe the beloved's arched brow, while the cloud is within
the beloved's eyes: a fine shift in the use of the simile:

> O my incomparable one, your mother bore none like you.
> Your eyes are like the sea; your brows, like a nightingale's wing.
> In the dawn of your eyes, the Kingdom of Khorasan was a cloud.
> Your brows have made an arch and go as booty to Egypt.
> You have taken many prisoners: many hodjas and many merchants.

Line 5. Maten. MSS 7715, 1990 have čermak 'white' instead of urak 'pale'.

Lines 11-12. The corruption of priests and monks by the beloved is a constant
theme in T^{c}lkuranc^{c}i's lyrics: 'You are a snare for the monks, / A hook and
trap of priests. / You drive the monk out of his mind / Who even lived ever at
the hermitage' (Habełanun es orogayt^c, / K^{c}ahanayic^c aknat u kart^c, / Zmiakec^{c}in
xelk˜en tanis / T^{c}ē kac^{c}er ē zōrn anapat. P IV:17-20); 'Were a priest to see
you, / He would forget his learning and his many books' (T^{c}ē vardapetn zjez
tesnu, / Mořnay zusumn u šat grunk^c. P IX:9-10); 'Love takes shame from the
face / Of monk and priest alike; / It tears elders and deacons from their
orders / And takes sense from the head, shame from the face' (Sēren ku tani
zamōt^{c}n yeresēn / I habełayēn w' i vardapetēn, / Erēc^c, sarkawag ku jgē i
kargēn, / Tani zxelk^{c}n i glxun, zamōt^{c}n yeresēn. P XIII:18-21); 'He who tastes
sin / Gives no more news of God' (Ov or zmełac' čašakn ařnu, / Ayl astucoy č'i
tay xabar. P XIV:51-52). The image of Satan as a trap, or of sin as a snare,
is common in Mediaeval Armenian thought. The beloved, by contrast, is Nahapet
K^{c}uč˜ak's faith (LXII):

> Since my mother bore me, I have not confessed to a priest.
> Whenever I saw a priest, I turned and bolted.
> Whenever I have seen a beauty, I have gone to her arms, to her
>   breast and face.
> I have made a chapel of her breast; I have said my confession to
>   her teats.

Even this worshipful attitude does not ensure against rejection (LXIII):

> Your breast is a white cathedral; your teats, burning lamps.
> I will go and become a beadle, or the lamplighter of your cathedral.
> 'Go, stupid boy! You are unworthy to be lamplighter of my
>   cathedral.
> 'Go off and play, and leave my cathedral in the dark.'

As though this metaphor were not sufficiently sacrilegious, the lover devises
yet another (LIV):

> Your bosom is the Lord's pantry, your breasts a psalter.
> I will go and become a monk and live at your breast,
> Reciting the alphabet so far as I master your breast.

Nahapet K^{c}uč˜ak proposes an arrogant defence of such sacerdotal misbehaviour
before the highest Judge (LVI):

> What can I do, or what could I be? When I see a beauty, I love.
> Were I to learn the cause of eternity, still would I go and speak,
> And take the beloved in my arms, and go to God, and show Him:
> 'You created beauty. Of what sin do You accuse me if I love it?'

All this is written in a spirit utterly alien to T^{c}lkuranc^{c}i, and it seems also
more imaginative, certainly more joyous and entertaining.

Line 17. Nahapet K^{c}uč˜ak would never call this grace (XXII):

> Come out of your house! At least look at me, or love me.
> What will my love alone do, when yours does not befriend it?
> When love comes from two, it is sweeter than almonds and sugar;
> When it comes from one, it is harder than one's dying day.

Line 19. T^{c}ē č^{c}ē mnayi xew kapelu. See P VII: 8 (Es mnac^{c}i xew kapelu 'I remained spellbound', literally 'crazy to be bound'). NK LXV reads:

> A beautiful girl called from the high town, 'My kiss is for free'.
> Her voice reached the monastery; the monks turned into kızılbaš
> [habełnin kapec^{c}in łezēlbaš, literally, 'they bound kızılbaš].
> Many feet and heads were broken; many cowls were torn and broken.

G. R. Driver ('Religion of the Kurds', JRAS, 1922, p. 197) offers the following explanation:

> The word Quzilbash originally means 'red head' and was applied to certain Shi^{c}i Persians, who lived on the Turkish frontier near Adharbaijan and many of whom have settled in Asia Minor in the neighbourhood of Angora and elsewhere, from the red caps which they always wore. But the religion of the modern Quzilbash, who are said to number 45,000 persons, bears now but little resemblance to the Shi^{c}i faith and has become, under the influence of the Kurds, nothing but a very degraded superstition. They worship a large black dog, in which they see the image of the divinity, and seem entirely ignorant of any definite doctrines or religious practices. Once a year they unite in an isolated spot to celebrate a ceremony which leaves far behind in its shameless rites those of the Oriental Bona Dea at Rome. There, after prayers noteworthy only for revolting cynicism and an invocation of the deity of fecundity, the lights are extinguished and the sexes intermingle without regard to age or the ties of kinship. They have no legal existence in the Turkish Empire, and their scandalous rites enjoy only a secret indulgence. They avow no beliefs, but they always give themselves out for orthodox Muslims, that they may enjoy the civil rights permitted to the adherents of that religion.

The qizilbaş was originally the twelve-peaked crimson hat of the Persian Muslim religious leader Haidar; the twelve peaks symbolise the twelve Shi^{c}a Imāms (see Introduction to C. N. Seddon, trans., Hasan-i Rūmlū, Ahsanu't-Tawārīkh, II, Oriental Institute, Baroda, 1934). Haidar's followers devastated Armenian lands. A sixteenth-century Armenian chronicler wrote: 'All the provinces of Armenia which were under the rule of the Qizilbaş (Arm.: Karmraglxoyn 'red-head') were ruined and destroyed. And wherever any building was left standing, the homeless and the naked: men and women, old and young, boys and girls without shelter—went with tearful faces from door to door, beneath the roofs of strangers, to beg for food for themselves' (V. Hakobyan, ed., Manr žamana-kagrut^{c}yunner XIII-XVIII dd., II, Erevan, 1956, p. 243).

Line 21. T^{c}ē šat t^{c}ē k^{c}ič^c i yet jgem. The line is repeated verbatim in P. V:7.

Line 22. A reading of NK XX may suggest that the way to put out the fire kindled by love is the water of baptism (perhaps this is the water of P III: 23-24):

I call on high, O God; may my voice reach you!
Let not the generation of the baptismal font burn in love's
   conflagration [T^col awazani cnund i sirun pelan c̆^ci ēri].
Love indeed has hands and feet like a highwayman.
Come, behold your bandit; a bandit, and he has no arrow!
Arise, come; into iron have you made me. I come not, and she
   drags me.

Line 23. <u>Nay sērn i sirts i ners k'ert^cay</u>. The image of an external force
invading the hapless man could not be clearer. It recalls NK I:

When love came into the world, it came to my heart and dwelt there.
Then it fell from my heart, from earth to earth.
It came up into my head; it came and nested in my brain.
It asked tears of my eyes, and blood flowed down.

*   *   *

This song (P III, C, p. 13-14) is written in the same form and metre as
the foregoing. It is gentler than many of the other poems in its attitude
towards love, though: the lover does not rage against his beloved if she rejects him, nor does he condemn her for seducing him (Lines 3-4). In P XIV:53,
the poet declares, 'Love removed Adam from Paradise', but here, T^clkuranc^ci
reproaches himself not so much for speaking of love's delights as for failing
to remember that the hard realities of death and Judgment will inevitably
intervene; the prevailing attitude is one of perplexed resignation (Line 17),
not misogynist anger. The beloved, for all her power (Lines 1, 5, 6, 8, 14),
is modest (Line 16). She abounds in grace and mercy (Line 12); indeed, she
is 'an example to the good' (Line 9). Although his beloved is a woman of
virtue, T^clkuranc^ci must nonetheless choose between her and God (Line 19).

Perhaps the key to T^clkuranc^ci's understanding is to be sought in that
moment of choice. The Creator is greater than the created; however fine the
creation, its beauty is earthly (Line 20) and ephemeral, and to choose it
over a greater, immortal beauty would be a negative decision, towards ugliness
and evil; the choice between good and evil is difficult enough, for the temp-
tress lays traps for even the most pious men. But far more sublime is the
choice between good and better, although the principle is the same; the hand
that reaches towards earthly virtue, refusing the invisible, ineffable mystery of Heaven, is stamped with the 'sins of death' (Line 18).

TRANSLATION

1 They shed sunlike rays
    When you turn your eyes to love.
    If I remember love, if you forget love,
    I love you with my heart.

5 You shatter stone;
    You melt mountains.
    Him you look upon with love
    You ignite with undwindling flame.

    You are an example to the good;
10 Another mother has borne none like you:
    White-browed and black-eyed,
    Visage of light in grace and mercy.

    Ribbon-lipped, you shed roses;
    With your swaying neck you lay waste citadels.
15 In every member you are beautiful;
    Would that you would show yourself.

    But what can I do? There is no way;
    I lie beneath the sins of death.
    I look at you; I look at Him
20 Who has created you of earth.

    Crazy Yovhannēs T^{c}lkuranc^{c}i,
    You chatter idly all day long.
    You cast man into fire,
    Turn, pour water on him, and pass on.

Notes

Lines 5-6. Nahapet K^{c}uč^{c}ak expresses a similar thought (VIII):

    Look upon the stone, but bring grace from yourself.
    Nothing is stronger than stone; Behold! It gives forth a
        stream of water.
    A hundred-pound millstone shakes in fear of the water.
    My heart is a piece of meat; Alas! How will it oppose your love?

K^{c}uč^{c}ak's image recalls these lines from a ghazal of Sa^{c}dī (Kolliyāt-e šaīx Sa^{c}dī, Tehrān, 1334, AH, p. 759): 'O beloved, it would be strange if your heart of stone / Turned not by water from the eye of Sa^{c}dī, for a millstone turns.' It is perhaps not coincidental that water and millstone are mentioned together so often. According to an Arab proverb, water is life and the most precious stone is the millstone. There is, of course, no life either without bread. Yet man lives not by bread alone, but by love. It is the eyes which possess power over the lover. A Greek lianotragoudi 'short song' (N. G. Politou, Dēmotika tragoudia, Athens, 1975, p. 175) asks: 'Who has seen such war as the eyes wage? / Without knives and swords, one is shattered to pieces.' The imagery of love's power rivals T^{c}lkuranc^{c}i's apocalyptic vision of Tal i veray datastani 'Poem on the Judgment' (Covakan, p. 44, Lines 5-7):

> He will judge the whole world in a fire the measure of a torrent
> And the burning earth will burst aflame; rocks and hills will melt
> more swiftly than wax.
> The crack of thunder will be lightning: the rushing rivers will
> be swirled into clouds.

P Appendix V:3-4, 'I was a firm stone, and it shook me; / I was an iron fortress; like water was I melted,' presents a similar vision, but it is unlikely
to belong to any mysticism of which love is the dynamic principle, as described by Rudolf Otto in The Idea of the Holy (New York, 1973, p. 24):

> In mysticism, too, this element of 'energy' is a very living and
> vigorous factor, at any rate in the 'voluntaristic' mysticism, the
> mysticism of love, where it is very forcibly seen in that 'con-
> suming fire' of love whose burning strength the mystic can hardly
> bear, but begs that the heat that has scorched him may be miti-
> gated, lest he be himself destroyed by it.

The tone of the Armenian poet is one of condemnation, not transformation.

Line 7. Zov du sirov natar anes. Arm. Natar < Ar. nadar 'a look, glance;
attention.' Maten. MSS 7715, 1990 and 7712 have nazar, the Perso-Turkish
rendering of the word. MN II:11 reads Apa k^caram ara, ahli nadar es 'Then be
graceful, you are wise.' (Ar. ahl 'people' + idāfat + nadar "people of
nadar". The word nadar here has a connotation of wisdom and beneficence.)
Grigoris Aɫt^camarc^ci XXII:27 reads Yov or du nayis aṙnes natar, which we
translate 'He whom you look at, you give the eye to'; MN III:39 has the same
sense, Um or k^caɫc^cr nayes ew nadar anes 'He whom you look at sweetly and give
the eye to.' P XIV:38 reads Ew blbulin anenk^c nadar 'And [let us] gaze upon
the nightingale.' Here, Maten. MSS 9271, 7715 and 1990 have nazar. The meaning of the phrase nadar aṙnem in Mediaeval Armenian lyric poetry varies from
'I behold' to 'I look with favour upon' to 'I give the eye to.' Sa^cdī, in
the Introduction to the Golestān, seems to have the former meaning in mind
with the phrase nazar dāstan: 'When will you show grace to friends, who have
nazar for enemies?' But the nazar is also the evil eye, against which one
burns incense pounded of seeds of the wild rue (B. A. Donaldson, The Wild Rue,
London, 1938, p. 13). Again, the beloved's eyes are both enticing and
destructive.

Line 10. Ayl mayrn c̆^cē berer zēt zk^cez. Cf. NK XCVI:
> I took the world in my palm and went all over this earth.
> Another mother has borne none like you [Ayl mayr zet zk^cez c̆^ci
> berer], and there is none like you in foreign lands.
> You put on green and blackberry; you come and stand before me.
> White forehead, arched brows, eyes like the sea; you have light
> ablaze.

Line 12. Lut^cf u k^caramov luseres. Arm. Lut'f < Ar. lutf; k^caram < Ar. karam;
the words are virtually synonymous and form a pair-combination used in

MN III:61 Vardn i blbuln asac^C: Ē lut^Cf u k^Caram 'The rose said to the nightingale, "O grace and mercy"', and XIV:79: T^Cēpēt tesay amēn mardoy lut^Cf u k^Caram 'Although I have seen the grace and mercy of every man'; in MN III:11, 32 it is the beloved's nadar (cf. Note to Line 7) which provokes hope of her k^Caram in the lover. P XI:11-12 reads: Lut^Cfn ē cacker zamēn ašxarhs, / Šak^Car kat^Cēr iwr k^Caramēn 'Her grace has covered all this world; / Her mercy shed drops of sugar.' KE XX:14 reads Zeray i lērbēn č^Celnē lut^Cf u k^Caram 'For from the shameless one neither grace nor mercy comes.'

Line 13. Lar šrt^Cēnovēd vard t^Cap^Ces. Arm. lar 'string, ribbon, a string on a musical instrument'; Maten. MSS 7715, 2398 and 1990 have sar instead 'a row, series, or string,' as of pearls; the beloved's teeth are thus described in P IX:7-8 Šołayr k^Clap^Cn u lar šrt^Cunk^C / U margartešar atamunk^C 'Your jaw gleamed, and your ribbon-lips, / And your teeth, a strand of pearls'; Kosteneanc^C here reads lal 'ruby' instead of lar. Sayat^C Nova wrote of a 'Magic mirror, / Ruby and topaz', and two precious stones drawn antak covi mič^Cen 'from the midst of the bottomless sea'--cf. P XIV:19 Ayd anatak covud nman 'Like your bottomless sea'; the essence of the beloved's eyes is drawn from the depths of themselves--and the two eyes of the beloved, in which future and past are mirrored (Jam-halila, / Lal u t^Cila; see M. X. Naryan, 'Sayat'-Novayi gorcacac mi k^Cani artahaytut^Cyunneri masin,' Lraber, Erevan, February 1974, pp. 47-48). Frik wrote of the Virgin (Appendix IX:32) Du lal mecagin, or i Badašxan, / Ealut^C ew zērut^C u ayl patwaken / Akn lusatu 'You are the ruby of great price in Badakhshan, / A ruby and emerald (cf. P V:1 Hanc^Ckun ayl ov teser zmrut^C 'Who has seen another such emerald?' and other noble, / Light-giving jewel[s].' P XII:30 similarly reads Atamunk^Cd margarit, šak^Carberan es 'Your teeth are pearls; you are sugar-mouthed,' and P XIV:12 has Margarit atmunk^Cd šarēšar 'Your teeth are pearls in rows'). Thus, a lar, perhaps, of lal, conceals šar and šar, all beneath the kamar of the brows overarching lal u t^Cila, 'ruby and gold.'

Line 14. Čočan vzovēd berder k^Cakes. The berd 'citadel, fortress' is the vanquished lover (cf. Note to Lines 5-6); of the man who is assaulted by the agony of death itself, Mkrtič^C Nałaš uses the same imagery (XII:5-7):

> I knew I was a citadel in this world.
> The pain of death besieged my body:
> Behold! My whole rampart was agitated, and it crumpled.

Line 16. K^Cawēl t^Cē k'ez nēman du es. Arm. K^Cawel 'but, lest, if only, might'; cf. Frik XX:31 K^Cawel t^Cē ert^Cank^C ař Koysn 'Let us but go to the Virgin'; MN V:24 Bažin č^Cunis i K^Cristosē, k^Cawel dařnas 'w apašxares 'You have no portion from Christ unless you turn and repent'; P VIII:15 K^Cawel draxtn anmahut^cean 'Were it the immortal Paradise.' Ačaŕean derives the word from k^caw 'no, never, not at all' and k^caw lic^ci 'God forbid!' (Bedrossian); Maten. MSS 6159 and 2556 of P VIII have the alternate form k^caweal, Classical Armenian p. part. 'repented, innocent' of k^cawem 'I expiate'. The translation of the line is problematical; I have relied for the meaning of nman in this context on the Song of Songs II:17, which reads in Armenian Darjir nmaneac^c du, ełbawrordi im 'Turn and show thyself, O son of my brother'; a translation of k^cez neman du es as 'You are like yourself', and of the whole line as 'But that you are like yourself' seems too obscure.

Line 22. Zōrn i bun ĕnd ayl k'ases. Zōrn: ōr Mediaeval and Modern Armenian 'day', acc. sing. prefix z- + def. art. with a prepositional phrase i bun rendered 'radically, to the essence', i.e., 'completely', hence the idiom 'all day long'; ĕnd ayl xōsem 'I speak of another', i.e., of extraneous matters, hence 'idly', is another idiom proper to Mediaeval Armenian (Ačaŕean).

Line 24. Darnas lnus ĵur w'anc^c nes. The lover in an Armenian folksong, inflamed by his beloved, begs her to pour water on him as T^clkuranc^ci does here to the excited listener: Čermakec^c getin jĕnic^c, / Alĵi, durs ari tĕnic^c; / Jeŕoved ērvac sĕrtis / Kam deł ara, kam ĵur lic^c 'The ground is whitened by the snow. / Come, girl, out of your house; / Make a cure for my heart/ Burned by your hand, or fill it with water'. (Komitas Vardapet and M. Abełyan, Hazar u mi xał, Erevan, 1969, p. 29.)

* * *

In this poem (P IV; C, pp. 14-15), written in the same form and metre as the foregoing, T^clkuranc^ci declares his beloved pure to God and man alike (Lines 4, 5, 6, 15, 16), and one senses some variation in the poet's attitude to love; when first burned, he rejects it altogether (P I), or avoids it rather than be burned again (P II). He proposes love, but only that of higher things, claiming that though earthly love might be good, love of Heaven ought to rule it out in this life (P III). Here, though, he appears to accept the necessity to live within the terms of this world, at the same time in a way acceptable to God (Line 23); love, if it comes from thoughts of the heart (Line 22), is justified between the lover and the beloved. But the passion of the monks

(Lines 17-20) is another, darker face of love which is evil in its destructive effect upon the spiritual side of man.

TRANSLATION

A thousand Yusufs are your servants,
O sun and beautiful visage.
All the world is a sacrifice to you,
For there is no fault in you.

5   There is not a hair of fault in you;
You are pure and holy in person.
I inscribe myself a sacrifice to you,
Your servant, at your mercy.

Lily, basil and violet,
10 Water lily and rose at your breast,
Immortal apple and quince,
Pomegranate and orange and red rose.

Your breast is a paradise of immortality,
A paradise laden with immortal fruit.
15 You are an example to the good;
God and man love you.

You are a snare of the monks,
A trap and hook for priests.
You carry off the senses of the monk
20 Who even lived ever at the hermitage.

Crazy Yovhannēs T^{C}lkuranc^{C}i,
Open your ear with thoughts of the heart.
Make haste, and find a way in this world,
And you will take up a crown of glory in the next.

Notes

Line 1. Joseph (the normal Armenian for which is Yovsēp^C; the name appears in T^{C}lkuranc^{C}i's poem as Usuf, Yusuf < Ar. Yūsūf), to whom Sūra XII of the Koran is devoted, is the archetype of human beauty in the Near East (cf. P XIII:25 Yovsēp^C Gełec^{C}ik w' anōrinak mard 'Joseph the Beautiful and the man without peer'; XX:21-23 Kinn zgełec^{C}katipn Yovsēp^C / Aṙnē iwreann ordi anē, / Yetoy zsirtn č̌^{C}ar sermanē 'Woman takes Joseph of beautiful countenance / And makes of him her son. / Then she plants evil in his heart;' cf. also NK XIII:1 in Note to P I:1). I have reproduced the Arabic form in the translation; where T^{C}lkuranc^{C}i has used the normal Armenian form, it has been rendered as English 'Joseph'. Pivazyan's suggestion (Glossary, p. 297) that Usuf may mean 'Arab' seems wrong, as the literary connotation of the Biblical and Koranic name is clear enough to let it stand: the poet could have seen himself as an innocent of the holy people, lured by Potiphar's wife.

Line 3. Amēn ašxarhēs k^cez fētē. Cf. MN III:31 Aha es k^cez fida, im t^cači sarvar 'Behold I am a sacrifice to you, O crown of my commander;' Arm. fētē (fida) < Ar. fidā 'sacrifice'. Line 7 uses the Armenian equivalent mataɫ.

Line 4. Zeray č̌^cunis iski ɫalat. Ɫalat < Ar. ghalat 'mistake, transgression'; Aɫayan lists Armenian derivative forms anɫalat 'blameless', xalatwor 'culpable' and xaltil 'to err'. Cf. KE XXI:3 Na t^cewi im hogwoy xōsk^cn i yir srtin ǰumlay ɫalat 'Behold, it seems the words of my soul were an assembly of errors to his heart'. Ɫalat is repeated in Line 5. Xač̌^cikyan, Hišatakaranner, Vol. III, pp. 486, 531 cites Maten. MS 5440, fifteenth century Srti tarekusanac^cs, ah! Zamēn ɫalat grec^ci 'Of my heart's perplexities, yea every fault did I write down' and MS 6366, also fifteenth century T^coɫut^ciwn arēk^c, es em ɫalat, awrinak č̌^cunēi; zinč̌^c or č̌arec^ci ays č̌^cap^cs ēr; crec^ci, bayc^c du i teɫn hramē 'Forgive me; I am at fault and had no example. What I preached was so much: I wandered, but you, command [me back] to [my] place'. Cf. NK XL: Banik mi ɫalat ari, or sirun eɫa xašnarac 'I erred in being love's shepherd'.

Line 8. U k^cez caray u k^cez zak^cat^c. Zak^cat^c < Ar. zakat 'charitable tax', hence 'mercy, charity'.

Lines 9-10. Šušan, ěrēhan u manušak, / U nōnōfar, w'i coc^cn vard. The lily is a Biblical symbol of the beloved (cf. Song of Songs II:1 et passim. and P IX:3-4, X:30). Armenian ěrēhan (ṙahan) < Ar. raihān 'basil' (Hübschmann, p. 175) is mentioned in NK LXXXVI:

> Ah, my mouth of pomegranates and almonds, pomegranates and almonds, flowers and basil [Ay im nuṙ u nuš beran, nuṙ u nuš, caɫik 'w ěrahan]!
> You are like rosemary [hazrevard]; your mother has not borne one like you [cf. P III:10].
> Your lips are like lemon; you open the mine [matan < Ar. ma^cdan] of man.
> Your tongue is like a nightingale, singing praises like the spring.

And P XIV:9-10 reads Eresěd vaṙ ē cirani, / Vard, ěrēhan u nunufar 'Your face is burning purple: / Rose, basil and water lily'. The seed of basil (t^coxmi měrēhan, NP toxm-e raihān) was used in preparing potions against demons (Macler, L'enluminaire arménienne profane, Pl. LXI). Basil, the 'royal' herb, enjoys a place of great honor in many cultures. In Christian Greece, on Epiphany Eve, a priest dips basil in a copper bowl of water, ties the basil to a cross, and goes from room to room in parishioners' houses singing canticles and shaking drops of water, to get rid of the kallikantsaroi-demons. Basil--basilikós--is also held in high esteem in folk verses (see G. G. Abbott, Macedonian Folklore, 1903, repr. Chicago, 1969, pp. 75, 94). In Zoroastrian legend, the fragrance of basil is considered choice, sweet, auspicious, the very breeze of heaven (cf. Pāzand, Āfrin Ī wuzurgān, ed. and trans. by B. N. Dhabhar, Translation of the Zandī Khurtāk Avistāk, p. 411, n. 24, Šāyest nē Šāyest 10.7: pad šab may ud sparam ud hēč xwarišnīg tis ō abāxtar rōn nē rēzišn 'at night, cast not northwards wine, basil, or any other edible thing'; Mēnōg Ī Xrad 7.15; Do^{c}ā-ye Bahrām Varjāvand, in Āfrīnagān-e Gahāmbar: U-Tān may ō jam be dast, u-tān sparam andar bāzū, 'And may you have wine and cup in your hand, and basil at your arm'. The Qur'ān, 56.89, borrows this idea of basil in Heaven. In the ninth century, when the widow of the Kurrami leader Jāvīdān married Bābek, she offered a spring of basil to him (Cambridge History of Iran, 3.2, p. 1011), and the Fārs-nāme, twelfth century, cited by Christensen, Modi Mem. Vol., Bombay, 1930, pp. 327-328, has Anōšīrvān offer a sprig of basil to Kavād. Rūmī wrote (Nicholson, Dīvāne-e Šams-e rabrīz, No. 16, p. 64): bar man be vaz ke mozde-ye raihān-am ārzū-st 'blow upon me, for I desire the prize of basil,' and here we arrive at T^{c}lkuranc^{c}i's meaning: the beloved's breath is heaven, joy, and immortality. The Persian religious use of basil may be very old--perhaps Ezekiel 8:16 is alluding to it in the condemnation of those sun worshippers (= Zoroastrians?) at Jerusalem 'who put the branch to the nose'. (But note the nosegay in Persia today.)

The violet (Arm. manušak) appears in P XII:3, XIII:36 and SV:34. The water lily (here nōnōfar < Ar. nīlūfar, līlūfar, cf. Hübschmann, p. 279) is a holy flower of Zoroastrianism, and on the eleventh day of the fourth month Tīr the Jašn Ī Nīlōfar 'Feast of Water Lilies' is celebrated (J. J. Modi, The Religious Ceremonies and Customs of the Parsees, 2nd ed., Bombay, 1937, p. 437). It is spelled Nōnōfar as a girl's name in a MS of 1394 (Bodleian Arm. MS 69, cf. Baronian and Conybeare, Cat. Arm. MSS Bod., Oxford, 1918, p. 161). NK XII reads:

> Ah, my infidel's infidel [k^{c}yafuri k^{c}yafur], burn not before the infidel.
> Be fuller than a wine glass; do not spill out for every young fool.
> Do not be like the rose, the myrtle that will grow on every street.
> Be the water lily which grows from the bottom of the sea [Nunufar calik elir, or covun yatakn erewi].
> A thousand eyes will gaze upon you, but a thousand hands will not reach you.
>
> Your love is like the sea; by swimming, none can reach it.

P XV:39-40 reads Nawnawfarn i Jērēn i durs / Delin kanač^c erewec'aw 'And the water lily, rising from its pool / Appeared, yellow-green'. The water lily may be seen as the pupil emerging from the depths of the beloved's sea-like eyes (cf. Notes to P I:11 and III:13), visible but unreachable.

Lines 11-12. The quince (Arm. serkewil) and orange (Arm. narinj) are mentioned in the Song of Songs (IV:3; VI:6); Nahapet K^{c}uč^{c}ak saw the hand of his beloved as a pomegranate (XC: Zotkunk^{c}n al i jur idir, znṙna jeṙk^{c}ukn al luac^c 'She put

her feet in water and washed her little pomegranate hand'). P XV:59 Nuṙn ayl
ebac^c hazar akṙayn 'The pomegranate also bared a thousand teeth', would suggest the voluptuous, ripe, sweetness of the beloved's lips, forced open by the
heat of love--the summer of the metaphor--to reveal their pearly treasure.

Line 15. Du ōrinak es alēknun. This line is a verbatim repetition of
P XIII:9. Tewkanc^c published it as du annman es mēǰ aleknun 'you are incomparable amongst the good'.

Lines 17-18. Habelanun es orogayt^c, / K^{c}ahanayic^c aknat u kart^c. The Epistle
of James, I.14, speaks of men 'hooked and trapped by their lusts', and this
image of enticement and capture of the unwary is found also in texts from
Qumrān (see T. H. Gaster, The Dead Sea Scriptures, 3rd ed., New York, 1976,
p. 16). Here, the beloved is a trap for the lover. Cf. NK LXXXVIII:

> Ah, my snare and evil one, where have you come from, and met me?
> Your eyes are like a burning taper; there is a jewel at the end of
> your brow.
> You have taken pearl and ruby and sewn your lips' radiance [cf.
> Note to P III:13].
> With it you have taken my breath, but the soul in me you have not
> taken.

The sea of the beloved's eyes contains a hook for the fish that dares to plunge
into its waters; P XIII:26 compares the one captivated by the beauty of Joseph
(cf. Note to P IV:1) to such a fish: Zinč^c jukn i siroy yankarc ēnkni kart^c
'Like a fish, for love he falls suddenly onto the hook'. Brit. Mus. Or. MS
1608, Fol. 273b has this warning beneath the title of the hymn Olb ew xrat
pitani by Yovhannēs T^{c}lkuranc^{c}i: Ēndhanur mardkayin lselik^c: lēwaruk^c ēzbarbaṙ
beranoys. Heštut^{c}iwn ašxarhis ē patrank^c, orpēs kart^c i covu orsordac^c 'To be
heard by all men in common: Hear ye the speech of my mouth! The pleasures of
the world are deception, as a hook in a sea of hunters' (cf. Conybeare, Cat.
Arm. MSS Brit. Mus., London, 1913). 'Hunters' probably refers to fishermen
(Arm. ǰknors, literally, 'fish-hunter').

The clergy of the Armenian Church are often mocked and castigated by the
Mediaeval poets (cf. Note to P II:12); Mkrtič^c Nalaš (IV:65-74), himself an
archbishop, condemns the corrupt hierarchy of the Church at every level:

> Katholikoi swelled the fellowship of the lawless,
> Ordaining unlettered bishops, all for avarice.
> Newly-sprouted priests have become salesmen of the Word
> And preach the pleasures of men, all for avarice.
> Bishops transgress the canon concerning the house of prostitution
> And accept the red dekan [dahekan, a gold coin] as a bribe, all
> for avarice.
> The monks have abjured the monasteries and have forgotten all the
> psalms.
> They go round from door to door, all for avarice.
> The elders fight with each other, raising club and sceptre;
> They rip out beards and punch each other in the mouth, all for avarice.

In the Paulician <u>Banali c̆smartut^cean</u> (F. C. Conybeare, trans., <u>The Key of</u>
<u>Truth</u>, Oxford, 1898, pp. xxxix, 16, 17), the Devil's favourite disguise is
said to be that of a monk, and his twelfth disguise is that of a hermit; demons
become anchorites at remote sketes, the following ingenious explanation being
given for the latter: Nok^ca hanapaz zbanǰars ew zxotelēns siren . . . ew
zcomapahs pahen, k^canzi ew kerakurk^c noc^ca hanapaz i gic̆ayin telis busani.
Vasn aysorik ew bnakut^ciwnk^c noc^ca andr lini, k^cani yoyž siren zna 'They love
vegetables and grasses every day . . . and they keep the [meatless] fasts be-
cause their daily food grows in damp spots, wherefore their dwellings are also
there, because they dearly love it.'

Line 20. Several MSS have <u>anarat</u> 'pure, virtuous' instead of <u>anapat</u> 'desert,
hermitage'.

Lines 22-24. <u>Srti mětōk^c zakanǰěd bac^c. / Astēns aray k^cez c̆ar šutov, / Andēn</u>
<u>aṙnus psak p^caṙac^c</u>. These lines are repeated verbatim in P XVII:34-36.

* * *

This (P V; C, p. 15) is written in the same form and metre as the fore-
going. T^clkuranc^ci portrays himself as a wanderer distracted by passion, ar-
guing with himself and justifying his predicament to an invisible judge. He
is drawn to the candle of his beloved; her light is mirrored in his own face--
i.e., she transmits her happiness to him and bestows life on him--but he is
too fragile, a bit of thin plate, and he melts (Lines 13-14). The impossi-
bility of his predicament is literally reflected in this image: plate that
does not mirror fire will glow but dully; the lover will glow only in the
presence of the beloved, but he will also melt. Her love is terror (Line 9),
but the cure is harder to contemplate than the malady (Line 16). The beloved
is a narcotic indeed: she is pain itself and the only release from pain (see
Note to P I:9).

T^clkuranc^ci argues that his infatuation is not his sin; he is the instrument of another will (Lines 11-12), and even if he is driven to wrongful be-
haviour by love, he bears no responsibility for his actions. Nahapet K^cuc̆^cak
addresses a similar complaint to God (LVI: see Note to P II:11-12), and
T^clkuranc^ci's apology seems likewise addressed to either God or the listener,
rather than to the beloved herself (the 'turtledove' of Line 15). The

essential argument of the first four stanzas is informed by the plea of passivity and helplessness. The poet's passion is doomed to failure: 'The Lord will not bring your will to fullness' (Line 20).

TRANSLATION

Who saw another such emerald,
A topaz gem and pearl.
She arose before my unsuspecting eyes,
Reaped my breath and took my mind away.

5   She leaves no patience in me;
I have no cease at home or outside.
Whether I draw back more or less
Her image never leaves my mind.

So much as I look I am affrighted;
10   My heart in my stomach turns around.
Of what crime do you accuse me?
He who sees does not remain just.

Like gold foil held close to the taper
I have caught fire; there is no way out.
15   Ah, my turtledove, what will become of me,
When the potion for this wound is so severe?

Crazy Yovhannēs T^clkuranc^ci,
Give not the whole day over to idle talk.
Draw love of this world from your heart;
20   The Lord will not fulfill your will.

Notes

Lines 1-2. Hanc^ckun ayl ov teser zmrut^c / Tpazion akn u čuhar. Arm. čuhar < Ar. juhar 'jewel, essence' (loan-word from Middle Iranian gōhr); Arm. akn likewise means both 'jewel' and 'source, origin' (Bedrossian), although the nom. pl. for the former is akank^c, while for the latter meaning it is akunk^c. T^clkuranc^ci may have intended a subtle play on the two words, but P XIV:14 (Bernēd i vayr t^cap^ci juhar 'Gems drop down from your mouth') clearly intends juhar as 'jewel'; on the beloved as a jewel, see P III:13, XIII:46.

Line 7. T^cē šat t^cē k^cič^c i yet jgem. This line is repeated verbatim in P II:21.

Line 10. Tewkanc^c instead of i p^coris k^carnu 'in my stomach turns' has k^canc^cnu krcic^cs 'passes from my breast'.

Line 13. Zēt ēzt^cit^cełn i momn i mōt. The lover is a fragile piece of gold foil which melts in love's fire; in the poem 'Parting' by the Mediaeval Hebrew

poet Yehudah ha-Levi (Nina Salaman, <u>Selected Poems of Jehudah Halevi</u>, Philadelphia, 1946, p. 48, Line 35), the lover is thin plate upon which the beloved's words are stamped. Cf. P XIII:40.

Line 15. <u>Ay im ɫumri es inč^c linim</u>. Arm. <u>ɫumri</u> < Ar. <u>qumrī</u> 'turtledove'.
Compare Song of Songs I.10, K̄^canzi geɫec^ckac^can cnawtk^c k^co ibrew ztatrakē.
T^clkuranc^ci in another poem (<u>Xrat pitani ew awgtakar</u>; Covakan, p. 35,
Lines 17-18) rebukes himself for the mellifluousity whereby he deceives his
listeners into believing his talk of earthly delights: <u>Xew Yovhannēs
T^clkuranc^ci, ɫumri t^cut^ca es ew blul</u> [Covakan: t^cut^ca <k>, NP. tūtī 'parrot';
bl <b> ul], / <u>Marmnawori es p^coyt^c i gorc, hogewori es šil ew gul</u> 'Crazy
Yovhannēs T^clkuranc^ci, you are turtledove, parrot and nightingale; / Hastening
to the deeds of the body, you are squint-eyed and dull to the things of the
soul.'

Line 15. Cf. KE, p. 180, Line 9: <u>Ekayk^c mankunk^c i paɫč^canin, / Caɫkunk^cn i
mēj vĕran zarnemk^c</u>; / <u>ɫumrin erger mez eɫanak / Aysor eɫev paycaṙ garun</u> 'Come,
children, into the garden, / And let us strike a tent of flowers! / The turtledove was singing us a melody; / Today it was a glowing spring' (on the last
line, cf. P VIII:1 <u>Aha eɫew paycaṙ garun</u>).

* * *

This (P VI; C, p. 15-16) is written in the form and metre of the foregoing, but it differs from P I-V in that its final stanza does not contain any
condemnation or warning or counsel; there is no clear progression of thought
or attitude to be discerned in it, no widening illumination. Each quatrain is
a fine, almost self-contained expression of the beloved's beauty. As the
scribe of Maten. MS 1990 wrote, it is a love poem <u>yuž azniw</u> 'noble indeed'.

TRANSLATION

     I am your desire, of your face's light,
     City of Khotan, China and Mahāchina.
     If they of Hindustan beheld your tresses,
     Wherever you went they would call you back.

5   The hundred year old monk
     Whose white has turned yellow
     Severs the sacred girdle of the Mass
     And desires you before the Cross.

But you are the potion of happiness.
10 When they take you into the garden,
You shake your locks and tresses loose
And reveal your breast in the garden.

How will the one who loves you ever die
Or turn yellow of face?
15 Pride and acclaim to your parent;
Glory and honour to your maker.

How can crazy Yovhannēs T^clkuranc^ci
Praise you?
A Coptic slave befits you;
20 A Bulgar, Cherkess, Greek or Latin.

Notes

Line 1. <u>Loys eresac^cd em k^co p^cap^cak^c</u>. The implication here seems to be that the lover's desire for his beloved is her own desire; what is the light of the Sun if there is none to behold it and no Moon to mirror it? The beloved desires the light of her own face, and the lover is her moon. The Persian poet Maghribī wrote (cf. Browne, Vol. III, p. 334): 'When the one enamoured of your beauty looked in the mirror / And saw the reflected image of his cheek, he became wild and mad. / At every glance he displayed the perfection of his cheek / To his own eyes, in a hundred ornaments and vestments.' Several MSS contain the variant reading <u>Loys eresac^cd ē k^co p^cap^cuk</u> 'The light of your face is soft.'

Line 2. <u>K^całak^c Xut^can, Č^cin u mač^cin</u>. Praise for the beauty of a city and comparison of the beloved with it is common in Armenian literature (see Note to P XIII:24). T^clkuranc^ci uses this conceit frequently; indeed, P XIV:29 is a verbatim repetition of VI:2: 'O beauteous city, lofty and firm fortress.' Or a city may be the beloved's ransom. The nightingale declares to the rose (MN III:44): <u>K^co mēk hayild aržē zk^całak^cn Mač^cin, / Č^cē Č^cinumač^cin mēk hayelud gin</u> 'Your one glance is worth the city of Mahā China; / Nor is China and Mahā-China the price of one look from you.' KE, p. 180, Line 8: <u>Du es k^całak^c Č^cinumač^cin</u> 'You are the city of China and Mahā-China'. Similarly, T^clkuranc^ci writes (XIII:55-58): <u>Pag mi yeresēd ažē zEznkan, / zHapaš u zEaman, zTil u zHndustan. / Erku varsd ē gin, ē Č^cin u Xut^can, / Pułłar u zĒstmbol u šahri Eaztan</u> 'One kiss from your face is worth all Erznka, / Ethiopia and Yemen, Delhi and Hindustan. / O China and Khotan, your two tresses are the price of China and Khotan, / Of Bulgaria, Istanbul and the city of Yazd.' Khotan was famed for its musk, cf. Frik, Appendix IX:36: <u>Du mušk, or goven Xut^cayi xudan</u> 'You are musk that the lord of Khotan praises'. On Khotan, see V. Minorsky, trans., <u>Hudūd al-^cĀlam</u>, London, 1937, pp. 85,255; before its conquest by the Turks <u>ca</u>. A.D. 1000, Khotan was a great Iranian centre of Central Asian Buddhism; it traded also in jade (see H. W. Bailey, <u>The Culture of the Sakas in Ancient Iranian Khotan</u> in E. Yarshater, Series ed., Columbia Lectures on Iranian Studies, No. 1, Caravan Books, Delmar, N. Y., 1982). Arm. $\check{C}^c$in u ma$\check{c}^c$in is 'China and Mahā-China'. Cf. KE, p. 180, Line 8 <u>Du es k^{c}a</u>+<u>ak^c</u> $\check{C}^c$inuma$\check{c}^c$in 'You are the city of $\check{C}^c$inuma$\check{c}^c$in'; the beloved is exquisite and exotic amidst things commonplace and prosaic. In the days of Mongol invasion, the faraway and unknown land of China was thought to be the source of the scourge that devastated much of Armenia. The Chronicle of Sebastac^{c}i (<u>circa</u> A.D. 1937) relates (as translated by A. G. Galstian, <u>Armianskie istochniki o Mongolakh</u>, Moscow, 1962, p. 23):

> In the Armenian year 669, 20,000 Tatars came out of the country of $\check{C}^c$in and Ma$\check{c}^c$in, crossed the valleys of Albania and reached Gugark^c. Destroying everything in their path, they reached Tiflis but turned back quickly, as the Georgian king Lasa pursued them.

Davit^c Ba+i$\check{s}$ec^{c}i's <u>History</u> is more guarded (Galstian, p. 103):

> In the year (Armenian) 670 the Tatars came from the northeast; according to some, they were from the land of $\check{C}^c$in and Ma$\check{c}^c$in; others consider them barbaric tribes who came from the region lying beyond the gates of Derbent; yet others consider them Scythians from the extreme north, and all these tribes are called Tatars, according to the prophet; Scythian barbarians, strong and great in number.

The 'prophet' referred to is probably Nersēs the Great. We learn from a colophon of A.D. 1248 that he (Galstian, p. 46)

> predicted the time of their invasion, saying: "After my death, when seventy years shall have elapsed, this will take place." And behold, fifty years after the holy man's prophecy, they became strong conquerors, and then they advanced on the East, and twenty-eight years later appeared in the Armenian land. . . .

The Armenians regarded the catastrophe as a divinely ordained punishment for their sins, only preceded by Old Testament-style prophecies of doom, so in a sermon of A.D. 1251, Kostandin Catholicos Barjrberdc^{c}i (Galstian, p. 44) admonished his flock to regard the Khan's power as proceeding from God. During the Mongol period many Armenians, including King Het^{c}um of Cilicia, visited Karakorum, the Mongol capital, and recorded their wonder at the exotic splendor of $\check{C}^c$inuma$\check{c}^c$in.

Line 4. Maten. MS 9597 instead of <u>ko$\check{c}^c$in</u> 'call' has <u>ku gan</u> 'come'.

Line 20. <u>Pu</u>+<u>ar</u>, $\check{c}^c$ark^{c}az, ho+om, la$\check{c}^c$in. Arm. <u>ho+om</u>, lit. 'Roman', i.e., a Greek of the Eastern Roman Empire. Several MSS instead of <u>la$\check{c}^c$in</u> have <u>latin</u>, but perhaps one should reject the <u>lectio facilior</u> and translate 'Laz' tentatively.

* * *

This (P VII; C, p. 16) is written, again in the form and metre of the foregoing. It is about death; love might be a thing of some importance, but death overshadows it (Lines 1, 2), and with death comes the judgement of man's deeds (Line 20), and love adds no virtue to these. (Line 15) Indeed, the world is of so little account compared to the awesome weight of Judgement Day that it is better for a man to kill his feelings and renounce the sight of beauty (Lines 9, 10) than to neglect thought of the next world even for a moment, even in the most trivial way (Line 19). Spring, T^clkuranc^ci assures us in another poem, would also be very beautiful, were it not for death's day, Hell and the final judgement (P VIII:17-20). But in that poem, the dire warning comes in the last stanza of a five-stanza poem, and all that comes before it is loving description of the beauty of Spring. Here only one stanza (Lines 5-8) is devoted entirely to the beloved, while death threatens from the start.

TRANSLATIONS

> Were there neither death nor dying
> I would have many other cares, but
> I dare not embark on some foul deed;
> I fear my eye will not cease from crying.
>
> 5 I saw you as the light,
> Like the sun that rises anew.
> My heart was ignited with sharp flame.
> I remained spellbound.
>
> I will put a knife to my heart;
> 10 I will give my eyes to the needle to poke out.
> May this world not fill me with shame;
> In the next world, my portion is Gehenna's food.
>
> But man gains naught in love,
> Nor does he partake of glory from God.
> 15 This world fills man with shame;
> In the next world, his portion is Gehenna's food.
>
> Crazy Yovhannēs T^clkuranc^ci,
> Do not lay for yourself foul words.
> For every empty, negligible word
> 20 You have an account to give in the next world.

Notes

Lines 1-2. Mkrtič^c Nałaš echoes this sentiment in III;77-80: K^{c}anzi sēr ašxarhis awurk^c mi kałc^{c}r ē, / Yetoy bažak mahu ew dzoxoc^c ē, / Zi mah kay ew meranil, yetinn lac^c ē, / Ew sarsap^c dzoxoc^{c}n zis xist ku mašē 'For the love of this world is an ephemeral sweet; / Then is the cup of death and Hell. / For there is death and dying, the last is crying, / And the terror of Hell greatly wearies me'. Those with many plans are surprised by the arrival of death, which makes naught of their cares. A dying youth pleads (MN XI:41-44): 'Inǰ č^{c}ē aten, oč^c žamanak meraneloy, / Oč^c nel zntan ew gerezman mtaneloy, / Kamk^c č^{c}unim es im tanēn elaneloy, / Zi šat hasrat^c unim u šat ban hogaloy 'It is not the hour, not the season for my death, / Not for me to enter the narrow prison and the tomb. / I have no will to leave my home, / For I have much longing and much to worry about'. Cf. P VII:2: Es uni šat ban hogalu. Mkrtič^c wrote his tragic lines after he had witnessed the plague that carried off many of the young at Diyarbakir. A man overtaken by death laments (MN XII:4) Zinč^c t^{c}atpir unēi, kiskatar mnac^c 'Whatever plans I had remained half-completed'.

Line 3. Č^{c}išxem dner zis piłc gorcoy. Compare with Line 18 Mi dner zk^{c}ez piłc baneru. Several MSS instead of dner have dnel; the infinitive ending -er instead of customary -el may be observed in P XIII:64 šiner 'to build'.

Line 4. Mkrtič^c Nałaš demands (VIII:8) Du vasn ēr dadaris zac^{c}erd i lalu 'Why do you stop your eyes from crying?' in an admonition to his listeners to prepare for death and Judgement.

Line 8. Es mnac^{c}i xew kapelu. Cf. P II:19. On binding, cf. Matt. 18.16-18; on the 'bond' (Gk. desmēn) of excommunication in magical practices within the Greek and Arm. churches, see M. Summers, The Vampire, repr. New York, 1960, 91, citing Christophorus Angelus, Encheiridion peri tēs katastaseōs tōn sēmeron euriskomenōn Hellēnōn, Cambridge, 1619; C. F. Abbott, Macedonian Folklore, repr. Chicago, 1969, 211; and the Legend of Narekac^{c}i infra.

Line 11. Astēns č^{c}ēne zis amōt^{c}ov. Compare with Line 15 Astēns k(')ēnē zmardn amōt^{c}ov; as with Lines 3 and 18, these lines are essentially the same, with a change of person. T^{c}lkuranc^{c}i stresses his point while expanding it from his own experience (zis 'me') to a general principle (zmardn 'man').

Line 12. Andēn bažin ker gehenu. Line 16 is a verbatim repetition of this.

Line 19. Amēn oč^{c}inč^c datark bani. The use of oč^{c}inč^c 'nothing' as an adjective by itself seems unusual in Armenian usage. The poem contains several

syntactically obscure lines (cf. 3 and 11), which I have interpreted on the
basis of comparison with others like them, when they did not yield a sensible
translation otherwise.

Line 20. <u>Andēn hamar unis talu</u>. Mkrtič^c Naɫaš indulges in a bitter pun while
castigating himself (VIII:61): <u>Tēr koč^cis, tur hamar gorcoyn tirakan</u> 'You are
called "Lord" [<u>Tēr</u>, the customary title of a <u>vardapet</u>]; render a lordly account
of your deeds', and adds (VIII:64) <u>Vay awurn, or hamar tas teaṙn tesut^cean</u>
'Alas for the day you render an account to the Lord's scrutiny'. The 'empty
word' (<u>datark bani</u>, gen.) of T^clkuranc^ci is a reference to Matt. XII:36 <u>Bayc^c</u>
<u>asem jez t^ce, Ënd amenayn datark bani zor xawsic^cin mardik, dac^cen hamar yawurn</u>
<u>datastani</u>.

*   *   *

This (P VIII; C, p. 17) is written, again in the form and metre of the
foregoing. Although it is a love poem there is no overt mention of love, lover
or beloved. Possible allusions to lover and beloved (Lines 11-12) and to the
beloved's beauty are left to the reader's own imagination; Lines 17-20 recall
P VII:1-2, which are nearly identical and refer specifically to the evil of
earthly love. Maten. MS 7717 has the title <u>Taɫ garnan</u> 'Poem of Spring';
MS 9597 calls it <u>Taɫ siroy</u> 'Poem of Love', and of course it is both, for
earthly love is the flowering of the senses, the vernal season of earthly
existence, while for the earth, springtime is the equivalent in nature of love
in man. The phrase <u>sēr ašxarhis</u> (P V:19) here means both 'earthly love' and
'love of this world'. A poem written by Kostandin Erznkac^ci on the beauty of
Spring is found in Venice Matenadaran MS 103, A.D. 1336. It was attributed to
Yovhannēs T^clkuranc^ci, probably mistakenly in Venice MS 559 (written at a later
date) because of the similarity of its opening lines to P VIII.
KE XI: <u>Yovanēs T^curguranc^coy asac^ceal vasn yarut^cean K^cristosi</u> 'Spoken by
Yovanēs T'urguranc'i on the Resurrection of Christ'

1 Today it was a glowing spring; the flowers rejoiced in their
        splendour
  And the small birds clothed themselves in blossoms tribe after
        tribe
  Over peaks of the mountains spread the flowers of many hues,
  And they cover the face of the earth, the plains and gardens.

2   The small birds in the flowering gardens are decked in fine plumage
    And sing sweetly in myriad ranks the never-ending round.
    They are drunk on the delicate perfume and sit atop the flowers.
    They are created of love, and love is in them that speak.

3   The orchard is adorned, and the birds chorus in flocks,
    And every bird has love and much longing in his heart.
    The ceaseless, sweet voice has banished sleep from the night,
    And every bird speaks of his own gentle love.

4   The violet assembles the flowers, saying,
    'Arise ye in accord. Let us go and cut down the rose bush,
    Lest the red rose come and spread wide his handsome petals,
    Else at the shining vision of him the sons of men will not look
        upon us!'

5   Now hyacinth and snowflower depart for the search
    And despatch the fig and summon the lily in the meadow.
    The waterlily at the heart of the sea arises, hears and comes.
    And they call the amaracus, and the narcissus with him.

6   Now the rose is happy; he rejoices, exults
    And enters the garden, gathering all the flowers.
    All the blossoms that sprang up upon the vernal earth assembled
        there,
    And they took counsel to wreak evil and treachery against the rose.

7   Suddenly the nightingale rises, lofty from amidst the flowers and
        cries,
    'The rose has awakened from sleep in his tent of green!'
    The rose hears the nightingale's voice and opens the door of his
        tent,
    Shakes free of his green bonds and puts on crimson.

8   Then the flowers wilted; half shed their leaves
    And half fled into the high mountains hard of ascent.
    And half for shame put on blue and went into mourning,
    And half for fear shook with terror and yellowed.

9   Then the rose adorned the orchards and gardens
    And arrayed his thousand petals like seeds of the pomegranate red.
    So came the nightingale and rested, intoxicated by the sweet
        fragrance,
    And thus he spoke ceaselessly night and day to the rose:

10 'Love is the tree and the flower, and love the bird's voice in the
        trees.
    Love is the rose and love is the nightingale who sits above the
        rose in love
    The multicoloured, lovely flowers abide in love,
    And for love the little birds sit atop them.

11 Now the nightingale is happy and rests above the rose,
    Chanting a thousand welcomes to him, king of the flowers.
    The rose turns to the nightingale and clasps him fast in his green
        embrace,
    Saying, 'I, too, am a master of love, and my heart is yellow for it.

12 Were there no love in my heart and I had ease,
    Why would I hang night and day amidst the thorns?
    I live by love and have glorified my leaves;
    If love leave me, let the wind sweep me away.

13 Nightingale! Do not marvel at my glowing, handsome face,
    For he who has no love has no beauty either.
    Water pressed upwards by my roots rises into me in love,
    And from the light of the Sun I gather my beauty.

14 Those who breathed inhaled life with my sweet perfume;
    They rejoiced in my comely sight and movement animated them.
    All the cares, the illusions and the gloom of this world
    Scattered when they beheld the vision of my grace.

15 Let them lead me willingly to the one with love in his heart,
    And so long as he gazes upon me, it shall rest there.
    Let them take me away and scatter me amongst the company in love;
    May they rejoice at the shining sight of me and drink their wine!

16 Now I stand decked out in glory, and my petals burn like fire,
    And I have cloven the depths of my heart bared to your yellow gaze.
    Come, kiss me and slake your primeval love!
    Then let them come and reap me, to be found in the garden no longer.

17 Let the doctors come and pulverise me
    And mix the rose-sugar and save it as a potion against heartache.
    Let them fry me in fire and hawk me as sherbet in the marketplace;
    Let them take me and give me as a medicine to all the sick.

18 Let them pound my heart in water and fill the bottles with it
    And sell me as rosewater, for I hold the scent of immortality!
    Therefore I tear open the yellow of my innermost heart.
    Whoever sees my open heart, let him heed my complaint!'

TRANSLATION

    Behold, it was a glowing spring.
    Orchard and garden flowered.
    The plains and mountains were adorned,
    And the meadow(s) brought out kingly robes.

5   Buds flower and intertwine;
    Breeze and wind grow sweet.
    Small birds in the garden make melody;
    Sweet comes the voice of the nightingale.

    The tree's shadow thickens;
10 Abundant rushes the water in the stream.
    He entwined his arm round its neck;
    He drank in love the sweet wine.

    And beyond all price is that rosebush
    Where one might meet such joy:
15 Would it were the Paradise of immortality
    In which the first man was placed.

    Were there neither death's day nor Hell
    Nor the terror of Judgment,
    Then this were beautiful,
20 Which crazy Yovhannēs T^clkuranc^ci has said.

Notes

Line 4. **Arōt hanin ĕzxilanin.** Cf. Song of Songs V:7 <u>Hanin yinēn zxlayn im.</u>
If the line means that the fields have decked themselves (Arm. <u>arōt</u> 'meadow' is
in the singular, and does not then agree with its verb) in a mantle of green,
T^clkuranc^ci has completely misunderstood the Biblical idiom; the Bride is
stripped of her cloak by the watchmen on the walls of Jerusalem, not adorned
with it. In P X:36, T^clkuranc^ci declares <u>K^cajanc^c tanēn berac du inj xilay es</u>
'You are a kingly robe brought to me from the house of the <u>K^cajk^c</u> [cf. Note to
P I:5-6 and XIII:7],' perhaps referring to events in Armenian legend. Usually
the <u>k^cajk^c</u>, who are unable to make anything, take robes and the like from the
habitations of men.

Lines 11-12. <u>Zt^cewēn berēr bolor vĕzin, / Sirov xĕmēr zanuš ginin.</u> The subjects of these two lines are unclear, but I interpret the first as the quick-
rushing brook embracing the roots of the trees (taking Arm. <u>viz</u> 'neck' as a
metaphor); and the second, as the root itself, which drinks the life-giving
water.

Line 13. <u>Ayn vardenum gēm č^ckay gin.</u> The rosebush (Arm. <u>vardeni</u>) may be
either the beloved embraced in the preceding two lines, or it may be merely a
rosebush; the poem's subtlety is in this ambiguity. For the beloved may well
be the whole garden; Nahapet K^cuč^cak's beloved is Adam's paradise (NK LV, cf.
Note to P I:13), and T^clkuranc^ci wishes the same were true of his own <u>golestān</u>
(Lines 15-16 <u>K^cawel</u> [cf. Note to P III:16] <u>draxt anmahut^cean</u> [cf. P I:13,
IV:13-14], / <u>Yorum edaw mardn arajin</u>). <u>Gēm</u>, a Mediaeval Arm. interjection
meaning 'indeed, truly' (Ačaṙean) is usually found at the beginning of a sen-
tence or clause, as in KE XV:21 <u>Gēm t^cagawork^c en lel sovor</u> 'As has been the
custom of kings' (compare with the ancient epic fragment cited by Grigor
Magistros <u>Orpēs awrēnn ē t^cagaworac^c</u> 'As is the law of kings' in the Intro.),
Frik I:7 <u>Gēm Abēl ēr ardar, zawakn Adamay</u> 'Truly Abel, son of Adam, was
righteous,' NK LXIX <u>Coc^cud loysn durs cagē, gēm elnē meṙeln i holēn</u> 'The light
of your breast glimmers forth: truly it is a dead man rising from the earth'
(the resurrection of Lazarus is probably recalled here), but C XXI:2 'I consider it thus even if no other say it, for surely [<u>gēm</u>] I know what I have
done,' and P XII:31 <u>Yašxarhs xōrōtik gēm du minak č^ces</u> 'Could you be in truth
the only beauty in this world?' are exceptions, as is our original example.

* * *

This (P IX; C, pp. 17-18) is written in the form and metre of the foregoing. It is animated by subtly contrasting imagery: in the first stanza, all
is glowing and bright; in the second, at least in the first two lines, the dark
colours of sea and cloud predominate. In the third stanza, a priest trembles
with cold; in the fourth, the beloved's fiery heat melts the mountains. In the
third stanza, there is a picture of passivity and the evaporation of memory;
the fourth stanza flares up with images of violence and conquest. The fifth
and final stanza ends with the poet's self-condemnation. The fifth mentions
also the two breasts, the final point on the beloved's body that the poet here
reaches. We began with the two eyes, and here, too, is the duality of the
poem: the two above and the two below. The eyes in the earlier part of the
poem flood the earth with their light and attract the lover to them; the
breasts at the end are casks of gold, shut and hidden, that deny their love
to him.

TRANSLATION

> With love I saw you seated,
> Sunlike little suns,
> Like a garden in whose midst
> Are rose and lily, glowing little flowers.
>
> 5 You have eyes like seas;
> You have brows darker than clouds.
> Your jaw gleamed, and your ribbon lips,
> And your teeth, a strand of pearls.
>
> If a priest sees you,
> 10 He forgets his learning, and many books.
> He trembles throughout his person,
> And turns his summer to winter.
>
> How much can I oppose you,
> When you cause the mountains to melt
> 15 And lay waste with your love high citadels,
> And cause rocks and boulders to tumble down.
>
> Crazy Yovhannēs T^{c}lkuranc^{c}i
> Praises you, casks of gold.
> I fear the fire will consume my soul
> 20 Inextinguishable, and sleepless worms devour me.

Notes

Line 2. <u>Arewnman aregakunk^c</u>. (On Arm. <u>aregakunk^c</u> 'little suns', see Note to
P I:5-6) and the marvellous assonances of Gregory of Narek's 'Melody of the
Nativity' (cf. P XXIII). T^{c}lkuranc^{c}i immerses the reader in the radiance of
his image; each word has <u>arew</u> or <u>areg</u> as its first two syllables, and each word
swells to fill half the line.

Line 4. <u>Vard u šušan, paycar całkunk</u>^{C}. The face of the beloved is a vernal garden; her sunlike eyes are like bright flowers at its centre. Her eyes are fire (Line 2), earth (Line 4) and water (Line 5); the wind, perhaps because of its association with the holy spirit, is the only one of the four elements in which T^{C}lkuranc^{C}i is not pursued by his beloved's eyes. The beloved embraces all the earth and drags the lover down to the earthly; his only refuge from her is the spiritual.

Line 5. Ac̆^{C}er unik^C zēt ĕzcover. Cf. Notes to P I:11, and II:5, XII:21, XIII:2, IX:2, and XIV:3, 19. The sunlike eyes are transformed into seas, and these may be luminous; Mkrtic̆^{C} Nałaš describes thus the death of a young man (XI:65-66): <u>Gełec^{C}ik goyn eresac^C t^{C}aramec'aw, / Ew covayin ac̆^{C}k^{C}n i lusoyn</u> <u>pakasec^{C}aw</u> 'His face's lovely colour faded / And the light of his sealike eyes drained away.'

Line 6. <u>Uner unik^C k^{C}an zt^{C}ux amper</u>. Cf. P XI:5, and NK C: 'Your fingers are like candles; your brows are like a dark cloud. / Your eyes are like the sea; there is none in the world like you.'

Line 7. <u>Šołayr klap^{C}n u lar šrt^{C}unk^C / U margartešar atamunk^C</u>. Cf. Note to P III:13.

Line 12. <u>Anc^{C}ēnē zamaṙen jmerunk^C</u>. Valerii Briusov translates this line (L. M. Mkrtchian, ed., <u>Armianskaia srednevekovaia poeziia</u>, Leningrad, 1972, p. 248) <u>Zima ž im kažetsia vesnoy</u> 'Winter seems spring to them'. A. Tchobanian (<u>Les Trouvères Arméniens</u>, Paris, 1906, p. 189) has nearly the same rendering, 'L'hiver pour eux se change en été,' with the same discrepancy in number (which is strange, as Kostaneanc^C, the published version they doubtless used, has <u>vardapetn</u> nom. sing.; only Maten. MSS 1990 and 9597 have <u>vardapetk^C(n)</u>). In any event, one does not usually tremble (Line 11) because one's winters have changed to summers, but vice-versa; so I interpret the line as '(he causes to) pass the summer [<u>zamaṙen</u>, acc. sing.] (into) winters (winter).' Cf. NK XLIV:

> When love remained to me, I lived in garments of love.
> In the winter I lived in the snow and still sweated.
> When love left me, I wore seven furs.
> In summer I lived at the furnace's grate but shook still.

Cf. also NK XXXVIII:

> I sigh and blood comes, by the happy sun of the beautiful one
> My sigh ascended to heaven; from heaven snow comes down.
> Who has seen snow in summer, coming down on the son of man?
> I do not know whether it falls on me alone, or descends evenly
> over all.

Arm. <u>šat arewun</u> 'happy sun': <u>šat</u> is usually translated as 'much' (Bedrossian), but cf. Av. šaiti- 'rich', NP šād 'happy' and H. W. Bailey, Zoroastrian Problems in the Ninth-Century Books, Oxford, 1971, p. 4, n. 2. May be 'abundant sun.'

Line 13. Jez inč^c łatar es dimanam. Arm. Łatar, Ar. qadr, Tk. kadar, 'amount'; inč' łatar is parallel to NP. če qadr and Tk. ne kadar 'How much?'

Lines 14-15. Erb duk^c i hal hanēk^c zlerunk^c, / Sirov k^cakēk^c barjr berder. Cf. Notes to P III:5-6, 14; here, as the plural indicates, it is the eyes which possess such destructive power. Cf. NK LXXVIII:

> Such eyes you have: the right boils, the left roasts.
> Such eyebrows you have: they lay waste Shiraz at its foundations.
> Anyone who hears your voice in the cities of Aleppo and Damascus
> Gives up the Sun, and beholds you with passion.

Erevan Matenadaran MSS 9271, 7715 read i gil hanēk^c 'make into pebbles' instead of i hal hanēk^c.

Line 18. These are the breasts of the beloved (says Tchobanian).

Line 20. Ansēj uten ank^cun ordunk^c. In his more didactic verses, T^clkuranc^ci is fond of this common image of corruption, cf. C XVI:18 'I have furnished the worms' feast; I know, full eagerly I go to be their food'; XVIII:6 'Where there is darkness and Tartarus, sleepless worms and the fiery furnace;' XIX:ii:22 'To sinners (he gives) unextinguishable fire and Tartarus, the pit of worms;' and XXVI:25-26 'I whored, I lusted, and I bore the worm; / I kindled an unextinguishable fire; the worm will not die.' Sleepless worms are popular in mediaeval Armenian theological works; see H. S. Anasyan, Haykakan matenagitut^cyun, I, Erevan, 1959, col. 1002. Mkrtič^c Nałaš IX:57-60 presents this gloomy scene:

> The evildoers fear the Creator;
> Trembling, they will be cast into the fire of torments.
> 'Alas!' they cry, mingled with the sleepless worms
> In viscous darkness, below the ice.

Do earthly worms ever sleep, though, one wonders. The spectacle of sinners frozen into the ice recalls the ninth circle of Dante's Hell; the xaṙnelov of Line 59 may imply illicit union, recalling the punishment of Sodomites described in the Ardāy Wīrāz Nāmag (to be associated with the story of the white snakes which entwine themselves about King Pap in P^cawstos Buzand IV:43; see B. L. Č^cugaszyan, Hay-iranakan grakan aṙnč^cut^cyunner V-XVIII dd., Erevan, 1963, p. 89). The coiling, twisting snakes are, indeed, a characteristic of Satan himself. The worm in Ancient Iran was a demonic creature (Phl. xrafstar), even the useful silkworm, which one might think a friend to man. Zoroastrians thus preferred cotton to silk (M. Boyce, A History of Zoroastrianism, Vol. I, Leiden,

1975, p. 299 n. 28). But for the Armenian Christians, the worm was a reminder
of the transitory life of man and the eternity of God, sleepless like the
zuart^cun 'awake' angels.

* * *

This poem (P X; C, pp. 50-52) differs from the foregoing in meter and
rhyme. It is abecedarian (each line begins with a successive letter of the
Armenian alphabet, from A to K^c, a total of 36; twelfth-century additions to
the alphabet, Ō and F, are not included by the poet), and is divided into
quatrains; each line is eleven syllables long, with the caesura falling after
the sixth syllable. The poem is written in monorhyme.

It describes a bond between lover and beloved with virtually no negative
overtones. In P IX (cf. Note to Line 4), the lover was pursued through three
of the four elements of Creation by the vision of the beloved's burning eyes.
In this poem, the fourth element, that of the spirit, confirms his love in its
three aspects (cf. Note to Line 11). Although the heading of this poem in
Vienna Matenadaran MS 343 reads Tał siroy Yovanēsin 'A Love Song of Yovhannēs',
the customary epithet xew Yovhannēs is absent perhaps because for once the poet
sees no need to rebuke himself, but more likely because of a corrupt MS
tradition.

TRANSLATION

> Your face is fine and round and you are beautiful.
> Your mouth is full of sugar; you have a parrot's tongue.
> Your colour is the red rose's; you are sweet in smell.
> You are Paradise and garden, like a flower.
>
> 5 Heaven and earth are my witness that I love you.
> Awake, open your ear that I may complain to you.
> I have come as your guest; you are my shelter.
> Why do you not look at me? Surely you do not disbelieve.
>
> I leave you far away, just as you deceive me.
> 10 Gather me back in time; I am your servant.
> My heart, sense and mind apply to you in love.
> As you love me well, so I love you.
>
> I am greatly agreeable to you, as you are to me.
> I am your servant in my soul, that you do not wound me.
> 15 Desire me, my soul, and I desire you.
> Say 'My soul!' to me, and I will say it to you.

Your voice is like a partridge's when you call me.
On my pledge and faith and oath I love you.
Lively, fine and elegant when you walk,
20 You laugh delicately and reap my breath.

Stand, ardent and happy, if you are master of the pledge.
I behold you in love; God is our witness.
Swiftly you shall reach my love if you do not lie.
As you love me, so do I love you.

25 With a poisoned arrow from the bow you have wounded my heart.
Lick my heart with a kiss, as you are willing.
Grant water to my thirsty liver; I am a thirst to you.
Bountiful water of the fountain, I behold you.

My heart was filled with love; do not lay sin on me.
30 You are a fragrant rose, the flower of the lily.
Give me counsel; you are very wise.
In the assemblage of men, I am a servant to you.

You are the vernal dew and sweet you fall.
With your juice, you are red apple and imperishable rose.
35 With your plumage, you are a peacock, like a bird.
You are a kingly robe brought to me from the Titan's abode.

Notes

Line 2. Berand šak^crov i li t^cut^cak lezu es. Cf. Note to P I:9. We have already seen the virtue of women with sweet mouths (cf. P I:12, XII:30). It was sometimes believed in Muslim Persia that one who ate the flesh of a parrot attained eloquence (B. A. Donaldson, The Wild Rue, p. 166). T^clkuranc^ci, boasts of his eloquence and prowess in love, perhaps with some sarcasm, 'Crazy Yovanēs T^clkuranc^ci, you are turtledove, parrot and nightingale' (C XXV:17). The poet Frik lamented the approach of death thus: Im t^cut^cak lezus ku kapi 'My parrot tongue is bound' (cit. in M. Abełyan, Erker, IV, Erevan, 1970, 336).

Line 3. Goynd ē karmir vardin, hotovd anuš es. Arm. karmir 'red' was probably a shade of pink. Cf. NK LVII:

> I saw a beautiful girl walking, and I called 'Red face [karmir
>   eres, cf. P XII:5, XIII:36]!'
> She turned and answered: 'I am beautiful, where have you fled?'
> 'God gave to me a face; to you, eyes. Stand and gaze!
> 'He gave to me beauty; to you, fire. Burn yourself!'

Line 5. Erkink^c w'erkir vēkay, or ku sirem zk^cez. In Line 22, God is vkay 'witness' to both lover and beloved. Such quasi-legal terminology is frequently employed by the poet; oaths are mentioned four times (Lines 18, 21), and Lines 9 and 13 display the principle of strict reciprocality in affection, despite the admission of the lover in Lines 10 and 32 that he is the beloved's servant. Perhaps this legalistic language is meant to parody vows of marriage.

Line 11. <u>Im sirts u xelk^cs u mitk^cs sirov ē ar̊ k^cez.</u> The lover addresses his beloved not in <u>kamk</u>^c 'passion', but through the faculties of the soul: feeling, knowledge and wisdom.

Line 17. <u>Jaynd ē kak^cwoy něman t^cē zis ku jaynes.</u> The partridge (Arm. <u>kak^caw</u>) is a popular image of the beloved. Cf. NK LXXVII:

> They lie, O brothers, saying that the partridge is untamed.
> I saw one yesterday, and happy is her master.
> She had pen-traced brows, and her mouth was full of sugar
>   [Unern ēr l̵alamov k^casac, 'w ir berann šak^crov i li. Cf. P X:2.
>   <u>L̵alam</u> < Ar. <u>qalam</u> 'pen'. Cf. Sayat^c-Nova, Part I, II:1
>   Patkirk^cět l̵alamov k^casac 'Your visage, pen-traced' and, in Greek,
>   Giannēs Ritsos, <u>Epitaphios</u> III <u>Phrydi mou gaitanophrydo kai</u>
>   <u>kontylogrammeno</u> 'My eyebrow, ribbon-browed and pen traced'. The
>   latter work, although written in this century, employs traditional
>   Greek dekapentesyllabic distiches and makes use of traditional
>   imagery dating back to mediaeval days.]
> Even if she were to take a dead man in her arms, she would remove
>   him from her breast alive.

Cf. also NK XCVIII: 'I saw a little partridge yesterday -- her master is most blessed.'

Line 18. <u>L̵awl u hawat w' erdumn, or ku sirem zk^cez.</u> <u>L̵awl</u> (also in Line 21) Ar. <u>qaul</u> 'speaking, promise, contract'. Maten. MS 3202, of A.D. 1417, contains a colophon with the following lines: <u>Zl̵awin u zerdumn iwreanc^c p^coxec^cin ew</u> <u>surb xač^cin tugank^c hasuc^cin</u> 'They changed their pledge and oath [apparently a a pair-combination; cf. Note to P III:12] and paid compensation to the Holy Cross;' and Erevan Maten. MS 4515, of A.D. 1461, has a colophon which reads in part <u>Ov i yays l̵avlēs i durs elanē, R̊ [1000] t^cangay tugank^c tay</u> <u>amirin</u> 'And whoever violates this pledge, let him pay damages of 1000 t^cangs to the Emir' (L. S. Xač^cikyan, <u>ŽE dari hayeren jer̊agreri hišatakaranner</u>, Erevan, 1955-67, I:198, II:161). The disappointed lover of P Appendix I:23 cries <u>Ur ē</u> <u>l̵avlěd, ur ē erdumn, or br̊nec^cak^c zastuac věkay</u> [cf. Line 5] 'Where is your pledge? Where is the oath we took with God as our witness?' These citations underline the quality of a covenant or contract that pervades the poem.

Line 19. <u>Čapuk, čox u čartar, erb or du k^cayles.</u> The assonance of č recalls another epithet previously encountered, <u>čōcan</u>, which is associated with the beloved's swaying hips as she walks.

Line 25. <u>Č^carxi del̵ac netov sirtěs xoc^cer es.</u> <u>Č^carx</u> < NP <u>čarx</u> 'wheel, bow'. Cf. NK XVII:

> I attended your love: it came like an arrow from the bow
> [K^cu sirud mtik ari, na zēt net i č^carxēn elaw]
> I stood, sinless, and it came and nailed my heart through.
> Children, by your sun I say this little arrow nailed me.
> Make haste and cure it with some potion, lest they say 'He died of
>   that'.

Line 26. Maten. MS 7714 <u>Sirov kᶜo vařeal em, du hečᶜ xapar čᶜes</u> 'I burn with love for you, but you (give me) no news.'

Line 27. <u>J̌ur tur carwac lerdis pᶜapᶜakᶜ em es kᶜez</u>. The syntax of the last four words is parallel to that of P VI:1, and somewhat problematical. It may mean 'I thirst for you', or it may imply reciprocity yet again: lover and be-loved thirst for one another. The liver (Arm. <u>leard</u>) was perceived by Eastern poets as a centre of one's physical and emotional being, much as we view the heart alone. Cf. NK XIV:

> A little bough greeted me, and my wound was re-opened.
> I said 'I love you', but my words found no reply.
> She turned and answered thus: 'What can I do?
> 'Your love rose to my head, and my liver boiled in my stomach.
> 'It (your love) descended from my head and was nailed to my heart.'

In NK XCVII, we read <u>Gner em karmir kᶜimxa u zčikyars tver em tamła</u> 'I have bought red silk and made a banner of my liver'. The lover dying of love plans his funeral feast in P Appendix I:18. The fire in his soul will eliminate the need for charcoal: <u>Im čikareš kᶜapap herikᶜ, ariwns tᶜoł gini linay</u> 'My liver will suffice for kebab; let my blood be the wine'. In the Armenian folksong <u>Kapel es hiwsovd bant es ǰgel</u> 'You have bound me with your braids and cast me in prison', the beloved is <u>ansirt, anǰigyar</u>--'heartless and liverless'.

Line 31. <u>Tur dun inǰi xrat; du xist xikar es</u>. The maxims of Ahiḳar, chamber-lain of Sennacherib at Nineveh, were well known in Mediaeval Armenia (cf. F. C. Conybeare et al., ed., <u>The Story of Ahiḳar</u>, London, 1898; A. A. Martirosyan, ed., <u>Patmutᶜiwn ew xratkᶜ Xikaray Imastnoy</u>, Book I, Erevan, 1969), in both Armeno-Turkish and Armenian versions. The name came to be synonymous with wis-dom, hence the adjective <u>xikar</u> and Frik XVI:42 <u>Ałēk manuk, mec hawr ordi, u łarip, dawst u xist xikar</u> 'A good boy, son of a great father, an exile, a friend, and very wise' and KE XVII:4 <u>Xelōkᶜed ler du, ayd xikar</u> 'Be intelligent, that wise one. . . .'

Line 36. <u>Kᶜaǰancᶜ tanēn berac du inǰ xilay es</u>. On the <u>kᶜaǰkᶜ</u>, see Note to P I:4, 6. In Movsēs Xorenacᶜi III:60, Artašēs curses his son Artawazd, who is unwilling to provide him a proper funeral, telling the youth that he will be seized by the <u>kᶜaǰkᶜ</u> when he rides to the hunt on Azat Masikᶜ (Mt. Ararat): see also P XIII:7. For <u>xilay</u>, see Note to P VIII:4. But the <u>kᶜaǰancᶜ</u> or <u>ǰoǰancᶜ tun</u> is also the name of the heroic house of Sasun. The <u>kᶜaǰkᶜ</u> were thought to steal luxury objects from human beings, as they could not make any-thing themselves. Like the dragons or deceased chieftains of Nordic Europe, they were probably imagined to guard hoards of ancient and fabulous treasures.

* * *

This poem (P XI; C, p. 18) is written in the same form and metre as
P I-IX; it is similar in structure and imagery to many of the other lyrics.
The beloved's face is luminous (Lines 2-4), melting the lover by its heat
(Lines 13-14). Her step is fine and her body sways (Lines 7, 9), crushing the
lover. As in other poems, images of delicacy and beauty become images of power
and destruction; T^{c}lkuranc^{c}i yet again describes the contradictory nature of
love. These seeming antitheses reside in the same beloved.

But the poet admonishes himself (Lines 17-20) not to 'step out of line',
not to be deceived by the lovely hues of earth that death turns gray and dry.

TRANSLATION

1   Suddenly I saw one
    Whose face shed dew of many hues.
    I withered and collapsed from the vision.
    Light glowed and dripped from her neck.

5   Her eyes are a sea; her brows, a dark cloud.
    Her hair is of light golden thread.
    She swayed like a willow branch.
    With her fire she consumed every land.

    Elegant in her movements and dainty in her step,
10 Rending the soul from the body,
    She covered all the world with her grace;
    Sugar dripped down from her mercy.

    When my eyes lit upon you,
    I was ignited like candlewax.
15 I took leave of my senses, astonished;
    I was filled with dread at the vision.

    Crazy Yovhannēs T^{c}ulkuranc^{c}i,
    Do not step too far out of line.
    When the splendid visage dies,
20 Colour flees to dry earth from the face.

Notes

Line 14. Nay varec^{c}ay zēt momełēn. Cf. P XII:14 K^{c}o sērd zis mom arar, du inj
połpat u k^{c}ar es.

Line 18. Xist mi haner zotk^{c}d i crēn. The expression 'to step out of line' is
found in Modern Armenian (from the daily Hayrenik^c, Boston, 16 May 1975, p. 1)
Mełmac^{c}man ayn k^{c}ałak^{c}akanut^{c}iwnĕ, or kĕ hetapndui ōruan artak^{c}in naxararut^{c}ean

ko<u>l</u>mē, piti karenay oč̆^c-mij̆amtut^cean cirēn durs gal 'Will the policy of relaxa-
tion pursued by the present foreign ministry be able to step out of the line of
non-interference?' But it probably comes ultimately from an old Armenian form
of oath-taking mentioned by Mxit^car Goš in his <u>Datastanagirk</u>^c ('Law Book'),
Va<u>l</u>aršapat, 1880, 51 and cited by G. Tēr-Pōlosean, 'Naxni Hayoc^c hogepaštut^cean
šrj̆anic^c', <u>Yušarjan-Festschrift</u>, Vienna, 1911, 233: '. . . Or the way those of
other nations swear disavowal: either by entering the church and extinguishing
the light, or by blowing on water and oil [i.e., on the fire of an oil lamp],
or by tracing a cross on the earth and treading upon it, or by holding a dog's
tail, or by holding a bone in one's hand, or by tracing two lines in the earth
and stepping from one onto the other. For all these are kinds of disavowal
which a Christian must not undertake even if death or the destruction of his
house threaten'. The expression <u>aylazgik</u>^c may refer here to non-Christian Armenians. Tracing lines in the earth for swearing is a custom mentioned with
approval for Zoroastrians in the <u>Sōgand-nāme</u> ('Book of Oath-(taking)'), published in M. R. Unvala, <u>Dārāb Hormazyār's Rivāyat</u>, I, Bombay, 1922, p. 45 (long
version, p. 51).

* * *

This poem (P XII; C, p. 49-50) is written in quatrains of eleven-syllable
lines, with caesura after the sixth syllable and monorhyme in <u>-es</u> or <u>-ez</u>. The
author calls himself Yovhannēs, but does not employ the epithet <u>xew</u>. The poet
complains that his mind is gone (Line 20) and that he forgets himself (Line 23),
and his confused exclamations reflect his state; the 'beloved' and 'friend' of
Line 17 commits villainies no enemy would undertake, in Line 18. The beloved
of Line 29 is 'incomparable' in her beauty, but in Lines 31-32 T^clkuranc^ci
tells us that beauty is the most commonplace of things, always present in quan-
tity and repeated <u>ad infinitum</u>.

TRANSLATION

        Your eyes are dark and commanding; you are beautiful.
        You are fragrant, like a white rose.
        You are a bunch of violets, roses and flowers.
        You are green as the year-old willow.

5   You are white and red, bitter and sweet apple.
        With your sweet fragrance you have intoxicated me.
        You are almonds and sugar mixed with honey.
        It seems a full moon; you are like the Sun.

You are melted, poured gold and silver.
10 You are a treasure of silk; how much shall I praise you?
Your love has touched me; in truth, I burn.
Come and make me a potion; you are my cure.

You have severed sleep from my eyes; you are rest.
Your love made me candlewax; you are steel and stone to me.
15 Night and day you are in my heart;
You have plucked out my immortal soul without warrant.

You are my beloved, and a friend to me.
None of evil will might do what you have done.
Swordless and knifeless, you have spilled my blood.
20 My wisdom fled; you have taken my mind away.

I am a handful of earth; you are a being of fire.
How long will you bloody my heart consumed by flame!
Wherever I sit, I forget myself.
Have you poisoned me? Are you a witch?

25 You have filled those two seas of your eyes with a potion;
You have plucked up the arch of your brows.
You are a green spring; you are like the sea.
How long shall I live thirsting for that sea alone!

There is none like you; you are incomparable.
30 Your teeth are pearls and your mouth is sugar.
Are you really the only beauty in the world?
In this world, many have arrived and yet more will come far
    lovelier than you.

Speak your piece, Yovhannēs. Why do you hold back?
You are slave and servant of St. Karapet.
35 St. Karapet, I beseech you
To save my reciters and listeners from evil.

Notes

Line 1. Ac̆ᶜerd e tᶜux u pēt, du xōrōtik es. Pivazyan, in his Glossary, explains pēt as 'great, big' (Arm. mec, xošor); it may come from pet 'chief, commander' (Bedrossian). Xōrōtik 'beautiful' is from the pair xorotik-morotik with diminutive-affectionate -ik, ultimately from Av. Haurvatāt and Amĕrĕtāt, the divinities of the waters and plants, who give their name to the Arm. hōrot mōrot flower. The flower became synonymous with beauty; thus the nineteenth-century writer Aristakēs Tewkancᶜ, Aycᶜelutᶜiwn i Hayastan, 1878, printed at Erevan, 1985, refers in a description of the beauties of nature to hōrot-mōrot nerker 'lovely hues' (p. 31).

Line 2. Kᶜafur vardi nĕman anušhotik es. Kᶜafur < Ar. kāfūr 'camphor, white'. Cf. P XIV:37-40 Ar'ek ijnunkᶜ i bal̆c̆ᶜenin / Ew blbulin anenkᶜ nadar, / or i kᶜafur vardi sirun / I šur ku gay kᶜan zdiwahar 'Arise, come! Let us descend into the gardens / And gaze upon the nightingale, / Who for love of the white

rose / Wanders about more than a man possessed'. Camphor is mentioned in Song
of Songs I:14 Eškōl ha-kofēr dōdī 'my beloved is unto me as a cluster of cam-
phire' (A.V.), Arm. oɫkoyz nočoy, LXX botrys tēs kyprou. Camphor was used as
an antaphrodisiac and for cosmetic purposes. But it seems evident that the
word, in association with a rose, means only 'white', cf. NK LXXIX:

> Your eyes are like the sea which stands at Egypt's gate.
> Your tresses are like the wind-blown wave.
> You have shot up higher than a poplar and grown redder than an apple.
> You are more brilliant than the white rose, which has filled the
>   world with its fragrance.

Line 7. Du meɫrov šaɫēlac nuš u šakᶜar es. The beloved is almonds and sugar;
her love is even sweeter than that mixture, cf. NK XXXIV:

> If there be a price for love, pay it. Do not live without love.
> If my soul is the price, then take that and give the other, I
>   beseech you.
> Come close and sit by me, that I may give you news of love.
> Nothing is sweeter than love, even if you eat almonds and sugar.

Šaɫēlac 'mixed': not content with only one substance as the metaphor of his
beloved, the Armenian poet mixes essences, cf. NK XCI:

> The Sun is your creation: it gives light to all the world.
> They say that your little white breast mixed with milk you have
> Gives musk-scented nourishment, that sweet fragrance you possess.
> You speak more sweetly than the sweetness of your fruit.

But Nahapet Kᶜučᶜak finally rejects the metaphor altogether; his love tran-
scends it (III):

> I believe there is no sweeter fruit on earth than love.
> Sugar mixed with almonds next to love is bitter and sharp.
> I tasted something else: I was a master of love with you.
> Give your love to my heart, too; I am the prisoner and slave of
>   your love.

The same delectable blend is declared bitter, not for love this time, but for
the grief of separation, in Mkrticᶜ Naɫaš' Song of the Exile (XIV:13-16): 'The
exile's bread is bitter to the taste, / Bitter and sour is the water mixed with
tears he drinks. / Even if they ever give him almonds and sugar to taste, /
Blood rains from his heart when he sighs'.

Line 8. K'tᶜui bdri lusin, zēt aregakn es. Bdri < Ar. badr 'the full moon'.
Cf. KE XXV:2: Kᶜu tesovd es du lusin patri tamam / Or im sērtis xawareal 'By
your glance, a full moon you are / Causing light to awaken in my darkened
heart!' Arm. zēt 'like', from Classical ziard cf. P II:2 Zet zaregakn, IX:5
zēt ēzcover, XI:7 zēt zuři čeɫ.

Line 10. Ɫumaš es xazēni, kᶜani govem zkᶜez. Ɫumaš < Tk. kumaş 'tissue, fab-
ric, material, cloth'. Cf. NK CXIV Kᶜo sērn ē angin ɫumaš, i vačar vasn kᶜez
ekay 'Your love is priceless silk; I came to buy you'. Xazēni < Ar. xazine

(St. Malxasyanc^C, Hayeren bac^{C}atrakan bararan, Vol. II, s.v. Erevan, 1944); Riggs, Modern Armenian Vocabulary, Smyrna, 1847, lists the form xazna.

Line 13. Ketrer k^{C}un yač^{C}werus du faralat^C es. Cf. P XI:14 Nay varec^{C}ay zēt momelēn. Nahapet K^{C}uč^{C}ak likewise is transformed by love into a flaming candle (LI, LII):

> He who is master of love and has no cure for it--
> Let him go and dig his grave and enter alive therein
> And leave his heart's face open that the scarlet flame escape.
> And may the passerby say: 'A man, master of love, is burning.'
> * * *
> I sang so many hayrens that I taught the Titans in their caves
> [Hanc^{C}ank^C es hayen asi, or zk$^{\check{c}}$ajern i k^{C}arn usuc^{C}i, lit. 'I
> taught them into stone'; a variant of XXXVIII, cf. Note to
> P IX:12, p. 322, reads Hanc^{C}ank^C hayreni asi, or elaw srtiks
> k'arē tun 'I said so many hayrens that my heart became a house
> of stone'; this version has hayen, which is probably a scribal
> error for hayren. As the main import of the quatrain is unaf-
> fected either way, we leave the first line as it stands.]
> I returned, bringing jewels, and erected [kapec^{C}i, lit. 'I bound']
> a pillar from Heaven.
> I ascended and sat on it, and complained to God:
> 'God, look down for a moment at what pitiful things there are.
> 'A child of ten melts like candlewax for love [Tasn tarekan manukn
> i sirun zēt mom ku hali].
> 'His bone has become a wick, and his skin burns like olive oil.'

Line 16. Anmah u angrol zhogis haner es. Maten. MS 5623 has Anmah u k^{C}ralawl zhogis k'utis u hanes 'You devour and pluck out my immortal and k^{C}ralawl (?) soul'. An+grol lit. 'grol-less' may be a lectio facilior of k^{C}ralawl, which was perhaps the pres. part. act. of a lost verb k^{C}ralem. If such a verb existed, I cannot determine its meaning. The grol, 'writer', is the recorder of God's decision when a man is to die, and, apparently, also whether he is to go to heaven or hell. In an Arm. magical MS ca 1808, the grol is shown as a winged man with a frightening expression: in his left hand he holds a sword which is shown about to stab an old, bedridden man upon whose chest the super-natural being stands. In his right hand the grol holds a scroll open to show the words amenayn melok^C 'with all (his) sins'--the victim seems doomed to damnation. The angel Gabriel in various other, roughly contemporary MSS is shown as a martial, winged youth with sword aloft and the little soul, swathed like an infant, cupped in his left hand. He stands on a whitened corpse. As the angel Gabriel is regarded, like the grol, as a psychopompos, and indeed may be identical to him, the different scenes may represent not a contrast, but episodes before and after death on one visit. (For the MSS, see F. Feydit, Amulettes de l'Arménie Chrétienne, Venice, 1986, Plate 11.) V. M. Manoyan writes ("Elementy predstavlenii o vnutrennem stroenii zemli u obitatelei armianskogo nagor'ia (Po materialam fol'klora)," Lraber, Erevan, Jan. 1974, p. 68):

The 'writer' (groł) in Armenian also signifies Satan, the devil, and according to the general opinion of philologists (M. Emin, G. Łap^can^cean, etc.) the Armenian expression grołe k^cez tani "The devil take you" is a relic of pagan days, and its primordial meaning seems to have been "May Tir take you down to the subterranean kingdom."

Nahapet K^cuč^cak wrote of the groł (XXIII, L, LV):

> Little soul of mine, if only you allowed me to uncover your breast,
> I would make it a garden, and by your leave would go within.
> I would take an oath not to violate your conditions.
> How faithless is the groł who comes and takes me from your breast!
> * * *
> In this world there are two pitiful, lamentable things:
> One is to be a master of love, and the other is the coming of the
> groł, who carries you away.
> The dead man is not to be lamented: his wound is clearly seen.
> Come, behold this wretched one who is neither dead nor alive.
> * * *
> I had need of wine of your colour; I would drink and get drunk.
> Your breast is Adam's Paradise; I would enter and pick apples there.
> I would lie between your two breasts and sleep;
> In that hour would I consign my soul to the groł, would he but
> come and take it away.

The groł is sent, of course, at the command of the Christian God, and is therefore the agent of justice. But the beloved is unjust, and takes away the lover's soul without divine sanction, an-groł, lit. 'groł-less'. I have followed Artin Shalian, David of Sassoun, University of Ohio Press, 1964, in translating the term as 'without warrant'. In ancient Iran, the planet Mercury (Ar. ^cUtārid, Ir. Tīr, Arm. loan-word Tir) was because of its swiftness seen as a heavenly messenger, the scribe (dabīr, Arm. dpir) of the gods who recorded and announced man's fate, see, e.g., the couplet of the early NP. poet Rūdakī: zīr-aš ^cuṭārid ān ke naxwānī-š ǰoz-e dapir / yek nām-e ū ^cuṭārid ō yek nām-e ū-st Tīr 'Beneath it is Utarid, that one you call not other than the Scribe. / One name of it is Utarid and one name of it is Tīr.'

Line 32. Astěwors šat eker w'aylwi gay k^can zk^cez. Compare this sentiment with Virgil, Eclogue II:75: 'invenies alium, si te hic fastidit, Alexim'. T^clkuranc^ci may be saying that the grapes are sour.

Line 35. This is a reference to St. John the Baptist, whose shrine at Muš was revered by Armenians and Kurds and was considered second only to Echmiadzin in Armenia in sanctity. It was founded on the site of the temple of Vahagn and Astłik at Aštišat by St. Gregory the Illuminator himself, according to Arm. tradition. It was a place of pilgrimage for poets, musicians and wrestlers. It is quite likely that Yovhannēs T^clkuranc^ci himself made a pilgrimage to the place at least once in his life.

* * *

This poem (P XIII: C, p. 21-24) is the record of a lover's confused emotions: pleas and accusations alternating with fulsome praises of the beloved, who is addressed in Turkish as c̆ēllat ēfēnti 'my lord executioner' in the refrain which follows each stanza. The stanzas contain four or five eleven-syllable lines with caesura after the fifth syllable. All the lines of each stanza rhyme, but there is no rhyme scheme amongst the stanzas as a whole, nor does the refrain rhyme with any other line in the poem. The poet's angry admonition to himself at the end contains the usual denial of all that has come before: 'A thousand demons back up these words of yours' (Line 62).

TRANSLATION

> You are a vernal rose and garden.
> Your eyes are potent, intoxicating seas.
> Your breast is Paradise, an orchard of fruit;
> You are my judge; pronounce judgement.
> 5 Do not kill me with your love, my lord executioner.
>
> You hold greater dominion than the mighty Cross.
> Are you of fire, of earth, or a Titan of human face?
> I am sick; I will recover when you sit at my right.
> O shining neck and tulip cheeks,
> 10 May you remain more untried than the green hornbeam.
> Do not . . . .
>
> Our forefather Adam does not resist love.
> Eden's Paradise lost its flavour for love.
> I remember David's deeds and tremble more than the willow.
> 15 Solomon grieves, and I weep with him.
> How will I relate news of Farhād and Šīrīn?
> Do not . . . .
>
> Love takes shame away from the face,
> From monk and from priest.
> 20 It tears elders and deacons from their orders.
> It takes sense from the head, shame from the face;
> It makes man base and removes him from the Sun.
> Do not . . . .
>
> O face of a city and ornament of the land,
> 25 Joseph the Beautiful and man without peer
> For love falls suddenly like a fish for the hook.
> What counsel do you offer, unfading rose?
> There is no further obligation of your praise upon me.
> Do not . . . .
>
> 30 O honey, butter and pared almond,
> A thousand thorns in the eye of him who gazes with cunning upon you.
> O cypress and plane tree and white cheek!
> O arched brows, curve of a bow!
> Do not . . . .

35 O beauteous city, lofty and firm fortress!
O bouquet of violets, petal of a red rose,
You have consumed the liver of many a son of Adam.
As I praise you, you grow stronger, fortress.
Do not . . . .

40 Swifter than foil curling in the fire
Have I come to burn and turn to ash.
When I saw you, O sunlike one,
My soul was terrified, and I still tremble.
Do not . . . .

45 Who depicted you and revealed your face,
Carnelian gem, ruby and garnet?
Do not accuse me, O Shah, Sultan,
For loving you, O rose garland.
Do not . . . .

50 Your face is the Sun, and Venus is your brow.
Your jaw is an apple and your breasts, melons.
What does Eden's Paradise hold? It is at your bosom!
When the sugar is with me, what is Egypt?
Do not . . . .

55 One kiss from your face is worth Erzincan,
Ethiopia and Yemen, Delhi and Hindustan.
O China and Khotan, your two tresses are the price
Of Bulgaria, Istanbul and the city of Yazd.
Do not . . . .

60 What nonsense do you spout, crazy T^clkuranc^ci?
Your mind is lighter than a mite's wing.
A thousand demons back up these words of yours--
They let no trace of holiness remain in man.
You can make a thousand faces black with love.
65 What nonsense do you spout, crazy T^clkuranc^ci?

Notes

Line 2. Ac̆^cerd ē cover, xumar u mēstan. Xumar 'crazy, drunk' < Ar. xumār
(Ałayan); the same author cites the verbs xumrel, xumril 'to become intoxicated' and the substantive xumrut^ciwn 'insanity, intoxication'. Ac̆arean considers xumar a noun 'grogginess, one newly awakened from drunkenness [zart^cxum,
arbec^cut^ciwnic^c nor st^cap^cac]'. In the History of King P^cahlul (Patmut^ciwn
pɩnjē k^caɫak^cin, Tiflis, 1908, pp. 62-67), we read P^cařk^c Astucoy kendanwoyn,
or kay ew mnay yawitean, zi xumarn aync̆^cap^c xelōk^c kĕ xōsi 'Glory to the living
God, who is and remains eternally, for [even] the drunken man speaks with that
much sense'. A variant of the above substitutes xew 'crazy' for xumar; the beloved's xumar eyes in our poem communicate their quality to xew T^clkuranc^ci.
The word refers specifically to intoxication, however, and an Aramaic loan of
the same Semitic root xmr gives us Classical Armenian xmor 'leaven' (Exodus
XII:15, XXXIV:25). Mēstan < NP. mestan, mast 'drunk, intoxicated', cf. Sayat^c
Nova XXIV K^cu ēsxĕn inji mast arav 'Your love made me drunk'.

Line 5. <u>Sirov mi spananer, c̄ēllat ēfēnti</u>. C̄ēllat < Ar. ǰellād 'executioner'.

Line 6. <u>Siasat^c unis k^can zōrawor xac̆^c</u>. Siasat^c < Ar. <u>si yāsa</u> 'power, domin-ion, policy' cf. MN III:12 <u>K^cani siasta^cov inji xēnǰer ēnes</u> 'With such power do you run me through' and 69-70 <u>Vardn i blbuln asac^c: Inč̆^c siasat^c ē, / Or alams bolor dēm k^cez hasrat^c ē?</u> 'The rose said to the nightingale, "What state is this / That all my world is but longing for you?"' T^clkuranc^ci's words are subtle, for the holy sign (Arm. <u>surb nšan</u>) of the Cross had supreme power. Crosses of various holy places are invoked in lists in magical MSS. The Muslim word is in direct conflict with the Christian--<u>siyāsa</u> defeats zōrut^ciwn; com-pare the tragic love of Yovhannēs and Ayša.

Line 7. The poet refers to angels (<u>hrełēnk^c</u>, cf. Heb. seraphim, 'burning ones'), men (of earth, relying on the folk etymology of Adam from Heb. adāmāh 'earth'), and the <u>k^caǰk^c</u>, who are neither earth-born men nor angels of heaven, but are in between. They have, T^clkuranc^ci usefully informs us, human faces (we are acquainted already with their treasure).

Lines 12-13. <u>Sirun c̆^cdimanay naxahayrn Adam, / Vanc^c siroy elaw yedem draxtēn ham</u>. Erevan Maten. MS 8968 does not have <u>ham</u>: the subject may not be Ar-menian <u>ham</u> 'flavour', then, but the Adam of Line 12. <u>Ham</u> could be read as NP. <u>ham</u>, 'also', yielding this reading: 'For the sake of love he left even the Paradise of Eden'.

Lines 14-15. <u>Dawt^cay gorck^cn yišem ew k^can zuṙ dołam, / Sołomon i sug w'es i het lam</u>. Cf. P XX:9-10 <u>Kinn ēzDawit^c ark^cayn płcē, / U zSołomon apakanē</u> 'Woman pollutes King David / And ruins Solomon'. This is probably a reference to David and Bathsheba.

Line 16. <u>zVahrat Širinin zxaparn es onc^c tam</u>. Farhād, the legendary Kurd im-mortalised in Nizāmī's poem 'Khusrō and Šīrīn', carves the rock face at Behistun for love of Queen Šīrīn, but kills himself by jumping from the same rock when thwarted by the evil designs of the ministers of the Iranian king Khusrō. The story was known in Armenia, cf. Sayat^c Nova XLVIII: <u>P^cahradēn miṙac, Širinn asac^c łaren ērvac im; / K^cašvil e vart^cēn mod c̆^ci t^cołnum, xaren ērvac im. / Bēlbulēn asac^c 'Vart^cis xat^cri k^caren ērvac im.' / Tasnumek amis munǰ im kac^ci; taren ērvac im. / Astvac ku siris, zar mi hak^cni, zaren ērvac im. / Meǰlumi nēman man im gali, yaren ērvac im</u>. 'Farhād dead, Širin said "The daphne burns me. / I do not draw near the rose; its turns burn me." / The nightingale said, "For the love of my rose, [ascetic life amongst the] stone[s] burns me. / Eleven months have I lived mute; the year burns me." / If you love

God, do not wear yellow; the yellow burns me [see P Appendix III:iii, in which
indigo is the offending colour that calls to mind the beloved, and Appendix II:
11-12, in which it is orange]. / When I go in amongst the company, my beloved
burns me'.

Line 22. Šinē malamat^c, hanē yarewēn. Malamat^c < Ar. mālāmāt 'blame', which
the Sūfīs sought to efface self-pride.

Line 24. Ē šahri sivat^c ew asxarhi zard. Sivat^c (spelled siwat^c in Areg, 1924,
pp. 659-661) < Ar. sifāt 'face' (Aɫayan, who provides an Armenian spelling
sēfat^c). Kostandin Erznkac^ci seems to make a distinction between surat^c 'face'
and sifat^c, cf. XXI:12 I surat^cn mi nayel . . . sifat^cin ara mtik 'Do not look
at the surat^c . . . attend to the sifat^c'. The Ar. sifāt can mean 'characteris-
tics, attributes, qualities', that is, features of a personality more profound
than outward physical appearance. The beloved is similarly likened to a city
in Line 35, and Lines 55-58 provide a list of the cities which are the beloved's
ransom. Movsēs Xorenac^ci (II:42) compared the city of Eruandakert to a human
face in all its details. Such metaphor, rather hyperbolic even in small doses,
is used to ultimate effect in a Mediaeval Armenian folksong from a MS of 1691,
Taɫ i veray geɫec^ckoyn 'Song About A Beauty' (Mnac^cakanyan, p. 285):

> Yesterday I saw a beauty
> In the city of Angora.
> A king desired her
> In Muscovy and Portugal.
> To see her face he gave
> Salonica and Edirne.
> As the price of her sea-eyes he gave
> Scutari and Galata.
> He got up and gave her as a gift
> The city of the Sun by Egypt.
> For a sweet chat [he gave her]
> Šahraɫul, Baghdad and Basra.
> The lovely one arose to speak
> And said her piece:
> 'King, welcome.
> Your steps be on my head:
> Salonica turns round,
> Edirne shakes at its foundations
> And Scutari's mountains tumble down.
> Let Galata remain in its place.
> Do you want to give me a fine gift,
> A Sun-city surpassing Egypt?
> If you do, give me Constantinople,
> Venice or Spain.
> Many Saints' bodies rest there
> With the body of Tēr Yakob.
> Or give me the Bounds of the Mother of God
> Built in Alikurnay [Angora?].
> 'Girl, you are from the city
> Whose name they call Polis [Constantinople].
> They say great Constantine

Lives as king there.
One edge sits on Aleppo,
One on Amida, one on Amasia.
Egypt is your lot,
With Bursa and Kafa thrown in.
Tokat is the price of your walk,
With Erzurum and Gandja thrown in.
Your sweet laughter
Is worth Xorasan and Hormuz.
Moscow is your likeness,
Or great Rome, where the Pope lives.
There is none like you
All are the price of one look at you.'
Deacon, reciter of these things,
I have greatly exceeded myself.
So many cities as all these
Must not be given to the lovely one for free.
When love comes to a man,
It says neither child nor boy
Nor layman
Nor elder nor anchorite.
Children, do not accuse me!
Demoniac [tiwanay, from NP. dīvāne, cf. P XIII:62] love has overtaken me.
All these cities
Are slave and servant to the lovely one.
Anything you give is worth it, brothers!
For a beauty has no price.
And to that beauty who loves you
Give your soul, with your eyes thrown in.

Line 25. Yovsēp^C Gełec^Cik w'anōrinak mard. Cf. NK XIII and P XX:21 (in Note
to P IV:1).

Line 30. Ē mełr u karag ew kełewac nuš. Karag 'butter' most probably refers
to the beloved's white skin, described as urak 'pale' in P II:5. Cf. also
NK LXXXII Caṙay k^Co dnč̌in meṙnim, or čermak ē zet karag eł 'I would die a
sacrifice to your chin, which is white as butter oil (ghee)'.

Line 31. K^Co neng hayołin yač̌kēn hazar p^Cuš. In P VII:10, the poet declares
he will have his eyes put out with a needle--presumably because he cannot bear
the sight of the beloved, whose glance transfixes and enchants him. Here, in a
reversal of emotion, he would protext her from the evil eye of another. Com-
menting on this line, M. Abełyan says (II:129) 'The people always would utter
curses and oaths, or oaths in the form of curses', and cites this line from a
bolk quatrain: Inč̌^C p^Cuš gay im aṙjewē, č̌^Car ač̌k^Ci srtovē xri 'May any thorn
that comes before me pierce the evil eye to its heart! It is to protect against
such thorn-like assaults that many Middle Easterners keep a thimble strung together with the blue mati (Gk. 'eye', for 'evil eye') as a talisman.

Line 32. Ē salvi č̌^Cinar ew spitak t^Cuš. Salv < NP. sarv 'cypress'; č̌^Cinar <
NP. čenār 'plane tree'. The i of salvi is probably ezafe. The cypress is the

beloved's slenderness and grace; she herself is the pleasant, shady plane tree
as well.

Line 33. Cf. KE, p. 177, Line 23 Yunert aɫeɫan nēman, / Gaɫtuk neterov zaxmes
'Your brows are like a bow; / You wound with secret arrows'.

Line 37. Šatoc^c es lap^cer du admordu lerd. Maten. MS 9271 and Areg have
ardmordu. The word is to be read as the genitive of adam ordi 'son of Adam',
cf. P XV:64 Ew zardmordun bark^cēn banay (Maten. MS 3498 Or zardmordu bark^cn
banan 'Which open the fruits of Adam's son') 'And opens the fruits of Adam's
son'. Tk. adamoğlu 'son of Adam', has the added sense of 'a righteous man',
but this is not necessarily always so in Armenian, as in a song of the minstrel
Ɫul Egaz, eighteenth century. (H. Sahakyan, Hay ašuɫner XVII-XVIII dd., Erevan,
1971, p. 43): Adamordus mitk^cn šat a ulor mulor, / Min damn gohar šnas, min dam
čgnawor 'The thoughts of this son of Adam are turbulent indeed; / One moment he
is an expert about jewels, and the next he is an ascetic'. The intrusive -r-
of *ardmordi is evidently a feature of spoken Armenian, not grabar; cf. for
ease of pronunciation the form candrut^cenē (abl. sg.) for canrut^cenē (Feydit,
Amulettes, 15). The form adamordi, if a calque from Tk., is late, but a parallel construction arewordi 'child of the Sun' (see P XX) is found in the writings of St. Nersēs Šnorhali (twelfth century).

Line 40. K^can zt^cit^cexn i hurn or ē i varman. Cf. P V:13.

Line 48. T^cē sirem zk^cez, ē kuli tastan. Kuli tastan (Maten. MS 9271,
tēstan) < NP. gol-e dastān 'rose of the garland'; T^clkuranc^ci may be implying
that his beloved is the finest rose of the garland. The phrase may also be
read as 'garland of roses', with Arm. kuli the gen. sg. of kul.

Line 50. Eresd ē area, čakatd ē Zōhran. Zōhran (Kostaneanc^c, zohra) < Ar.
zuhra 'Venus', cf. the NP. epithet zohreh ǰebīn 'Venus-browed', of which čakatd
ē Zōhran is most probably an Armenian translation.

Lines 51-52. Kělap^cd ē xncor, cěcerd ē šamam, / Zinč^c yedem děraxti i k^co
coc^cd kan. The same images are to be found in equal proximity to each other in
this Greek lianotragoudi 'short song' (N. G. Politou, Dēmotika tragoudia,
Athens, 1975, p. 171):

> Your lips are sugar; your cheek, an apple.
> Your breasts are a Paradise; your flesh, a lily.
> Might I kiss the sugar, bite the apple;
> Might the Paradise open; might I embrace the lily.

Line 61. <u>Xelac^cd es t^cet^cew k^can znělěrku t^cew</u>. The poet's thoughts are light as a mite's wing; he scorns their triviality and vanity. They are also, like the insect's wing, all aflutter with the confusion of passion, as in an Armenian folksong (Komitas Vardapet and M. Abełyan, <u>Hazar u mi xał</u>, Erevan, 1969, p. 27): <u>Čenčełkan t^cew a sirtěs</u> 'My heart is a sparrow's wing'.

Line 64. On the infinitive in <u>-er</u>, cf. P VII:33.

Line 65. <u>Inč^c ěnd ayl ku tas, T^clkuranc^ci xew</u>. A verbatim repetition of Line 60 in place of the refrain following the earlier stanzas, which would be out of place in this concluding denial of former emotions.

* * *

This poem (P XIV: C, p. 19-21) is written in the same form and metre as P I-IX. The second and fourth lines of each stanza rhyme in <u>-ar</u>; except in the first, where all four lines end in this syllable. The worldweary wisdom of the poet in matters of love is apparent from the first: this spring will be like the others. Once again, the lover will be overcome by love, and his sufferings will be the same as before.

But the initial, cautionary lines of the first quatrain are followed by a deluge of metaphor in which the beloved is described in exquisite and delicate images. In Line 37, she is finally invited by the poet to descend into the garden, where the nightingale wanders about like a madman for love of the white rose. But this vision in the poetic garden of delights reminds the poet of woman's sinister power over men, which is so great that even priests cannot oppose it (Lines 47-48; cf. P VI:18-20, VI:5-8, IX:9-10, XIII:18-20). The poet's attitude changes, predictably, and he now condemns woman as the source of man's perdition; her carriage, which reminded him of a swaying willow (Line 18) now conjures up the image of a twisting serpent (Line 70).

In the closing quatrain, T^clkuranc^ci appeals in his own name to the reader, urging him to resist temptation. The customary epithet <u>xew</u> is omitted from this envoi; presumably, the poet has for once resisted temptation and does not feel deceived. The same cannot be said for his lady, wooed into the garden only to be rejected.

(A translation of this poem appeared in <u>Ararat Quarterly</u> 20.3, Summer 1979, 61-2: 'Yovhannēs T^clkuranc^ci: Master Minstrel'.)

TRANSLATION

Spring passes into yet another spring;
Again the news of love they bring:
Two seas, the eyes, and lyre of light,
And eyebrows' curve beyond the arch.

5   Your brow is light, giving light,
A full moon, sun and moon.
Your hair, drawn back with golden thread,
Descends evenly over you.

Your face is burning, purple.
10 Rose, basil and water lily.
Your breast is a garden, with roses full;
Your teeth are rows of pearls.

Sweet and mellow is your voice,
And from your mouth gems drop down.
15 Your fingers are of light;
Even the sun does not give such radiance.

You have flourished, a luxuriant plane tree;
It sways more than the green willow branch,
Like that bottomless sea
20 Where you made me my rest in you.

With such an arrow have you wounded me
That I have none else to cure me,
O face of beautiful form
That painter and artist have created.

25 You are a flowering sycamore;
You bear fruit, musk and ambergris;
You dress in muslin and purple.
All your fringes are rows of pearls.

The cities of Cathay, China and Mahā-China
30 And the stores brought from Bursa:
The road over which you walk
Sprouts lilies, water lilies.

You have bound your necklace as a bridge
And a river of wine bringing joy.
35 He who drinks of you
Rejoices with glad heart.

Arise, come, let us descend into the garden
And gaze upon the nightingale
Who for love of the white rose
40 Wanders about more than one possessed.

When the month of spring comes
Dry and green, as a flower
Your waters take their boisterous course
And rush down from the mountains.

45 When a man meets love
He is more inflamed than a fire,
But it is not prayers that come to his mind,
Nor does he read homilies and menologia.

Your lips are a beam of light;
50 Gems drop from your mouth.
He who takes a taste of sin
Gives no more news of himself to God.

Love removed Adam from Paradise,
Cast him into the world and made him giddy,
55 And betrayed him to Satan,
Who tortured him six thousand years.

The children of Seth were confounded,
They who were eager ascetics;
They heard the horn and the cymbals
60 And all came down from the mountain.

The woman decapitated John
For foul Herodias.
He who was inflamed with desire
Hastened to carry her will to completion.

65 Love parts a man from his senses,
So that there is no other news for him.
His wisdom is confounded
And he becomes worse than a man possessed.

Woman has sweet talk:
70 She walks, swaying more sinuously than the snake.
Suddenly she spills poison
And like a trap seizes the hapless.

She plucks her eyebrows and mascaras her eyes,
Adorning herself more than an almond tree.
75 She twists her waist and purses her lips,
Enticing men into the rocky mountains.

You created woman from the rib
For the sake of Adam's love:
'Be fruitful and multiply--
80 And go through the rocky mountains'.

And still with this love burn
These evil earthborn men,
Who go whoring every day
And become the food of eager worms.

85 T^curkuranc^ci begs of you
That you master not a woman's love
Lest you be deprived of the ineffable light
And no more cure come to you from God.

Notes

Line 1. Gēnay bahar aylw'i bahar. Bahar < NP. bahār 'spring'. The stress on
bahar at the caesura and at the end of the line creates a rhythmic image of the
succession of the seasons. The rhythm is communicated to xabar ('news' < Ar.
xabar) in Line 2, and an ironic tension is drawn: is news really news if it is
repeated endlessly, spring after spring? On Arm. aylw'i < ayl vayr 'another

place', Mod. E. Arm. eli, see M. Abełyan II:44, and Ałayan, Aknarkner, I, 410-11. I take aylw'i as ayl ew i, cf. note to P XIV:19-20.

Line 4. Unk^cn ē keŕer k'an ĕzkamar. Maten. MSS 9271, 7715 and 1990 have unert ē keŕ 'your brows curve'; the impersonal form Pivazyan prefers better illustrates the generality of the siroy xabar 'news of love', which we receive in a few telegraphic images.

Line 6. Bolor lusin, šams u łamar. Šams < Ar. šams 'sun'; łamar < Ar. qamar 'moon'. For 'full moon' T^clkuranc^ci, perhaps to avoid too many foreign words in the line, uses Armenian bolor lusin, instead of Arabic bdri, cf. P XII:8. Cf. Grigor Ałt^camarc^ci (apud M. Abełyan, II:143): Ē šams u łamer, astł aŕawōtin, paycaŕ aruseakn lusov ilin 'O sun and moon, star of morning, glowing full Venus!' Kostandin Erznkac^ci describes the play of light and dark; the moon of the beloved's face glows in the night of her black tresses (XXIV:10): Lusin surat^c siah mazov 'Her face, a moon, with black hair' and XXIV:4 Zerd ĕzlusin surat^c bolor, / Šurǰ eresin mazern olor 'Like the moon is her round face, / And roundabout it, her curling hair'.

Line 7. Varserd oski t^celov k^cašac. T^celov k^cašac may mean either 'drawn back with a thread' or 'drawn [i.e., written] with a thread'; for the latter sense, cf. Sayat^c Nova II Patkirk^cĕt łalamov k^cašac 'your pen-traced visage'.

Line 10. Vard, ĕŕēhan u nunufar. Cf. P IV:9-10.

Line 17. Anǰĕd k^co ĕox buser ĕ^cinar. The beloved is herself a plane tree, cf. P XII:32.

Lines 19-20. Ayd anatak covud nman, / Or zis i k^cez arir łarar. Kostaneanc^c has anyatak 'bottomless' for anatak; the Armenian dialects of Loŕi and Xarberd have the forms atak, adag 'bottom', and the dialect of Zēyt^cun has a verb atkenal 'to dive, to be submerged deep beneath the water' (Ačaŕean). A Mediaeval Tał pilpuli ew vardi 'Song of the Nightingale and Rose' (Mnac^cakanyan, p. 156) contains the line K^co sērn, im sēr, i yanatak coverun 'My love, your love is in the bottomless seas'. The modern minstrel J̌ivani wrote, Ĕnknołĕ durs ĕ^ci galis, vih ē, anatak hor ē 'The one fallen does not re-emerge outside; it is a chasm, a bottomless pit' (ŽHLBB). The image of the beloved as a bottomless sea seems a constant theme in Armenian lyric poetry, from Mediaeval days up to recent times. For Line 20, Erevan Maten. MS 3751, Srvanjteanc^c, Mananay, pp. 269-272, and Kostaneanc^c have Geris i meǰn zarwēzar 'I, the prisoner, tumbled down and down in its midst'; zarwēzar is probably to be interpreted as

zar < NP. zīr 'below' + Arm. we=ew i 'and into/from' (cf. P XIV:1, aylw'i=
ayl ew i) + zar (as above). MS 5668 has ZGeris i mejn ɫarɫēɫar, the last word
of which Kostaneanc^C interprets as ɫarɫ arar 'you drowned (vb. trans.)'. ɫarɫ
< Ar. gharq 'setting, sinking' (Aɫayan provides alternate Armenian spellings
xaɫɫ, ɫaɫɫ), NP. loan-word with aux. vb. Kostaneanc^C would then have 'You
drowned me, the prisoner, in it', a meaning not substantially different from
that of the versions of MS 3751 and Srvanjteanc^C. But ɫarar < Ar. qarār 'decision, resolution, resolve, stability, calm' in Line 20 implies not only the
stability and harmony of lover and beloved (cf. Sayat^C-Nova XXX Irek^C harur u
vac^Cun u vic^C amen andamět ɫarari 'The 366 members of your body are all in
harmony'), but also a mooring place. But can there be any place to drop anchor
in a bottomless sea? As in Lines 1-2, there is a shadow of irony. The image
of love as a bottomless sea appears in an Armenian mediaeval folksong of which
many variants exist, Aṙawotun k^Camin elnē 'The wind of the morning arises'.
Mnac^Cakanyan, pp. 160-166, prints three versions from MSS of the seventeenth-
eighteenth centuries. One is attributed to X̄ev (sic!) Yovhannēs, i.e., probably T^Clkuranc^Ci. It would seem that T^Clkuranc^Ci, the earliest of the three
Ašuɫs identified, reshaped an existing song, perhaps adding the image of the
bottomless sea as in P XIV.19, in line 9. But it is not, one thinks, the
poet's own song: it contains no condemnation of Woman.

> The wind of the morning arises and sweeps me away, sweeps me away.
> Your love was a fire: it burns me away, burns me away.
> 3 Don't let my enemy come and pluck me away, pluck me away.
>
> REFRAIN: My rose, don't fall; my rose, don't fall.
> Alas, I am burned by your wound.
> My rose, don't fall; my rose, don't fall.
> Alas, I am a stranger and have no land, no flock.
>
> 8 Now came the winds of the Kingdom, the winds.
> Your love is like the bottomless seas, the seas
> (k^Co sērn nman i yanatak covern, covern).
> The nightingale pitched his tent close, close by the rose.
>
> REFRAIN
>
> 15 The cloud of morn descended, down upon the mountains, down.
> The nightingale mourned at your fading, your fading,
> And fears death, death from the wound of love no more.
>
> REFRAIN
>
> 22 The dew of morn came down; you grew moist, moist my rose.
> You were filled, filled with the mercy of Christ, my rose.
> The rays of the Sun shone forth and you opened, opened, my rose.
>
> REFRAIN

29 Crazy (X̄ēv) Yovhanēs (sic) spoke these words for himself, yea,
   himself.
   They took my dear love away, yea, away
   (Im sirakan ears aŕin, taran, hay, taran, hay).
   I mourn for her and I cry, yea, I cry.

   REFRAIN

The abduction of the beloved (line 30) is an enduring theme; cf. Sirec^{c}i, yarĕs
taran, / Yara tĕvin u taran 'I loved and they took my love away; / They wounded
me and took her away', written by Avetik^c Isahakyan in 1898 (Lirika, Erevan,
1968, p. 46), now a folksong as well. Neither poet says who these enemies were,
and one is inclined to agree with the literary critic and scholar Ōšakan
(Oshagan), who commented at Jerusalem on Isahakyan, 'Had he been a real man
(/ erkek mart /) they should not have taken her away!' (oral comm. by Prof. K.
Maksoudian, Columbia University). The clouds and dew of morning are, I think,
the lover (cf. the poem in Bodleian MS Arm. f.7, fols, 150a,b-151a).

Line 26. Ptuł ku'tas mušk u ampar. Ampar < NP. ambār 'ambergris'.

Line 29. K^{c}ałak^c Xat^{c}ay Č^{c}in u mač^{c}in. Cf. P VI:2, which has Khotan. Here
instead is Cathay (Khitai), cf. Rus. Kitan 'China'.

Lines 33-34. Karmunǰ kapac es apiki / Ew get gini uraxarar. Maten. MSS 9271
and 7715 have instead of Line 34 Getn u ginin uraxanayr 'River and wine were
glad'. Karmunǰ=kamurǰ 'bridge'. H. Ačaŕean writes (Classification des
dialectes arméniens, Paris, 1909, p. 4): 'Certains cas de métathèse de r sont
communs a tous les dialectes; garmunǰ en face du classique kamurǰ "pont" . . .'.
The form krmanǰ-umĕ 'on the bridge' is attested in the dialect of Agulis
(S. Sargseanc^c, Agulec^{c}oc^c barbaŕĕ, Moscow, 1883, part II, p. 39). T^{c}lkuranc^{c}i
uses the form zkarmunčn (Ł. Alisan, Hayapatum, Venice, 1901, pp. 539-541,
zkarmunǰn; Maten. MŠ 515, zkarmučn) in P XXIII:113, 124; in one mediaeval song,
the beloved is called k^{c}arē karmnǰni 'bridges of stone' (M. Abełyan, II:132).
French rivière can mean 'necklace'; the apiki (=apaki 'glass', for which
Ačaŕean has ulunk^c 'necklace' as a secondary meaning) of Line 33 may be the
'river of wine bringing joy' of Line 34. But Line 35 suggests that the river
is the beloved's mouth, and the necklace the red bridge of the lips over it.
Cf. NK LXXX:4 Bernikd ē i šiš nman, or vardin ǰrovn ē i li 'Your little mouth
is like a bottle which is full of rosewater'. The modern Armenian poet
Hovhannes Siraz uses the same images of bridge and river--in reference to his
arms and his beloved's hair--in the poem C^{c}erekners k^{c}ristonya, gišerners
het^{c}anos 'A Christian by day, a heathen by night' (K^{c}nar Hayastani, Vol. III,
Erevan, 1974, p. 5, Lines 5-8):

Cold sister, what have I done to your swan's neck moon?
'Happy is he!' say the swans to the holder of your loins.
You are in my arms and I am in you; thus I give my soul
And a bridge of both arms to the flood of your scented hair
[Zuyg t^cevers kamrǰac buyr-mazerid heɫeɫin].

Line 38. Ew blbulin anenk^cnadar. Maten. MSS 9271, 7715 and 1990 have nazar; MS 5668 and Srvanjteanc^c have natar, see P III:7.

Line 39. Or i k^cafur vardi sirun. On k^cafur, see P XII:2.

Line 40. I šur ku'gay k^can zdiwahar. Maten. MSS 9271, 7715 and 1990 read Zōrn linar (1990: linin) xēv (1990: xew) u xumar 'All day he is [was, they are] crazy and drunk'; on the interchangeability of xew with xumar, see Note to P XIII:2.

Line 54. Yerkir jgec^c w' arar siwar. Šiwar=šuar 'giddy', cf. Frik XXXI:80 Fērik, anyoys mi kenar, or čenknis i hogs w'i šiwar 'Frik, live not bereft of hope, lest you fall into worry and giddiness'. The word is probably a borrowing, cf. NP šurīdan; swr could be read as either šūr or š(e)v(a)r; a similar case is Armenian sulul-sulval < NP. swlwl, cf. Note to P XXIV:64. (On *šureloy 'of the wanderer', p. part. gen. sg., see Russell in the Annual of Arm. Linguistics, 8, in pub.).

Lines 53-56. See the chapter 'Songs of Creation and Adam'.

Lines 57-60. Set^cay ordikēn xaṙnakec^can, / Or čegnawork^c ēin yōžar / Zp^coɫn u zc^cnceɫaysn lsec^cin, / Amēnn ekin leṙnēn i var. Cf. the Armenian Apocryphal Book of Adam (in T^cangaran hin ew nor naxneac^c, I, Ankanon girk^c hin ktakaranac^c, Venice, 1896, pp. 319-21):

> And the nation of Seth and his older brothers multiplied, but they pursued the nation of Cain and did not cohabit (oč^c xaṙnakēin) with the nation of Cain, but abided in purity. But the daughters of the nation of Cain multiplied mightily, so that there was one man for every hundred women, and they circled about him and fought over him and took him away from each other, for men were few, but women and girls were many. The nation of Seth and his brothers did not mingle with them, and the nation of Seth abided in purity. There were so many good men: five hundred and twenty virgin ascetics there were amongst them, nor was there any means of their mingling with the nation of Cain. And in inventiveness the daughters of the nation of Cain contrived red paint (zkarmradeɫn) and white paint, wherewith they reddened and whitened their faces. They plucked their eyebrows (zunk^cn kasec^cin) and put antimony on, and they fixed their hair and tresses, and made various contrivances and musical instruments. They adorned with henna (xinec^cin) and reddened their feet and hands, and they adorned their bodies and made them resplendent with other decorations. And thus resplendent in clothing and every manner of fashion they went gaily into the mountain, rejoicing and dancing, clapping their hands and

sounding the trumpet, long and in varying voices. They mingled with the
sons of Seth and deceived them all. They were five hundred and twenty
ascetics, and one Noah alone remained a virgin, while all the other com-
mingled with them and became even worse than them, and became the doers of
deeds filthier than dogs', but a father did not know his daughter, nor did
a mother copulate with son, nor brother with sister. And they lived a
daily life of this adultery, and they did not remember God. And for their
many sins God was wroth against them, and wished to suffocate them by
water. God ordered Noah to build an ark, and to marry. . . .

The birth of Cain and Abel as described in the same text curiously parallels
the Zurvanite legend of the birth of Ahura Mazdā and Angra Mainyu as narrated
by Eznik, and may contain traces of old Iranian beliefs: . . . zanloysn or
koč^ci Kayēn ew zbarexorhn or koč^ci Habēl 'The lightless one called Cain and the
one of good thoughts called Abel' (p. 1). To Arm. barexorhn cf. Av. vohumaitē
(dat. sg.), an epithet of Ahura Mazdā in the Zoroastrian confession, Yasna 12.
Also, the forms of sexual union specifically denied in this story of Seth are
the same that by the Zoroastrian practice of next-of-kin marriage, Phl.
xwēdōdād, are considered the most meritorious (cf. Bahman Yašt II:57, 61;
Šāyest nē šāyest VIII:18, XVIII:3, 4; Ardāy Wīrāz Nāmag II:1-3, 7-10; Mēnōg ī
Xrad IV:4, Agathias II:31; Dēnkard III:82).

Lines 61-64. Kinn zYovhannēsn glxateac^c / Herovdiay płcoyn hamar, / Or na
vaṙeal ēr c^cankut^ceamb / P^cut^cov taraw zkamk^cn i katar. Cf. Mark VI:17-28,
esp. . . . ew č^cogaw glxateac^c zna i bantin. According to the Evangelist, however, the dreadful deed was carried out not for love, but out of a sense of the
king's word of honour, which cannot be broken; out of the same Persian concept
comes the command and counter-command of *Xerxes in the Book of Esther.
T^clkuranc^ci refers to John's martyrdom in P XX:11; the following poem, Vasn
surb Yovhannu glxatman 'On the Decapitation of St. John' (C, p. 8) is attributed to him:

> When the merciful Father willed the liberation of the face of men,
> He sent Gabriel to Zak^caria, the High Priest.
>
> When he kindled the temple incense in honour of the divine glory,
> He saw at the table to his right the unsubstantial form of flame,
>
> Which said, "Zak^caria, a voice of rejoicing brings you glad tidings.
> A great child will be born unto you, more honourable than the prophets,
>
> A servant of the immortal Word, of the unreachable, uncreate Son
> Who is born of the holy Virgin, for the salvation of mankind."
>
> His wife was barren, and was not persuaded of these things.
> Zak^caria was stricken dumb until she bore him a son clean.
>
> Then the Son of His Father's nature, without beginning and end,
> Took body from the Holy Virgin for the salvation of mankind.
>
> When Lord and servant were born, Heaven and earth were full of grace.
> The shepherds and Magi set off to bow to the ground at the Holy
>   Nativity.

When St. John grew up, he made the mountains his home
And ate locusts and honey; he covered himself with camel's hair.

In body he was bodiless; angelic were his life and privations.
He preached baptism and gave the commandment of repentance.

He baptised the immortal Word, God, and from above he heard a voice.
The Holy Spirit in the form of a dove descended towards the Jordan.

He was witness to the immortal word, and gestured with his finger to
  the people:
"This is Christ, the lamb of God, who takes all sins upon Himself.

He who believes and calls Him the Son enters into judgement;
He who refutes Him is condemned to inextinguishable fire without
  end" [i hur anšej u anvaxčan, cf. P I:28].

He opposed Herod and all the nation of the Jews,
saying, "It is not the law that you take your brother's wife, O
  vipers and beasts!"

That one was angered against John and bound him and cast him into
  prison.
One day he honoured the princes on the birthday of his perdition.

The insensate woman [Anēzgam kinēn, cf. Pivazyan I, entitled Tal . . .
  i veray . . . anēzgam kanancᶜ in Maten. MSS 2394, 8605, 3081 and
  Srvanjteancᶜ] heard. She was the daughter, the demons' pitfall.
She arranged her tresses and locks in the shape of a wondrous arch.

She darkened her eyes and brows, and anointed her face with demonic
  mascara,
Decorated all her person, and made a luxurious throne for the demons.

She said, "Go and move about there, so the crowds will be amazed.
Request John's head when they promise you reward."

The foul one went amongst the company, there where the princes were
  crowded together [cf. P XXIII:147-148 Yortel nstin . . . sat išxan].
She craned her neck more than the basilisk-serpent and twirled her
  hips more than a bow [. . . kᶜan zalelan, cf. P XIII:33].

She swept the revellers with her eyes and brows, flung out her arm,
  more supple than a willow,
Lifted up her foot and pranced about like a soldier of the Legion.

She stupefied the king, infected him with the passion of fornication,
And he swore: "Ask, girl, and I will give you a reward from me."

She asked for the head of John, holy friend of God.
He was very sad, not wishing to give it, but did so because of his
  oath.

The king sent an executioner, who went off, loudly sobbing,
And entered the prison atremble, crying "Woe!" with a thousand
  mouths:

"What will become of me, pitiful and wretched, where will I go?"
Until St. John, eager for his (own) murder, gave the command.

Shaken greatly with fear and remorse, he severed the head,
Took it and gave it to the foul girl, and she gave it to her
  haughty mother.

His disciples heard, and put the body in a tomb.
The soul went to the prophets, saying "The immortal king comes.

May he come and free us all of Hell and the abyss,
And take us to the ranks of angels in unending bliss."

On the morrow, that foul girl took her evil work to the cold house,
Which opened its maws to house two bodies now: the head, and a
    dog [i.e., adulteress].

The corpse became the food of fish; the head remained in the ice's
    mouth
As a cause of his mother's mourning, that she might know diverse
    sorrows.

They took it and put it in the mourning place in accordance with
    his mother's pleas.
The mother saw and howled aloud, and stared up towards the face of
    God.

She began to speak twistedly, reviling St. John.
Her sense fled, her eyes turned askew, and her face's colour became
    blue.

Her hands and feet were bound, a stone fell from the ceiling
Onto her head and killed her, and she was laid low like a foul bitch
    [Jeřkĕn ew otk^cĕn kapuec^caw . . . On the kap 'bond', cf. P II:19,
    VII:8].

The servants came and took the sacred head and put it in the window
That the disciples might come and pay a bribe for it.

Punishment came to the foul one: her house collapsed on her body
And she was lost, like a lewd demon, without a tomb.

And for a long time it remained there, until two monks came
And found the sacred head, slung it over their shoulders, and went
    on their way.

They met a potter and sold that gem.
The potter took it and made a holy sign of it, like the Cross.

I, Yovanēs T^curkuranc^ci, spoke shortly these words concise;
God give you peace and keep you unshaken and untried.

The above poem is published in couplets, each line containing sixteen syllables,
with caesura following the eighth syllable. The lines of each couplet rhyme
with one another, but not with the lines of adjacent couplets. One notes the
infrequency of Arabic loan words, the more Classical style of diction, the
absence of xew in the envoi, and the poet's faithfulness to the Gospel in re-
cording Herod's motives. These elements would tend to place the poem in a different genre than these lyrics, despite T^clkuranc^ci's fanciful and vivid
description of Salome's prancing and strutting. The poem belongs to the
narrative-heroic genre of P XXIII and XXIV, or to the wisdom poems, as a retelling of a Biblical tale.

Line 70. K^Can zōj k^Caylē w'aṙnu galar. So, too, the dance of Salome in C III above.

Line 79. T^Cē ačec^Cēk^C ew bazmac^Cēk^C. Cf. Gen. XXXV:11 ačesǰir ew bazmasǰir, 'be fruitful and multiply'.

* * *

This poem (P XV; C. p. 39-42) is written in lines of eight syllables, with caesura falling after the fourth syllables. Pivazyan has not divided the poem into four-line stanzas, but I have done so, excepting Lines 105-106, for the following reasons: Full stops are placed fairly regularly every four lines throughout the Armenian text, although there are several exceptions. While punctuation cannot be taken as a reliable guide to the meaning of a Middle Armenian text, the use of full stops in T^Clkuranc^Ci's poems is fairly consistent. The transition of themes in the poem (see esp. Lines 89-92) supports such division.

The second and fourth lines of each stanza rhyme in -an, with the notable exception of Lines 37-40, where the rhyming syllable is -aw (changed in -an, however, in the version of the Taɫaran of 1513); other exceptions, also in -aw and similarly rationalised in the Taɫaran, are Lines 60 and 62. Such cases occur in connection with the number of a verb, about which T^Clkuranc^Ci is sometimes inconsistent; changes in transmission of the poem may have happened either way, and the mangled form ēṙēɫnan (see Note to Line 21) indicates how much this poem may have suffered at the hands of scribes.

The poem is a veritable catalogue of flowers, and most of these are connected with one or another Armenian belief, sometimes hinted at by T^Clkuranc^Ci. The pilgrimage of the flowers of Lines 33-36 is a journey to Christ, the rose (cf. KE XII, Ban vardi ōrinakaw zK^Cristos patmē 'These words tell of Christ through the example of the rose'. The poem is attributed to Yovhannēs T^Clkuranc^Ci in a MS of A.D. 1469 [see M. Abeɫyan, II, 127; a similar attribution exists for KE XI, see P VIII]. KE commented on another of his poems, Meknut^Ciwn vardin hamaṙōt. Vasn angitac^C šinec^Ci, zi karcēin et^Cē marmnaworac^C bank^C vardis, Ew vasn ayn grec^Ci 'A brief commentary on the rose. I made it for the ignorant, because they thought my poem on the rose concerned carnal matters, and for that reason I have written it'.). MN II, Taɫ i dēms margarēic^Cn ew K^Cristosi ew Lusaworč^Cin 'Poem in the persons of the Prophets, Christ and the

Illuminator', is yet another example of this frequently encountered extended image:

> The beautiful flowers that existed once
> All went away.
> Another flower, too, departed, one such
> That all the flowers lamented him.
>
> That flower had a sweet fragrance
> That all the world sensed,
> And the flowers of all the world
> Turned to that flower's love.
>
> Some from that flower's love
> Turned dry and yellow.
> Many in that flower's love
> Flowered more than the hornbeam.
>
> God gave that flower,
> And many did not see its worth,
> He who gave the flower, took it back;
> Many remained in vain below.
>
> The flower passed on to a place
> Where all the flowers rejoiced.
> A thousand multicoloured flowers
> Gathered to that flower's love.
>
> The flowers from that flower's love
> Gathered dew and shone;
> Every flower with his colour
> They placed upon that flower's head.
>
> A flower opened anew
> With that colour, in that flower's place.
> Christ preserves the flower,
> That flower at the Cross' base.
>
> The flowers were the prophets,
> The patriarchs, and the first saints.
> The flower that was with them
> Was Jesus, the Father's only-begotten.
>
> A flower opened anew
> With the same colour in that flower's place.
> That flower was our Illuminator,
> Scion of St. Thaddeus.
>
> Naɫaš, if you have sense,
> Think of the spring flowers
> So brilliant in colour,
> Which dry and turn yellow.
>
> Do not be such a flower,
> Lest wind and tempest bear you away
> Be a flower of good deeds,
> That your soul may bear fruit.

The Illuminator in this poem is St. Gregory, who established Christianity as the state church of Armenia. The Church claims also an earlier Apostolic foundation under Sts. Thaddeus and Bartholomew. As for their banner, the cyclamen, Iranian Muslims believe that Mary grasped it under a date tree while giving birth to Jesus, and call it panǰe-ye Maryam 'the five [fingers] of Mary'; it is placed in the hands of women in childbirth (Donaldson, The Wild Rue, p. 27). The red spot at the center of the flower is believed by Christians to be the blood of Mary's heart (George Ferguson, Signs and Symbols in Christian Art, New York, 1966, p. 30).

T^clkuranc^i lingers over each detail out of love for the earth and its delights, the 'kindness' (Line 95) of the Divine, who provides eternal spring in the world to come. Even the grape is praised (Lines 69-70). The slow, cyclical turn to autumn comes gently in the poem, not as a ringing denunciation of earthly vanity. T^clkuranc^i is here the observer, not the storm-tossed lover seeking to tear himself away from the object of his obsession, and we see him mellow, devoting barely a few lines to hellfire and doom.

TRANSLATION

God, without beginning or limit,
Inconceivable, inexplicable:
Such a noble spring You have made.
Like Eden's Paradise.

5   Trees and orchards waxed verdant
And, gleaming with fruit, were adorned.
Small springs hastened forth;
Seas and rivers were quickened to motion.

Four-footed beasts that were confined
10 Burst out of their stalls and emerged:
The camel's young do leap about
And circle round the places of their frolic.

The masters of love strut about,
Glance over their shoulders, and pass;
15 Girls beautify their tresses,
Promenade, walk about and rejoice together.

All the birds were gladdened
And came to their perches;
The swallows came and set their nests--
20 They sang Psalms, completely at home.

There is the *John-bird, and glow-worm,
And the turtledove has a very sweet voice;
They know sermons, canticles and poems,
Melodies, and many hymns.

25 Stork, goose and duck
And shoveller-duck made merry,
Nightingales arrived with their desires
And tumbled into the rose bush.

The earth bubbled and grew tender.
30 Myriads upon myriads of flowers sprang up;
All the plains were full of blossoms
At whose fragrance men rejoice.

Lily, green myrtle and astragal
And violet came together
35 And went to bow down to the rose:
The cyclamen was their banner.

The narcissus exuded balmy fragrance,
The poppy was resplendent in its crown
And the water lily, rising from its pool
40 Appeared, yellow and green.

The hamasp^ciwṙ amongst the flowers
Was the one said to be the mother of wisdom,
Which cures scabby leprosy
And appears on Ascension Day.

45 Sentient and vegetable creatures
And all the sons of men,
All in a single voice
Bless the increate, existent Word.

The branches of the trees grew soft
50 And their fruits ripened one by one,
The mulberry before the aloe;
The cherry tree was like a bow.

The apricots on the tree grew yellow
And the apples reddened.
55 The fruits scorned the pear
Until it was ripe and firm.

Walnut, jujube and chestnut,
Almond and hazelnut grew sweet.
The pomegranate also bared a thousand teeth;
60 The date hung from the tree.

The quince grew yellow;
The plum weakened and fell from its bond.
Orange, bitter orange and lemon comes
Which open the fruits of Adam's son.

65 When that cavalcade has passed,
The praiseworthy grape comes,
For this one removed us from Paradise
When Adam ate him.

The shut gate of Paradise
70 The grape has opened again to men.
Our Lord Jesus Christ in respect of the wine
Said to the Apostles in the upper room,

"Take and drink in hope;
This is my saving blood.
75 He who drinks it in purity
Never tastes eternal death.

He will live in me
And I in him eternally."
The last days of autumn came,
80 Which is the passing of every seed.

The plains grow empty of their plants,
Flowers pass and appear no more,
The trees are stripped of all their fruit,
And branches now have shed their leaves.

85 Birds form flocks and cry,
"Who else will be worthy of the spring?"
However much they eat or drink,
Still they long for the spring day.

Autumn is like old age:
90 The old die, and pass, and go.
We must await the eternal,
The everlasting, the unending,

Every day of which is spring,
When glory and honour are unbroken.
95 Who does not recall this kindness
And render glory to the Divine--

I call him possessed,
Or arrogant Satan.
He who gave this boon to us
100 Asks in return today

That you love your brother and love prayer,
Pure, submissive and penitent.
If you preserve this, in this world you have it,
And in the next world it is yours as well.

105 But if you remain in sin, never turning (from it),
You will be given over to Gehenna's fire.

Crazy Yovhannēs T^{C}ulgorĕnc^{C}i,
Full of grievous sins,
Asks of you that with thoughts of the heart
110 You say "Lord, have mercy" for his soul.

Notes

Line 13. Siroy tērnin ku čoxanan. Siroy tēr 'master of love', i.e. 'lover',
cf. P XIV:86; NK III:3 Zhamn al ari es ayl, siroy tēr ełay het k^{C}ezi 'I tasted
something else as well: I was master of love with you'; and NK LXXXIV, in which
the poet addresses the beloved: K^{C}o tiroǰd ayl inč^C ernek, du herik^C es xałlu
xnjor 'What else does your master need? You are enough of an apple to play
with.'

Line 9. Č^{C}orkotanik^C or argelan. The Tałaran of 1513 has instead of or argelan
'that were confined', arogac^{C}an 'were sprinkled'; Maten. MS 1990 reads or
orogec^{C}an 'were watered'.

Line 21. <u>Ohanahawn u ĕrĕłnan</u>. <u>Ohanahawn</u> is Mod. Arm. <u>Hovanahav</u> 'a kind of songbird' (ŽHLBB). MS 1990 has <u>Ahaynayhawn ew ĕršnan</u>; MS 3498 reads <u>Yovaynayhawn u ĕrĕłnayn</u>; I connect tentatively the third word with NP. <u>rōšān</u> 'radiance' as a noun, 'glow-worm'. The similarity of written ł and š (ɳ and ℓ) in Armenian script would account for the variants in MSS. The <u>yovanahaw</u>, possibly the Yellowhammer (<u>Emberiza citrinella</u>), a type of bunting, is mentioned in the <u>Tał T^cṙc^cnoc^c</u> 'Poem of the Birds' of Yovhannēs <u>vardapet</u>, Maten. MS 3595, fol. 69a-79b, cited by J. Greppin, <u>Classical and Middle Armenian Bird Names</u>, Delmar, N. Y., 1978, 243 (translation mine):

> 'The <u>yovanahav</u> took flight,
> His voice like a reed flute.
> Arrayed in blue-green and yellow
> He fluttered round the gardens.'

On <u>ĕrĕšnan</u>, cf. Arm. <u>ĕrušnayiay</u>, from NP. <u>rōšanāyī</u>, a kind of eye-medicine (Ałayan, <u>Aknarkner</u>, I, 279).

Line 29. <u>Eṙac^c erkir ew kakłac^caw</u>. Cf. Matt. XXIV:32 <u>zi yoržam nora ostk^cn kakłasc^cin ew terewn c^cc^cuic^ci</u> . . . . Trees become <u>kakuł</u> 'tender' in Spring, P XV:49.

Line 36. <u>Ztełtn unēin iwreanc^cn alam</u>. <u>Alam</u> < Ar. <u>a^clām</u> 'marks, signs'.

Line 41. <u>Hamasp^ciwṙn i mēǰ całkanc^c</u>. The <u>hamasp'iwṙ</u>, a twelve-stemmed white or multicoloured flower of the Melandrium family, is the subject of a mediaeval treatise, <u>Patmut^ciwn hamasp^ciwṙ całkin</u> 'History of the flower <u>hamasp^ciwṙ</u>', in which we read, 'If you put it to your ear, you will hear heavenly voices and speech, and you will understand all the languages of men and will know the tongues of animals, beasts and birds. If you put it to your eye, you will behold all creation before your eyes. If you hold it to your palate, you will experience the sweet taste of Heaven. If you put it to your tongue, you will converse and speak in every language, and will tell of the knowledge of wise men and priests. If you touch it with your fingers, you will gain every art. . . . And much has been said of the great and powerful miracles worked by this flower'; according to Mxit^car Goš, the <u>hamasp^ciwṙ</u> 'will fill the ignorant with widsom' (<u>imastut^ceamb ztgēts lc^cc^cē</u>) (cf. S. Avdalbekyan, "<u>Patmut^ciwn hamasp^ciwṙ całkin</u>"', <u>Patma-banasirakan handes</u>, Erevan, 1976, 3, pp. 258-9, and N. Taławarean, <u>Hayoc^c hin krōnnerĕ</u>, Constantinople, 1909, p. 16). In a mediaeval Armenian wedding song cited by H. Hakobyan, <u>Haykakan manrankarč^cnt^cyun</u>: <u>Vaspurakan</u>, Erevan, 1978, 12, the bride addresses the groom: 'King, what shall I bring like you, / Your green [i.e., new] Sun, like you: / The flowering <u>hamasp^ciwr</u> / Blossoms like your Sun.' Bp. Tirayr, ed., <u>Frik diwan</u>, N. Y., 1952, 654, cites the line 'This is the <u>hamasp^ciwṙ</u> flower, which saves man from death'

(also poem XVIII.3); the editor translates the name of the flower as Eng.
Campion, Tk. yalan garanfil çiçeği (lit. 'false clove flower') (see also Ēd.
Aḷayan, Ardi hayerēni bac^C atrakan baṙaran, Erevan, 1976, I, 804). Fr. Ḷ. Ạlišan,
Hin hawatk^C kam het^C anosakan krōnk^C Hayoc^C, Venice, 1910, 84-5, cites Mxit^C ar
Goš (twelfth century) and Mxit^C ar Herac^C: on the flower. Herac^C i wrote that
the hamasp^C iwṙ has one root and sends out twelve shoots; each of its flowers
has a different colour. If sought at night, it appears aglow. Ališan con-
siders it the lychnis orientalis.

Line 51. T^C ut^C n yaṙaǰeac^C k^C an ēzhalwan. Halwa < Ar. halfā (Ačaṙean).

Line 58. Nušn u fēntuxn k^C aḷc^C rac^C an. Fēntuxn < Ar. findiq 'hazelnut, filbert'.

Line 62. The Taḷaran reads Deḷc^C n i caṙin . . . 'The peach on the tree . . .'.

Line 64. Ew zardmordun baṙk^C ēn banay 'And opens the words of Adam's son'. The
reading of MS 3498, Or zardmordu bark^C n banan, as 'fruits' seem more appropriate than 'words' in the context, although the possibility of a pun is not
denied: spring does give vent to poets' mellifluosity. On the form zardmordu,
see Note to P XIII:37.

Line 65. T^C ē ayt hecelt ēr or anc^C aw. This is probably a reference to carpets
of spring flowers, cf. KE XXVI:2.

> Like the sultan's many-horsed troop,
> Tribe upon tribe, they build their summer residence;
> Half coming through the mountains,
> The congregate.in the garden.

The grape of Line 66 ripens after the multicoloured encampments of the flowers
have gone.

Line 66. In Armenia, grapes ripen in August, that is, after the flowers of
spring and early summer have gone. Autumn there is the 'golden season', the
time of rich harvests and pleasant weather. The grape represents all the other
fruits of the earth, and the rite of blessing the first grapes, xaḷoḷōrhnēk^C,
is performed on the Feast of the Assumption (Verap^C oxumn S. Astuacacnin), which
is celebrated on the Sunday closest to 15 August. The prayer recited over the
grapes was composed by St. Nersēs Šnorhali, and invokes the power of the holy
cross (surb xač^C, nšan) against pestilence and insects. It seems that the
important Christian festival was made the occasion for an older, distinct
ritual blessing of the first fruits, because the two coincide in season; cf.
the feast of the Transfiguration and its association with the summer holiday of
Vardavaṙ. Nonetheless Armenians have sometimes drawn symbolic parallels between

the blessing of the grapes and the rôle of the Virgin: just as Mary redeemed womankind from the curse of Eve, so did Christ by the shedding of his blood, as he called the Paschal wine, redeem the grape that had made Noah drunk.

Line 85. <u>Hawern eram kapen u lan</u>. <u>Eram kapel</u> 'to form a flock, flock together', cf. KE XV:12 Jagōk^c hawerd elnen paren ew en miaban eram kapel 'The birds with their young rise, dance, and form their flocks together.'

* * *

This poem (P Appendix I; C, p. 53-4) has been published in couplets of two sixteen-syllable lines each, with caesura following the eighth syllable of each line; all lines rhyme in -<u>ay</u>. This is the joyous, extravagant work of a lover in spring. Yovhannēs made <u>xew</u> with wine (Line 23), compares his ruin to the beloved's glory; his spilled blood is her smeared henna (Lines 19-20). Wound and cure become one: he is pelted--with the apples of love; he is wounded--by a sweet tongue. She is čalat 'executioner' (cf. P XIII:5), but as her weapon is love, so her victim's funeral is a minstrel's, with wine instead of water for the washing of the corpse, a green leaf instead of linen for the winding sheet, and a <u>mtrup</u> 'minstrel' instead of a priest. The beloved's cruelty is a violation of the <u>ɫawl</u> 'word, pledge' and <u>erdumn</u> 'oath' of love (Line 45, cf. P X:17), but the poem ends on a positive note: with patience, the poet's suffering will end and harmony with the beloved will be restored.

The optimism is uncharacteristic of T^c lkuranc^c i, and the vivid contrasts of the imagery of the poem recall K^c uč^c ak instead. The other lyrics end with a warning against woman and a rejection of love, except for P X, which, as noted above, refers to a contract undertaken, maybe a reference to a truly successful liaison which, for all its passion, did not around T^c lkuranc^c i's misogynous anger. Uncharacteristic, also, is T^c lkuranc^c i's description of himself: the clouds of his abundant tresses touch the mountains of his muscular chest (Lines 37-38). In his wisdom poems he is old--maybe he wrote them much later. He seems obsessed by the vision of the dismemberment of his own body and the outpouring of his blood (Lines 25-40). This self-description, almost narcissistic in comparison to T^c lkuranc^c i's absorption in the qualities and features of the beloved in the other lyrics, together with the mock funeral, find their closest parallels in certain quatrains of Nahapet K^c uč^c ak, in which the poet parodies the established religion; his only religion is his beloved (LXII,

LXIII, LIV, cf. Note to P II:11-12). T^clkuranc^ci condemns this same attitude
in a wisdom poem against women (P XX:13-16) which clearly belongs to a much
later stage of his life than this. Nahapet K^cuč^cak seems to have written long-
ingly, not angrily, of his youth: <u>Erb or es pztik ēi, kanč^cēin inj oski tłay</u>
'When I was little, they called me golden boy' (XXV). This poem of dreams,
wine, gardens and longing for a faraway beloved seems to be of T^clkuranc^ci's
golden time, if indeed he is its author.

TRANSLATION

    I cannot withstand your love: Grant me your love; it is as though
        I had died.
4 Take a golden spade along; come, dig a grave for me.

    Let them burn me with the <u>tarapul</u>: That my heart's conflagration
        might roar.
8 Many a man falls into this fire and burns dry, the green above him.

    Let them wash me in wine, let them bring me a minstrel as my priest.
12 May the green leaf be my winding sheet; let them take me to be
        buried in a new garden.

    Behold, bandit and murderer, the executioner comes to be your pupil!
16 You have cast many into the prison of love; your door and gate are
        a slaughterhouse.

    You burned and crushed my heart and daubed your eyes with antimony.
20 You turned, spilled my blood, and smeared henna on your feet.

    Pelt me with apples--the sweet tongue has wounded me!
24 Make me crazy with sweet wine--I was imprisoned in your breast.

    This night in my dream they cut me up piece by piece.
28 Beasts were sated on my blood, birds on my corpse.

    Above me is the lion's maw; my blood spurts like water.
32 Whoever thirsted for my blood, let him come and drink his fill.

    From my brave feet to the ground I have one soul to sacrifice.
36 My liver will suffice for kebab; let my blood be the wine.

    The clouds of my head have descended upon the mountains of my heart.
40 My heart's rancour exhales a fog and sprinkles tears of blood.

    We ate from the same table and drank from the same bowl.
44 In one place we got up; in one place we sat down. Where is that
        time now?

    Where is your pledge? Where is the oath We held God as witness to?
48 You fell away, estranged. Death to him who wished us ill!

    May God bring our evil-wisher evil, that he have his fill of evil.
52 May He grant good to our friends, that our word be made good again.

    God give my heart a way; let the tree blossom green,
56 Or let my heart's tree spring, and the small bird chirp and speak.

Deeds are completed with patience: Crazy Yovanēs, be patient.
60 The time will come, by her own will she will come, and kiss her,
however far away.

Notes

Line 2. Halal ara, hansĕ mer̃ay. Halal ara, 2 pers. imp. sing. of halal aynel,
anel, ar̃nel 'to make worthy, to grant love' (Aɬayan). On halal 'permissible'
see Note to P XIX:31.

Line 4. W'eko p^{c}orē inci t^{c}urpay. T^{c}urpay 'grave' (Pivazyan); Tk. türbe from
Ar., a Muslim tomb.

Line 5. T^{c}oɬ zis eren tar̃aypulov. C. Dowsett suggests a derivation from NP.
dar-e behāl 'firewood', but it is more likely Arm. darap^{c}ul, a wooden box (see
G. Sruanjtreanc^c, 'Groc^c-broc^c', Erker, I, Erevan, 1978, 71), or a stringed
musical instrument. The latter is most likely. In Erevan Matenadaran MS 7782,
A.D. 1471, fol. 1-b, from Arckē (Pl. XLVII and p. 28 in A. Gevorgyan,
Arhestnern u kenc^{c}aɬĕ haykakan manrankarnerum, Erevan, 1973), a woman is shown
plucking the instrument, with the caption Kin mi or tarapulay kĕ zarnē 'a woman
who is playing the tarapul.'

Line 6. Kanač^c terewĕn t^{c}oɬ patnen . . . . The imagery is the same as that
used by KE XI:7 in describing the risen Christ as a rose: Hanē zkananč^c kapan u
hagni zir xĕrmĕzin '[the rose] removes his green bonds and puts on his crimson.'

Line 10. Mtrup beren inj k'ahanay. Mtrup < Ar. mut̤rib 'singer' (Aɬayan).

Lines 13-14. Hay harami u mardĕspan, / Čalatn i k^{c}ovd aškert ku'gay. Harami <
A harāmī 'bandit' (Aɬayan); čalatn, cf. Note to P XIII:5.

Line 16. Dur̃d u dĕrunk^{c}d ē ɬanaray. Ɬanaray < Ar. qannāra 'abattoir' (Aɬayan).

Line 18. U k^{c}asec^{c}ir yač^{c}k^{c}ĕd surmay. Surmay < NP. sormeh 'antimony'. Oriental women encircle the eyes with a collyrium of antimony, which is thought to
'make the eye-lashes grow, to beautify the eyes, and to incite the heart to
love' (Elgood, Safavid Medical Practice, p. 203).

Line 20. W'i otvĕnid dĕrir hinay. Hinay < Ar. ḥinnā 'henna'. According to
Muḥammad, a believer ought to do four things: use perfume, take a wife, clean
his teeth, and 'bind henna'; some Muslims are said to believe that the merit of

one dirham spent for henna exceeds one thousand spent on charity. Henna drives pains from the ear, strengthens sight, keeps the membranes of the nostrils soft, gives the mouth a sweet odor, strengthens roots of the teeth, removes body odor, lessens satanical temptation, gladdens angels and believers, infuriates infidels, ornaments the user as a sweet fragrance, and diminishes the trials of the grave (Donaldson, The Wild Rue, p. 188).

Line 45, Ur ē łavlĕd, ur ē erdumn. Cf. P X:18.

* * *

This poem (P Appendix II; C, p. 52-53) is bilingual: the odd-numbered lines are in Armenian, while the even-numbered lines are in Turkish, written, of course, in Arm. script. The poem is printed in quatrains of octosyllabic lines or hemistichs with caesura following the fourth syllable. All lines within a quatrain rhyme (however loosely; the final syllable of Line 2, -im, is found with Lines 1, 3 and 4 in -um, for example, while the quatrain beginning at Line 17 has the final syllables -in, -ĕ, -i, -ĕ), but the rhyming syllable (or syllables: Lines 1, 2, 4 rhyme in -rĕtum, -ērtim and -awrtum; Lines 5, 6, 7, 8 rhyme in -amar, -umar, -amar and -ēmēr; Lines 10, 11, 12 rhyme in -ēnči, -ēnči and -ēnči; Lines 15, 16 rhyme in -arman, -ērman; Lines 17, 18, 20 rhyme in -axtin, -ahtĕ, -ahtĕ; Lines 21, 23 rhyme in nman, nman; Lines 26, 28 rhyme in -erman, -ērman, cf. Lines 15, 16; Lines 29, 30 rhyme in -usin, -ulsink (reflecting the gen. ending -ing preserved by Ottoman orthography); Lines 33, 34, 36 rhyme in -iǰin, -ēǰin, ičcun) differs from quatrain to quatrain.

The imagery of the poem is familiar from other poems of Tclkurancci: the beloved is perceived as healer (Lines 16, 28) and the cause of pain and suffering (Lines 2, 3, 14, 32); her brows arch (Line 5, cf. P XIV:4), her teeth are a string of pearls (Line 15, cf. P IX:8, XII:30, XIV:12), her breast is paradise (Line 17, cf. P XIII:3), she is basil (Line 22, cf. P IV:9), her eyes are like the sea (Line 27, cf. P II:3), her face is a full moon (Line 29, cf. P XII:8), and she is the city of čcin u mēǰin (Line 34, cf. P VI:2). The poet does not rebuke himself for his love at the end of the poem; although the familiar epithet of his envois appears in Line 7, Xew ełay es noray hamar 'I was crazy for her', Tclkurancci at the end calls himself simply Ergołis Yovanisin 'This singer Yovhannēs' (Line 35). And the relaxed tone of this

work of the singer Yovhannēs is best summed up by Line 20, Surēlum awmrumuz
vahtĕ 'Let us enjoy the time of life'. The Turkish lines were translated by
Ō. Eganyan (Pivazyan, p. 287). Maten. MS 5668 has the following stanzas in
place of quatrains 5, 7 and 9:

> Come, let us go into your garden,
> And I will pluck the sweet apple.
> The rose sleeps in the bud;
> The nightingale comes, and desires the rose.

> It ran to and fro, searching:
> 'They have stolen my rose!
> Tell me the news, if you have seen it,
> Else my soul will depart from me!

> My heart is devoured by your love
> My pains are legion.
> Come to me with your sleeping breast
> And your high and slender waist.

> How much more will you judge me;
> Behold your prisoner!
> If you have an answer, speak it plain.
> Forget me not, light of my eyes.'

'Light of my eyes', ač^{c}k^{c}i loys, is the way Sayat^c Nova was, centuries later,
to address his beloved in his song, Mi xōsk^c unim iltimazov, which is still
popularly sung by Armenians.

TRANSLATION

> Today I was very sad;
> My old pain was renewed.
> My rejoicing ended
> When I saw my beloved taking a walk.
>
> 5 She had brows, arched brows;
> Her intoxicating eyebrows are black.
> I was crazy for her;
> Her face is a brilliant moon with a rose garden.
>
> You gave me measureless love,
> 10 O bud, young one of the roses!
> Again you wore orange,
> And made me weep.
>
> Like the wild hind
> You cast my heart into doubt.
> 15 Your teeth are a string of pearls;
> Make me a cure for my pain.
>
> Your breast is like Paradise.
> Come, do not mutilate my heart!
> My soul and the light of my eyes,
> 20 Come, let us enjoy the time of life.
>
> You are like a pomegranate seed;
> You are clove and basil.
> Lovely flowers are like you;
> Whom does the gracious lily resemble?

25 When I see you, incomparable one,
No command remains for me.
Your lovely eyes are like the sea:
Make a potion for my wound.

Your face is a full moon.
30 Let the bud smile on my wound.
Come, approach your servant,
O my cruel one, subtle and sweet.

In this world
You are the city of Č^cin u mējin.
For this singer Yovhannēs
Have mercy, for the sake of your head.

Notes

Line 11-12. Tk. <u>Alvay hagar narĕnči, / Ēylētink peni zarĕnči</u>. The conceit of the colour of the beloved's attire calls to mind P Appendix III:iii and Sayat^c Nova XLVIII (cited in the Note to P XIII:16).

Line 14. Tk. <u>Tušurtunk konklumē ku mēn</u>. <u>Ku mēn</u> = NP. <u>gumān</u> 'thought, doubt'; <u>anguman</u> (<u>an</u> 'not' + <u>guman</u>) is used in KE XV:15 <u>Gay varden gałt ew anguman</u> 'the rose comes secretly and suddenly' like Arm. <u>yankarc</u> 'suddenly', lit. 'without thought'.

* * *

This poem, <u>Hayrenik asac^ceal ē T^curkuranc^cu i veray siroy</u> 'A little <u>hayren</u> that T^curkuranc^ci has spoken on love' (P Appendix III), was first published by Č^copanean in <u>Hayrenneru burastanē</u>, with the following note:

> These five little poems belong to a privately owned poetical MS at Aleppo, a copy of which Archbishop Artawazd Siwrmeyan was kind enough to send me . . . the copyist of the MS has given the group of poems the title <u>Hayrenik asac^ceal ē T^curkuranc^cu i veray siroy</u>. But the little poems differ from Yovhannēs T^clkuranc^ci's true verses, and certainly belong to K^cuč^cak. (p. 323)

He may well be right. Appendix III:i reads <u>Caṙay ayn čaktin linim, margartē k'ĕrtink^c ku c^cōłay; / Asc^ci t^cē pagik m'aṙnum, na tełikn ē xist łalapay</u>; NK CLXXI is identical, except for the fourth word of the second line, which reads <u>m'aṙnem</u>, a more modern form. III:ii reads <u>Im earn erku duṙ unēr; mēken gałt u mēkn alani. / Nēstēr i gałtuk dĕṙnakn, ku kanč^cēr hayerēn łazali</u>; NK CIV is identical, and the first line of CCCLXXXIV reads <u>Srtiks erku duṙn uni; mekn gałt u mekn alani</u> ('My little heart has . . . '). III:iii reads <u>Ov spitak coc^c</u>

uni, t^{c}oł lĕrĵuk šapik č^{c}i hagni; / Ert^{c}ank^c anicenk^c k^{c}ałak^{c}n or lełakn i mĕĵn
ku busni. / Pōyačun karasn awiri, iwr sirtĕn t^{c}oł hali patři; / Pōyačin ayl
inč^c anē, ir tartern k^{c}anc^c ĵern aweli. / Ert^{c}am ałač^{c}em zastuac, or lełkan
ĕntikn anc^{c}ani, / Oč^c spitak coc^c lurĵ hagni, oč^c mankan sirtĕn nĕwałi; NK CXCV
reads Ov or čermak coc^c uni, t^{c}oł kapoyt šapik hagni; / Kočakn ayl arjak t^{c}ołu,
ov tesni, srtikn aruni. / Ert^{c}am ałač^{c}em zastuac, lełakin hantn hatani; / Oč^c
na ayl kapoyt hagni, oč^c mankan sirtn aruni 'May she who has a white breast
wear a blue chemise / And let the buttons loose; whoever sees it, may his
little heart bleed. / I will go and plead with God that the indigo field perish, / That she not put on blue anymore, that a boy's heart bleed not'. III:v
reads Eresd ē serov macun, pagd anuš er k^{c}anc^c amenun; / Ber pagnem loys
eresĕd, or č^{c}ert^{c}as gangtis k^{c}o nerun. / K^{c}o nerd al šat varjk^c arer u kaper
karmunĵ geterun; / Dun ayl ayd varjkunk^c ara, k^{c}o mekik ałbōr arewun; a variant
of NK CCCLXII (p. 331, n. 67) is identical. One notes that III:v:3-4 is preserved as a couplet in the text of NK CCCLXII: Kozal, mi hagni kaput, mi xałar
u tar t^{c}ewerud; / Mi gar 'w i dřnakn anc^{c}nir, mi čočar, kozal, arewud. / K^{c}o
harn al sat varjk^c arer, šat karmunĵ kaper geterun; / Dun al mek varjkunk^c ara,
pag mi tur dnč^{c}id moterun. 'Beauty, do not wear blue, do not play and move
about your arms; / Do not come and pass through the gate. Beauty, by your Sun,
do not sway. / Your father paid many wages and built many bridges over the
rivers; / Pay a wage yourself, and give a kiss to the ones close to your chin';
although with slight variations. The building of bridges was a recognised form
of philanthropy in Mediaeval Armenia, as earlier in Sasanian Persia. Frik
wrote (L. Miriĵanyan, ed., Margaritner Hay k^{c}narergut^{c}yan, Erevan, 1971, p. 110):

> 'One is incomparable with his hands,
> Skilled in both study and craft;
> He makes foundations at the bottom of the sea
> And builds bridges over the river.'

TRANSLATION

i.

I am a servant of that brow which sprinkles sweat of pearl.
I said 'I will take a kiss,' but that place is very crowded.

ii.

My love had two doors: one secret and one known.
She sat at the secret gate and sang an Armenian ghazal.

iii.

May she who has a white breast not wear a sky-blue chemise.
Let us go and curse the city in whose midst indigo sprouts;
May the dyer's equipment be wrecked, may his heart melt and break!
What else will the dyer do? He has more wounds than you.
I will go and plead with God that the indigo type perish,
That the white breast not put on sky-blue, that a boy's heart not swoon.

iv.

I say 'You are comely.' She says, 'The Lord has granted it.'
I said 'Give me a kiss.' She said, 'My kiss has a price.'
I said 'What is the price of your kiss?' She said, 'The price of my
    kiss is your soul.'
My soul wants your soul, too. I will not say no; I will take it out
    and give it to you.
I fear you want my eyes; with what will I gaze upon you then?
Seven and six eyes were necessary, seven and six or forty and six.
With one will I observe the rest of the world; all the others I will
    turn towards you.

v.

Your face is yoghurt with cream; your kiss is sweeter than all.
Bring me the light of your face that I might kiss it; do not go and
    complain to your sister-in-law.
Your sister-in-law also paid a huge wage and built a bridge over the
    rivers.
Pay the same wage yourself, for the sake of your only brother's Sun.

Notes

i.2.   Łalapay < Ar. ghalaba 'battle, confusion' (Ałayan, who lists the form
xalapay). The sense of crowding or confusion of many lovers at the cheek of
the beloved is understood, while the idea of a great number may perhaps be
associated with Ar. gholb 'thickly-planted orchards'.

ii.1. Alani < Ar. ^{c}alanī 'manifest' (Ałayan).

iii.2,5. On indigo, cf. H. Razi, ed., Dīvān-e Jāmī, Tehran, 1341 AH, p. 452
ān gabāye nīlgūn bīnīd dar sīmīn bareš 'Behold that indigo chemise upon her
silver bosom'.

iii.3,4. Pōyači < Tk. boyaǰĕ 'dyer' (Ałayan).

*   *   *

This abecedarian poem Aybēn minč^{c}ew i k^{c}ēn gankat anem es (P Appendix IV)
is divided into four-line stanzas, each line of which contains eleven syllables
with caesura following the sixth syllable. All lines rhyme in -es, -ēs or -ez.
In all the above particulars, the poem resembles P X very closely; indeed, the
theme is the same as well--the contract of love, which the lover begs the

beloved to keep faithfully (cf. Line 18 in both poems). Maten. MS 9271 contains a variant of Lines 13-36, a translation of which follows the translation of the poem.

TRANSLATION

      I will make my complaint from A to Z.
      Why do you not greet me? You are falsely agitated.
      You know that I have suffered evil on your account.
      Why do you deceive me? Surely you are not an infidel.

5   To whom will I go to complain? You are my cure.
      You keep the sun of your face from me;
      When you come, you are like the morning light.
      I am amazed at this: why do you spare me?

      I left you far away; you have not left me.
10 It is time you cured me, else I am lost.
      Mine is not that house which treats you cruelly;
      It is well for you to understand in your mind that you are false.

      Where is the pledge and oath you made to me?
      You have strayed from your promise; your faith is slight.
15 The blue is our witness that I love you.
      I am the earth at your feet where you tread.

      I heard your voice and rejoiced.
      You made a pledge with me, and you have forgotten it.
      I am neither dappled stone nor iron, that I might oppose you.
20 I am flesh, hide and bone; why do you melt me?

      You deceived me before, saying 'I love you'.
      Then you showed yourself false, and your pledge a lie.
      Many have deceived me; you are not alone.
      Merciful is God, who will not ignore me.

25 I have suffered many evils, which you know full well.
      You, faithless one, are the cause.
      You try to drink my blood, but cannot.
      Why are you not generous, since I love you?

      You are fine-feathered as a peacock;
30 You have put on rosy-coloured satin.
      Behold me in submission to you, whatever you say.
      Amongst the multitudinous race of men, you are the crowned head.

      I delight and rejoice when I see you,
      Whether anointed with your love or standing before you.
35 I will give glory to the Maker who renewed you.
      You are my sermon, my hymn and my teaching.

Maten. MS 7715: Variant Readings

13 You have no pledge and you have sealed no pledge.
      You have strayed from your oath and are utterly faithless.

15 The blue Maker in the sky above is witness.
The earth that you tread--to you is my soul.
Freely I abide with you; you are my face.
My pain is my sorrow; another do you rule.
I am not dappled iron, that I might oppose you,
20 But flesh and raw skin; you melt my bones.
Arise and come outside that I may see you.
When you enter the house anew you take away my soul.
Soon you will turn around and come out through the door.
I rejoice greatly when I see you.
25 I do not understand why you hate me.
You must come to me, if you love me.
Try to come quickly, that I may see you.
Your visage is bounteous; you are red as a rose.
What they say is a lie; you must not fear.
30 They lead her out of my city that she might speak ill of us.
Give me one little kiss, or else I will die.
They struck me with a lance; you are my potion.
I long for your breast; you are a white, spouting tower.
You shine with pride; you are like a bow of light.
35 I will give glory to Christ; he created you beautiful.
What cause can I assign to you, when you are incomparable.

Notes

Line 1. I have used 'A' and 'Z' in the translation for ayb and k^{C}ē, the first
and last letters of the Armenian alphabet (two additional letters, ō [Classi-
cal aw] and f, were added in the twelfth century, see A. G. Abrahamyan, Hayoc^C
gir ev grč^{C}ut^{C}yun, Erevan, 1973, p. 75). They are not used by T^{C}lkuranc^{C}i in
his alphabetic poems, but a folksong of Tarōn (K. Sasuni, Patmut^{C}iwn Tarōni
ašxarhi, Beirut, 1957, p. 501, 'Geḷǰuk erg' 'Village Song') goes through the
Arm. alphabet from A to F beginning Ayb, ben, gimov govam zaḷjik, / Da, ēc^C,
zayov zardrem zglxik / . . . Ōn, ōrhnakan hazar barev, / Fēn, u fēlēk^C farfuṙ
fnčan / Igan bazmin i mer seḷan 'With a, b, g will I praise the girl, E with d,
e, z will I adorn her head / . . . O, a thousand good blessings, / F, and a
porcelain coffee-cup of fortune / Came and sat upon our table'. Armenians and
other Orientals practice divination of Turkish coffee grounds.

Line 8. Ĕnd ays ku zarmanam, t^{C}ē inj yēr ku xnayes. Maten. MS 9271 reads
. . . t^{C}ē du zis ater es 'that you have hated me', cf. MS 9271 Line 25 Č^{C}em
imnar i k^{C}ēn t^{C}ē du zis ates, 'I don't know from you, whether you hate me.'

Line 11. Im tun ayd č^{C}ē čafay zor du ku k^{C}ašes. Čafay < Ar. Jafā 'cruelty';
the Armenian idiom is probably borrowed from NP. Jafā kesīdan 'to suffer
cruelty.

Line 15. Kaputn ē mez vkay, or ku sirem zk^{C}ez. The blue is the Almighty in
Heaven, cf. Var. Line 15 Kaputn i ver vka ararōḷn yerknis.

(Var.) Line 18. Ꮮams ē im ꞁusay, mēk m'ayl ku tires. Ꮮam < Ar. ghamm 'sorrow, grief'; ꞁusay < Ar. ghussa 'sorrow'. Cf. Nahapet K^c uč^c ak (Kostaneanc^c , Hayerg, p. 39 Grē, č^c karnay kardal, zinč^c i yim sirts kay ꞁusay 'write the sorrow within my heart, but none can read!' KE XIX:1 Ew yerak zōrn i ꞁusay hogōk^c mašem zis andadar 'And always, ceaseless, all day long, I wear out my soul with sorrow'. The second half of the line probably means 'you love another' (one 'masters' love; cf. P XIV:86 T^c ē knoj siroyn mi tiranayk^c).

Line 19. Čarti k^c ar č^c em w' erkat^c , or dimanam es; Var. Čatu [or Čartu] č^c em erkat^c , or es dimanam k^c ez. MS 7714 has Čawrĕd k^c ani k^c ašem erkat^c u k^c ar č^c em or dimanam k^c ez 'How much can I bear your cruelty; I am not iron and stone that I might oppose you'. Čawr < Ar. ĵaur 'tyranny, injustice' is probably a lectio facilior substituted for čart, čartuk 'dappled' (Bedrossian).

Line 22. Nay yetoy sut elar, ꞁavli ealan zk^c ez. Ealan < Tk. yalan 'false'. The odd accusative construction ꞁavli ealan zk^c ez may be a vocative 'You whose pledge is a lie'; cf. Line 26 anhawatik zk^c ez '[o] faithless one!' or Mod. Arm. ay kez glux!

Line 29. Siramargi nman našxac p^c etur es. Note metathesis of xš to našx-ac, part. of naxšem 'I portray < Ar. naqqaš (cf. P I:4).

Line 32. Rameal yazgĕs mardkan sart^c ačĕs do es. Sart^c ač < NP. sar 'head' + tāĵ 'crown'. Var. Line 32 R̆empĕov zis harec^c in, im deꞁĕn du es. R̆empĕ, cf. 'The Lay of Brave Liparit', P XXIII:58, 73, 127.

(Var.) Line 33. C^c ankam es k^c o coc^c ut, čermak bꞁ(x) buč es. The latter half of the line is clearly a problem. One is tempted to add x to bꞁ as Pivazyan has done and reconstruct bꞁxawꞁ 'sprouting'; buč may be read as burč < Ar. burĵ 'tower' (Aꞁayan). The resulting image is striking, recalling Song of Songs VIII:10 stink^c im ibrew zaštaraks 'my breasts are like towers'.

Line 34. W' iwceal i sēr k^c oyin dam yandiman k^c ez. Iwceal=awceal past part. of awcanem 'I anoint'. Var. Line 34 Wisoy nĕman p^c ayles, zerd loys aꞁeꞁ es wisoy is here read as gen. sing. of vēs 'proud'.

CHAPTER TWO

YOVHANNĒS AND AŠA

This love poem (P Appendix V; C, p. 58-62) is published in quatrains of octosyllabic lines, with caesura following the fourth syllable of each line. All four lines of each quatrain rhyme, but the rhyme differs from one stanza to the next; lines 121-4 do not rhyme. Pivazyan's text is based on Mnac^{c}akanyan's edition (Hay miǰnadaryan žoġovrdakan erger, pp. 183-190) of Maten. MSS 9271, 7717, 7715 and 1990. The title of the poem in MS 7717 (A.D. 1695) is Taġ Erznkac^{c}i Yovanisē asac^{c}eal 'Poem spoken by Yovhannēs Erznkac^{c}i', and the poem is accepted as Erznkac^{c}i's by Armenuhi Srapyan YE III. The title of the poem in MS 9271 (17th cent.) is Taġ asac^{c}eal xew Yovanisi i veray Ašayin 'Poem spoken by crazy Yovhannēs on Aša', hence its attribution to T^{c}lkuranc^{c}i, with whom the epithet xew is usually associated. According to Mnac^{c}akanyan, the variant reading of P Lines 77-8 = Mnac^{c}akanyan Lines 70-1 Xew Yovannēsn erb zayn lsec^c, / Br̄nec^c zčamp^{c}an i yotvnin 'When crazy Yovhannēs heard that, / He set out on foot' as Xew Yovhannēsn erb zayn lsec^c / Bĕtnec^c zčamban i Ezĕnkin 'When crazy Yovhannēs heard that, / He set off for Erzincan' (MS 7717) is a scribal change to justify the attribution to Erznkac^{c}i. And indeed Yovhannēs Erznkac^{c}i does not call himself xew.

Love between Christian and Muslim was not entirely unknown in Armenia and adjacent regions. Mxit^{c}ar Goš, for instance, condemned intermarriage between Armenians and foreigners (Arm. aylazgik^c) in a fable: the owl asks the hand of the eagle's daughter. When they try to hold the wedding in the daytime, the bridegroom cannot see his bride. The eagle's daughter gropes for the owl in vain at night, and the marriage is dissolved. The fable is repeated in the Proverbs of Vardan with the heading C^{c}uc^{c}anē zhawatac^{c}eal mardik, or zdsters tan aylaseric^c xawareloc^{c}n i lusoyn K^{c}ristosi '[This] displays the believers who give their daughters to foreigners buried in darkness from the light of Christ.' In the presence of the Armenian prince Zak^{c}arē, who had married his daughter to the Muslim Emir of Aleppo, the same Mxit^{c}ar castigated the Armenians of Ani for marrying Georgians, who were Christians (M. Abeġyan, Erker, Vol. IV, Erevan, 1970, p. 221, citing the historian Kirakos Ganjakec^{c}i). A Muslim emir from Syria once became a Christian, it is told, in order to marry a girl of that faith, despite his mother's angry objections. The product of that marriage was Digenēs Akritēs, epic folk hero of the eastern Byzantine borderlands (cf. John Mavrogordato, Digenes Akrites, Oxford, 1970, p. 24). The Persian poet Rūmī, himself a resident of the cosmopolitan Anatolian city of Konya-Iconium, wrote, 'In love all things are transformed; Armenian is changed to Turk' (A. J. Arberry, Mystical Poems of Rumi, Chicago, 1968, p. 18). And sometimes not. Galēmk^c earean, Nōtark^c Hayoc^c, 1888, cites a Menologium of 1416: When the forces of Timur the Lame were entering Van, an Armenian youth died in the defence of the city. A young Kurd, beholding the modesty of the Armenian widow, offered her the place of a servant girl in his house. At first she refused, but later relented, seeing no other way out. The Kurd's wife died, and the Armenian girl married him. The Kurd's relatives insisted that she become a Muslim, but he replied Es i na hawan em, na ziwr hawatn pašté ew es zim 'I am agreeable to her. Let her practise her religion, and I, mine.' The tolerant Kurd was overruled by his family, who stoned the girl to death. The story of Yovhannēs and Aša was very popular, as the following Armenian folk tale recorded by G. Šerenc^c, Vanay saz, Vol. II, Tiflis, 1899, pp. 112-117 (apud Mnac^c akanyan, pp. 191-195) indicates. One notes the verse fragments of an earlier version in the narrative; the Armenian hek^c iat^c (< Ar. hekāyat 'tale') may be based on our poem. It is curious to note also the supernatural elements of the prose version: Aša's replacement by an Islamic succubus, Salč^c um P^c aša; and resurrection from the dead through the imbibing of pomegranate wine. Unlike T^c lkuranc^c i's Aša or Digenēs Akritēs' father, Salč^c um P^c aša does not desert her faith; she and her lover are bound by death in eternal love, while the Armenians and Turks, rather like the Montagues and Capulets, continue their feuding. The comparison with Shakespeare further suggests a sort of Friar Laurence figure in the ascetic; the meeting of star-crossed lovers from hostile families or nations is a widespread folktale-motif, to which is added in the Armenian the folktale-motif of the supernatural wife.

SALČ^c UM P^c ASĒ: TRANSLATION

There was and there was not a mother, and a son. The son was very well-read, so that indeed neither a moment nor an hour passed free of reading.[1] Night and day he had a book in hand, and wanted to know everything concerning the existence of the stars of Heaven, of Heaven and earth. One day he piled all his books under his arm,[2] gathered all his writings and took to the road, in order to go to a monastery and become an ascetic.[3] He went and reached a halfway point on the road. Sleep was upon him;[4] he put his books underneath his head and made a pillow of them that he might sleep a bit and rest. God knows whether he slept a little or slept a lot, but several beauties came, gathered all around him above his head, and whispered and tittered.[5]

One said, 'Let's strike him,[6] let's weaken this boy;[7] let's not let him live.' One said, 'Let's not weaken him or destroy him or do anything to him.' One other said, 'Come, let's cast[8] the love of Salč^c un P^c aša over him. Then let him torture and torment himself, as long as he lasts.'[9]

Salč^cum P^cašē is queen[10] of the _houris_; whoever falls by her love or her fire goes mad, gnashes his teeth,[11] strays and goes into the mountains.[12] The boy got up, awake, and just then it was as if trembling had seized his body, and he himself didn't know what had happened to him; he was like a madman. He took a few steps here and there in the boundless, endless plain,[13] but it was no use, and he understood that he had been possessed by evil ones, that they had stricken him. He gathered his books up as best he could and filled his bag and took to the road. He barely[14] reached his house, and called his mother:[15]

> Mother, mother, my mother!
> A fine[16] lamb, and some wine!
> Feed the poor
> So that Salč^cum P^cašē will love me.

The mother, when she heard her son's voice, ran quickly out of the house, opened the door and saw that her boy was not the same; his aspect,[17] form and face had changed; she cried with pity:[18]

> My deacon, my only son![19]
> May the _grol_ and death seize you;[20]
> You were on your way to the monastery and hermitage!
> Go, enter into a hole in the ground!
> Why should I sacrifice a fine lamb
> And distribute it amongst the poor?
> Who is Salč^cum P^cašē? Who is she?
> What has she to do with my house?

The son saw his mother's anger, and that there was no use, so he said to her again:[21]

> Alas, mother, help me![22]
> Put on your bonnet; go through the market.
> Mascara your eyes, that they become lovely.
> Help your only son!
> Behold how difficult the business of love is!
> Put on your clothes and ornament yourself well.
> Go to bazaar and market:
> Behold how difficult the business of love is!

His mother got up, put on her bonnet, tied it at the ends,[23] put mascara on her eyes, perfumed herself and went to the markets. She stood here and there and listened to this and that news;[24] she heard many good and bad things. The young men fell in step behind her. One pinched her,[25] another insulted her,[26] another grabbed at her hem, another did this and another that, until finally[27] her heart got sick of it. She turned back, came home, and understood how difficult the business of love was, that a boy falls willy-nilly into love's fire. She embraced her boy at her heart and said to him:[28]

> Ah, my boy, my only son,
> I will go and sacrifice a fine lamb
> And lay it at the feet of the poor;[29]
> May Salč^cum P^cašē love you!

That morning they sacrificed a lamb in the good light and fed all the poor, and believed that in this way Salč^cum P^cašē's love might fall on the youth;

that she might be bound in love to him and be crowned with him.[30] The next
day the boy went, shouting and acting crazily,[31] and stood under the palace[32]
of the Pasha of that city, perhaps because[33] that Pasha's daughter's name was
also Salč^c um P^c ašay. He called the Pasha's daughter from under [the walls
of] the palace:[34]

> Salč^c um P^c ašay, I am your servant!
> I burn with love for you.
> Whatever may happen, I have fallen to your fate;
> Make one my love for you and your love.

Salč^c um P^c ašē, when she heard his voice, knew things were difficult with him.
She answered him from the dome[35] of the palace, saying:[36]

> Hey, crazy boy, Armenian boy,
> Who are you? Get lost, go!
> I am a musulman, you are an ērmani;
> What can your love have to do with me?
> Go! Stand at my father's door;
> Take your dagger[36] and cutting sword,
> And when he comes, give him a cut[37]
> And say, 'Give your only daughter to me!'

Salč^c um P^c ašē's heart also grew wretched and went out to him; she loved him,
and indeed they were inflamed with love for one another, dreaming of one
another night and day.[38] There was no sleep or help; the girl began to waste
away. Salč^c um P^c ašē's mother learned of her daughter's state,[39] and wished
to get rid of the girl rather than wed her to a poor boy, but she had no
means. One day, while the girl was washing her head, she secretly mixed
poison[40] into water and gave it to her daughter to drink, that a remedy[41]
might be effected. Whe her daughter had drunk the poison, she went out of
her mind and died. They took her and buried her secretly, that no man might
find out.

As soon as the boy learned of the girl, he lost his head and went and
secretly removed her from the tomb, slung her over his shoulder, and took her
off to a remote spot, where he deposited her in the cave of an ascetic. Every
day he went and brought her pomegranate wine. He fed it to her at every
drinking time, and drank some himself, as well.[42] He would drink, then look
around at Salč^c um P^c ašē's face and say 'Salč^c um P^c ašay, your health! May you
be well and happy.' One day, when he had gone out to bring the wine, he was
late. When the ascetic returned, he beheld a fiery houri in the form of a
girl standing behind the table in his cell. The ascetic sat down next to
her and they broke bread together. Then he cautiously tugged at her hem and
said 'My Nanē, sit down, you've been standing enough.' No sooner had he said
it than the girl fell flat down her whole length,[43] spread out on the sofa.[44]
The ascetic was terrified unto death:[45] 'Alas, I have sinned, sinned, sinned
against you, God! All my forty years of asceticism have gone for naught!'
He prayed and said, 'O Lord God, give soul to this one!'

By God's command the girl arose, got up and stood in her place. The ascetic stood there as well; she ran off to another corner. The next day, the boy returned from the city and saw Salč̣ᶜum Pᶜašē standing straight as a candle. When he saw this from the road, he lost his wits and was so happy that he didn't know what to do, and rose up by one world. He filled a cup of wine and drank, saying, 'Your life, Salč̣ᶜum Pᶜašay!' Salč̣ᶜum Pᶜašay, who had kept her mouth shut all that day, now awakened from the sleep of death by God's command. Her mouth opened, and she cried, 'Sweet, sweet, beloved of my heart, may your drink be sweet.' She said this,[46] and the words had barely left her mouth when both boy and girl fainted away in their places, fell down, and died burning with love for one another.

An arc of light was bound above them, and the cell shone[47] with that radiance.

After a few days, the ascetic came to himself and said, 'Was this a dream that I saw? I will go and have a look at my dwelling to see what happened to that girl.' He came and saw that a brave youth lay by her side. He was terrified,[48] and wanted to flee from there, but by God's command the angel Gabriel came to him and said, 'Fear not, O ascetic. Theirs was a holy death; it was written on their foreheads that it be so. They will remain in sacred love so long as they are dead. Take them up and bury them.'

The ascetic fulfilled the angel's command and buried both of them in one coffin, and lowered a splendid tombstone over them. An arc of light was bound in the cell. The coffin had great force and power. May the one who seeks find his desire.[49]

Salč̣ᶜum Pᶜašē: Notes

1. Ēskun, or mēy taʾn u shatᶜ kardalucᶜ parap č̣ᶜi mnay: taʾn < NP dam 'breath, moment'; shatᶜ < Ar. saᶜat 'hour'.

2. Ōr mʾēl ur gyrkᶜerĕ kʾžani hiwntᶜ.

3. Ur xamar č̣gni: xamar = hamar, as čambax = čanaparh in this text.

4. Kᶜiwn kʾtani: lit., 'sleep is carrying [him] off'.

5. Inč̣ᶜx or kᶜeanj me aḷēknerĕ ku gean, kʾlecᶜven vēr inor gylxun, kkzan, kkzvĕzan: inč̣ᶜx appears to be an armenised form (with inč̣ᶜ 'what') of Armeno-Turkish henč̣ᶜa(kᶜ) 'so much', cf. Sayatᶜ-Nova XXXI Hencᶜakᶜ ĕli dun v ĕres las mazĕt šaḷ talov, ač̣ᶜkᶜi lus 'If you so much as cry over me and shake your hair down, light of [my] eyes'; the last two words of the line

seem onomatopoeic, perhaps related to Mod. E. Arm. kzmt^{C}el 'to pinch'
(A. S. Łaripyan, Hay-r̈useren bar̈aran, Erevan, 1947).

6. Zanenk^C, 1 pers. pl. pres. subj. act. of *zanem, pre. stem zan- of NP
zadan 'to strike'.

7. Lačun.

8. Iskenyk^C.

9. K^{C}ani sał i: Sał < T sĕgh (Ałayan) 'whole, healthy'.

10. Malak^C.

11. K'dandaxori: pres. ind. 3 pers. sing. medio-pass. of *dandaxorim NP dand
'tooth' + xordan 'to eat'; i.e., 'to bite one's teeth, to gnash one's
teeth'. Cf. Clas. Arm. dandanawand 'bit' (Middle Iranian dandānawand).

12. K'ini sarer: cf. P XIV:76 zMardik jge i sar w' i k^{C}ar '[Woman] casts men
amongst the mountains and rocks'.

13. Ancer, anxlis dašti mēj̈: ancer = ancayr; anxlis = Arm. an- 'not' xlis <
Ar. xalās 'clean, free' (Ałayan); the sense of anxlis is perhaps 'unbroken,
unrelieved'.

14. Anĵax-anĵax.

15. The next four lines are in octosyllabic verse.

16. Susun.

17. Didarn < NP dīdār 'sight, vision, look'.

18. Ēler i inč̈^{C}-or nmuš geotac^{C}ac: The last word may be connected with gut'
'pity'.

19. This and the next seven lines are in octosyllabic verse.

20. This sort of imprecation, particularly with the familiar groł 'psychopompos', is considered by M. Abełyan (II:129) an important feature of Armenian folk poetry. It is seen often in the historiolae and spells of

magical texts. On curses involving the groł see most recently
S. Harut^c yunyan, 'Mahvan patkerac^c umnerĕ haykakan aneck^c nerum,' <u>Lraber</u>
<u>Hasarakakan Gitut^c yunneri</u>, Erevan, 1985.12, 53-65.

21. Ēlĕm.

22. This and the next seven lines are in octosyllabic verse.

23. Lač^c ik k'čori, k'čot^c i.

24. Xabrin, dat. with def. art. < Ar. xabar 'news'.

25. K'kĕmti: I connect this with Mod. E. Arm. kčem 'I prick, sting'.

26. Xakar k'ini: xakar < ? Ar. haqīr > Arm. kak^c rem 'I insult' (Ałayan).

27. Axĕr < A-NP āxer 'finally'; cf. Ełišē Č^c arenc^c, Tałaran XV (A.D. 1920-21)
Asi t^c ē mark ēk^c axar duk^c, č^c ēk^c tesnum marmins cuat 'I said, "You are
men after all! Can't you see my wasted body?"'

28. The next four lines are in octosyllabic verse.

29. Ałk^c eytnerac^c p^c ay kĕ xanem: P^c ay < NP pāy 'foot'; xanem = hanem.

30. I.e., marry him. The bride and groom are crowned in Orthodox churches.

31. Xēvalov.

32. K^c eŏski, gen. sing. < Phl. kŏsk (MacKenzie, p. 51) 'pavilion, palace'
Tk. kŏsk. Note the umlauted vowels and palatalization of Armenian words
as well as Turkish loans in this text.

33. Maear k^c i < NP magar ke 'perhaps because', via Tk. ğ > /y/.

34. The next four lines are in octosyllabic verse.

35. Kubic^c, abl. sing. < Ar. qubbah 'cupola, dome'.

36. Xanč^c aln < Ar. xanǰar 'dagger', Rus. kinžal.

37. Mēy xat tur: xat < Ar. hat 'cut'? More likely Arm. hat 'piece', as in
'I'll give him a piece of my mind!'

38. Gišer u c^c̣erek xieal ziealin: <u>xieal</u> < Ar. <u>xayāl</u> 'thought, dream'. Cf.
KE XIV:4 <u>Eraz ē xaboł ew xayal anc^c̣awor</u> 'It is a deceptive dream and a
passing fancy'.

39. Ēyut'en 'existence', i.e., 'state', Ar. hāl.

40. Ału-zēhir: <u>zēhir</u> < Ar. <u>zahr</u> 'poison, venom' (from Middle Iranian), <u>ału</u> <
Tk. <u>aǧu</u>, <u>aǧi</u> 'poison'.

41. T^c̣ēslim < Ar. <u>taslīm</u> 'submission, health'.

42. Zĕmēn xmc^c̣nelu geahin: <u>geah</u> < NP <u>gāh</u> 'time, one of the five watches of the
day'.

43. Bōyov, inst. sing. < Tk. <u>boy</u> 'stature, height'.

44. Taxti, gen. sing. < NP <u>taxt</u> 'chair, throne'.

45. Lełin k'kdri: lit., '[his] bile is cut off'.

46. Haman ēsa kandar k'xōsi: <u>kandar</u> < ? NP <u>kandar</u> = <u>ke andar</u> 'which is within'.

47. P^c̣lp^c̣st^c̣ray: possibly connected to <u>p^c̣ałp^c̣ałim</u>, 'I shine, glitter', but
an unknown word to me.

48. K'zaxaxori.

49. Murazĕ < Ar.-NP <u>murad</u> 'desire' (Ałayan); this is a stock ending for Armenian folktales, just as the beginning is a common one.

YOVHANNĒS AND AŠA: TRANSLATION

What fire is this that burned me,
Or what shade has hemmed me in?
I was a firm stone, and it shook me;
I was an iron fortress; I melted like water.

5 She came, passed, and walked in splendour.
She swayed and minced her hips.
She turned and stared long after;
My soul beheld and was frightened.

The day was that luminous Sunday of the week;
10 I was strolling above the monastery
With a censer in hand, with incense full,
And I had a psalter there as well.

I walked and read
Until supper time might come.
15 I came and started, as if at a fire;
I neither wrote nor read.

She rode a grey Arab steed;
She came and passed, surpassing beautiful.
Her eyes would take away Tabriz;
20 Her eyebrows stole my sense away.

She threw me an apple; I did not come near.
She threw me another; I bent down and picked it up.
'You are a Moslem, a Mollah's daughter.
I am Yovhannēs, a priest's son.
25 What has your apple to do with me?'

'Come, come O infidel's son!
Bring from us beautiful speech.
I am a Moslem, a Mollah's daughter.
You are Yovhannēs, a priest's son.
30 Let's love one another; that will be fine!'

Yovhannēs' mother: 'O my child!'
She put on her clothes and furs;
Every day she wanders from one monastery to the next,
Vowing incense and candles.

35 'Deacons! Say "I have sinned!"
Monks, say "Lord have mercy!"
Will his senses come back to him?
Will my Yovhannēs return home?'

He said no 'Lord, I have sinned!'
40 He said only 'Allah' and 'Sheydullah!'
Then they answered thus:
'This Yovhannēs has no sense.'

'Hey, Yovhannēs, hey, my boy!
Return home, say "I have sinned!"
45 Your priest is shouting there
That "Ašа has become his lover."'

'O my mother, I am your servant.
If my priest shouts against me,
Let me show him Ašа;
50 He will become crazier than I!'

'Hey, Yovhannēs, hey, my boy!
Return home, say "I have sinned!"
You are alone; there is no other way.
There is no other way to exist!'

55 'O my mother! I am your servant.
I drank your milk; be kind to me.
They took my senses away, and I became crazy.
There is no cure for me from you.'

'Hey, Yovhannēs, hey, my child!
60 Come back home, say "I have sinned!"
I will bring you an Armenian girl,
And give you to a priest for blessing.

Hey, Yovhannēs, hey, my child!
Come back home, say "I have sinned!"
65 Aša is a lawless Turk;
She strives against your faith.'

'Ah, mother! Don't be a fool.
There is none like Aša!
Her tongue is a nightingale; her voice, a turtledove.
70 Her waist is as narrow as a Frank's.'

Aša sat at the window
Very sad, her hand over her face,
For her father the Kadi beat her today:
'Why do you love the Armenian's son?
75 See if anyone arises and comes.
The ear of Yobhannēs is deaf!'

When crazy Yovhannēs heard of that,
He set out on foot
And bareheaded, hat in hand,
80 Went and stood before the Khan.

He greeted the king,
And they made their salutations short.
He grabbed the grey horse by the tail
And sang a <u>kafa</u> to every dale.

85 Aša sat atop the fortress,
Listening for Yovhannēs.
One other stood by dressed in yellow.
She was dressed in scarlet and green.

'Hey, Yovhannēs, listen!
90 What moves atop the fortress?
You clothed in yellow, I am your servant.
Tell me the name of the one in green,
Else I will be the king's falcon
And fly and sit upon your arm.'

95 'My grandfather's name they call Mollah.
My brother is called the city's Shahnah.
My name they call Aša;
My other sister is called Zulutha.
My mother's name they call Fathma,
100 And my father they call Kadi Mollah.'

Crazy Yovhannēs is your servant.
Make a cure of my wound,
For I have gone crazy and wandered through the mountains;
I melted like wax in my place.'

105 'Hey, Yovhannēs, you must enter the mosque
And raise your little finger
And wander around with the mollahs,
And then you will be lord of my breast.'

'Ašа, may your love be forbidden me
110 If such things truly come to pass.
Ašа, may you find your death's day
For contesting my faith.

I learned eight canons of psalms,
And for love of you I forgot them.
115 Not a day did I say "Lord, I have sinned!"
Only "Allah" and "Sheydullah!"'

'Yovhannēs! Young in years,
Young in years but weighty in thought,
You have not betrayed your God,
120 Nor have you been at a loss for words.

Go build a church
That I may enter with my shoes on therein.
Let them put the crown upon us and bless us,
And may the will of your heart be fulfilled.'

Yovhannēs and Ašа: Notes

Line 7. Darjaw i yet xošor nayec^c. MS 7717 has xolor = xolor 'fierce, wild'.

Line 17. Mēk mi hecer pōz pētawi.< Tk. boz 'grey horse'; petawi 'Bedouin'.

Line 18. Ekaw anc^{c}aw k^{c}aȷ̌ muhali. MS 7717 had muɫali. Muɫal < Ar. mughal 'beautiful' (M. Abeɫyan, ed., Sasna crer, Glossary, Erevan, 1951).

Lines 24-29 are in Turkish.

Line 50. K^{c}an zis u ayl xew ku linay; xew is also found in Lines 57, 77 and 101.

Line 71. Ašan nstēr p^{c}ančarayin. P^{c}ančaray < NP panȷ̌are 'window'.

Line 74. Ēr ku sires zčayun ordin. Mnac^{c}akanyan reads zHayun.

Line 105. Before this line, Mnac^{c}akanyan adds the stanza Xew Yovhannēs, es k^{c}ez caṙay, / Du im xoc^{c}us čar mn aray, / T^{c}ē č^{c}ē hogis k^{c}aktaw, meṙay, / Im meɫk^{c}s k^{c}oy viz ku mnay 'Crazy Yovhannēs, I am your servant; / Make a cure for my wound, / Else my soul is destroyed and I am dead, / And my sins remain around your neck;' in which Ašа appears to be speaking.

Line 116. Probably šahīd Allāh 'God be my witness!'

Line 117. C$\bar{\text{o}}$ Yovann$\bar{\text{e}}$s, p^{c}ok^{c}r i p$\bar{\text{o}}$yac^c. Lit., 'small in height < Tk. <u>boy</u> 'height, stature'. Is this <u>xew</u> Yovhann$\bar{\text{e}}$s T^{c}lkuranc^{c}i as a youth?

Line 122. Muslims remove their shoes before entering the mosque.

CHAPTER THREE

WISDOM POEMS OF YOVHANNĒS T^CLKURANC^CI

Here are poems (P XVI-XXII) without the breath of spring or the
enchantment of love. Love, even simple friendship, is deceptive (cf. P XXI:
1-4). T^Clkuranc^Ci was at least seventy years of age when he wrote P XVI
(cf. Lines 51-52), and it seems unlikely that he wrote the other poems in this
chapter when he was a young man. Picturesque lines and images can be found
in these poems, sometimes drawn from Scripture, often to be found in Armenian
homilies, but they are terrible rather than exquisite, and repetition makes
them dull. Death, in the presence of which the acquisition of the goods of
earth is vanity, before which the great men of the world are as dust and the
beauty of the young is a passing dream, dominates T^Clkuranc^Ci's every thought.
The grape, extolled in P XV, is here condemned (P XIX), and woman, ultimate
fount of sin, is excoriated in a poem whose refrain pleads 'God save us from
her evil!' (P XX). Of all earthly activities, only repentance finds favour
in the poet's tired eyes. Numerous comparisons are to be drawn with the al-
most exclusively admonitory verses of Mkrtič^C Naɫaš, while Nahapet K^Cuč^Cak's
joyous and vivid quatrains of youth and love, so often cited in discussion
of the lyric poems, become suddenly remote in style and subject matter, for
these are the lines of the poet in winter.

P XVI (C, pp. 38-39: TRANSLATION

      O death, as oft as I remember you
      I tremble and am terrified.
      There is none bitterer than you,
      And you are the bitterest of all that is bitter.

  5 Bitterest of all that is bitter,
      Can you resemble yourself?
      Hell is bitterer than you,
      But afterwards you bring that, too.

      Solomon remembered you
 10 And said, 'Alas! Woe is me!'
      He condemned wisdom
      And said to himself, 'Fie on you!'

      What profits wisdom?
      I died more wretched than the ignoramus.
 15 Sinless I came into the world
      And I go, my face blackened with sin.

Solomon the King said
"Do not say I am a king.
I have many treaures and riches,
20 And many palaces with gold inside."

In vain do you amass treasure in your agitation;
You know not for whom you gather it.
You have enbraced this world,
But dig yourself down deep into Hell.

25 Ah, Death, is it that you hold rancour,
And snatch away Adam's son,
Or are you the scourge of sin
Born of the fruit of death?

You say naught of Moses the Prophet,
30 Nor indeed are you ashamed before David;
You carry off your father Abraham
And crush Isaac into the earth.

You toss King Trdat from his throne
And have no respect for Constantine.
35 Were a thousand horsemen to take a stand,
Or multitudes, you fear naught.

Were one to wear six suits of armor,
You still cast the arrow and penetrate.
You take him off, lead him to prison
40 And cast a stone before the door.

You are an eagle; swiftly flying,
You cast your wide-spreading wings
Over every powerful child of this world
And envelop him in their domain.

45 A thousand times blessed is he
Whom you transport with his good works,
For whomsoever you seize you have carried
Through the fiery torrent of sins.

Yovhannēs T^c1kuranc^ci,
50 You speak in vain, you preach in vain!
At the fullness of seventy years
You have reached death's door.

P XVII (C, pp. 39-30): TRANSLATION

How long will you abide in sin,
Insensate, savage man!
Enough of measureless evil have you done:
Turn from sin!

5 No living breath has been spared
From Adam down to you.
I know you will not heed the advice of Scripture
And that which it has preserved concerning sinners.

Whoever held fortress or city
10 Or palaces adorned with gold
Later left all without their master
And lies beneath the earth.

Whoever drank sweet wine
And stuffed himself more than a bloated pig--
15 I saw him most hateful,
Casting a foul stench.

He who rode with his neck up high,
Wielding his sword in every clime--
I saw him most regretful,
20 Lying between boards of wood.

Many girls and comely women
Had their locks and tresses fashioned.
Their attire is dazzling;
They are rounded as the sun.

25 They sway and slowly twist,
Beloved of every man.
On their death's day they are hateful,
Foul and nauseating to the beholder.

Christ sits on the throne of glory,
30 Dispensing reward to those who love Him;
To the righteous He gives a diadem,
The same also to the repentant sinners.

Crazy Yovhannēs T^{c}lkuranc^{c}i,
Open the ear of your heart in thought.
35 Make yourself a remedy fast in this world,
And you will take up a crown of glory in the next.

P XVIII (C, pp. 32-33): TRANSLATION

The Holy Scriptures taught us
That there is no holy priest.
Death is sufficient teaching for us:
It has spared no living thing.

5 Neither king nor prince--
Even with a hundred thousand horsemen--
Neither priest nor ascetic,
Neither magnate nor sufferer.

I have seen great and powerful kings
10 Lying in a space of two ells,
The world-famed tongue
Of which no reliquary remains.

The body nurtured with dainty viands
Stinking like putrefying carrion;
15 The seams of the body rent,
And a rotting side reclined between the boards.

I saw the princes and the magnates
With far more than their measure
Now not even the lords of two coppers;
20   They were not worth two coppers themselves.

He who said 'I am Solomon'
Now submitted to the ant.
Now his feet are washed,
But his eyes are full of dirt.

25   I saw strong, brave children
Who struck terror into wild beasts
Without the strength of a fly
To take, to give or to speak.

I saw brides and bridegrooms
30   With their beauty gone
And the spider plundering in his web
Above the grave.

The mother who sat up with her child:
"Alas for my son, who cried so much!"
35   He lay in a coffin
And she never embraced him again.

From Adam down to you,
All who have lived have died.
If there is wisdom in you,
40   Do not let this out of your mind.

St Gregory saw this
And betook himself to the Cross;
St James understood this
And undertook many hardships.

Anthony knew this
And fled into the mountains.
The ascetic Paul recognised this
And left his wife and home.

All the saints were weighed
50   And reckoned at naught.
And everyone knows this;
Woe to the fool who does not!

Crazy Yovhannēs T^clkuranc^ci,
You have displayed true examples.
55   Seek to flee from this world;
To your exemplars be a friend.

P XIX (C, pp. 42-43): TRANSLATION

I give you counsel of the spirit:
Listen, O my useless soul.
As the fruit-bearing tree is to its root,
So be you planted in your heart.

5 If you have love of God,
　Hate wine and the whore.
　Wine is the mother of all sins,
　To which every book bears witness.

　Wine is accessory to adultery,
10 And motivates the sodomite malaise.
　Wine incites one to murder;
　Leave it, such evils does it bring upon the soul!

　Wine-drinking is lunacy,
　More evil than demonic possession.
15 It amazes the head from its natural state
　And wounds the other half with pains.

　Then he bellows more than a savage wolf;
　He does not know the measure of satiety.
　He vomits and puts his face in it,
20 And the dog comes and licks his mouth.

　He takes long strides on his way,
　Hiccoughs foully and grimaces,
　Throws his arms this way and that,
　And strikes whomever he meets.

25 It drags him up onto high walls,
　Makes things spin before his eyes,
　Tumbles him headlong from it,
　And swiftly removes him from the sun.

　Paul commands us:
30 Intoxication is a great evil.
　Whoever calls it just
　Is like a dog barking at his master.

　Wine brings shame upon a man
　And casts evil on his tongue.
35 With wine before the bread,
　Two and three are no profit still.

　Crazy Yovhannēs speaks concisely.
　He who listens gains much.
　He who partakes of the taste of this counsel
40 Inherits the kingdom.

P XX (C, pp. 56-57): TRANSLATION

　Blessed is the name of the Word immortal
　Who created woman from the rib.
　The rib, O brothers, has no marrow,
　Nor has woman a brain to bring her sense.

5 Woman is sweeter than others in speech
　And swiftly exiles Adam from Paradise.
　Woman is Satan's comrade;
　God save us from her evil.

Woman pollutes King David
10 And ruins Solomon;
She beheads St John--
God save us from her evil.

Woman hesitates not from Arewordi,
From Jew and from Turk.
15 The one she loves--that is her faith.
God save us from her evil.

Woman throws brothers into turmoil
And casts dispute and conflict in their midst.
She says her own, and heeds not others;
20 God save us from her evil.

Woman takes Joseph of beautiful countenance
And makes of him her son.
Then she plants evil in his heart:
God save us from her evil.

25 Woman ruins the child,
And yet again turns and calls "Brother!"
When the heart loves, it hates faith.
God save us from her evil.

Woman mascaras her eyes and lashes,
30 And rubs red on her face.
Our Armenian people owe naught to her;
God save us from her evil.

Woman opposes the law;
When she enters the church,
35 She does not listen to the Gospel.
God save us from her evil.

Woman has no desire for prayers.
She longs for her relatives
And wants to go and see them.
40 God save us from her evil.

If woman repents today,
She is fouler than a demon tomorrow.
Her eyes cry; her heart is stained.
God save us from her evil.

45 Woman makes an oath, explodes with it:
"Death rules me for you!"
Don't believe it; it comes from her rib.
God save us from her evil.

A woman who is merciful and good
50 Is like the holy virgins,
But when she is evil and unrepentant,
Hers is the demons' place.

Yovhannēs has drunk
Many toasts to his beloved
55 His heart is excited after women without measure--
God save us from their evil!

P XXI (C, pp. 30-31): TRANSLATION

    Listen, O my heart, and take heed,
    For there is no one truly dear,
    Neither neighbour nor brother,
    Neither monk nor priest.

5   For this very time has brought--
    He who knows not, let him know--
    The one whom you hold most dear
    With flame issuing from her mouth.

    Though you make her very dear,
10 Do not believe in her in your soul.
    Try her from every side and see,
    Then relate to her your considered thoughts.

    Many men speak sweetly to your face;
    In their hearts, flame smoulders.
15 A false beloved may dine at your table
    And deny you in the hour of your trials.

    Keep yourself as healthy as you are;
    Be ruler of your head and person,
    If you be a powerful physician.
20 Your life will sweep past, fluttering, swifter than the wind.

    He who gives and takes a word or two
    With a beloved both unlettered and untrue:
    Let him hear and take heed,
    And set his mind, and be amazed.

25 One brave and warlike amongst princes
    Stands always sadly in his place
    If an angel comes and sits by your side,
    He arises and departs, quicker than Satan.

    Keep your love firm;
30 Let your heart abide in love.
    Give no place to hatred,
    Lest love go and stay away.

    Crazy Yovhannēs T^{c}lkuranc^{c}i,
    Keep good watch over your thoughts.
35 He who loves man loves God;
    He who hates his brother is Satan.

P XII (C, pp. 26-27): TRANSLATION

    Now might you heal with great art,
    Who have remained slenderer than a hair.
    Every man's body is a wound,
    But your soul is the very parable of a wound.

5   You declare yourself shepherd to the sheep
    And say, "There is none like me."
    When you are more mindless than all the world
    What do you boast of, evil cultivator?

Is there anyone so adept in counsel,
10 Counselling the world threefold,
Himself outside all adivce,
Every man's laughter and scorn.

You say "Do not kill,
Do not steal and do not fornicate."
15 Behold! You kill, you fornicate and deprive,
And you have remained evil's spawn.

You are leader of the blind,
Binding burdens on men's backs
And not lifting a finger to help,
20 Deceptive and corrupt merely.

You counsel every man,
While the face of your soul is turned:
"Try to do good."
And you oppose him, to his harm.

25 You have dug yourself a deep pit,
And a torrent boils at its floor.
You have kindled fire and flame
And have no remedy at all.

Body, have your fill of evil;
30 Do not stand as the adversary of good.
God is forgiving and merciful
If you pour out a stream of tears.

I am most sinful,
And you have no example for yourself.
35 Exhaust yourself in mortification,
Or be a martyr in the body.

Are you not sick of sin?
Repentance is your cure.
You have tried sin and have seen;
40 Do not tread over another such fire.

Do not boast, crazy Yovhannēs
T^clkuranc^ci with your swift tongue.
You have befouled my soul with sin
And remained darker than a black candle.

P XVI: Notes

This poem is written in quatrains consisting of eight-syllable lines, with the caesura falling after the fourth syllable. The second and fourth lines of each stanza rhyme in -es.

Line 3. Č^cĕkay k^can ĕzk^cez lełi. MN XII:41-42 echoes these sentiments: 'And in truth there is no evil more bitter than death, / Which separates the bridegroom from his new bride.' T^clkuranc^ci introduces the sombre image of newly-weds parted by death in XVIII:29-32.

Line 6. Mit^{c}ē du i k^{c}ez nĕman es. Perhaps this means death is comparable only to itself, and is so dreadful that it surpasses even itself. An analogous, equally puzzling construction, K^{c}awēl ţ^{c}ē k^{c}ez nĕman du es is discussed in the Note to P III:16.

Line 9. Soɫomon yiŝeac^c ak^{c}ez. With this appeal to the wisdom of the ancient king of Israel, expressed in the world-weary lines of Ecclesiastes, Mkrtič^c Naɫaš wrote the following poem (IX), whose similarities to T^{c}lkuranc^{c}i's are striking:

> All man's glory is empty and vain:
> Solomon says this with lordly grace.
>
> If you are the lord and prince of all,
> Still will you descend to earth and prison later on.
>
> Be not deceived by nauseating, mephitic sin.
> The thief awaits you ever [yerak; cf. P XVI:41, C II:9], perceive
>   it well.
>
> Cease from evil, follow the good,
> Open the gates of your heart and confess.
>
> If you are seduced by sin in this world,
> O miserable one, you will regret it on death's day.
>
> You will be as a dream of the passing night.
> You will awaken later on, but attain naught.
>
> He who knows this not is stupid and ignorant,
> Nor does he turn from sin, the demons' servant.
>
> He is ensnared in Satan's net,
> And that one does not leave him as God's portion.
>
> If you have no good man to counsel you,
> Remember death's day and thereby recognise.
>
> Time like a flower shines,
> But then goes weeping down to earth.
>
> Emtombing the dead, lay a plan for yourself;
> His hour has come. Yours will, as well.
>
> Behold your body with good thought,
> Which is alive today and earth tomorrow.
>
> All counsel is confounded on the day of death.
> What you think and will remains to you.
>
> All glory was hidden until the end,
> For man went to his eternal home.
>
> When the guest arrives for commendation of the soul,
> Invitation will be given to the patient man alone.
>
> With sighs, he observes all the nations.
> Most pitiable, he is apart from them.

He does not lend a hand to the dead,
Nor is he of any help at the hour of the end.

He will flee, hiding from the terror of the angel;
But in that terrifying hour he will not be freed.

For certain, death is an evil to the sinful man,
Who did not make a remedy for himself in this world.

Death, having come, seizes him suddenly,
Like a thief in the night, covert and unseen.

They bear him up to Heaven's path;
Demons come and battle there against his soul.

And the wretched, sinful soul remains
Which Anthony [cf. P XVIII:41], holy ascetic, saw.

There is no profit from this world, whoever be judged;
But may he follow only good deeds.

And he remains, undending, unfading,
Fruitful, his soul ornamenting.

On Judgement Day to the merciful Father of the Son
And to Abraham [cf. P XVI:31] the rich man is your witness.

The rich man thirsted in the firest of Gehenna,
And longed for the tip of Lazarus' finger [cf. Luke XVI:19-31].

Try to pray while yet you live,
That your soul be freed of inextinguishable Gehenna.

Much does he dispense to the hungry at your table,
Which you take in return by Jesus' hand.

Evildoers fear the Creator;
Trembling, they will be cast into the fire of torments.

"Alas!" they cry, mingled with the sleepless worms [ank^cun ordanc^c, cf.
    P IX:20]
In viscous darkness, below the ice [a vivid image indeed, recalling
    Dante, Inferno, Canto XXXIV and Frik XXXIII:28-31, 'The ranks of the
    angels are angry; / They have prepared the ice / And saved Tartarus
    for you, / And piled up sleepless worms.']

All the righteous see Christ,
Full of rejoicing; in mirth they ascend to Heaven.

In harmony with the angelic throng
They bless the Lord, God everlasting.

They share in the desirable table of life,
And are sated in the appearance of the Creator's glory.

And they will be woven in unity in the love of the Immortal,
Wedded in love to the invisible bridegroom.

They sing the glory of God eternal,
In ever-pleasing ecstasy, terrible glory.

This counsel come to you O sensible man,
That you repent and be worthy of the Lord.

Do not remain, do not stay unturned from sin.
Do not betray, do not betray your soul to torments.

Lines 15-16. Anmelk^c i yašxarhs eki / U melōk^c genam seweres. These lines occur nearly verbatim in Yovhannēs Erznkac^ci's Tal Adamay 'Poem of Adam' (Srapyan, ed., X:25-26): 'Innocent into the world I came, / And I leave, my face blackened with sin [Ew melōk^c k'ert^cam seweres].' The word seweres is used by Erznkac^ci in Line 10 of the same poem, K^cēnē arin seweres 'They made me black-faced before you.' It appears to mean 'shameful, outrageous' and is used in the following context as a substantive seweresank^c (A. A. Martirosyan, ed., Patmut^ciwn ew xratk^c Xikaray Imastnoy, Vol. I, Erevan, 1969, p. 23, citing Patmut^ciwm planjē k^calak^cin, Tiflis, 1857, p. 81): Ordeak, law ē aljik or cnani ew šut merani, k^can t^cē apri ew azgin iwroy seweresank^c berē 'My son, it is better that a girl be born and soon die, rather than live and bring disgrace upon her people.' According to Martirosyan, a MS once in Conybeare's possession read naxatink^c 'wrong, affront, injury, opprobrium' (Bedrossian) instead of seweresank^c.

Line 26. 'W Adamay ordin ku hanes. On the son of Adam, cf. Notes to P XIII: 37 and XV:64.

Line 32. zIsahak i holn ačeres. Ačeres, 2 pers. sing. pres. ind. act. verb, probably from NP ajār 'ardent', hence Arm. ačerem 'I hasten (sm.).' Maten. MS 1990 has ačares.

Line 33. zTrdat yat^coroyn jges. The poet probably refers to Tiridates III, the Arsacid King of Armenia who is reputed to have introduced Christianity as the state religion of his country circa A.D. 301. Mkrtič^c Nalaš also speaks of the fall of the great and powerful (I Nalašē asac^ceal vasn unaynut^cean ašxarhis 'Spoken by Nalaš on the Vanity of this World,' VI):

> All the things of this world, brothers, are a dream and a lie.
> Where are the kings, princes, barons, sultans and khans?
> They built fortresses, cities and palaces, and enjoyed high esteem.
> Then indeed they left those lordless and entered earth and the
>   prison.
>
> Nalaš, do not be deceived by sin, do not be judged an animal;
> Do not embrace the things of this world, do not think they will
>   remain to you.
> Soon they will come demanding you, and will wound your soul with
>   death;
> Your soul will be separated from you, and your body will remain in
>   prison.

There is no certainty, for sure, in this world, nor does it keep
    faith with man.
One day it allows him rejoicing, but it is acrid and bitter for him
    thereafter.
Do not believe in this world; it lies ever.
It never keeps what it promises.

To many it promises peace, and keeps them always in vacillation.
To many it said "Greatness", and kept them poor and hungry.
It lies: "I will keep you happy and make good your days",
And takes them into the midst of the sea, and keeps them in
    Tartarus.

Days pass over, and only death's day comes,
And drains you empty of the sun, and makes you pitiful, lamentable.
Alas for those fine children who turned into earth and dust;
Their time passed like a dream of the dark night.

When you knew, O captive, that your love would turn to grief,
Might you love this world no more than you can!
Do not long for possessions. You have no need of greatness.
You have food and clothing; any more would bring you pain.

O miserable Naɫaš, strive to do good.
Listen to your own counsel, that it pass into others' deeds.
You knew you were a raft, and the river of sins bore you.
You are judged with the cares of the world, and have no gain therefrom
    save harm.

Lines 47-48. Maten. MS 7057 contains this version: 'You seize him boldly /
And lay him to rest at the breast of Abraham.'

Line 51. E̅ōt^{c}anasun am le̅c^{c}er. A curious variant of this line was published
in Bazmave̅p, 1859, p. 375, Zet anasun tarin lc^{c}er 'Like an animal you have
come into fullness of years.' The z probably comes from the misreading of the
word zewt^{c}anasun or zeawt^{c}anasun 'seventy', acc. sing., cf. the Taɫaran of
1513 and Maten. MS 1990, 2672, 7508, 9271, 7273. The line seems to be reliable evidence of T^{c}lkuranc^{c}i's age when he wrote this—and most probably—
the other wisdom poems. T^{c}lkuranc^{c}i's poem Ban xratakan 'Words of counsel'
(C XVIII) is full of an old man's feelings of regret at a misspent life; particular attention to the line I cerut^{c}eand glorec^{c}ar, yoržam zmeɫk^{c}d e̅ir
k^{c}aweloy 'In your old age you toppled, at the time when you should have repented your sins' is warranted in this connection:

    My self, why did you fornicate? Your voice reaches every street.
    When you were filled with innumerable evils, you became the inheritor
        of evil Hell.

    What help or profit has it got you that you are estranged from
        sacred acts?
    In this world you befouled your name; you kindle fire and flame for
        yourself in the next.

    Do not count on another kingdom; the abysses of the deep await you,
    Where is darkness, and Tartarus, sleepless worms, and the fiery
        furnace.

I knew you before, my self, who were to tumble head over heels
When you became a lover of wine, when you learned much barking.

For you preached to many, and were a teacher of the Holy Scriptures.
When you did not begin to do good, everything went away with the
    waters.

I accuse none other; you make yourself stripe and wound.
Although you forgot your precious loss, you are the cause of many
    sins.

What you built, you ruined. You will not build anything new again.
Alas and woe to me, the prisoner! I said, "What is to become of me?"

In your old age you toppled, at the time when you should have
    repented your sins.
You had no way of turning back, and I fear you will stay the way
    you are.

Wisdom without fear plunged Solomon into the abyss [Imastut^{c}iwn aṙanc^c
    zerkiwł zSołomon yandunds ijoyc^c; the prep. aṙanc$^{\bar{e}}$ takes acc. instead
    of customary genitive];
Although in this world he was glorious, he was small and abject in
    the next.

Body! Have enough of evil. From this world to the next we must
    carry
The bad and the good we have done, which they will place before us.

Cry and shed tears every day, plead to the Lord of creation,
The merciful and forgiving God, expiator of sinners' sins.

He cares for every man and sets aright the tumbled and the fallen;
He grants good gifts, the return and shelter of those gone astray.

Crazy Yovhannēs, full of sin, whether you are to hear or to speak,
Go and inhabit the mountain, or follow the pathways of the holy.

Line 52. Several MSS read 'you have lived in sin' or 'you still abide in sin.'

P XVII: Notes

The poem is written in quatrains of four octosyllabic lines each, with
caesura falling after the fourth syllable. The second and fourth lines of
each stanza rhyme in -ac or -ac^c. The poem is published as C XIX in couplets
of sixteen-syllable lines, together with the following variant:

How long will you abide in sin, O perfectly insensate man?
    [K^{c}ani datis i het mełac^c, ē anzgam mard katarac; the last word
    replaces Pivazyan's katałac.]
Have enough of the immeasurable evil you have done, and turn from
    sin.

See and hear the Scriptures' counsel: What is saved of the sinners'?
To the righteous are kingdom, glory, and swift-abundant honour.

Take terror and cast it in your heart; you, too, know what is saved.
From Adam to this day, it has not spared a living soul.

He who had fortress, and city, and a palace trimmed with gold:
Now all has remained half worn out, and he himself has gone down to
   a pit already dug.

He who rode a charger and brandished his sword in every face
Was later pitiful indeed, lying between two boards.

He who drank sweet wine and stuffed himself more than a bloated pig
Now has become most hateful, cast out like a foul good-for-nothing.

Many was the brave youth, his beard fresh-sprouting, or yet one
   with beard already grown--
I saw that beautiful face mixed with earth.

Many girls with lovely locks, their tresses arranged in order,
Were dressed in cloth of gold thread like the round Sun.

See what they have suddenly become, thrown between unplaned, unhewn
   boards;
Their death's day hateful, and they beloved of every heart
   [Urenc^c mahun ōrn ateli, urenk^{c}n amēn srti sirac: a construction
   contrary in meaning to P XVII:27].

But this is not the later accounting; that is perfect.
When the Cross is borne from Heaven, Christ sits on the throne of
   glory.

He gives a crown to the righteous, who moritified themselves and
   lived in tears;
To the sinners: unextinguishable fire and Tartarus, the pit of
   worms.

Crazy Yovanēs T^{c}lguranc^{c}i, open your eyes in thoughts of the heart.
Make confession with steadfast heart, repent, and live in tears.

Line 1. K^{c}ani datis i het meɫac^c. The idiom k^{c}ani datis, lit. 'how much
would you be judged' occurs in a similar context in MN VIII:13-14 Ēr datis,
eɫkeli, het anc^{c}aworis, / Erb hetoy p^{c}ošiman trtum ti linis 'Why do you abide,
O wretched one, with these transient things, / When later you will be regretful [p^{c}ošiman < NP pašīmān, lit. 'repentant'] and gloomy?'

Lines 7-8. MN VIII:67, rather than accusing the sinner of ignoring one
Scripture, accuses him of following another: Hin taftarn meɫac^c du ēr ku'nores
'Why do you renew the old ledger [taftar < NP daftar 'ledger, office'] of
sins?'

Line 10. Darpěsni oskov cep^{c}ac. Cf. T^{c}lkuranc^{c}i's 'Lay of St Alexianos'
(C II), Line 8, Darpas unin oskov cep^{c}ac, šar ganj unin ordi č^{c}unin 'They had
a palace trimmed with gold. They had many treasures and they had no son.'

Lines 11-12. Maten. MS 5623 contains the variant <u>Nay i yetoy mnac^c antēr, /</u> <u>Berac i neł: gub mi jĕgac</u> 'Remained then without a master's / He was carried to a narrow pit and cast in.'

Line 16. <u>Č^canuŝahot gēs mi jĕgac</u>. The same sense of physical revulsion is conveyed in P XVIII:14 <u>Nĕman giŝoy mĕxgay hotel</u> 'Stinking like putrefying carrion'.

Line 22. Maten MS 9271 has <u>vardern</u> 'roses' for <u>varsern</u> 'tresses'.

Lines 26-28. The death and decay of 'girls and comely women' (Line 21) recalls the ruin of the 'beautiful visage' of the beloved in P I:27.

Lines 33-36. These lines are identical to the last four lines of P IV.

P XVIII: Notes

The poem is written in quatrains of octosyllabic lines, with caesura following the fourth syllable of each line. The second and fourth lines of each stanza rhyme in -<u>er</u>, -<u>el</u>, -<u>il</u> and -<u>ēr</u>.

Lines 33-36. The death of the young demonstrates the uncertainty of man's lot and the illusory nature of any sense of security he may nurture in his vanity. <u>Ołb i Nałaŝ Mkrtič^c episkoposē vasn tłayoc^c mahuan</u> 'Lament by Bishop Mkrtič^c Nałaŝ on the Death of Children' (MN XI), translated below, treats of this theme. The woeful spectacle, one notes, must have been one familiar to most people of T^clkuranc^ci's day; R. Lewis relates that plagues were commonplace in Ottoman Turkey, and the number of dead in Istanbul alone each day during one of these exceeded one thousand (<u>Everyday Life in Ottoman Turkey</u>, London, 1971, p. 107).

> The Creator of creation was wroth against us.
> Sweet divine nature was embittered against us.
> Today a sword of flame swept over the earth:
> Fire burst forth from the house of God.
>
> Cries of woe broke from a thousand mouths at the deeds wrought,
> For the new love of bride and bridegroom was rent in two.
> How many down-faced youths turned to earth!
> And how many mothers of dead sons rent themselves in grief!
>
> Sinless children were wounded by the angel,
> And tumbled pitifully before their parents:
> Wasting away, wretched, before their mothers' faces,
> They withered like the flowers of the spring.

But who can tell with word of mouth of the calamity
And the bitter grief, the heart's laments.
For the visages, so beautiful and splendid, died,
And beloved sons were parted from their mothers.

Let all cry and lament today,
With bitter tears groan in one voice,
For rational man has never beheld such grief,
Which every mountain, valley, tree and branch bewail.

A handsome youth of fine visage, like the Sun,
His eyebrows, arches; his eyes, lanterns to behold,
In all his person and stature incomparable,
Was lovely and beloved of every man.

Deacons, beautiful and sweet-voiced,
Who read the psalter every day,
Becoming to the church, like flowers,
Have died today, and enter the narrow prison.

A bitter order and judgement has arrived this day.
He had neither help nor remedy from any quarter.
The angel of death, terrible in form and fearful,
Pities neither bridegroom nor child.

The boy fell, writhing piteously,
For the day of death's violent court had come.
He glanced to right and left, wretchedly, and crushed his soul;
He had neither help nor remedy in that court.

Then he rose and spoke in tears: "Have mercy on me.
I am wretched. Please, leave me,
And free me from the holy angel's hands.
For I am still a child. Please, ransom me.

It is not the hour, not the season for my death.
Not for me the entry of the narrow prison and the tomb!
I have no will to leave my home,
For I have many longings yet, and much to worry about."

The child rose and groaned aloud, but there was no relief.
He turned in bitter tears and beheld his father:
"Father, please bring me help, my soul is ruined.
I had a thousand longings in my heart, and not one has come to be."

The father turned and said to his son, groaning,
"I have no cure, ransoming you with silver and gold.
I will give my soul in exchange for yours with ready heart.
Please do not wound me with the fiery sword."

The father could not save his beloved son.
The son arose and groaned, and parted them from their souls,
And filled their eyes with tears of misery and bitterness.
He bewailed his green Sun of youth.

Crying, he said: "Farewell, fathers and brothers!
Farewell, my dear ones, all of you alike!
For this hard and bitter path I take
I ask you lay in a Mass in store.

Farewell, holy priests divine!
Recall me in one voice with sacred prayers.
With Masses conciliate the divine Word,
That He make my soul worthy of the Kingdom."

The lovely hue of his face faded,
And his sealike eyes' light drained away.
His comely, strong arm slackened,
The silver tendon of his golden neck shrunk down.

Then the terrible command arrived, set down by God.
The angel came from the Creator, demanding the soul.
The holy angel took the soul by laying on his hands,
And the beautiful body crumbled to dust in the earth.

I, Bishop Naḷaš, the Virgin's servant,
Saw with my eyes the bitter and piteous grief.
Crying, I cried and lamented in tears;
With bitter tears I said laments for the newly dead.

In the great year of the Armenians nine hundred,
And slightly, but more than eight and ten [A.D. 1470],
I saw with my eyes' lamentation and bitter groaning
That which brought the city of Mardin to tears.

Most blessed Virgin Mary, Mother of God,
I beseech your person for our deceased,
That you make them worthy of the Kingdom's holy crown,
And to you, Mother of God, we all prostrate ourselves upon the ground.

P XIX: Notes

The poem is written in stanzas of four octosyllabic lines, with caesura following the fourth syllable and the second and fourth lines of each stanza rhyming in -e.

Line 6. Du zginin u zbozn atē. T^clkuranc^ci wrote another poem on the damage done to his soul by early indulgences in these two evils, Xrat pitani 'Useful Counsel' (C XXIV):

O wicked man, enemy of righteousness,
Changeable in good, unmoving and steady in sin!

Humble and sweet-tongued to sin, haughty towards righteousness,
Vessel of wine and drunkenness, prisoner of a thousand harlots!

Valiantly righteous and fresh, a preacher one hour and a minstrel
    [Arm. gusan; a reference to his lyric poems] the next,
You are tongue-tied in righteousness, spouting words at useless
    deeds.

Who has seen honey and butter mingled with the potion of death?
Or who has heard of evil and good, light and darkness in unison?

He who has served two masters is not worthy of the Kingdom,
Neither patriarch nor priest, nor leading layman.

You have hoped in God, O my soul, for "Thou are merciful and
    forgiving";
If you do not turn and have mercy on yourself, who will be your
    expiation?

That which was not spared by Adam, who was commanded with the
    commandment,
For tasting once went up out of the paradise of Eden.

This is an example of the sinners who sin and repent not.
They go to eternal fire, into the unextinguishable and endless
    flames.

Always you counsel the world: "Turn to God, O sons of men."
Why have you not heeded your own sermon, O scatterbrained, insatiate
    beast?

Wine and the minstrel corrupt many a wise man and scholar;
That is your daily activity, from which you have no return or cease.

If you give thought to death's day, and the call to judgement,
To warnings and to Gehenna, you have desire of the Kingdom.

With these you free yourself of torment, and find some small place
    of rest,
O Yovanēs T^clguranc^ci, but you live in keeping with your counsel.

Line 17. Maten. MS 3751 instead of 'more than a savage wolf' has zet zarǰ
katłac 'like an enraged bear.'

Line 26. Maten MS 7717 reads kanač^c dašt c^cuc^canē 'shows [them] as a green
plain'; three other MSS instead of Yarǰew ač̆ic^c darjuc^canē 'Makes things
spin before his eyes' have . . . dur c^cuc^canē 'shows a door before his eyes.'

Line 28. Maten. MS 2079 has datark 'empty' for šut mi 'swiftly.'

Line 31. Ov zharbenalĕn halal asē. Halal < Ar. halāl 'permissible,' i.e.,
not harām (Ar. 'forbidden, impure'), cf. Vičabanut^ciwn hogoy ĕnd marmnoy
('The Argument of the Soul with the Body', Mnac^cakanyan, p. 402, Lines 115-
116): Mi ert^car haram utĕr, / K^cani kay halaln drac 'Do not go and eat haram /
When halal is set [before you]'; KE XX:14 Yanamōt mardun utel hac^cn ē haram
'It is haram for the shameless man to eat bread'; for the idiom halal aṙnem
'I make halal,' cf. Note to P Appendix I:2.

P XX: Notes

The poem is written in stanzas of four octosyllabic lines each, with caesura following the fourth syllable of each line. All lines rhyme in -ē, except for Lines 1-2, which rhyme in -in, and Lines 49, 50 and 52, which rhyme in -i; the last word of Line 3 is ełbayrk^c. The poem bears a much greater resemblance to T^clkuranc^ci's lyrics than to the other wisdom poems in its tone and vigour, and indeed its imagery affords closer comparison to the lyrics than to Mkrtič^c Nałaš' wisdom poetry. It is treated separately from the lyrics because of its didactic intent, and because it lacks the praise of beauty and description of spring which the lyrics have: the essential topology of the lyricist's imagination.

Line 3. Maten. MS 33 has cacuk 'hidden' instead of cuc 'marrow'.

Line 4. Maten. MS 7709 has xabel ē 'is/has deceived' instead of xelk^c berē 'brings sense'.

Lines 5-7. Maten. MSS 3751 and 9271 read, 'The serpent speaks sweetly to the woman, / And exiles her swiftly from Paradise; / Woman strives to deceive Adam.'

Line 6. zAdam draxtēn šut artak^csē. On this theme, cf. P XIII:12, XIV:53, etc.

Line 8. Astuac p^crkē knkan šaṙē. Šaṙ 'tumult' could also be Ar. šārr 'evil'. The twelfth-century Persian poet Xāqānī of Širvān asks pardon that he comes from a town (whose name is also pronounced Šarvān) whose name begins with šarr 'evil'; he adds, defensively, that it also has the two letters with which šar^c 'religous law' begins and bašar 'humanity' ends. It is thus a šīr-van 'abode of lions', nay, šaraf-van 'place of honour' (see V. Minorsky, 'Khāqānī and Andronius Comnenus', BSOAS 11, 1943-46, p. 557, n. 3). In Armenian, the Arabic loan-word šaṙ 'evil' is found in the expression xer ew šaṙ 'good and evil' (see A. Srapyan, Hay miǰnadaryan zruyc^cner, Erevan, 1969, 39). There may be a pun in the Armenian on šar 'rank, row': stay away from the crowd of women. As is seen in the story of Aša, the lure of woman breaks barriers between Armenians and infidels, and this poem accuses women of leaving their faith for love. It is therefore most likely that an amulet published by Feydit (Amulettes de l'Arménie Chrétienne, Venice, 1986, p. 268) protects i yanōrinac^c šayṙē 'from the evil of infidels' and not from their šariat (sic) as the editor suggests, but still note Khāqānī.

Lines 9-10. Cf. P XIII:14-15.

Line 11. Cf. P XIV:61.

Lines 13-14. Kin č̆^cgani ew oč̆^c ok^cē, / ŏ^c i J̌htē, oč̆^c i t^curk^cē. Maten.
MSS 7707 and 7709 have oč̆^c pšgay, and Ł. Ališan, Hin hawatk^c. . ., Venice,
1910, p. 103, reads pēzgay 'hates'. The g of pšgay may be a scribal misreading of d (զ and դ), for bštem, Muš dialect 'I reprimand, reproach' (cf.
Ačařean): Giwlēsērean has suggested in connection with P XII:34-35 that his
T^clkuranc^ci was associated with the Surb Karapet monastery at Muš. Č̆^cgani may
be corrupted by haplography from č̆^cč̆^ck^canay 'does not flee'. At any rate, the
verb is something she doesn't do--the infidel is not shunned. The reading of
MSS 7707, 7709, 3081, 8605, 2394 and 33 and Kostaneanc^c of Arewordi seems
preferable to the blander ew oč̆^c ok^cē 'from no one'. The Arewordik^c, or
Children of the Sun, were a non-Christian Armenian sect. Another heresy cen-
tered at Awan in the poet's own T^clkuran region, Amayk^c province (Gr. Hakobyan,
Nersēs Šnorhali, Erevan, 1964, p. 21) derives from the earlier T^condrakite
heresy. Both were severely condemned by Nersēs Šnorhali; both seem to have
survived down to recent days in some form (see Russell, Zoroastrianism in
Armenia, Ch. 16). T^clkuranc^ci suggests that a woman for love will not scorn
even the hardened heretic. In Line 14, MS 7709 has instead of J̌htē 'from Jew'
the reading J̌haye = (?) č̆'hayē 'from non-Armenian'.

Line 21. Kinn zgełec^ckatipn Yovsep^c. Cf. P IV:1, XIII:25.

Line 27. Several MSS have 'That is the greatest of sins' or 'Falls into the
greatest of sins'.

Lines 29-30. Kinn zač̆^ck^c u zunk^cn dełē. Cf. P XIV:73.

Lines 53-55. Yovhannēsn i kĕnkanē / Šat ē xmer tōstōk^canē, / Anč̆^cap^c srtovn
yet grgřē. Tōstōk^can < NP dōst-kām 'a cup of wine which a lover drinks to
his mistress's health'; MSS 33 has tōstkanē (C. Dowsett). Nahapet K^cuč̆^cak
wrote (cited by Abełyan II:96) Coverd k^cez gini anem, / U nawerd i tōstok^cani
'I will make the seas wine for you / And make the ships goblets to drink your
health', a much more vivid image. See also KE XXVI: 8:

> Palpul imastun saxi,
> Saxi lusełēn mez kan
> Kangnin u gini mez tan
> Or es xēmem tōst ōk^can
>
> 'Nightingale, wise winebearer,
> Our winebearers of light
> Stand and pour our wine
> That I may drink a cup to my beloved.'

A version published in <u>Bazmavēp</u>, 1954, No. 3-4, pp. 70-77 has instead of these lines, Ē Yovhannēs, č̌^car knkanē / Du šat heṙu k^cez mišt pahē, / Na ir srtov k^cez grgṙē 'O Yovhannēs, from evil woman / Ever keep yourself far away; / With her heart she excites you.'

P XXI: Notes

The poem is written in four-line stanzas of octosyllabic lines in which caesura falls after the fourth syllable. The second and fourth lines of each stanza rhyme in -<u>ay</u>.

Line 19. <u>Et^cē hak^cim kari linis</u>. <u>Hak^cim</u> < Ar. <u>hakīm</u> 'wise man, esp. doctor'.

P XXII: Notes

The poem is written in four-line stanzas of octosyllabic lines in which caesura falls after the fourth syllable. The second and fourth lines of each stanza rhyme in -<u>ay</u>.

Line 2. <u>Ormn . . . k^can zma . . . barak</u>. Pivazyan's source, Maten. MS 2676, is deficient here. XVII contains a complete reading, <u>Or mēnac^cir k^can zmaz barak</u>, which I have used in the translation.

Line 22. <u>K^co hogoyd ēres p^caxerak</u>. <u>Paxarak</u> < Ar. <u>bakara</u> 'spinning-wheel' (Ałayan). Armenian <u>x</u> may be a misreading of <u>t^c</u> (<u>խ</u> and <u>թ</u>) from <u>p^cat^cerak</u> 'disaster', Phl. <u>petyārag</u> 'oppression, opposition' (see Hübschmann, <u>Arm. Gr.</u>, p. 254).

CHAPTER FOUR

THE LAY OF BRAVE LIPARIT

Kostandin IV, second Het^{c}umid king of Cilician Armenia, son of Marshal
(Arm. marajaxt) Baudouin (Arm. Paɫtin, died 1337), died in 1363. Petros, king
of Cyprus, who had interfered before in Armenian affairs, sought to gain the
ground for Pemund, but it passed to Kostandin V, paternal cousin of Kostandin IV
and son of the Chamberlain (Arm. jambṙlay), Het^{c}um, lord of Aɫtik^c. Kostandin
had maternal relations on Cyprus, and he attempted to reach an agreement with
Petros on mutual defence against the Egyptian Mamelukes, whose anger had been
aroused by the Cypriot sack of Alexandria in 1347. Cilician Armenia bore the
brunt of the Egyptians' wrath. In 1367-69 Mančak Šahar-oğlu, Mameluke Emir of
Tarsus, led thousands of Turkoman and Karaman tribesmen in repeated assaults
against the Cilician capital, Sis. After the attack of 6-9 May 1368, the Armenian Latinising party suggested that the crown be taken from Kostandin III
and offered to Petros. Others thought help might best be obtained through the
marriage of Kostandin IV's widow Mariwn to a powerful European prince. Petros
met representatives of the Latinising party in Venice in August and September
1368. Accepting their offer of the crown of Armenia, he hastened back to
Nicosia, where the minting of coins bearing the legend 'Petros, King of Armenia' was already underway. His plans never saw success, however, because he
was killed on 16 January 1369 by members of his court.

Despite all this political manoeuvring, Armenia remained without foreign
assistance, and Sis fell in May 1369. In April 1373, Kostandin III was murdered by relatives. Mariwn assumed the throne; Lewon V was heir. The latter
was captured by the Mamelukes in 1375 when all Cilicia fell and the last Armenian kingdom ended. Lewon was ransomed from Egyptian captivity; he came to
Paris in 1382 and died there at peace in 1393.[1]

Baron T^{c}oros (Kapnec^{c}i), Grand Marshal of Armenia (paron T^{c}oros awag
marajaxt Hayoc^c ('Grand Marshal' is the translation adopted by A. K. Sanjian,
Colophons of Armenian MSS, 1301-1480, Cambridge, Mass., 1969, p. 95), a native
of Sasun, had three sons, Vasil, Likos and Liparit. Liparit married Dame
Anna (Arm. Tam Anna) and had a son, Sir Yohan. In 1367, Liparit replaced his
deceased father as Marshal of the Cilician Armenian kingdom under Kostandin V
(1365-1373). In this position, the young man assumed the burden of defending
the country almost singlehandedly for a suspicious and ungrateful king. It
must be remarked in fairness to Kostandin V that Petros of Cyprus was plotting
with Latinising Armenians against him, as we have seen. John Dardel, confes-
sor, advisor and secretary to Lewon V,[2] records the participation of Liparit's

brother, Vasil, in the plot that led to the assassination of Kostandin V,[3] and
it has been suggested that Liparit was a member of the noble Orbelean clan,
eager to advance to a position of supreme power on the prestige of his deeds
and his ancient name.[4] Liparit routed 12,000 of Mančak's warriors at the
bridge over the river of Anc^cmnc^cuk, southeast of Sis, on 6 May 1367, wounding
Manč^cak's son.[5] Mančak attacked again on 20 May 1369, this time with a force
of 60,000. Contemporary Armenian chroniclers assure us that the treachery of
the Armenian king in failing to hold the Anc^cmnc^cuk bridge, and not the vast
numbers of the enemy, was the cause of the disaster at Sis and, specifically,
of the martyrdom of Liparit at the hands of the Muslims.[6]

The story of the intrepid commander's desperate defence of the Armenian
state in its last days and the tragedy of his martyrdom found their place in
the popular imagination. The story in all its vivid details was recorded in
many chronicles of the fall of Cilicia, and several prose accounts of a
literary character survive as well. One such narrative, 'The History of Brave
Liparit and His Sister' (Patmut^ciwn k^caĵ Liparitin ew k^ceṙ norin), may be
found in Maten. MSS 3569 (17th cent.) and 6951 (A.D. 1762):[7]

> Brave Liparit was from the province of Sasun, and he came to live
> in Cilicia at the time of the last Armenian king, who was from the
> Rubenid house of Het^cum and T^coros and their grandchildren. And he
> was brave, like Trdat and Mušeł [cf. P XXIII, Lines 54-55]. The
> nation of the Tačiks came from Egypt with many armies against Tarsus
> and the province of Cilicia. Liparit alone rose up against them
> and slaughtered them all, piling up the corpses [Arm. laš; P XXIII:119
> reads laškern arar dizan dizan. Laškar < NP laškar 'army', differing
> from laš by one syllable--the eight-syllable line does not permit the
> reading of Arm. suł vang 'laškarën'--and just as valid in meaning in
> context, may be a scribal error; Ališan in Sisuan reads 'lašk'] hill
> by hill.
>
> And he came to the end of the bridge, to the King's forces, and
> he and his horse sat and rested there. And again he went to war
> and slaughtered them and caused them to flee, and preserved the Arme-
> nain kingdom unshaken and undisturbed for a long time; he made pri-
> soners of armies and of the king and massacred armies and chased them
> off and harried them. And for fear of him no horseman dared to raid
> Armenia.
>
> And the Armenian king was afraid of brave Liparit lest he come and
> kill him and become king. But Liparit, who was brave in soul and
> body, did not have such evil thoughts, but was singleminded in the
> love of Christ and of the holy faith of the Illuminator and of the

holy churches, and with manly courage he opposed the forces of the
Taciks. But then a certain Mančak from Misr [Misr 'Egypt'], a mounted
fighter, brave and of giant stature came to ask of the Sultan that he
be allowed to come forward and kill the brave Liparit. And he came
with fifty thousand horsemen and flung his army against Sis. And then
the king of the Armenians called the brave Liparit and said: 'These
forces have come for you.' And he cried and said: 'My life [ǰan < NP
ǰān 'soul, life'] is for the churches and the Christians, and not for
the crown; of what do you accuse me, who have harassed and destroyed
your enemies? But I hope in Christ, that He give strength to His servant to oppose and drive away the enemy of His cross.' And at the
same time he entered the church and kissed the holy altar, crying and
saying: 'Deal well with me, that I fear not my enemies nor those of
my own who have taken counsel against me in enmity. But I commend
myself in sincerity to the Christians.' And he kissed his brother
Vasil and his son Yohannēs and his wife Anne and praised them with
much lamentation, and said: 'They knew not my heart and my bravery,
but when my foot departs from the palace gate, it shall be surrounded
by wild beasts thirsting for blood, and they will destroy the churches
and palaces and spill innocent Christian blood without measure.'

And he brought his horse and saddled it, and he mounted it, brave
Liparit did, and with his lance [cf. Note to P XXIII:58] in hand he
led the armies of the Armenian king, and he blessed God. And the
enemy was terrified by the sound of his call, and their hearts were
shaken as by a lion's roar [cf. P XXIII:16]. And it was customary
for him to keep two or three stout horses saddled behind him. And
when his horse tired of running and walking, he would turn to a
horseman, dismount, and then ride the other into battle again. And
very often in battle the horse would fall, and then he would fight
horsemen and lance-bearers and armored men on foot, and, slaughtering
them, he would emerge from their midst, go to his armies and mount a
new horse, to return shouting like a lion.

And I insist that many for fear of him died on horseback. And he
killed the fighters like fire [consuming] reeds. And he took no notice of those who attacked him with sword, javelin and arrow, considering them as naught, and their blows seemed to him like so many
swipings of a handkerchief. Also many times he stepped into battle on
foot amidst the horses and turned back the enemy merely by stoning
them, he himself returning happy, blessing God.

And a certain brave man, Mančak by name, came to battle with a force
of fifty thousand. And brave Liparit arose shouting and blessing the

awful name of God and marched against [Mančak's] forces. And they
were terrified when they saw the conquering martyr [cf. P XXIII: 128].
And plunging into the battle and flailing he drove them off and massacred them and killed Mančak and turned back, piling up the corpses
heap by heap. And when his steed was exhausted, he turned back towards
the Armenian lines. Then the king turned malign [cf. P XXIII:121],
took the Armenian horsemen and turned back; he crossed the bridge and
pulled it down with a chain. And when brave Liparit came and saw this
mischief meant for him, he undertook to die for Christ and turned back.
He dismounted from his horse, flung away his sword and sat down in the
middle of a field. Then they surrounded him, and none dared to approach him. And from far off they hurled lances and javelins and
spears at him until he was buried in them, and only then did they un-
sheath their swords and cut him and kill him. And they began to
slaughter the nation and lay waste the churches and kill the king and
kill or capture the men and women—whose number is known to God alone—
and they took the head of the brave martyr to Egypt.

And the Sultan felt very sorry, and said: 'Why didn't you bring
him to me alive that I might give him a woman to bring forth offspring?
I would make him king and set him up as a bulwark against my enemies.'

And that was how they martyred brave Liparit and massacred the
Christians and the land of Armenia, and the nation of the Tačiks ruled
and reigned over the country.

And Liparit had a sister who had fled to a village and had married
there. She was fifty years old when an Ishmaelite champion [pēhlēvan <
NP pahlavān 'hero, champion, strong athlete'] came and said to the Baron
of Sis, 'Bring me someone from your province or your armies like me,
that we may wrestle. If not, then give me one hundred red dahekans
from your lands.' And he did not know any wrestler who could grab the
Tačik's belt. And the sister of brave Liparit came and said: 'What
will you give me to tread on the champion?' And the Baron said: 'I'll
give you whatever you desire, if you tread on him.' The woman said:
'All the cotton I can carry, let that be mine.'

And they undertook it. When the champion arrived, he saw the gigantic woman and was afraid, but because she was a woman he scorned
her. And the champion approached; he put on his clothing and began
moving about as though mocking a man and asking him to fight him. And
the woman came forward in her womanly garb, and, seizing the champion
by his two ankles [? Arm. lcakac^cn] with her fists and raising him up,
she brought him before the Baron and pushed his face in the dirt;
pulling off one ear, she threw it away. Then all, captivated by fear,

[asked] 'Where is she from, or of what nation?' And the king ordered that she be given all the cotton she could carry. And they piled onto her shoulders nearly a hundred litres. And she took it happily off to her home. And when she opened up the cotton, she saw that they had put in forty litres of stones. And all remained deaf to the woman's pleas for aid.

The episode of Liparit's sister parallels his own experience very closely: a strong, faithful individual is deceived by the man he is serving and defending; he meets his end through treachery, not through the failure of his own power. Perhaps one can discern through these the dim, gigantic form of Mher of Sasun, the muscle-bound, frustrated epic hero of the Armenians stalking into the rock-cut chambers above Van for an eternity of brooding after a lifetime of disappointment.

The Lay of Brave Liparit (P XXIII; C, p. 5-11) is published in quatrains of octosyllabic lines. To Line 49, the first three lines rhyme and the fourth is a refrain. Lines 49-154 do not contain a refrain, and the second and fourth lines of each stanza rhyme. P. M. Xač̌ᶜatryan (Telekagir, No. 11, Erevan, 1964) published the Venice Matendaran MS version of A.D. 1371, which begins with Line 49 of our text; Tᶜlkurancᶜi must have written the poem within two years after the fall of the Cilician capital. The poet's moving description of the hero's farewell to his young son (P XXIII:103-103) is described in the same words as a similar scene in the Lay of St Alexianos.[8]

Notes

1. H. P. Tēr-Pōlosean, H. N. Akinean,'Kᶜajn Liparit', Handēs Amsōreay, No. 1-3, Vienna, 1965, pp. 20-22. See also H. N. Akinean, 'Patmutᶜiwn kᶜaj Liparitin ew kᶜeṙ norin', HA, 1933, p. 130.

2. Armenuhi Srapyan, Hay mijnadaryan zruycᶜner, Erevan, 1969, p. 94.

3. P. M. Xač̌ᶜatryan, 'Hovhannes Tᶜlkurancᶜu "Tal kᶜaji Lipartin" patmakan olbē,' Patma-banasirakan handes, No. 2, Erevan, 1964, p. 114.

4. Ibid., p. 116.

5. Xač̌ᶜatryan, pp. 112-113; Jerusalem Matenadaran MS 1205, fol. 197a-b (published in Srapyan, p. 95); Tēr-Pōlosean, p. 24.

6. Xač̌ᶜatryan, p. 113.

7. Srapyan, p. 238, Pivazyan, p. 271.

8. C II:35 'Crying, they kissed their son, so that they moved the crowd to tears'.

THE LAY OF BRAVE LIPARIT: TRANSLATION

You are holy in soul and unsullied;
The Lord had chosen you in Heaven.
You have been the Christians' pride,
O great and strong and brave Liparit.

5   You were brave Samson himself;
When you put your breastplate on
The Turk for fear of you turned to ash,
O great . . .

Brilliant as the sun,
10 Your face was an arc of light;
Your ways were kind and your speech was sugar,
O great . . .

By nature good to the poor,
You paid heed to the priests.
15 Your word was lauded in every land,
O great . . .

You gave yourself for the Law,
Standing one against a thousand.
Your sword clove open many hearts,
20 O great . . .

You were a guardian against thousands;
No man has seen another like you
Among the earthborn in this world,
O great . . .

25 Light-giving star of this land of Sis,
You stood at every hour:
The Turk trembled to death for fear of you,
O great . . .

When the evil moment reached you
30 There was no one to come to your aid.
Your body was daubed in red,
O great . . .

At the evil death you faced
Your birth became your mother's grief;
35 A thousand mouths cry 'Woe!' for you,
O great . . .

Garden and tree of the land of Sis:
Colours lost their hue and the flowers
Exchanged sighs,
40 O great . . .

Catholicos and priest
And all the holy priests together:
Their hearts trembled with many tears,
O great . . .

45 Now the north wind
Remembering Sargis came to you.
You were a pillar to us, the Armenians,
O great . . .

* * *

O blessed name of God
50 Without beginning and end
Who gave strength to brave Liparit
And strengthened His holy servant.

Like brave and holy Sargis,
Like holy T͡oros, like holy Vardan,
55 More victorious than Mušeł,
Than Trdat, the Armenians' king.

When he mounted his galloping charger
And took in hand his supple lance
The nation of the Turkmans, yea,
60 All Turkmanstan was shaken.

There was no stopping the coming of war;
It came ten, twenty times every year.
Alone, he scattered a host
And caused blood to flow like the river Jihan.

65 Then that obstinate infidel . . .
Like a serpent and scorpion and viper . . .

They were full of evil as a skin of vinegar;
They gathered and came against Sis--
Mančak by name, storehouse of evil--
70 They came and reached the city.

Sixty thousand men in unison
Put on their armor and mounted their horses.
In their hands they grasped the supple lance,
The sword, and the buckler, and made their stand.

75 Sixty thousand Turkmans arose
And cried out in rage;
They blew the war trumpet
And played pipe and trumpet together.

Those lawless, evil animals,
80 Those outlandish creatures
Even for fear of brave Liparit
Tremble like the willow and do not advance.

Then the holy king speaks:
'Brave Liparit, great warrior!
85 My horsemen have come for you
To this place where they stand.

You slaughtered sixty thousand
And seized Mančak's famous son.
You carried off the Sultan's throne
90 And much spoil, and horses.'

He gave this sweet reply:
'It was in return for the evil to my city.
But it is not fitting to converse,
Although the day of my death has come.'

95 He got down and saddled his charger,
Put on his armor and the breastplate thereon,
And placed the conquering shield over his head,
And grasped in hand the supple lance.

He bowed low to the holy throne
100 And knelt before every altar.
He glorified the Trinity
And praised the princes as one.

He sighed, kissed his young son
So that the horsemen were moved to tears.
105 He said: 'My son Yovhannēs,
Vasil my beloved brother!

My lady Mananay,
Sunlike princess,
Behold my image in first youth's glory
110 Who am to descend into earth, my tomb.'

Brave Liparit addressed the king:
'Noble king of the Armenians,
Hold the bridge fast and strong
That I go into their midst and return.'

115 He remembered Christ of the awful voice.
He left and proceeded like a lion;
Scattering horsemen,
Pursuing them like a leopard.

He heaped up armies on each other
120 So that rivers of blood rose.
The king's thoughts turned to evil,
He took his horsemen and departed.

The Turk cavalry advanced,
Took the bridge and made their stand;
125 When Liparit turned back,
Behold--the evil horsemen rose up to meet him.

They hurled the lance from every side
And sorely wounded the conquering martyr.
He looked pitifully to right and left
130 And found none to help him.

The beast-faced lawless ones
Thirsted for holy blood.
They left his holy body there,
Took his head, and bore it away.

135 When the horsemen returned
The people of Sis came out again.
Again they seized and entered Sis,
Set fire to the city, and departed.

They ruined many palaces
140 And diverse churches
And made prisoners of elders
And deacons alike.

The light beamed down
On the holy body at rest.
145 Brave Liparit and Sir Yohan
Died for the Christians.

There at the tables where they sit and break bread
In the company of many, with many princes,
The holy priests remember him
150 And say 'Lord have mercy' for him.

Crazy Yovhannēs T^{C}lkuranc^{C}i
Spoke these pitiful, brief words.
Remember him every day;
With one voice speak of his example.

Notes

Line 37. Palc̆^{C}a < NP bāghče 'garden'.

Line 58. I jeřn ařnoyr zĕřum čōčan. Sanjian (Colophons, p. 107) and Alayan mistranslate Arm. (ĕ)řum(b) as 'bomb'; it means 'slingshot' (cf. KE XIV:18 Xalin t^{C}ur 8w ĕřumb u guzov zhet irac^C 'They play together with sabre, slingshot and pike') and is not to be connected to Gk. rhomphaia 'broad sword' (LXX Gen. 3:24, pace C. Dowsett). Frik (XXVII:30) writes of fate Hĕnc^{C}kun k^{C}ar ap^{C}ov aces, or cawgnē hazar řembawor 'You cast the stone by hand so, that a thousand sling-shooters cannot help.' Matt^{C}ēos Uřhayec^{C}i, Žamanakagrut^{V}iwn, Jerusalem, 1869, pp. 251-252, describing a battle of the eleventh century, writes: mi omn i yaylazgeac^C i t^{C}agstean kayr, hareal zT^{C}ořnik řmbovn i sirtn galtabar, ew andēn meřanēr k'ajn T^{C}ořnik 'One of the foreigners lay in hiding. He struck T^{C}ořnik stealthily in the heart with a řumb. The brave T^{C}ořnik died of it.' T^{C}ovma Arcruni, Patmut^{C}iwn tann Arcruneac^C, Tiflis, 1917, pp. 219-221, mentions řmbak^{C}ar-k^C 'ballistic stones'.

Line 60. T^{C}urk^{C}manstan. Maten. MS 515 has ōtarastan 'foreign land'.

Line 78. Nafir < Ar.-NP nafīr 'trumpet'.

CHAPTER FIVE

THE MARVELS OF NAREKAC^{C}I

St. Gregory of Narek (Arm. Grigor Narekac^{C}i) is best known as the author
of a series of mystical poems called the Book of Lamentation (Matean
oɫbergut^{C}ean), or simply Narek. Many Armenians ascribe magical properties to
the pages of this book; they tear these out, fold them into diamond shapes,
and hang them on their children's necks as talismans. Different poems are
believed to have different powers and properties. A 1926 edition of Narek
has, in addition to a printed list of poems according to the power of each,
another list scrawled in ink opposite by a former owner: "(6-3) For protec-
tion from a demon; (91) And the destruction of the latter's power; . . .
(18) For all kinds of cures"; and so on. A number of popular legends have
grown up around Narekac^{C}i's life, about which a few facts may be stated with
relative certainty.

Maten. MS 1567, written in A.D. 1172, states that Narekac^{C}i flourished
around A.D. 983, during the reign of the Arcruni king Senek^{C}erim. Tradition
records that he was born circa A.D. 951 to Xosrov, bishop of Anjewac^{C}ik^C; he
spent most of his life at the monastery of Narek, and died as a hermit in a
cave overlooking Lake Van shortly after he had completed the Book of Lamentation, in 1003.[1] As a young man, Grigor studied under his uncle, the priest
Anania, to whom the honorific epithet Happy (Arm. erǰanik) is applied in a
Menologium; Grigor 'studied the scholarship of the Godly writings with con-
siderable zeal,'[2] and his understanding of certain Greek words which entered
Armenian as proper names indicates that he may have known Greek.[3] The Menologium cited above records an accusation of heresy levelled against Narekac^{C}i
by certain 'lazy and lascivious' priests.[4] The three priests from Sis of
P XXIV were probably the inquisitors charged with investigating this accusation; the miracle of the doves (P XXIV:69-92) is adduced as tangible proof
of Narekac^{C}i's holiness, as a result of which the charges against him were
dismissed.

Numerous legends concerning Narekac^{C}i's life and miracles survive in
Armenian folklore. He works for seven years as a shepherd (cf. P XXIV:56)
in the valley of Ⱡazid to feed a shepherd's orphaned children; he leaves
there and goes to Muš, where he works for a villager to free the latter from
debt; then he arrives in a village where a bridegroom has just died.
Narekac^{C}i revives the young man, to the delight of the mourning parents.[5]
The latter legend, involving the bridegroom dead on his wedding day, is drawn
from a theme familiar to T^{C}lkuranc^{C}i and other Medieval Armenian poets,

Mkrtic$^{\check{c}c}$ Naḷaš in particular.[6] Another poem,[7] involving two priests from Sis instead of three, as in our poem, relates yet other miracles of the saint:

> There were two priests in the village of Sis[8]
> Who went up higher than Masis[9]
> And filled a small measure.
> By God's grace they stopped
> And sent to Narekac^{c}i.
> We, too, have seen his grace;
> I will be a servant to Narekac^{c}i.[10]
> The small measure of water they had sent he changed
> And wherever his hand grasped carded cotton
> A leaping fire wreathed about;
> He placed that in the small measure of water[11]
> And sent it back to the priests.
> When the priests saw it
> They were sore amazed there:
> 'Let us go and see Narekac^{c}i.'
> They came and reached Narek's mountain;
> An angel gave the news to Narekac^{c}i:
> 'Your priests have come as guests.'
> I will be a servant to Narekac^{c}i.
> He took his cowl off his head
> And took a shepherd's crook under his arm.
> He went halfway down his mountain
> And met the two priests;
> He looked at the two priests.
> The priests wanted water.
> I will be a servant to that shepherd.
> He made the sign of the Cross over that mountain
> And struck the dry rock.
> He caused water to spring forth from the rock[12]
> And gave it to the priests to drink.
> Their old white[13] beards became young;
> They were sore amazed there;
> They became immortal there.
> I will be a servant to Narekac^{c}i.

P XXIV is written in monorhyme; each fifteen- or sixteen-syllable line is divided into hemistichs of seven or eight with caesura following the third or fourth syllable of each. The hemistichs are not broken into quatrains-- as is the case in many of the love poems--however.

Notes

1. M. Mkryan, Grigor Narekac^{c}i, Erevan, 1955; see also J. R. Russell, Introduction to Grigor Narekac^{c}i, Book of Lamentation, Classical Armenian Reprint Series, Delmar, NY, 1981.

2. Ibid., p. 119: 'ew usuc^{c}eal zusums astuacayin groc^c anyag baḷjanōk^c.'

3. Ibid., p. 121.

4. Ibid., p. 122; the word used, cayt[c] 'heretic', originally was applied to Armenian-speaking Gypsies who embraced Greek Orthodoxy; see G. Tēr-Mkrtčᵛ[c]ean, Hayagitakan usumnasirut[c]yunner, I, Erevan, 1979, pp. 482-483: 'Cayt[c]eri masin'.

5. M. Abełyan, Erker, Vol. I, Erevan, 1966, pp. 506-507.

6. P XVIII:29-32; cf. also Mkrtičᵛ[c] Nałaš, 'Lament by Bishop Nałaš over the Death of Young Men,' Ēd. Xondkaryan, ed., Mkrtičᵛ[c] Nałaš, Erevan, 1965, p. 150.

7. Mkryan, p. 123.

8. Armenian keō 'village' < Turkish köy.

9. I.e., Mount Ararat. On the word Masis in Armenian, see J. R. Russell, 'Armeno-Iranica', Acta Iranica, 25, Leiden, 1985.

10. Caṙa k'elnem Narekac[c]un. A similar refrain is found in an Armenian folk-song, Caṙa kělnim Karos xačᵛ[c]in 'I will be a servant to the Karos-cross' (Komitas Vardapet, M. Abełyan, Hazar u mi xał, Erevan, 1969, p. 118).

11. The medieval Greek story of Belthandros and Hrysantza speaks of a magic spring in which a fire burned, plēsion Armenias . . . eis tēs Tarsou to kastron 'near Armenia, in the fortress of Tarsus' (J. Mavrogordato, Digenes Akrites, Oxford, 1956, p. xxiv, n. 2). A similar miracle in Armenian tradition is recorded in Agathangelos, Patmut[c]iwn Hayoc[c], para. 544 (cf. II Macc. 1, 19-22).

12. Cf. Numbers XX:11, Nehemiah IX:15, etc.

13. Sivtak = Arm. spitak 'white'; similar metathesis may be observed in P XXIV:88, t[c]ep[c]ur = Arm. p[c]et[c]ur 'feather', and is characteristic of Armenian minstrel poetry, cf. G. Levonyan, Erker, Erevan, 1963, p. 197.

P XXIV (C, pp. 64-66): TRANSLATION

> There was a village they call Narek
> And on its throne the holy priest sat.
> There was a householder there;

They call his name Gorgik.
5 He lived a hundred years
And did not go to church.
The priest got up
And set after Gorg, asking,
Saying 'Gorg, you are a householder.
10 Why don't you come to church?'
He gave him this answer:
'I have much farming to do and I can't leave it.'
The priest cursed him:
'May your body not rest in the earth.'
15 A year came to fullness.
Gorg died in the night.
Four men took him on their shoulders
And took him to the outskirts of the land.
They opened seven graves;
20 The earth did not admit Gorgik.
They made iron links
And slipped them around his ankles from his feet.
Three days and three nights
They hung him on the wall in the Sun.
25 Then the body stank;
Gorg fell into the street.
No dog would eat of his flesh
And birds would not pass over him.
He had many men, many relatives.
30 They made another plan
And arose and went together
And fell at the feet of the holy priest.
The priest came forward
And remembered the living God.
35 He leaned on his staff
And asked the dead man,
'How did you arrive, Gorg?
How did you come to the outskirts of the land?'
Gorg raised his head
40 And fell at the feet of the holy priest
'Lord, pardon me.
They lead me down a false path.'
He raised his hand:
'Gorg, rest in the earth;
45 May He grant you the Law in rendering account,
That you be judged on Sunday.'
The fame spread even to Sis
Of the miracles of the priest
'There is a priest Narek
50 Who gives a dead man his soul back.'
Three priests of Sis,
Three in the city of Sis
Arose and journeyed
To come to the priest and see him.
55 They arrived and looked at each other;
He was pasturing sheep in the mountain,
And was somewhat nearsighted.
They glanced at each other and laughed.
Narekac^ci was holy in soul
60 And understood their thought in his heart.
'My lord, pardon me.
I am a disciple of the priest.'
Eight wolves sat in the mountain
On the fringe of the fold.

65 Behold, he called down the wolves
    And left them over the sheep as shepherds.
    He gestured with his staff to the three
    And they went before him to his cell.
    He took three doves--
70 It was a fast day, Wednesday--
    He cooked them and skewered them well
    And placed them before his guests:
    'Help yourselves, good guests.
    Let us dine at this table.'
75 They clapped their hands together
    And put their fingers over their mouths,
    Saying 'Lord, what have you done?
    Today is Wednesday, a fast day.'
    'Either eat, good guests,
80 Or command that they fly away.'
    The three priests from Sis
    Were amazed at these words:
    'My lord, how will we command them?
    They are cooked and skewered on the table.'
85 The priest came forward
    And remembered the living God.
    Behold, he raised his right hand
    And gave the plucked to feather.
    Seven times they winged their way
90 Over the holy priest's head;
    He blessed them,
    And they flew off to rejoin their flock.
    The three priests of Sis
    Fell at the feet of the holy priest,
95 Saying 'You are worthy, Lord,
    Of the praise of thousands.
    Let us go and bring the news
    To the Catholicos of Sis:
    "They say rightly and in truth
100 That he gives a dead man his soul back."'
    Yovhannēs said these words,
    Yovhannēs who is Turkuranc[c]i.
    He who heeds my words--
    May God forgive him his sins.

Notes

Line 2. Or yat[c]oṙn er vardapetin 'Which was at the priest's throne'
(Pivazyan's reading). We prefer Maten. MS 7709, Iwr yat[c]oṙn . . . 'On its
throne . . .'

Line 14. There is an Armenian proverb: 'When a girl dies, the ground must
approve; while she lives, the earth must approve' (David Kherdian, The Road
from Home, New York, 1979, p. 7). According to C. F. Abbott, Macedonian
Folklore, repr. Chicago, 1969, p. 211, an archbishop in Salonica once cursed
a man, saying 'May the earth refuse to accept you' (hē gēs na mē se dekhtē).
Such banned ones are called in Greek alyta 'not loosed' (M. Summers, The
Vampire, repr. New York, 1960, pp. 91-92); cf. the Armenian spells called

'binding' (kap), especially against wolves. Narekac^{c}i himself seems to have used the form of the gaylakap 'wolf-binding' in one of his poems, see J.-P. Mahé, 'Echos mythologiques et poesie orale dans l'oeuvre de Grigor Narekac^{c}i, REArm, 17, 1983, 249-278.

Line 21. Maten. MS 5623 instead of ōłer 'links' has zĕnǰil < Tk. zenǰil 'chain'.

Line 25. Ahay hotec^{c}aw marmin. Maten. MS 5623 has instead ktrec^{c}aw znǰiln 'the chain broke'.

Line 28. In place of this, Maten. MS 7707 has Ayn k^{c}o canr u meǰ xawčayn / Ēr parkac i meǰ žahahotin 'Your heavy and great hodja / Lay in putrefaction.'

Line 30. T^{c}ētpir < Ar. tadbīr 'plan'.

Line 34. Maten. MS 5623 instead of zastuac kendani 'the living God' has zastuac astuac 'God [who is] God'.

Line 37. Maten. MS 7707 reads T^{c}ē ayt inč^c aǰēp ban ēr 'What a wondrous thing it was'; Arm. aǰēp < Ar. ^{c}aǰab 'wonder'.

Lines 43-44. Maten. MS 7707 reads Vardapetn yaraǰ ekō / Ew yišec^c ēztēr kendanin, / Surb jeřōk^c xač^{c}akĕnk^{c}ec^c: / Gorg, hangč^{c}is du i mēǰ hołin 'The priest came forward / Recalled the living Lord, / [And] made the sign of the Cross with his holy hands: / 'Gorg, rest in the earth.'

Lines 44-45. Maten. MS 5623 reads Asac^c t^{c}ē hangist kac^{c}ir, / Minč^c or gay datołn amēni, / Erb ga datastan ařnē, / Patasxan xndrē yatenin, / J̌uap du nora tac^{c}es / Or banir i yōr kirakin 'He said, "Rest / Until the judge of all / Comes to execute Judgement / And asks for an answer before the Court. / Reply to him / That you open [the Court] on Sunday."'

Line 45. zAwrēns k^{c}ez hamarov tay. Hamarov = inst. sing. of Arm. hamar 'account'; two MSS have hamar ov 'who renders account', two others have hraman ov tay 'who commands', and one has hraman tayi 'I commanded'.

Lines 52-55. Maten. MS 7707 reads, ĕzNarek i tes gnac^{c}in, / P^{c}orjel kamēn zna, / Sk^{c}anč^{c}eleac^{c}n oč^c hawatayin 'They went to see Narek, / And wanted to test him. / They did not believe in miracles.'

Line 64. U alas kenin oč^{c}xarin. It was not customary, of course, to make wolves shepherds; Frik complains (App. VI, 168): 'You have given us a prince / like a ferocious wolf over sheep.' Arm. Alas (Maten. MS 7707, halas; YE X:28 xalěs(es) as verb meaning 'to let alone, release') < Ar. xalās 'free, end, edge'. Maten. MS 2270 has U sulval kaner; Arm. sulval < NP sulul 'end, edge' (Aḷayan). NP vav can be pronounced u or va, cf. P XIV:54, Arm. šiwar, šwar 'mad' and NP šurīdan 'to go mad'.

Lines 75-76. Maten. MS 7707 reads, Erek^c vardapet sesc^{c}i / Ays xōsic^{c}n i vayr mnac^{c}in 'The three priests from Sis / Were dumbstruck at these words,' cf. Line 82.

Line 78. Maten. MS 2270 has yurbat^c 'on Friday'.

Line 79. Maten. MS 7707 reads before this line, zErkus ap^{c}n al ver ikal / Ew edir zmatn i beranin 'He raised both palms, / And put his finger to his mouth.'

Line 82. Maten. MS 7707 reads, Mēk i mēk nayin cicaḷin 'They glanced at one another and laughed'.

Lines 89-90. Maten. MS 7707 reads, Goyn hazar p^{c}etur aŕin / Ew bolor ekin seḷanin 'They sprouted feathers of a thousand colours / And all came to the table.'

Lines 89-91. Maten. MS 5623 reads, Aḷawnik^c kendanac^{c}an / Eawt^{c}ēn man ekin seḷanin, / Glux drin vardapetin 'The doves were revived, / Seven came to the table / And rested their heads on the priest.'

Line 98. Maten. MS 7707 reads, Sk^{c}anč^{c}elik^c surb vardapetin 'The miracles of the holy priest'.

Line 104. Astuac iwr meḷac^{c}n aŕnē t^{c}oḷut^{c}iwn. The final diphthong -iwn was evidently pronounced -in on occasion (cf. Karst, pp. 22, 26, 28 on the pronunciation of diphthongs in Medieval Armenian). Maten. MS 5623 reads Astuac ziwr meḷk^{c}ēn t^{c}oḷu ew iwr cnōḷin 'God pardon his sins, and his parent.'

CHAPTER SIX

THE LAY OF ST. ALEXIANOS

This poem which retells a hagiographic legend, Taɫ srboyn Alēk^csianosi
'The Lay of St. Alexianos' (C, p. 4-7) was recorded in Jerusalem Matenadaran
MS 1485, circa A.D. 1636-42. It is written in couplets of sixteen-syllable
lines with caesura after the fourth syllable of each octosyllabic hemistich,
with monorhyme in -in, and contains an envoi by 'xew Yovanēs T^culk^curanc^ci'.
It was apparently written to be recited aloud; Line 4 reads Tērēn tay
xaɫaɫut^ciwn, ew inj i cayr elnel banin 'The Lord give [you] peace, and me the
beginning of this tale'. It also contains a descriptive aside characteristic
of T^clkuranc^ci's other heroic poems (Line 35): 'Crying, they kissed their son,
so that they moved the crowd to tears' [Hanc^c or žoɫovk^cn i lac^c hanin] (cf.
'The Lay of Brave Liparit', P XXIII:104 Hanc^c, or zheceln i lac^c ehan 'So that
the horsemen were moved to tears'). The tale appears to be of East Christian
origins; it is well known in Syriac literature (see H. J. W. Drijvers, 'Die
Legende des heiligen Alexius und der Typus des Gottesmannes im syrischen
Christentum,' East of Antioch: Studies in Early Syriac Christianity, London:
Variorum Reprints, 1984), and became popular in mediaeval Europe (see G. Paris,
La Vie de St. Alexis (thirteenth century), Bibl. de l'Ecole des Hautes Études,
7, 8; T. Nöldeke, 'Zur Alexiuslegende', Zeitschrift der Deutschen
Morgenländischen Gesellschaft 53, 1899, 256-8; and F. M. Esteves Pereira,
'Légende grecque de l'Homme de Dieu S. Alexis,' Analecta Bollandiana 19, 1900,
241-53).

The epic of Alexianos is very popular amongst Armenian Christians (see
H. A. Anasyan, art. 'Alek^csianos kamavor aɫk^cat,' Haykakan matenagitut^cyun, I,
Erevan, 1959, col. 405-413; Abeɫyan, III:124-129), and a version of it is to be
found in Vark^c haranc^c ('Lives of the Fathers'), Venice, 1855, Vol. I, p. 138 f.
According to this account, Alexianos' father was a prince in Rome under the
Emperors Arcadius and Honorius; his mother's name was 'Aɫlayis, according to
the Greeks; and Ak^cila, according to the Romans; and Anna, according to us'.
The Vark^c haranc^c provides the following description of Alexianos' father:

'The blessed Alek^csios [sic] was the son of a great prince and glorious
patrician. . . . And Ep^cimianos himself had many provinces, and was
greatly extolled. He had three thousand servants with gold-accoutred
steeds and brocaded garments. As he feared God greatly, he had many
churches built, with galleries; there Ep^cimianos sat, and the poor congre-
gated there, as they knew it was customary for him, when he was free after
dinner on feast days of the Lord and of the Saints, to come to the church
galleries and observe the poor through a window, that none might depart
without having received charity from him. And the poor came to him, and

he gave to all of them his possessions with his own hands. And he con-
structed hospitals and infirmaries for the poor, and provided for them
with his own income, which he entrusted to stewards whom he directed, and
he was compassionate even with the meekest of them. And in his palace he
caused a church to be erected to the Holy Mother of God, and had his tomb
built at its gate; every day he would enter his sepulchre and behold his
resting place and say to himself, "O my soul, this is your resting place
and dwelling; do not be deceived with senseless pride over these vain
glories." And only then would he speak to men; such was his wont.'

The same text relates the following concerning Alexianos' mother:

'And his wife . . . was pious and God-fearing and merciful and very
affectionate. And she was barren and had no child; she was compassionate
towards children and blessed their parents. But as she had none herself,
she languished in sadness, and every day she cried and lamented against
God, until Ep^cimianos, saddened by the straitened state of his sweet
spouse, was no longer able to make her cease from crying. Wherefore he
rebuked her before the Emperor Honorius and the Queen, and the great
priests. Then the pious Aꝉlayis, when they were alone, said to Ep^cimianos,
"My lord, why do you act haughtily and forbid me to cry? And why should I
not cry over my childlessness, for I see the beasts and animals and birds,
which give birth, and, rejoicing in their offspring, are consoled with the
gifts of God. And the same is God's blessing to newlyweds and to the parents of the Mother of God. And I see myself deprived of it, wherefore I
cry and lament, and wail against God, that He might take pity upon His unworthy prisoner and grant me a child, who will be good and God-fearing.
But if not, then let Him not give it, and I will not demand it. But you,
my lord, have been haughty towards me as though I were a suppliant in some
indecent matter, and you do not allow me to bewail my misfortune freely
against my abundant and merciful Lord and Creator." She said these and
similar things to her husband when they were alone, as the blessed Aꝉlayis
was adorned with great modesty. And when the God-fearing Ep^cimianos heard
these things from his sweet wife and was convinced by her of their justi-
fication, he himself was filled with sadness, and petitioned the Lord in
tears.'

Finally, God granted the couple a son:

'Alek^csianos was adorned with every virtue, and thought nothing of
greatness or of the visible glory of his parents, but was meek and submissive and peaceful and very wise, and thoughtful, and full of the Holy
Spirit, and was obedient and docile before his parents.'

At the age of eighteen, Alexianos was married. At the wedding feast, he vanished into a side room and sat sulking. His father came to him and admonished
him:

'Son, why have you come in here? For have not all the multitudes of
the city, together with the king, come and gathered today on your account?
Arise, my son; go to your wife, and speak to her, and be happy.'

In the nuptial chamber later on, Alexianos prayed and heard a heavenly voice
saying, 'Leave your house and follow after Me on the path of My poverty.' He
gave his wife his ring, telling her he was going to the church to pray, but he
escaped to Edessa, and became a beggar at the gate of the church there, refusing to enter the building, as he considered himself an unworthy sinner. His
parents, upon hearing of his disappearance, sent their servants to the ends of the
earth after him, and one gave him charity in Edessa without recognising him. He
remained abroad fifteen years; throughout this time his mother sat in her room,

vowing not to leave it until she might see her son again.

The priest of the church of St. Mary the Virgin at Edessa had a vision in which he was told that the prayers of the holy man who sat outside the church had been heard by the Almighty, who had ordered that the beggar be conducted into the church with great honour. Alexianos got wind of this and fled out of modesty, hoping to board a ship for Tarsus. The ship was blown off course and arrived at Rome, Alexianos' native city. When he arrived, he came incognito to his parents' house, where the servants mocked him and tore his beard. He had a vision in which he saw that three days were left to him. He demanded pen and paper (kałamar ew k^{c}artēz, Mediaeval Gk. loan-words), wrote down his life's history, and expired. When he died, a deacon read out the paper to the crowds. Alexianos' father heard it and wailed:

> 'What have you done, my son, who were the hope of my soul and the light of my eyes; the place of greatness was established for you. Why did your heart not show pity at my going out and my coming in, and why did you not tell me of yourself, and why did you accept humiliation from your servants?'

His mother came out of her self-imposed imprisonment, and cried to the people:

> 'Make me a path, that I may go and see my darling beacon, which was lit but is now found dark. Let me see the brilliant star that is now extinguished. I pray of you, mothers who have given birth to children, and the fathers, of whom they are the sons: my entrails shrivel in pity over procreation and over the rose that wilted in the garden and has no strength of fragrance remaining to it. Behold me and pity me!'

His widow spoke:

> 'I, the sufferer, entered the nuptial chamber yesterday and am a widow today. Indeed I have become like the turtledove whose spouse has died, who retires into a safe corner and perches no longer on the green boughs. So shall I go down to a cavern and wear black the rest of the days of my life, at your death.'

St. Alexianos died on the fifth day of February. Those who came close to his corpse on the day of his funeral were cured of their maladies. Many more were cured who took soil from his grave. In a less tragic Syriac version of this tale, St. Theophilos, son of a wealthy Antiochene, declines to marry the bride chosen for him, but takes her on his wanderings through Syria, circa A.D. 530. They live together in holy virginity, but pose as jester and prostitute in order the invite the contempt of the public, who humiliate them wherever they stop (T. Nöldeke, Sketches from Eastern History, Beirut, 1963, pp. 233-35). (One notes that malāmāt, the invitation of contempt, is a basic spiritual exercise of the Şūfīs of Islām.)

It is interesting to note a certain variance between the story as related above from the Armenian 'Lives of the Fathers' and T^{c}lkuranc^{c}i's version. According to the former, Alexianos' return to his homeland was an accident, as the ship on which the holy beggar travelled was blown off course. T^{c}lkuranc^{c}i, however, considers the return as a failure, whereby the saint succumbed to demonic temptation (Lines 60-61). It is characteristic for T^{c}lkuranc^{c}i to give the powers of evil their due even at the risk of diminishing the purity of the reputation of a holy man. The lyric poems are full of fallen priests (cf. Note to P II:11-12), and no mortal is safe from the harmful influence of the demons. The ship that, according to legend, was to carry Movsēs Xorenac^{c}i to Athens, was blown off course and landed at Rome; a similar mishap, again according to tradition, resulted in the arrival of the Virgin Mary at Mt. Athos. The topos is evidently very ancient, and one imagines that not a few ships that sailed Mediterranean waters had similar accidents when they did not travel by the conventional ancient method--following the coastline. We therefore consider the version of 'Lives of the Fathers' the earlier form; T^{c}lkuranc^{c}i's innovation (or, perhaps, his choice of another narrative that was current at the time) is rather a reflection of his own skeptical attitude towards human nature.

THE LAY OF ST. ALEXIANOS: TRANSLATION

Merciful God, who loves mankind, is quick to heed His servant
Who asks favours of Him in faith, and He hastens to fulfill his
    desire.

Think of the life of the ascetic Alēk^{c}sianos which I relate:
The Lord give you peace and me the beginning of this tale.

5   There was a prince who loved God, Ep^{c}rianos by name,
In the vast city of Stambōl, where kings were anointed.

He and his wife were good people who kept the holy commandments.
They had a palace adorned with gold. They had many treasures, and
    they had no son.

His wife desired a son; her eyes were ever shedding tears.
10 Thus she went from monastery to monastery, crying her heart's
    complaint.

She gave gifts to the churches: golden covers for the holy tables,
Dekans for the priests, and mercy to the bitter poor.

And the merciful, forgiving God had compassion for His servant.
He gave them a blessed son, a god boy, Alēk^{c}sanos by name.

15 When he was big and fully grown, a good seven years old,
They took him to the monastery of the priest John Chrysostom.

They said, 'Teach our son, O Lord, the holy, godly doctrines!'.
When he had learned and finished his education, the Gospel was
    familiar to him.

Nor was he idle in prayer, and he did not spare his body.
20 He desired an interpretation of the Psalter; they hastened to give
    him one to copy.

Then his father and mother wished to marry off Alēk^{c}sanos.
They went to a powerful prince, and asked for the daughter of that
    prince.

With glad thoughts in their hearts, they gave gifts and presents,
And said, 'We will give our Margarit to the splendid person of
Alēk^csanos'.

25 Then they returned, giving thought and preparation to the wedding.
They adorned horses and mules, and sacrificed oxen and sheep.

They gathered many priests and princes and went in to Alek^csanos,
Saying, 'Son, the Baron commands: Enter into the laws of the
first-created'.

He entered the church in tears and bowed to the ground before the
holy table:
30 'Lord, save me from [evil] designs, that I may triumph over my
enemy'.

Then he came out again and bowed his head before the people:
'I have promised myself to God; I cannot take a woman to wife'.

They said many shameful things, seized him, and put him on a horse,
And took him to his parents' court, and presented them with their
child.

35 Crying, they kissed their son, so that they moved the crowd to
tears.
Then they took him to his bride, and entered the church in glory.

He bowed to the ground before the holy table and glorified Father
and Son.
Then he fell crying at the feet of the elders and implored them:

'Do not place this transitory crown upon my head: I cannot wed a
woman.
40 I know full well that her blood is red, and passes, dainty food for
the earth'.

The holy priests were amazed; they put the crown on him and blessed
him.
And when they had finished the [deed of] love, they hauled them off
to the golden chamber.

Then they closed and locked the doors, and, exhausted, they fell
asleep.
The woman moved to embrace him, and awakened the innocent soul.

45 He had the crown of virginity and paid attention to naught, saying:
'My wife Margarit, here, as a sign to you, is my ring

Whilst I am away; I will come back'. But the blessed one never
returned.
Silver and gold are the food of rust; the silk of a carpet is the
moth's food.

The blessed one saw a poor man; he gave him muslin and purple.
50 He put on the poor man's sackcloth, and wished to go to the seashore.

When the blessed one did not return, she cried and called his mother,
Anna:
'Go, find your son, the light of my eyes and of your soul!'

They rushed outside crying, and searched for Alēk^csanos;
His father and mother and his wife, and all the city with them.

55 When they could not fine him, they cried so that their tears
turned to blood;
Alēk^csanos boarded a ship and went to Mount Horeb in Sinai.

Forty years he fasted and prayed in the desert;
Then he came to Jerusalem and bowed to the ground before the
[Holy] Sepulchre.

He came and reached the city of Edessa, and the blessed one prayed
much there.
60 Then the dragon of the abyss and the demons, cruel enemies by
nature,

Cast the thought of mercy for his parents in him, and thus tried
the blessed one.
He wished to go to the seashore; he boarded a ship and went to his
country.

He went to his parents' court, there were the poor were wont to
stay,
And bowed to the ground before his father, the prince, and saw his
mother and his good wife.

65 The blessed one cried and spoke, asking his father's mercy:
'Give me a place in your court for the sake of your longing for
Alēk^csanos'.

His mother groaned, and spoke through her tears: 'Eyes and eyebrows
of my boy!
Give him a place to rest, fulfill his wish!'

His mother and wife came out with the wanton girls and the servants;
70 They came out and tore his hair and dragged him along by the face.

They heaped ashes upon him, so that he cried out to his parents:
'Free me, holy lady, for the longing of Alēk^csanos!'

The Lord give you peace and make good your end.
He prayed night and day, and never rested.

75 When the day of his end came, by the will of the poor ascetic
Ink and much paper were produced, and he wrote his heart's complaint
thereon.

The blessed one died; they burned sweet incense,
So that all came to see him in hope, the whole city behind him.

The angels took his soul and transported it in glory to Heaven
80 For union with the band of fiery gender on the celestial nuptial
couch.

Then the multitude there went and called for his father,
Saying, 'Come, see this poor man lying dead with paper in hand.'

He came and took the paper, read it and saw the first words:
'I am Alēk^csanos, your son: in tears, I greet my parents!

85 My Psalter is a sign, my ring to Margarit,
But may my mother hear my complaint concerning that which your
servants did to me.

Wife Margarit, witness that they dragged me by my face'.
His father fell, his sense fled, so that they had to raise him up
by the arms.

His mother was like a lunatic, and would not go in to her son;
90 She turned, and flung away red dekans, so that the gates were
mobbed.

She went and fell upon the boy, crying and moaning piteously:
'Alēk^{C}sanos, woe to your mother, a thousand times alas to your
father!

'How awful is your wound!' she moaned incessantly to Margarit,
Who was never free of wounds until death's day came.

95 They took him and buried him, and built a holy church.
They named it Alēk'sanos, and it brought healing to many.

I, crazy Yovanēs T^{C}ulkuranc^{C}i, wrote down this ascetic's life.
This is the path of the kingdom; he who does not know it, let him
learn.

Notes

Line 8. Darpas unin oskov cep^{C}ac, šat ganj unin ordi č^{C}unin. The first half
of the line resembles P XVII:10 Darpēsni oskov cep^{C}ac. The walls of the homes
of wealthy Armenians were often gilded, as in the Bagratid capital, Ani: 'In
another hall, war and hunting scenes adorned the walls, which had been thickly
gilded where not painted on; the ceiling had carvings of geometrical forms'
(J. Orbeli, Razvaliny Ani, St. Petersburg, 1911, p. 41).

Line 48. Oski w arcat^{C}n i ker žankin, naxu k^{C}imhayn i ker c^{C}ec^{C}in. Nax < NP
nax 'carpet'; k^{C}imhay < NP kīmxā 'silk' (cf. NK XCVII Gner em karmir k^{C}imxa u
zčikyars tver em tamła 'I have bought red silk and made a banner of my liver').

CHAPTER SEVEN

SONGS OF CREATION AND ADAM

Ephraim Syrus wrote (Hymns on Epiphany, VIII:16): 'He has created the
heavens anew, because sinners have worshipped all the heavenly bodies; has
created the world anew, which had been withered by Adam; a new creation arose
from His spittle.' To the Eastern Christian, the cosmic drama of Creation is
re-enacted yearly, with the cycle of festivals commemorating the episodes of
the redemptive life of Christ corresponding to the procession of the seasons;
and the first Creation is emblematic of man's sinful natural state, which
needed to be saved through Christ. East Christians believe that Golgotha is at
the very centre of the world, that Adam was created and buried there, that
Christ was crucified there, and that the blood that flowed down from the Cross
onto Adam's skull revived the first man even as it redeemed all mankind.

T^{c}lkuranc^{c}i's poems refer often to Adam and to the Paradise of Eden (P I:3,
XIII:12-13, XIV:53, 78, XV:67-68, XVI:26, XVII:5, XX:6). Adam and Eve were the
archetype of human love; all future relationships between men and women were
informed by this earliest, flawed liaison. The cycle of infatuation, love, be-
trayal and disillusionment would repeat itself generation after generation. It
was as regular as the coming of spring, and, indeed, often coincided with it.
T^{c}lkuranc^{c}i (cf. P XIV:1-4) beheld this destiny with an attitude of world-weary
foresight. ^{c}Omar Khayyām wrote, 'This is the wheel (NP čarx) that reveals its
secrets to none, / That in its cruelty has killed a thousand Mahmuds and
Ayāzes'. For the fatalistic Persian poet, there was no breaking free from the
wheel, and he advised his listeners to drink wine and enjoy what they could.
But to the Christian, return to the Kingdom and liberation was possible through
repentance, asceticism and wisdom. Nor was fate itself to be feared, as it was
itself an instrument of God's will. Frik wrote on the Wheel of Fate (č^{c}arx i
falak^c < NP čarx-e falak) circa A.D. 1286 (Frik XXVII:47-55): Falak^{c}n pac^{c}xun
ku'tay: Mi haǰel, angēt alewor, / K^{c}ani es falak^c em lel, / Č^{c}em tesel k^{c}an
zk^{c}ez molor. / zAriwnd i veras jges, / T^{c}e falak^{c}n ē meɫawor . . . / Hazar t^{c}ē
falak^c em es. / Č^{c}em karoɫ or tam k^{c}ez ktor. / Hramank^c astucoy lini, / Es
aṙnem zk^{c}ez t^{c}agawor 'Fate answered: / "Stop barking, ignorant old man! / As
long as I have been Fate, / I have never seen anyone more confused than you. /
You cast your blood on me, / [saying] that 'Fate is guilty . . .' / Even if I
be a thousand fates, / I cannot give you a morsel. / If it be God's command, /
I will make you king."' Poems about Adam and the Creation of the world meant
more to the mediaeval Armenian than a simple retelling of a Biblical story.
They held out the hope of redemption from the cycle of death, or, apparently as

165

often, reflected the kind of accepting, fatalistic stoicism that Khayyām expressed and the Christian Frik dramatically decried.

Yovhannēs Erznkac^ci Pluz (flourished <u>circa</u> A.D. 1272-1293) wrote four poems on Adam (YE VII, X, XI, XII) translated below. It is interesting to note the mention of the six ages of the torments of Adam in YE XI: <u>Minč^c i vec^c darun, zordin or gay / Ew i kusēnēn marmnanay / Ew i eresun am linenay</u> 'Until in the sixth age, when the son comes / And takes his body from the Virgin / And lives for thirty years.' Early Christians believed generally that Christ came in the sixth world millennium, and an Arm. magical text is called <u>Vec^c hazareak</u> 'The (Book) of the Six Thousand'. Erznkac^ci Pluz derives the obvious lesson from the drama of Adam and Eve: <u>Mi hayir ač^c̆ōk^c yarat, or č^cnengē zk^cez</u> 'Cast not an amorous gaze with your eyes, lest it deceive you' (YE VII:117); T^clkuranc^ci agreed, but viewed the deception as inevitable. Every man, like Adam, must lament 'Innocent into the world I came, / And I leave, my face blackened with sin [YE X:26: <u>Ew melōk^c k'ert^cam seweres</u>; cf. P XVI:15-16].' But both poets praise the beauty of the material world: 'Blessed is the name of God, / Who opened closed doors, / Created the world beautiful . . .' (YE X:63-65). The nostalgic description of Paradise of YE XI:77-80 recalls T^clkuranc^ci's gardens of love, which are themselves images of Eden. T^clkuranc^ci says as much in P VIII:13-16.

A sweeping vision of Creation, from primordial chaos to the Deluge, is provided in the 'Song on the Creation of the World' (published by Y. K^ciwrtean, 'Yovhannēs T^clkuranc^ci, Talě Vasn Stelcman Ašxarhi', <u>Bazmavēp</u>, 1938, pp. 188-98; C, pp. 75-110). The poem was published at Constantinople in 1724; K^ciwrtean's MS is dated 1661, and a version is preserved in New Julfa MS 158, which has a colophon dated 1613. The story of Seth (Line 260) and the mention of the six ages before Christ (Line 114) both are themes familiar from P XIV; the rather detailed and fanciful catalogue of the beasts of Creation, some real, some legendary (Lines 68-94), recalls the lyricist T^clkuranc^ci's propensity for detailed listings of plants, precious stones, birds and fruits (see esp. P XV). Many other details, such as the mystical symbolism of the three tiers of Noah's Ark, the language of the serpent, and the failure of the Deluge to overwhelm Paradise (perhaps because it was in the lofty mountains of Ararat), probably derive from mediaeval Armenian commentaries on Scripture, and geographical details of Armenia are understandably the most abundant. T^clkuranc^ci's poem is published in couplets of two sixteen-syllable lines each, with caesura after the fourth syllable of each octosyllabic hemistich; all lines rhyme in -<u>an</u>. The poem is preceded by two couplets in the same form, except for rhyme in -<u>i</u>; the hemistichs of these lines also end in -<u>i</u>. Despite the scribal notation <u>Tunk^c.hariwr</u> '100 stanzas' after Line 196, we have separated the two introductory stanzas from the body of the poem because of their different rhyme and content, and because Line 1, as will be seen, is so clearly a beginning.

YE VII: TRANSLATION

1 All sons of Adam, generation of Earth,
Come, let me give you advice from God's wise words.
I know that not every man can learn from books,
For which reason I wrote this, that you hear it from me.

5 When God created Adam and Eve from the rib,
He made them in the luminous image of divinity,
He placed him in the garden in glory, planted by immortality,
And set in him the commandment to hold back from the ineffable:

"Eat of every fruit but one,
10 Else you soon die and go up out of Paradise.
If you keep my Commandment that you took from me,
I will transfer you to Heaven from Paradise, into the luminous
    ranks."

Satan, fallen from glory, having heard this,
Jealous of Adam and in opposition to the Lord of the worlds,
15 Took as his associate the serpent, from amongst all the beasts,
To tell Eve with treachery the teachings of sin:

"If you eat of that fruit which is in the midst of Paradise,
You will be gods, like the Creator."
The pitiable woman, captive listener of the vile serpent.
20 Ate of the fruit of that tree; her body was stripped.

Adam had seen this and had taken pity on his wife,
And took and ate of the fruit, and was stripped of light,
And took the fig leaf and covered his body,
And he--crowned by God--fled for shame.

25 The Creator of Adam came to see His image,
And called Adam, saying, "Adam, where are you?"
"Lord, I heard your voice and was shaken,
For I am naked and ashamed; I fled and hid myself."

"Alas for you, Adam, how were you deceived?
30 You did not heed the commandment; you partook of the fruit.
Get up, get out of Paradise, you are dead of sin.
This is no place for a dead man; you have fallen from it."

Adam's wretched words and sobbing gripped me.
Eve was the cause of his exile, and woe is me!
35 "This woman, when she gave me this, deceived me,
And from the Paradise of immortal glory has stolen me!"

The pitiable woman, prisoner to the serpent, was deceived,
And sin's deadly poison then spilled from Eve.
God's likeness, Adam, took pity and ate,
40 And died all the death of his progeny.

Sweet and beneficent God who created them,
The door of life and death: the two He revealed;
The free will of Adam with the fruit he tried;
They kept not the commandment, and He condemned.

45 Again to Adam He says, "Adam, you were earth.
You did not keep the commandment: to earth return!
You lived not with glory in Paradise; fall down into the world!
Work the earth with sweat and toil.

Instead of immortal plants, thorns shall spring up for you,
50 And in place of luminous Paradise, darkness will reign over you.
You had neither pain nor care: now cares will wear you down
Until the day of your death comes, when you will be entombed."

So pity yourself, my dear brother.
Your father Adam sinned and left his debts to you.
55 The one who sinned condemned you,
And with that one death imprisoned you in turn.

A certain one, of Adam's nature, we needed
To free us from Eve's debts of sin.
She kept not the commandment, while He kept and spoke:
60 Had we kept it, He would have taken us to Paradise.

Many righteous, chosen patriarchs came:
Abraham, father of the righteous, who loved God;
Moses the lawgiver, who spoke to God;
Prophets of godly teaching chosen from the soul.

65 But as they were of earth, and born of men,
They could not help men and free them from death,
Nor could then erase the book of sins of soul and body,
Nor turn those fallen prisoners of death back from earth.

For this great sickness we needed a physician
70 In whose soul no pain of death held sway;
In whose body there was no smell of sin.
Would he might prepare some medicine for our great pain!

But who is greater physician or more powerful lord
Than He who created us and is the king:
75 He who made in our bodies a reasoning soul,
The same pitied us with heavenly love.

The omnipotent Father, who gives birth to the Word,
Sent His son, sole-begotten, into the world;
The Holy Spirit, consubstantial with the father and offspring,
80 Assisted the Son to take bodily form.

The lord Christ was born of the Holy Virgin,
From a parent perfect, pristine, and pure.
The fire which burned from Adam's rib
Was extinguished in the water of life of the Virgin born.

85 Virgin-born, he blessed us,
And, descending to Bethlehem, he returned us to Eden in the cave.
Seated in the manger of the Word, he opened to us Paradise.
Baptised in the Jordan river, he granted us new birth.

In deathless divinity, he trampled death;
90 With his innocent and holy body he atoned for sin;
With his pure hands on the Cross he rubbed out the writing
And summoned us by his burial and resurrection to Heaven.

Adam, sick with sin, he turned from his pains,
And lifted man, fallen prisoner of death, from Hell.
95 He gave a new commandment to the sons of Adam:
"Love one another and this Lord of souls."

Now, my dear brothers and spiritual sons,
This sermon I have written is made of wise words:
Love God and the Lord, the heavenly Father.
100 Keep my commandment, the glorious light.

Be you a boy or a child, a servant of Christ,
Be you a man ripe with old age or a priest,
Be you a healthy or sick son of Adam,
Be you righteous or a sinner, this you must do for yourself.

105 Do not love this world and transient life,
And that which in this world seems to you good or comely,
That body made of earth with its fleeting pains--
Do not make these the lord of your soul, which is king.

The creator made you as a sapling in Paradise.
110 He made you that you might do good.
He gave you comprehending mind and eyes that see,
And two ears he formed for you, like the gates of a city.

Close your gates, and open your mind,
Lest evil enter and deceive your soul with sin.
115 Be opened with wisdom and good deeds;
Be filled with comely treasures and holy counsel.

Cast not an amorous glance with your eyes, lest it deceive you.
Heed not evil counsel, lest it sting you.
Strike not a man with your hands, lest the Lord judge you.
120 Consider not evil in your heart, lest it burn you.

Speak not evil with your tongue, else you are lost.
If you confess your sins, you are made righteous.
Prayer is speech with God; be not slow of heart.
Labour with your hands: for one, give a thousand.

125 This my brother, who asked this and I wrote it,
Was on the road; I hastened too.
But these few words I have written,
A remembrance for you of me, a good seed.

I have my hope in God, the Lord of all,
130 That He enter your heart and bring forth fruit,
The rain of the Holy Spirit's graces descend upon you,
And your soul, body and mind grow full of fruit.

May God have much satisfaction from you,
That His mercy be ever bestowed on you.

YE X: TRANSLATION

Our Lord came to Paradise
And called out to Adam, "Where are you?"
Adam replied from the fig tree,
"I am naked."
5 My Lord, I want you
To curse Eve and the serpent;
They deceived me
Of your light, so I was stripped,
And they gave me to eat of the fruit
10 And made me black-faced before you.
Merciful, merciful you are, and love men.
Do not ignore us, Lord!

My Lord, I am from that soil
By your own hands you created me.
15 Satan saddened me.
I ask you to dispel my pain.
I was scattered more than the water;
I ask you to gather me up.
Gather me up and fill a bottle,
20 And take power over me with your eye.
Merciful, merciful you are, and love men.
Do not ignore us, Lord!

My Lord, I am lost!
I have a hope that you will find me.
25 Innocent into the world I came,
And I leave, my face blackened with sin.
I encountered inextricable danger;
I ask you to rescue me.
Redeem me from my sins in this world,
30 And free me from the fire of the next.
Merciful, merciful you are and love men.
Do not ignore us, Lord!

Satan saw Adam
Standing at the gate of Paradise,
35 Pounding his two hands together,
And cackled caustically.
Adam addressed him:
"Have you seen your damned ways?
Although you removed us from Paradise,
40 Our Lord does not leave us from his hands."
Merciful, merciful you are and love men.
Do not ignore us, Lord!

Satan saw Moses,
Forbade him and cried much:
45 "My divine-speaking Moses,
Why is our Lord stirred up against us,
When we were disciples
Of God, Adam yet uncreated.
50 We have been deprived of our glory!"
Merciful, merciful you are, and love men.
Do not ignore us, Lord!

From the heavenly orders
Sadael had turned his face;
55 From Heaven he descended into the abyss,
And remained obscured from light.
He took Adam out of Paradise
And flung him into the world of beasts.
We are all strangers, brother,
60 Inhabitants of the beasts' land.
Merciful, merciful you are, and love men.
Do not ignore us, Lord!

Blessed is the name of God,
Who opened closed doors,
65 Created the world beautiful,
And divided into three faces;
Who arranged the angels in Heaven,
Gave Paradise to Adam
And the earth to beasts,
70 And made these places of the mindless.
Merciful, merciful you are, and love men.
Do not ignore us, Lord!

YE XI: TRANSLATION

Adam sat at the gate of Paradise,
Cried and called piteously,
Miserably at Paradise,
And sighed tearfully.

5 "Ah, seraphim! Ah, seraphim!
You who enter Paradise,
Implore the Divine
To give these sinners ease!

Yesterday I was in Paradise,
10 Covered with godly light.
There I was king,
Like the powerful King.

For Eve, partner of my rib,
Who was spoiled by the serpent's deception,
15 I, too, was persuaded by him,
And was expelled from Paradise.

They took away my beautiful ornaments.
They stripped me mercilessly
For the sake of one commandment,
20 The fruit of the immortal tree.

I am stark naked here.
Eve sits and cries terribly.
Why did I not say Lord, I have sinned.
You created me, have mercy!

25 This one time was I spoiled;
   I was deceived by a woman's words.
   When I saw Eve shamed,
   Stripped of glory like Satan,

   I was inflamed with compassion for her,
30 And, taking the immortal fruit, I ate of it
   And said, If my Creator comes,
   He will see me more naked than Eve.

   With paternal love He will show compassion
   And have mercy on me and on her.
35 When I heard the footfalls of the Lord
   Coming to Paradise, I was stupefied.

   I covered myself with a fig leaf,
   Fell amidst the trees, and hid.
   The Lord called, 'Adam, where are you?'
40 I called back, 'I am naked.'

   Lord, I heard your voice
   And, shamefaced, was gripped by fear.
   Now relate who told you that you were naked,
   And who deceived you!

45 Why did I not fall at his feet,
   Crying, saying 'Lord, I have sinned,'
   Rather than accuse Eve?
   It is I who have fallen from eternal good.

   From my rib you created the woman Eve,
50 Who gave me of the fruit and I ate.
   The last thing that I heard
   Was the Lord speaking to Eve:

   'I commanded you not to eat,
   But you ate of it: leave Paradise!
55 I placed you in eternal Paradise,
   But you loved that which is fleeting.

   I gave you the fruit of life,
   But you tasted of death.
   I adorned you in light,
60 But you loved the dark.'

   Eve answered him:
   'The serpent deceived me and I ate.'
   The Lord cursed the serpent and Eve,
   And I was trapped with them.

65 The Lord ordered us: 'Go!
   Earth you were. To earth return!'
   I implore you, cherubim,
   I have a complaint, hear me out.

   When you enter that Paradise,
70 Take a branch of the immortal fruit,
   Bring it and place it over my eyes,
   And cure my eyes cast into darkness.

When you enter Paradise,
Do not close the gate of Paradise.
75 Place me before it,
Let me look a moment, and turn me away.

Ah, I remember you, flowers,
Sweet-tasting springs!
Ah, I remember you, birds
80 Sweet-voiced, and the animals,

Who enjoy Paradise;
Go to your king and cry--
Who are planted by God in Paradise
And chosen from every species in the world.'

[Maten. MS 2190 continues after Line 18 as follows, with every second verse
repeated:]

They were expelled from Paradise,
Thrown onto thorny earth,
And ordered to return to earth
From immortality; they were to die,
And to till the soil of earth with their sweat
Until their return whence they came.
And after leaving this place,
You are to go to Hell with worries.
Live there and wander
Until in the sixth century, when the son comes,
And takes his body from a virgin,
And lives for thirty years,
He will go to the Jordan and be baptised
By the hand of John the prophet.
By Pilate he will be condemned,
By the will of Judas, his evil servant.
And he will be affixed to the Cross
For the sins of the first-created.
And he will descend from the Cross,
And in the soil of death he will be buried.
And he will descend to Hell,
And on the third day he will rise.
And he will free this one for you
And rest in his primeval glory.

[Maten. MS 4326 continues from Line 79 as follows:]

Ah, I recall the mother of faith,
The holy wedding and nuptial canopy,
The house of the immortal bridegroom
Who adorned you, eternal,
A miraculous second heaven.
May they rise in glory of glories,
That you give birth to us as light
To the sceptre of the son.

You share your cleansing bread
And give your pure blood to drink;
You raise beyond measure
The incomparable of things conceivable.
Come, sons of the new Zion,
Warriors for our Lord in might.
He divided the Jordan--
You, the sea of worldly sins.
To him, Jesus, is our strength--
You, Lord Jesus, of the existent Father.
You are ancient and fitting example
Of the highest altar,
Which planted the Paradise of Adam
And laid waste the foundations of Hell.
This bread is the body of Christ;
This cup is the blood of the new covenant.
The great hidden secret is manifest:
Mother of God, I have sinned before you!

YE XII: TRANSLATION

There, in the midst of Paradise, were three souls:
Adam, Eve, and the Commandment of the Lord.
The serpent ruptured the boundary of the orchard of life,
And banished Adam from luminous Paradise.

5   The woman showed disobedience by the deceiver's word;
They neared the tree of which He had ordered them not to eat;
By tasting of the fruit wherewith He had fashioned death,
They ate and knew that they were naked.

They desired leaves of the fig tree,
10 And made a covering for their bodies filled with shame.
The treat of the Lord was of God's coming.
Adam heard, fled, and hid.

YE VII: Notes

The poem, entitled Yovhannu vardapeti Ezenkac^coy, makanun Pluz koč^cec^ceal, asac^ceal ban šahavēt ew ōgtakar 'Profitable and useful words spoken by Yovhannēs Erznkac^ci the priest, whose surname is called Pluz', is written in four-line stanzas; each line contains twelve syllables, with caesura following the seventh syllable. All four lines within a stanza rhyme, but the rhyming syllable varies from stanza to stanza.

Line 83. This line probably refers to the passion aroused in men by women. It may also recall the Armenian belief that Adam's first companion in Eden was a fiery, one-eyed creature named Al; At^cam marmnelen, heč^c iraru c^cēin saze, ator hmar a At^camě heč^c č^cēr sire Alin. Astvac tesav or Alē č^ckrc^cav ěnkerut^cen ēne

At^camin het, Evayin stełcec^c '[Al was of fire, but] Adam was corporeal; they couldn't manage together at all, and for that reason Adam did not love Al. God saw that Al was unable to be Adam's partner, so He created Eve' (Erv. Lalayan, 'J̌avaxk^c,' Azgagrakan handēs, I, Šuši, 1896, pp. 344-45). Originally, Āl seems to be the Iranian name, meaning 'scarlet', of the demonic personification of puerperal fever, the child-stealing witch of Ancient Near Eastern mythology. In Christian and Jewish folk belief, the child-stealing witch seems to have been equated with Lilith, Adam's first wife, who after her rejection in favour of Eve showed her hatred of women by attacking them abed with child. The Armenians appear to have substituted for Lilith the Iranian Āl, against whom amuletic scrolls are prepared for women in childbirth. See J. R. Russell and Shāmlū, art. 'Āl,' Encyclopaedia Iranica, and Russell, Zoroastrianism in Armenia, Harvard Iranian Series, Cambridge, Mass., Ch. 14 (in pub.).

YE X: Notes

The poem, entitled Tał Adamay, Pluz vardapeti asac^ceal ē 'A poem on Adam, Pluz the priest has spoken it', is written in stanzas of eight lines plus a two-line refrain (except for the first stanza, with ten lines plus refrain); the even-numbered lines contain eight syllables and rhyme in -es, with caesura following the fourth syllable, while the odd-numbered lines (with the exception of the dekasyllabic first line of the refrain) contain seven syllables, and do not rhyme.

Line 10. Kēnē arin seweres. Cf. YE X:26 and P XVI:15-16.

Line 28. Kēn hayc^cem, or zis xalĕses. Xalĕsem 'I free' < Ar. xalās, cf. P XXIII:64.

YE XI: Notes

The poem, entitled Tał Adamay asac^ceal i Pluz vardapetē 'A Poem on Adam spoken by the priest Pluz' is written in four-line stanzas, each line of which has eight syllables, with caesura after the fourth syllable. All four lines within a stanza rhyme, but the rhyming syllable varies from stanza to stanza.

Line 14. Or łaltec^caw xabmamb ōjin. Łaltec^caw, aor. mid.-pass. 3 pers. sing. of *łaltanam, 'I err, am spoiled', denominative verb < Ar. ghalat, cf. P IV:5.

YE XII: Notes

The poem, entitled Taɫ Hovhannes Pluz vardapetē asac^Ceal 'A poem spoken by the priest Yovhannēs Pluz', is written in four-line stanzas, each line of which contains eleven syllables, with caesura after the fifth syllable. There is internal rhyme within Lines 1-3 and Line 12, but no overall rhyme scheme.

OTANAWOR PATMUT^CIWN YOHANISI VASN ĒSTEᵬCMAN AŠXARHI
'RHYMED HISTORY OF YOVHANNĒS ON THE CREATION OF THE WORLD':
  TRANSLATION

> The beginner is the beginning who began the Word: the creator,
>   eternal God;
> Which He revealed to Moses on mount Horeb in Sinai.
>
> Surely the nonsense they babbled concerning monstrous gods
> They spoke unwisely and absurdly, confused by many gods,
>
> 5 Which they call self-created, and heaven and earth false,
> Wherefore they prophesied that in a cloud He made known all this.
>
> God made them in the beginning; they are neither timeless nor
>   unreckonable in years.
> God alone is without beginning, without quality and unreachable.
>
> The earth was invisible; there was no day and nothing to be seen.
> 10 And the water covered the world, and created man was not apparent.
>
> And that is called unprepared: there was not yet any adornment,
>   nor were there any plants,
> Nor trees, nor mountains, nor plains, nor crawling things, nor
>   creatures that swim.
>
> Darkness was above the abysses, and the tenebrous shadow of the
>   years.
> Abysses is the name of water, and of the unreachable deeps.
>
> 15 The soul of God moved about, bestowing an impetus on the waters,
> For the Hebrews and Greeks say wind is not the proper term.
>
> That which God made in the beginning is the revelation of the
>   living Father
> And particular person of the Holy Spirit, creator, of the same
>   will with the Father.
>
> The things at the beginning of creation are not revealed to us,
>   the race of man,
> 20 But He who made them knows them: when they came to be, or when
>   they were·made.
>
> And God said, "Let there be light," and they spread,
> Even the highest good, which bore witness to the Word by nature.
>
> By him the arts were revealed, and the useful paths;
> By him the worst things were defined, the bad made apparent apart
>   from the good things.

25 There was no light that was useless or incongruous;
Glory to the giver of good gifts, endless and inexhaustible.

Out of light He made the beginning, creator and living light,
Evening and morrow, a complete day.

He told the water to divide, and the commandment bore result:
30 The seas became distinct and unmistakable separate fountains
burst forth,

Arching greatly above the firmament,
Nowhere thinning, nor slackening; united, equal and constant.

He made the firmament an interval,
A point equidistant between the lower and higher waters.

35 He created it in flight, ever moving, never stationary.
He established the dome of luminous bodies, uncountable and
innumerable,

And a second heaven of fire, abode of the incorporeal orders:
Triads of archpriests and enneads eternally singing praise.

The angels and archangels: these dominions are our guardians,
40 Principalities, powers and dominions invincible in strength;

Seraphim and cherubim and ever-kingly thrones,
Angels of joyous nature, ministers of the holy Trinity.

The third ether is out of reach, where is the sovereign Lord God,
Which Paul, having seen it, called indescribable and ineffable.

45 Angels and heavens and light are creatures of two natures,
Airy and fiery, endless and inexhaustible.

And the dry land appeared; dryness a sign of moisture.
He said, "Let the earth make spring forth tree, plant and verdure."

And the fruit-bearing trees came to be, and the flowers for the
adornment of men;
50 To be eaten and worn, pleasing, for the enjoyment of the eye.

And on the fourth day he made of the scattered, spreading light
A vessel of air, and gathered the light therein:

The pure one of the Sun, and the damp, medial moon,
And the other mass of the assembly of stars, both fixed and
wandering.

55 The sun is ruler of day and night;
When he departs, it is night; when he is born, the light of day
comes.

The darkness is not existence; the light is living and most
necessary.
With the scarcity of light, the tenebrous elements are
strengthened.

The sun rolls on its way, the moon sliding and gliding.
60 The fixed planets and stars by skips and jumps.

The Sun is the spring of light; the moon, its second mouth,
Which takes its light from the Sun or is hidden and unveiled.

These are the rules and measures, the counterpairing of natural
    forces and months,
Of hours and periods, of the cycle of the points of rest.

65 The Sun descended into Capricorn: then does winter come to us,
    and our nadir,
While in the South the summer comes, the time of fruits' ripening.

On the fifth day, the living creator and maker
Told the water to give birth to great whales and to swimming
creatures;

The first, at first, was Leviathan, dragon of the sea creatures.
70 Satan's image, he is crushed on the day of [Christ's] coming.

Innumerable and uncountable whales and reptiles wallow in the
    waters.
They are merciless, and forgetful of their birth.

So, too, the birds of the air, who have aquatic dwellings.
They leave their parents in the sea, and are pitiless spawn.

75 Animals are brought forth on earth: beasts and winged birds
Of wondrous form, for men who behold them are amazed.

Plants and pharmaceutic roots sown grant health,
But if taken after eating are the cause of death.

So the bands of beasts, who were not made man-eating;
80 In the beginning, they were submissive and beneath man's rule.

While yet Adam had not sinned, they had no hostile foe.
Panther, wolf and bear were in concert with the sheep.

Eating from fruit trees, all the animals, even the deer,
The beasts and creeping things and birds were at peace in universal
    love.

85 The deer are the ornament of the mountains; the fish, of waters,
The consolation and balm of seamen and travellers.

The _yaralez_ and chimaera and foul-mouthed harpy
Are said by some to be, and by others, not, but are not certain.

They are at earth's bottom, demoniac beasts with death-dealing
breath,
90 As the Lord advises us: "Their smell is death's potion."

There is a sea of all the world, and its name is Abyssal,
And the clouds draw water from it, and no one crosses it in ships.

All God's creations were made for man's honour,
That at the creation of man all might be in readiness,

95 Even as a man lovingly honours his king,
First adorning the house with diverse good things.

On the sixth day, the merciful Father who loves mankind
Spoke with the nature of the Son: "Let us make Adam like us."

We say the image of God, unity of the number three,
100 For we are inspired in word and mind, threefold personality and
single man:

So like His image; of genius in art,
Knowing and wise in gifts, immortal in rational soul.

It was not proper that we should make Him the person of the Father
only,
Although the will alone sufficed for all existing things to be.

105 The Son was not uninformed of His living Father's plan,
But acquiesces together with us, that we may learn all.

More graces were amassed in man, than in all existing creatures,
For with reason He made them, and this one with lordly honour:

Let us make the likeness of our image sensate prince of all
existing creatures,
110 For he is made of soil from the earth, but inspired with spiritual
grace.

Rational he is, and thinking, with eternal, immortal soul,
When in the sixth age He clothed the Word, son of the Father
by a virgin.

115 And according to the image of the spirit, man is an immortal soul.
The spirit is holy and unsearchable; so is the soul of man.

First He created the body, then the rational soul,
That it not be a witness to the matters of its creation.

He planted Paradise in the East, and called it the earthly Eden;
120 "Adam" is the name of Earth; Eden is translated the same.

On the third day, He planted it with the other growing trees.
This he called God-planted, only by another botanical term,

Beyond the trees of this world, and diverse in taste and colour,
Yielding bountiful good; glory to Him now and forever.

125 And He cast drowsiness upon the man, heaviness and slumbering sleep,
And took of his ribs and fashioned the cause of birth;

He knew of man's passing and did not want to relinquish him to death.
God made good; the serpent and Satan taught evil.

They accepted with blessing the command "Be fruitful and multiply";
130 So, too, all the reptiles, the ruler unlike the ruled.

In archpriestly honour he gave the animals their names,
But they, made by their Creator, were called to Earth.

"Earth" is translated as "fear", and "world" by "repentance",
For here you live in fear, while in eternity you remain fearless.

135 Paradise is the place of trees, bower of flowers rich in fruit,
High above the earth, a journey of six months,

Where is the tree called that of wisdom, the tree of death and
  immortality.
For man's sake it was planted, as a test of his love of God.

Four rivers flow forth, irrigating Paradise,
140 Called by the names Phison, Gehon, Tigris and Euphrates.

They irrigate Paradise, for it is level and even,
With luminous, unblemished fruit, ever green and never falling.

The waters descend from the mountain and level valley and floodgate,
Enter the bosom of earth and course beneath the mountains.

145 The Phison from mount Yemawon in the northeast
Flows to the Indian plateau, where there is noble gold

Which the antlions keep, and the gold is that plant
Which bounds the southern clime and keeps watch at the Red Sea.

And the gem called bdellium: that red spark is ruby,
150 Which may be found at night, for it burns unextinguishably.

No one can hide it, nor, having taken it, can one conceal it:
The scarlet corundum; it is the yellow-black sapphire.

The Gehon flows from the mountain of the moon, bursting into
  northern climes,
Cutting across Ethiopia, and Egypt grows fat on it.

155 The Tigris is from the province of Hašt; rising, twisting out of
  the countryside,
It cuts across Mesopotamia, hard by Asorestan.

Below Babylon, this and the Euphrates join together
In turbulent course and enter the Persian Gulf.

The Euphrates rises from Karin, and also at Oskeank^c,
160 And many rivers flow into it, and many waters join.

God placed man in Paradise, for they were made outside Paradise;
To labour and keep him they took command from their Creator:

To labour and care for him, and to guard the two gates,
And they accepted their Creator's injunction to fear him.

165 God commanded man in the sweetness of paternal mercy:
"It is sufficient that you eat all the fruit of the garden;

The unripe fruit of knowledge will be the cause of your death."
Adam and Eve were naked, without modesty or caution.

After they had sinned, they knew their nakedness,
170 For sin brings repentance, that they learn confession.

Satan saw Adam adorned with lordly glories
And, feeling oppressed, he laid a most grievous ambush.

Then he deceived the serpent and made his abode in him,
Promising him this gift, saying "I will make you strong in me."

175 He saw Eve standing apart and far from Adam.
They say the serpent was shortened: he exerted influence over Eve,

Either by words of men, like the ass of Balaam Peor,
Or as demons address their officers he spoke in the tongue of idols,

Saying, "Why do you not eat of all the fruits of your Paradise?"
180 For she was not informed of his plan; God alone knows the heart.

She said, "We eat all, but not from the tree of knowledge."
He asked Eve over her shoulder of that tree which is the occasion
of death.

Again the serpent spoke to Eve the words of deception and
perdition:
"God says one ate from there and became sovereign god,

185 Wherefore it seemed fitting to him to say 'That which is pleasing
to the eyes is always a sin'.
For let a man rejoice in what is his, in the glory and honour of
his greatness."

In ignorance Eve ate, and Adam came to love the woman.
They were naked before the ineffable light, and remained most
wretched.

The committed seven sins and were thus estranged from God.
190 They scattered the counsels of the Lord and placed those of the
tempter against them.

Thinking the word of the Lord a lie, they were pleased with the
serpent's talk
And remembered not the good of good, and loved the serpent.

Having eaten, they transgressed against the commandment and
stealthily sought to become divine.
When God questioned them, they spoke ill-fitting and insolent words

195 Which it was necessary to scorn, abuse and rebuke.
He accounted the woman well--over Paradise and lordly glory.

[ONE HUNDRED STANZAS]

He made one request for the thief, and three were brought forth.
They pleaded before god and became the sons of perdition.

With seven punishments were they punished, in accordance with the
transgression of the seven sins.
200 Thus sweat and labour, work and the earth were called a curse.

In gloom the labours of birth would be; thus the curses they
received from God,
And stripped of grace and glory they were hurled from Paradise
into exile.

They did not attain divinity, but were conquered under death by
death;
The heavens became clay, and light turned to darkness.

205 They were to remain immortal, but were changed from life to death;
They had lived in honour and glory, but became like dumb beasts.

Paradise remained without an inheritor, for it had none else
    remaining.
Alas for all that happened! Alas for the great loss of men!

For sinless had they eaten, without impulse towards divinity.
210 But where there was an "I have sinned", they were not very guilty.

God, regretful, mourned, for He was Lord, and merciful Father.
The fiery legions mourned, and all the heavenly ranks.

The creeping beasts mourned, and all the flying creatures,
For they saw their king all 'Woe!' and 'Alas!' and crying
    fearfully.

215 For they had remained sinless; they grew up in the Paradise of
    Eden.
The earth and Paradise were filled, and the era of Enoch began.

For they fell into sin, and still gave birth and multiplied,
Even as Eden in Paradise, which is impassable and inexhaustible.

He knows the cause of growth, all of which He made with His Word,
220 As the rib of Adam, which was birth without labour.

Man was estranged from God, and God, the cure, the merciful
    Father,
Made them garments of skins, and clothed Adam and Eve.

Specifically, there was neither mockery nor spiteful rancour,
But the promise of what will come to man, the future day's
    fulfillment of the Word.

225 He removed them and cast them out, and they settled near Paradise,
For they always looked towards it, towards the cause of their
    repentance.

A curse befell the serpent; his arms fell off and he crawled,
    wriggling, eating earth,
For he had made man into earth, and he had Satan at his breast.

Thirty years after the exodus, they received the command of birth
230 And bore first filthy Cain, the murderer, son of perdition;

Then the righteous Abel, and it was in the thirtieth year
When he ordained the priest and gave the honour of leadership.

Telling him, "Be good and a doer of righteous deeds,
And you will enter again into Paradise, there to be immortal."

235 Thus Adam advised his sons, and he lived prepared to love God,
To bring his portion of the offering of the goods of God the giver.

Abel rendered up his offering, and it was acceptable to the Lord.
Cain offered his, not a good one, nor pleasing.

Abel's was of choicest lambs, with ready, willing mind,
240 While Cain's was the rejected portion of his crops, useless and
    ill-fitting.

When God did not receive it, he abandoned brotherly affection
And said, "Go into the orchard, and I will remain outside".

Cain committed seven sins, and his punishment came of the same
    number:
The unworthy gift he offered and his jealousy against his brother,

245   The guiltless blood he spilled, a new, ungodly sin,
His mixing blood with earth, and the mournful grief he left his
    parents.

And for his answer in insolence, 'Am I his keeper?'--
For in mercy the Lord asked, as cause of his repentance--

God spoke to Cain, saying 'Immobile and powerless you will remain,
250   Wailing, shaking and trembling, disgusting to the race of men;

Your whole body becomes leprous, and you have no resting place.
Horns grow on your head. Cain comes and his voice is heard.

And he who kills Cain bears seven punishments.'
All these, all Cain's spawn perished in the deluge.

255   And Cain bore Enoch, and these were called the sons of men--
Enoch, you felt judgment--who begat the evil doer Malaliel,

And Malaliel began Methuselah; seven generations of the progeny
    of Cain.
Lamech had two wives, that nurturer of evil sins.

Lamech spoke with his wives: 'Break the covenant of divinity.
260   Commit adultery with the race of Seth, called the children of the
    Lord.'

On Sela he began Ubal, who was a musician and minstrel,
And on Ada he begat Tobel, who invented the smith's craft.

They took rouge and antimony, these female teachers of evil,
And fell in with the race of Seth, and it was just as they desired.

265   And Cain said, crying, "God, sovereign creator!
Speak to your beasts, that they grant me the day of death!"

This Lamech killed Cain--not the one who was Enoch's grandson--
And confessed to the women, lest he bear the punishment of Cain.

Let us return to the race of Seth, to Adam and primeval Eve.
270   He had sixty sons and daughters, whose names do not appear,

And Adam bore Seth, his parents' balm.
And of Seth was born Enoch, a good man, root of virtue.

Enoch hoped in God, who is a caring and merciful Father.
He does not forget us, visiting us on the day of resurrection.

275   The blast that stripped Adam and Enoch the same, did Enoch receive
And made these writings, testimony of existent beings,

A feast for the soul and mind and useful to the wise,
For God is the One who sees the pinnacle of wisdom's profundities.

This is choicer than gold, of more utility than silver,
280   More honourable than gemstones, and a fount of immortality.

In the five hundred thirtieth year Adam died;
In the same and tenth did Seth reach his end.

In his hundred and fiftieth he had borne Enoch, Kaynanayn.
Enoch by the same numeration arrived at his dying day.

285 Kaynanayn bore Malaliel, and Yared, Enoch's father,
And Yared begat Enoch, clear-minded and godly.

Enoch heard Adam: "Sin is the cause of death."
He bore Methuselah and made a beginning of repentance.

He ate neither meat nor fruit, but only grass and plants,
290 And set bounds for his own head, saying 'I am unworthy to see
      Heaven'.

He spoke of the day of resurrection, the terrible judgement of the
      Coming,
When the Lord will arrive with myriad legions and armies of angels.

The Lord God transferred him to immortal Paradise,
That Lamech, Satan in an evil doer's body, not murder him.

295 For on the seventh day God rested; this was a pause and stopping
      place.
Although sin conquered life, by good He conquered death.

And Elijah was with him, in return for the two who departed,
To the shame of the heretics, who do not believe in immortality.

After the transferral of Enoch, two hundred souls were reconciled
300 And went up to mount Ahermon, living as ascetics, that they might
      become immortal.

But they did not reach the extreme of their asceticism, descending
      and becoming polluted instead;
They fell in with the daughters of men, and went about in lustfulness.

The earth was stained, and none remained noble.
Twenty men copulated with one woman, but no semen flowed;

305 But one was born tall in height, and the mother choked on the day
      of birth.
They were giants, huge, forty cubits long,

With the breath of demons, fighters against God, cannibals and
      monstrous beasts.
Neither holy nor righteous men remained, only noble Noah.

Methuselah was clear-minded, without possessions or dwelling;
310 He begat Lamech, and Lamech gave Noah the royal crown.

Noah was perfectly righteous, beyond all his predecessors.
Five hundred years he was an ascetic, remaining a virgin.

In the mountains and waste places, he kept his bodily conduct
      angelic;
God was more pleased in him than in all the sons of Adam.

315 God spoke to Noah, saying "Build an ark.
Take a wife and beget a son, the cause of birth of a new world."

Noah bore three sons; Shem, Ham and beloved Japheth,
And they took wives, but Ham was from the race of Cain.

Noah was so righteous in his acts that in all six hundred years
320 He bore only three sons, for intercourse disgusted him.

Three hundred cubits in length and fifty cubits wide did he make
    the Ark,
And thirty cubits in height; of indestructible wood, with a sturdy
    hull;

And the sound of the carpenters' work reached every ear,
As though saying, 'Let us be ready, men! The flood has reached us
    and is coming on!'

325 The Lord God said to Noah, to my noble forefather:
'Enter, you and your children, the women and all your daughters-
    in-law.'

All having entered the Ark, this command was kept in holiness,
But He did not speak thus when they went up; men and women were
    called conjointly.

'Seven of the clean animals and the same number of birds
330 You will take to you in the Ark, while two of the unclean will
    suffice.'

He called for fewer of the unclean for He was Lord, first in
    wisdom;
That they might not afflict the clean, nor entrap men in deceit.

When it was completed, the whole construction of the Ark,
They plastered inside and out with red lead and cement of tar,

335 Letting a door in the side for the convenient entry of sensate
    species;
In amphoras at midship were food and various other necessities.

The upper, middle and lower houses were most secret,
The uppermost like the heavens, dwelling place of incorporeal
    powers.

The middle, like the Paradise of Eden, was the stopping place of
    the ranks of the righteous.
340 The lower house was like this Earth, where unholy and holy abide
    alike.

After this, the fragrance of sweet incense welled from the Ark,
And three turned towards it, and evil men understood not.

That which the Lord spoke came to be, and His command was fulfilled:
The Lord God sealed the outer door tightly.

345 Noah was five and a hundred when the command of wrath arose,
And in the six hundredth was the flood, after the day of repentance.

The abundant cataracts of Heaven were opened, and the springs
    burst forth from the abyss:
The floods of upper and lower water were united together.

And, rising above the mountains, the waters were heaped fifteen
cubits above them,
350 And Paradise alone remained; the water of perdition did not reach it.

Then was seen the tragedy, the sound of animals bellowing;
Many came towards the Ark, but what they wanted did not come to pass.

Fathers and mothers cried for their sons, and gained nothing by
crying.
Forty days and forty nights passed; all ages were blotted out.

355 It was no common rain, but a deluge from Heaven.
Inundated in their own sinful deeds, they were plunged into the
waters of the flood.

The Lord God remembered Noah and all His own in mercy.
God, who never forgets His noble servants,

Commanded that the cataracts and fountains be stilled by the wind
of the Spirit,
360 And after one hundred and fifty-six days, the mountaintops were
revealed.

Vasn Steɫcman Ašxarhi: Notes

Line 3. Gēm or aylandak č^castuack^c; barbanǰmunk^c or barbařec^can. Note the
expressive alliteration of the last hemistich.

Line 24. Were evil made by God apparent and visible as apart from good, Adam
should not have needed to discover the distinction by eating of the tree; the
theology here seems rather more Zoroastrian than Christian.

Line 87. Yaralez w eɫǰerwak^caɫn; yuškaparēn pēɫcaberan. The yaralez is a dog-
like creature of Armenian mythology said to revive soldiers fallen on the field
of battle; cf. the myth of Ara and Šamiram, Movsēs Xorenac^ci I:15. The etymology of the word is obscure. The yuškaparik is a harpy; the word comes from
Middle Iranian (see H. W. Bailey, Dictionary of Khotan Saka, Cambridge, 1979,
112).

Line 114. Zor i Z darun zgec^caw; i kusēn ordin hōr ew ban. Cf. P XIV:53-56.

Line 120. Adam ē hoɫoy anun; ew edemēn noyn t^cargēman. 'Adam' is compared to
Heb. adāmāh 'land'.

Line 129. Ačeloy zarganaloy; awrhnut^ceamb ařin hēraman. The same commandment
is cited in P XIV:79.

Line 131. K^cahanayapetakan patwov, kendaneac^cn koč^ceac^c zanuans. The Armenians tell the following story in this connection, which was recorded by

Bense, 'Bulanĕx kam Hark^C gavaṙ,' <u>Azgagrakan Handēs</u> VI, Tiflis, 1900, 27. When
Adam gave all the animals names, the ass couldn't remember its own name, and
kept asking Adam what it was. Adam finally grabbed the animal by its ear in
his anger and shouted 'Ass, ass! Do you understand?' That is why the ears of
the ass are long.

Line 133. <u>Erkirn erkiwł t^{C}argmani, ew asxarhn apasxarut^{C}ean</u>. Two fanciful Armenian folk etymologies, based on homonymy.

Line 145. <u>Yemawon</u>: i.e., Himalaya.

Line 146. <u>Gay i hapersah Hendkac^C; ur oskin ē aznewakan</u>. Hapersah: apparently
Phl. Abarsahr, 'realm of the Aparni', in the province of Xurāsān.

Line 155. <u>Hastēn gawaṙ ē Tigrēs; elanē gełjēn olorean</u>. The Tigris rises in
the west in Hasteank^C, in the land of Cop^{C}k^C, flowing down to Mesopotamia past
Amida, not very far from T^{C}lkuran.

Line 159. <u>Ep^{C}rat i Karnoy elnē; ew Oskeanc^{C}n i yerkuakan</u>. Karin: modern
Erzurum. The eastern branch of the Euphrates, the Aracani or Murat Su, rises
at Oskik^C (=T^{C}lkuranc^{C}i's Oskeank^C), see H. Hübschmann, <u>Die altarmenischen</u>
<u>Ortsnamen</u>, repr. Amsterdam, 1969, 460.

APPENDIX

THREE FESTAL HYMNS

Three Armenian Church hymns published by Abp. Norayr Połarean (C, pp. 69-74) are attributed to T^{c}lkuranc^{c}i in several MSS: their subject matter reflects the same liking for curious details of Christian traditional lore encountered in some of the lyric poems, and in the rhymed history of Creation. The language of the hymns is sometimes ponderously pseudo-Classical, sometimes strikingly beautiful in its vividly poetic imagery. There is a complete absence of Arabic, Turkish, and New Persian loan-words, but this is appropriate to the solemn, ecclesiastical form and purpose of the hymns, and need not imply different authorship.

The hymns are called Ganj 'Treasure' (1. Ganj vec^c awur cnndean; 2. Ganj hing awur hogoy galstean; 3. Ganj xač^{c}i erkrord awur). They are so called after the long spiritual hymn, originally called K^{c}aroz 'Sermon', of about 100-150 lines, as elaborated by St Gregory of Narek, many of whose k^{c}arozk^c began with the word ganj (e.g., Ganj lusoy 'Treasure of light . . .', Ganj bałjali 'Treasure of desiring . . .' Ganj ank^{c}nin 'Treasure unsearchable . . .', etc.; see Arminē K^{c}yoškeryan, Grigor Narekac^{c}i, Taler ew Ganjer, Erevan, 1981, p. 9). T^{c}lkuranc^{c}i's humns do not begin with the word, but the hymn for Pentecost, beginning Yawēt iskapēs, may be compared to Narekac^{c}i's Iskapēs anskizbn 'Truly without beginning . . .' (K^{c}yoškeryan, p. 141). The ganj usually begins with the description and praise of the attributes of divinity in the first stanza, followed by more specific passages on the occasion celebrated; each stanza closes with a prayerful refrain, or with liturgical passages (instructions for these are put in parentheses in the translation). The refrain in T^{c}lkuranc^{c}i's ganj for Nativity may be compared to that of Narekac^{c}i's for the same feast (Ganj anapakan, K^{c}yoškeryan, p. 131): 'Now intercede for us, we pray, for Christ the King to hasten aid.' The ganj is often accompanied in the Armenian liturgy by shorter spiritual songs, often composed together with the ganj by the same poet; these songs, called tałk^c, are generally 30-40 lines in length, and to them may be added further a mełedi 'melody' or yordorak 'homily'. These shorter songs are generally more lyrical in style than the ganj, reiterating its message (see J.-P. Mahé, REArm N.S. 16, 1982, pp. 464-467).

The hymn for Nativity is written in lines of nine syllables; the two for Pentecost and Exaltation of the Holy Cross are in lines of fifteen syllables. All three are in monorhyme, the ending varying between stanzas. The Nativity hymn repeats the apocryphal belief that Christ was born, not in a manger, but in a cave (Line 7, I Bet^cłahēm i yayrin cĕneal). Lines 44-45 of the Pentecost hymn appear to distinguish between the reactions of the representatives of various nations to the descent of the Holy Spirit, depending upon whether those nations later became Christians. The Arabs are mentioned disparagingly, and they are probably also the tačik Muslims in Line 50 of the third hymn, although by T^clkuranc^ci's time the word was applied also--and, in later centuries, exclusively--to Turks.

Line 18 of the third hymn mentions the tree (car̄ sabekayn) that was the place of hanging (kax-aran, 'gallows' in the translation, properly kaxałan) of the ram which was sacrified in place of Isaac (Sahakayn p^coxan). The ram was in the ancient world the archetypal animal of sacrifice. Christ the Good Shepherd (Luke 15:3-7) is shown carrying a ram, not a sheep, on a marble sarcophagus from Rome dated A.D. 250-275 (Metropolitan Museum of Art Bulletin, Vol. 35, No. 2, Autumn 1977, pp. 76-77 and illustration). In thirteenth-century Armenia are found great tombstones in the shape of rams (see for example plates 14 and 15 in Garegin Cath. Yovsep^cean, Xałbakeank^c kam Pr̄oŝeank^c Hayoc^c patmut^cean mēĵ, 2nd ed., Antelias, Lebanon, 1969). Amongst the modern Kurds, qŭč 'ram' is a synonym of sacrifice in the common proper name Qŭč Alī, which is given to a sick child so that God will not take him.

The ram is, then, a sacrifice, and is connected also with funerary rites and the afterlife. In the Classical world, the Odyssey describes a necromantic rite in which the blood of black rams was poured onto the earth (10.487 et seq.), and Pausanias (4.33.4) describes a statue in Messenia of Hermes carrying a ram; it is recalled that Hermes was the psychopompos, and Christ assumed later this role; in Armenia, for instance, St Gregory affirms that he is the ŝahapet gerezmanac^c 'sovereign of the tombs', in answer to the scornful question of Tiridates (Agath, para. 61). A large stone, perhaps a tombstone, in the shape of a ram's head, was found at Artaŝat (see B. N. Ar̄ak^celyan, Artaŝat I, Erevan, 1982, pl. 68), so the mediaeval tombstones mentioned above may go back to pre-Christian prototypes. The ram was a symbol of sacrifice, connected with the grave and the passage of the soul (Hermes carrying a ram), long before Christianity, and such pre-Christian conceptions seem to have contaminated the Christian image of the Good Shepherd in iconographic representations in the early period of Christianity. It would not be unusual, then, to find some similarly archaic conception or image altering Armenian representations of the ram.

It is a peculiarity of the Armenian translation of the story in Genesis of the sacrifice of Isaac that the ram, described in Hebrew and Greek as 'caught' by its horns (Genesis 22:13: Heb. ayil . . . ne'ephaz ba-sĕbakh

bĕ-qarnāv; Gk. <u>krios heis katekhomenos en phytō</u>ⁱ <u>Sabek tōn keratōn</u>) is in the
Armenian version 'hanging' by them (<u>ew aha xoy mi kaxeal kayr zcaṙoyn sabekay</u>
<u>zeḷjerac</u>^c). As though to underscore the difference between the versions, Ar-
menian manuscript painters depict the scene often, always showing the ram
hanging vertically by the horns from a tree rather than ensnarled or otherwise
caught (e.g., Maten. MS 4818, A.D. 1316, fol. 6a; MS 4922, A.D. 1447, fol. 3a;
MS 4778, A.D. 1462, fol. 1a). The ram is shown hanging also in a bas-relief
at Aḷt^camar, and T^clkuranc^ci calls the tree, as noted above, the <u>kaxaran</u> of the
ram. Perhaps the image of a ram caught thus and hanging in a tree possessed
some significance outside the Biblical story; a fine, richly gilded figurine
at the University Museum, University of Pennsylvania, from a Sumerian cemetery
at Ur, shows a ram standing on its hind legs against a tree, its horns free,
its forelegs braced against trunk and branch. The composition of the scene
is tantalizingly similar to the Armenian, but the details are not exactly the
same, and the extreme remoteness of age and culture would seem to preclude in
any case a direct tradition. But the contest between animal and tree, with
the tree victorious, is a commonplace of Near Eastern art (see E. Porada, <u>The
Art of Ancient Iran</u>, New York, 1965, p. 34) and literature (the Pahlavi-
Parthian poem <u>Draxt ī Asūrīg</u>). The Armenian artist, a mountain man, knew rams
get caught jumping, not crawling, hence, perhaps, the variation.

Line 64 invokes blessing upon the brave (k^caj) king of Armenia; this suggests that the hymn was written before the fall of Sis (see The Lay of Brave
Liparit, above) and the end of Armenian sovereignty. K^caj was an ancient
epithet of Artaxiads and Arsacids; in the lyric poems T^clkuranc^ci used the word
in its other but perhaps related sense, as the name of a supernatural being.

HYMN OF THE SIX DAYS OF NATIVITY (C, pp. 67-69)

> You, who descended from the ineffable light
> And came down to us from Heaven,
> Word apparent in the Father's place on earth,
> Enwrapt in body by the Virgin,
> God and man newly united,
> Man and God in simple unity,
> Born in the cave at Bethlehem,
> Swaddled and placed in the manger,
> Honoured by the eastern Magi,
> Who brought gold and frankincense and myrrh,
> By the intercession of your Mother and Virgin,
> Accept our rational offering,
> We pray thee.
>
> You pitied the creation of your hands,
> The sinful, defeated race of man;
> Serenely leaving your heavenly flock,
> You came to search us out, the lost,
> Returning us to the celestial fold.
> By the light of your body, a lamp aflame,

Sweeping out our defiled house,
You found your image renewed
And conjoined us in communion to the heavenly.
By the intercession . . .

Exalted in honour by the fiery hosts
Who cry 'Sanctus!' with unceasing voice,
Word of the Father at the beginning with God,
You were the fulfillment of the seers
And clothed yourself in the forms of the earth-born,
Description of your Father and light of glory.
What blessing of great wisdom, Lord,
Shall we offer you that is worthy?
Glory, honour, and obeisance to Thee,
Bread of life and our salvation.
By the intercession . . .

Today the highest heavens exulted
And the luminous ones shone.
Today the earth was renewed,
For the strife of evil was removed.
Today the darkness of idolatry
Was banished, perished without a trace.
Pains, imprecations, the labour of birth
Were lifted this day by the virgin Nativity;
On this day the angels with the sons of men
Glorify eternal God.
By the intercession . . .

New blessing was enthroned anew
For the new king born today.
The uncontainable was enclosed in body,
And the limitless was limited,
The timeless in time, and God,
The ancient of days, became a youth.
Fire in the rushes consumed naught,
And the bush was named the Virgin,
For in the beginning man wished
To be God, and reached Him not.
But the Creator came and became man,
Wherewith man was deified.
By the intercession . . .

Being ever from Being, ever born of the Father,
Revealed on earth in man's shape,
'Like rain upon the mown grass' [Ps. 72:6]
As David bore witness.
The Virgin conceived and bore Emmanuel.
He wandered amongst men on earth,
The rock from the mountain, uncut by hand
That shattered Belial.
That which the prophets predicted
He has come today, accomplished all,
Who sat on a throne with the Father
And is ever blessed with the Spirit.
[Remember, etc.]

Saintly, holy mother never married,
Blessed by the ranks of those of fiery form,
Golden trumpet, flowering staff,

Tablet of the Word inscribed with the finger.
Incense-wreathed peak and valley in blossom,
Closed door and sealed fountain,
Throne arrayed for the seat of the king,
Effulgent cloud, and dew sweetly spreading.
Hasten this song beseeching gifts
To the Word of God, made man in Thee!
Intercede with thy word made flesh,
(Remembering him who receives this hymn,
    Lord Yovannēs, who gave and composed it.)
And at His holy future coming
May we unite with the rank of the first-born.
[Have mercy, etc.]

HYMN OF THE FIVE DAYS OF PENTECOST (C, pp. 69-71)

Eternal indeed, with the Father as one, in divinity,
Truly risen, inexhaustible and indivisible,
In omnipotence and power ever lordly,
In the likeness of the Son yet still Creator, in glory,
Competent all things to complete in rationality,
Decisively and inseparably a single God,
Never to be analyzed or known, that came not into being,
Save us, now, O Lord, and justify us, O Spirit of God.
[Amen, etc.]

Existing and creating in the waters, declaring Thee,
Forming angels, rank and place, bestowing grace
Upon created earth, with plants, and flowers, grasses, grains,
Upon broad heaven, with beauty adorned, moon and sun,
Filling the seas with swarms of fish and great Leviathan,
And the air, blessed with shade, with the flutter of soaring birds,
And speechless beasts, those with four feet and those who creep,
Creating Adam, and shaping him to be like Thee,
And breathing into him, thy hands' creation, breath of life,
Granting him boons, bounty shown, to rule the earth,
Save . . .

Lofty to see, Adam in honour excelling,
To him wisdom, priesthood, kingship granting,
Placing him in Paradise with leafy trees of thick green leaves,
And fruits divers of colour unfading and sweet fragrance
With one commandment: to eat of many, but not of one,
But Adam transgressing was swiftly stripped, and dressed in a fig leaf;
Becoming him now in your brilliant light, adorning him anew,
Save . . .

Fount of wisdom, gift of good, mercy granted,
Thou spirit of power, wisdom, and knowledge,
Spirit of mystery, genius of realization,
Guide of awe, God-worship, and success,
The waters parted by thy power, ways opened out.
Finger fatherly and godly, receivest all,
Making all ever worthy as you wish, inexhaustibly,
Priest of the seven eccleasiastical mysteries.
Save . . .

Calling in new voice, fashioning new songs, you start the dance
Melodically, your spirit granted, today descended, resting in the
    Apostles,
Baptizing them, arming them with fire in the body, cleansing in the
    soul,
Promised Son and given Father, Thou entire Lord
Pourest down upon them gifts immense, bestowed in tongues.
Save . . .

Those who saw, prepared in that place, arrived from the realms:
The Parthians shuddered, Medes were amazed, Cappadocians elated.
The Cretans heard, the Arabs hid, others were bound fast;
Peter arose, brought Joel, and revealed the Scripture, [cf. Acts 2:16]
And three thousand affirmed and believed,
And more, number upon number, becoming countless.
Save . . .

Let us give glory to him, the new renewer, the spirit of truth,
Which was with the angel, in evangel to the Virgin, at the descent
    of the Word.
Fashioner of the temple, with the same in being, he made the body
And rested on the Son in the Jordan, in the shape of a dove.
Now they who berated God, the Holy Spirit, are therefore tormented,
And shall not have forgiveness, now and forever.
Save . . .

Let us sing, give glory, and implore Thee, Existent One
And be cleansed in spirit, in body pure, that we may be worthy.
Let us forgive sins and turn our cheeks if dishonoured.
Let us turn to God, do good, say prayers,
Respect our lords, honour our patents, love each other,
And serve, wait upon, and bow to Thee,
Confessing Thee, professing Thee, believing upon Thee,
Be filled with thy grace to guide ourselves and counsel others.
[Remember, etc.]

Holy Virgin Mary, in the rose's form glowing, unfading flower,
I pray of Thee, desirous I ask and burn with supplication,
Striving in soul, I tremble and shiver to be redeemed,
And strive in spirit, chaste of body, gaining strength,
And turn from sin, I sob, in tears to be made righteous.
I believe in my heart, and turned towards Thee I come, gracious,
    caring Mother,
That at the next time, at that coming, then renewed, I will rejoice.
[Have mercy, etc.]

HYMN FOR THE SECOND DAY OF THE EXALTATION OF THE HOLY CROSS (C, pp. 71-74)

In that Eden, garden of delight, of knowledge's tree,
The sprout of blessing, of our forebear's renewal, tree of salvation,
You were the altar and great teaching of the Father's word.
At the gush of the fountains of blood from His side that doused you
Hell defeated, foundations crumbled, and Paradise opened.
Darkness was yoked, light firmed and brightened.
Men became strong, and regained the paradise of delight.
We sing with them, the souls of salvation, new songs of blessing.
Receive, we beseech Thee, the worship of Thy saving cross.

He ascending, upon you by the Father's will, in uncreate body,
Drank of the sponge: bile with vinegar, bitter myrrh--
By tasting of them, made them sweet, against His deceiver.
By the lance's wound He released those born from the side, atoning
   their sins,
Freeing us by sacred commandment and kind deed.
Receive . . .

Staff of the Highest, tree of life, holy cross of power,
Thou crozier of victory, and ark of Noah, cause of salvation,
Tree of the thicket, gallows of the ram in Isaac's place,
Ladder of Jacob, descent angelic, ascent for the race of men,
Tablet-like, precious jewel, and weapon of strength,
By which the nation Israel was saved and freed.
Receive . . .

Awesome sign, stamp of the senses for the children of Moses,
Foundation of the Word, sacrificial altar of the Lamb, Paul's pride,
Mighty protector thou of the sons of men who hoped in thee
With loud songs, worship and prayer on bended knee,
Never blunted sword, great adversary, defender of souls,
Table of the holy bread that gives life to men, atoner of sons,
Receive . . .

Straightener of the straitened, comforter of grief, holy, vivifying
   cross,
Death dealing to the demons, banisher of tragedy, fulfiller of vows,
Bejewelled candleholder in the darkness of this world, light, maker
   of light,
Purifying table of life-giving bread, peacemaking intercessor,
Enlightener of the blind, causing the lame to walk, purifier from
   disease,
Remission of sins, reviver from death, our liberator,
Receive . . .

Moses beheld first the Lord hanging on thee, and named thee life,
Casting the staff that was made a dragon to swallow that of the
   sorcerers,
Staff stretched forth to split the sea and divide it in two,
And blessed tree plunged into the water, making it sweet,
Pointing out the goal and trampling the snake, prefiguring thee,
Marking David, named as light, rescuing him from the archers,
Sung of by Solomon, called the tree of life, made righteous,
Seen by Isaiah, an exalted throne bearing Thee aloft,
Thou holy and blessed cross, praised and exalted, glorified,
Receive . . .[1]

---

[1] These images of the holy Cross seem to be drawn directly from St. Gregory
of Narek, Matean Oɫbergutᶜean 73.a (discussed by J. R. Russell, 'Some Remarks
on Dragons in Armenia,' Journal of the National Association for Armenian Studies
and Research [forthcoming]). Might the mention of the archers be an oblique
reference to the azgn netoɫac 'nation of the archers', i.e., the Mongols?

Thou appearest as a sign, incomparable light, foreteller of the
   coming,
All beings rejoice in thy light and are glad,
But the nation of the Jews remains in shame, who believe in thee not,
And the tač̌ik Muslims, and all who apostatize the saving cross.[1]
But the hosts on high, cohorts of fire, myriads uncarnate
Honouring, rejoice in thee, dance, and are happy: Be our protector,
Make us worthy of thy blessing and thy mercy.
[Remember, etc.]

For the Holy Virgin, mother of the uncreated Word, Holy Mother
   of God,
And great John, the Holy Forerunner, and St. Stephen,
And St. Gregory, our Illuminator with the holy Cross,
May they prayers compose, and supplicate Thee, offering incense.
May they intercede, and be found pleasing to Thee, sole begotten Son.
May they seem sweet, their petitions mingled with our belief,
Thou Word become body, son of the Holy Virgin, crucified upon the tree,
Granting to mankind Thy peace and mercy,
Keeping Thy holy temple secure and serene,
Helping the Holy Patriarch and the brave king of Armenia,
Granting to our nation remission of sins, of every age,
To old and young, granting holiness to all,
And to the sayer of this hymn, Lord Yovannēs, in T^c̆elguran,
And to its receiver, Lord Martiros, and to his parents,
And to the corrector and copyist, forgiveness for their sins.
[Have mercy, etc.]

---

[1]Armenian tač̌ik was applied first to the Arabs, now to Turks--for they,
from the Arabs, adopted Islam. The name, with MIr. suffix in -č̆ĭk, probably
comes from the Arab tribe Ṭai (see H. W. Bailey, The Culture of the Sakas in
Ancient Iranian Khoban, Columbia Lectures on Iranian Studies, I, Delmar, NY,
1982, p. 88).

TEXTS.

In this section are reproduced the following texts of
Tᵒlkurancᵒi in the original Armenian:

1. P: all texts (P I-XXIV and P App. I-V). I am grateful to
Professor Pivazyan for permission to reprint, and for a
clean copy of his book.

2. C: Hymns (Ganjer) 1-3, pp. 67-74. I am grateful for permission
to reprint to His Eminence Archbishop Norayr Bogharian (Covakan).

3. Vasn stełcman ašxarhi 'On the Creation of the World' (VSA),
from Pazmaveb, 1938, pp. 189-98. I am grateful to the Editor for
permission to reprint.

Ա

Արբ՛ե՛կ, արբ՛ե՛կ իմ խում սուրաթ,
Փարք ու պատիւ քո ստեղծողին,
Եղկմական դրախտէն կու գաս,
Օրհնեալ անուն քո նախշողին։

5 Արբ՛ե՛կ արև գարնանային,
Արբ՛ե՛կ աշնան պայծառ լուսին,
Նիստ որ հայիմ լերեզդ ի վեր,
Տեսըդ հերիք է ինձ բաժին։

Տեսըդ բժիշկ է հիւանդին,
10 Առողջութիւն չերմընտուին։
Աչերըդ ծով է ծարուածին,
Բերանըդ քաղցր է քաղցածին։

Մոցդ է դրախտ անմահութեան,
Ի լեռ դարձնէ զելած հոգին,
15 Ոչ մեռանի, ոչ ծերանայ,
Ոչ երեսլին դառնայ դեղին։

Վաղվընէն ում որ հանդիպիս՝
Ի ձար եղնէ գորն ի բարին,
Ով որ սուրաթըդ համբուրէ՝
20 Խնդմով անցնէ զբոլոր տարին։

Զով դու սիրով ի նեռս ձենես՝
Ծաղկի քան գձառըն խրնկենին,
Ով կուռ միջացրդ դիրկ ածէ՝
Կանանչ մրնայ քան զնշդարին։

25 Եւ Յովհաննէս Թուրկուրանցի
Փառաւորէ զնայր և զորդի.
Աղվոր սուրաթն ի հող դառնայ,
Ի հուռն անշէջ իւր սիրելին։

ß

Տեսայ պատկերք մի դեղեցիկ,
Չետ գարեգակն որ լոյս կու տայ,
Տեսայ աչեր զետ ըղծովեր,
Ուներ քան դամպ ու գտարիայ:

5 Ուրակ ճակատ ու ճոխ բերան,
Ծամն ու վարսերն էր հոգեհան,
Ծոգն է լլըգած սպիտակ վարդով,
Մեջքն ու թիկունքն քան զլուռ ճօճան:

Ելից ի լիս հանց հուր ու բող,
10 Որ կու վառիմ գորն ի լըրման.
Մոցայ գւսումըն գոր ունի,
Մնացեր եմ լոկ աշխարհական:

Ասցի՝ Սիրէ զիս, ծով աչեր.
Նայ ատայ՝ Պահեմ գաչս ի վերան.
15 Նիստ որ հայիմ երեստ ի վեր,
Ար՛եկ կացիր ինձ լերեստն:

Ասուաձ ողորմէր ինձ, եղբայրք,
Որ գայն երեստ ինձ պատասխան,
Թէ չէ մնայի ինե կապելու,
20 Ի՛ ի շուրջ կուգի քան զգպայլ գաղան:-

Թէ շատ թէ քիչ ի լետ ձգեմ՝
Միթէ անցնի հուրս ի խափան.
Նա՛յ սէրն ի սիրոս ի ներս կերթայ
Ի՛ ես կու մրնամ մեղաց դարան:

25 Բերեմ անցընեմ գահն ի մրտիս,
Ու գդժոխոց հուրն անվախճան՝
Մի թ՛ագատիմ այս կրրակէս,
Որ յանկասկած ինձ վառեցան:

Խև Յովհաննէս Թուրկուբանցի,
30 Յրէ գխորհուրդըլդ դիւական,
Հան ի սրբաեկ սէր աշխարհիս,
Օրհնէ գանեդ բանն էական:

Գ

Արենըմ՜ան շողշող կրատան,
Քանի սիրով գայերդ ամՅես.
Թէ սէր յիշես ու թէ չյիշես,
Ես կու սիրեմ սրտովս դքեզ։

5 Դու բզվիմՅերըն խորտակես,
Դու բզեերունքն ի Յալ Յանես,
Զով՜դու սիրով Ծատար անես,
Ածանց կրակով դանձնիկն այրես։

Դու օրիՅակ Ես աղեկնուն,
10 Այլ մայըն չէ բերեր դԵտ դքեզ·
Սպիտակ Ճակատ ու սե աչեր,
Լունթֆ ու քարամով լունեբես։

Լար շրթընովլըդ վարդ թափես,
ՅօՅան վզովլըդ բերդեր քակես.
15 Ամէն անՅամըդ Ես դեղեցիկ·
Քաւէլ թէ քեզ նըմՅան դու Ես։

Բայց ինչ անեմ Ճարակ չըկալ,
Մ՜աՅա մեղաց Ներքե եմ Ես,
Յայիմ ի քեզ, Յայիմ ի Նայ,
20 Որ ի Յոդոյ ստեղծեր է դքեզ։

Եե ՅովՅաննէս Թուրքուրանցի,
Զօրն ի բուն ընդ այլ կասես,
Զմարդըն ի կրակըն կու ձդես,
Դառնաս լնուս չոր ւ՜անցընես։

Դ

Հագար ուսուՓ է քեզ ծառայ,
է՞ արեգակն ու խուպ սուրաթ,
Ամէն աշխարհրս քեզ ֆըրէ,
Չերալ չունիս ինկի դալատ։

5 Չըկալ ի քեզ մազ մի դալատ,
Անձամբըդ սուրբ և անարատ,
Ես կու գրեմ զիս քեզ մատաղ,
Ու քեզ ծառայ ու քեզ գաքաթ։

Շուշան, ըռեհան ու մանուշակ,
10 Ու նոնոֆար, է՛ի ծոցն վարդ,
Անմահ ինձոր ու սերկևիլ,
Նուռն ու նարինջ ու կարմիր վարդ։

Մոցդ է դըրախտ անմահութեան,
Անմահական պըտղով դըրախտ.
15 Դու օրինակ ես ուղէկնուն,
Չքեզ սիրէ սատուած և մարդ։

Հաբեղանուն ես որոգայթ,
Քանանայից ակնատ ու կարթ,
Չմիակեցին խեւըրն տանիս,
20 Թէ կացեր է գորն անապատ։

Ես Յովհաննէս Թուրկուրանցի,
Սըրտի մըռոք գականչըդ բաց,
Աստէնս արալ քեզ ձար շուտով,
Անդէն աննուս պսակ փառաց։

Ե

Հանգկուն այլ ո՞վ տեսեր զմրութ,
Տպագիրն ակն ու ճունճար։
Ինձ յանկասկած ի դեմս եկաւ,
Շունչս քաղեց ու զինելքս էառ։

5 Զի թող ի լիս համբերութիւն,
ի տուն ի դուրս չունիմ դադար։
Թէ շատ թէ քիչ ի լետ ձգեմ,
Տեսն ի մրտացս չի գնար։

Բանի տեսնում կու սարսափիմ,
10 Սիրտս ի փորիս կառնու գալար։
Ինձ մեղադիր լե՞ր կու լինիք՝
Ով որ տեսնու չի մնայ արդար։

Չեն ըղթիթեղն ի մոնն ի մոտ,
Ալրունն եկեր եմ, չկայ ճար,
15 Ալ իմ դումրի՝ եա ինչ լինիմ,
Երբ այս խոցոյս դեղն է դիժար։

Խև Յովհաննէս Թուրկուրանցի,
Զորն ի բուն ընդ այլ մի տար,
Հան ի սրտէտ սեր աշխարհիս՝
Տէրն չտանի զկամքդ ի կատար։

Ժ

Լոյս երեսացդ իմ քո փախաք,
Քաղաք Աութան, Չին ու մաչին,
Թէ տեսնուն գվարան Հնդըստան,
Ընդ որ կրթաս լիող կոչին։

5 Հարիւր տարւ Հաբեղանին,
Որ ճեղմակն է դարձեր դեղին,
Կարէ զքրստիկ պատառագին
Ու զքեզ ուզէ առջև խաչին։

Այլ դու դեղ ես ուրախութեան,
10 Որ զքեզ տանին ի պադչանին՝
Զծամդ ու գվարսելըդ ի վայր թողուս,
Զծոցդ բանաս ի մէչ պադչին։

Ով զքեզ սիրէ ո՞նց մեռանի,
Կամ երեսվին դառնալ դեղին։
15 Պարծանք ու վա՞շ քո ծընողին,
Փառք ու պատիւ քո արարչին։

Ո՞նց կարէ գովել զքեզ
Եւ Յովհաննէս Թուրկուրանցին։
Քեզ վայելէ ծառալ խալթի,
20 Պուլդար, չարքաղ, հոռոմ, լաչին։

Է

Թէ մահն չէր ու կամ մեռնիլ,
Ես ունի շատ բան հոգալու.
Չիշխեմ դնէր զիս պիղծ գործոյ,
Վախեմ չգաղրի աչս ի լալու։

5 Ես զքեզ տեսայ նման լուսոյ,
Չէտ զարեգակն որ նոր կելնա,
Սիրաս այրեցաւ բարկ կրակով,
Ես մնայի խև կապկելու։

Ես իմ սրաիս դանակ ածեմ,
10 Զաչքս ճաղի տամ հանելու՝
Աստէս չէնէ զիս ամօժով,
Անդէն բաժին կեր գենհենա։

Բայց չէ շանէր մարդ ի սիրու,
Ոչ փառք առեր ի յաստուծոյ.
15 Աստէս կէնէ զմարդն ամօժով,
Անդէն բաժին կեր գենհենա։

Խև Յուհաննէս Թուրկուրանցի,
Մի՛ դնէր զքեզ պիղծ բանկրու.
Ամէն ոչինչ դատարկ բանի
20 Անդէն համար ունիս տալու։

Ա.

ԱՆա եղե պայծառ դալուն,
Ծաղկեաց այգին ու պաղջանին,
Դաշտք ու լերունք գարդարեցան,
Արօտ ճանին ընձխիլանին։

5 Գունդքըն ծաղկին ու ճետ կապին,
Անուշանայ ճոխ ու քամին.
Զագերն ձայն աձեն յայգին,
Բաղցր կու գայ ձայն պլպուլին։

Կու թանձրանայ շուքն ծառին,
10 Ցորդոր գնայ շուրն ի յառին.
Զթեքն բերեր բոլոր վրգին,
Սիրով խըմէր գանուշ գինին։

Այն վարդենուն դեմ չկայ գին,
Որ այն խընդումն ճանդիպին,
15 Բաւել դրախտն անմաճութեան,
Ցորում եղաւ մարդն առաջին։

Թէ չէր մաճուն օրն ու դժոխն
Ու կամ սարսափ դատաստանին՝
Նայ այս աղեկ էր գինչ ասաց
20 Խե Ցովճաննէս Թուրքուրանցին։

Ի

Ես ձեզ տեսայ սիրով նստած,
Արենման արեգակունք,
Զինչ պաղչայ մի՝ որ կայ ի ներս
Վարդ ու շուշան, պայծառ ծաղկունք։

5 Աչեր ունիք գետ բղձովեր,
Ուներ ունիք քան գժուխ ամպեր.
Շողայր կլաին ու լար շրթունք
Ու մարգարտաշար ատամունք։

Թէ վարդապետան գձեզ տեսնու,
10 Մռունայ զսուունն ու շատ գրունք.
Ամէն անձամբն ի դող եղնու,
Անցրնէ զամառն ձմերունք։

Զեզ ի՞նչ դատար ես դիմանամ,
Երբ դուք ի հալ հանեք զլերունք,
15 Սիրով քակեք բարձր բերդեր,
Ի գիլ հանեք վէմք ու քարունք։

Ես Յոհաննէս Թուրկուրանցի,
Զձեզ կու գովէ, ոսկի տփունք.
Վախեմ թէ հուրն այրէ զհոդիս,
20 Անշէջ ուտեն անքուն որդունք։

ֆ

Աղէկ պատկեր բոլոր և գեղեցիկ ես,
Բիբանդ շաքրով ի լի թուքմակ լեզու ես,
Փոքնդ է կարմիր վարդին, հոտովկ անուշ ես,
Դրբախտ ես ու պաղչալ, ձաղկի նրման ես:

5 Երկինք է՛րկիր վրկալ, որ կու սիրեմ զքեզ,
Չարթիր, դականչող բաց, որ դանդատիմ քեզ.
Եկեալ եմ քեզի ճիւր՝ ասպրնչական ես,
Ընդ է՛ր լիս չես հալիր, դէմ անճաւատ չես:

Թողում զքեզ ի բաց, թանց որ ինձ նենգես,
10 Ժըմով զիս ժողովէ, ձառալ եմ ես քեզ.
Իմ սիրտս ու խիլքս ու միտքս սիրով է առ քեզ,
Եաւ որ սիրես դու զիս՝ սիրեմ ես զքեզ:

Ախատ եմ ես քեզ հաւան, թանց որ դու ինձ ես,
Մառալ եմ քեզ անձամբս, որ զիս չի խոցես.
15 Կամե՛ց դու ինձ հոգի՛, և՛ես կու կամիմ քեզ,
«Հոգիս ասայ դու ինձ, և՛ես կու ասեմ քեզ:

Չանգդ է կաքուղ նրման՝ թէ զիս կու ձայնես,
Դաւլ ու հաւատ և՛երդումն, որ կու սիրեմ զքեզ-
ձակպուկ, ճնխ ու ճարտար, երբ որ դու քայլես,
20 Մանրիկ-մանրիկ ծիծղաա ու շունչս քաղես:

Յորդոր կաց, ուրախս, թէ դալլի տէր ես,
Նալիմ սիրով ի քեզ, ասառւած վրկալ մեզ.
Շուսաով հանխս սիրուս՝ թէ դու անսուտ ես,
Որպէս սիրես դու զիս՝ սիրեմ ես ըզքեզ:

25 Չարխի դեղած նեստով սիրարս խոցիր ես,
Պագով սիրարս լաւէ, թանց որ հաւան ես.
Չոր տուր ծարւած լերգիս՝ փափաք եմ ես քեզ,
Աստ աղբիրի չոր և՛ես կու նալիմ քեզ:

Սիրով աւիրարս լցուաւ՝ ինձ մեղ չի գրնես,
30 Վարդ ես անուշահոտ, շուշան ծաղիկ ես.
Տուր դուն ինձի խրաա՝ դու խիստ խիկար ես,
Բամեալ լադգրս մարդկան՝ ձառալ եմ ես քեզ:

Յոյ ես գարնանալին և՛ անուշ կու ցօղես,
Ի՛ իւթովկ կարմիր խնձոր և՛ անխադամ վարդ ես,
35 Փետրովկ սիրամարգ ու հաւս նրման ես,
Քաջանց տանէն քերած դու ինձ խիլալ ես:

ԺԱ

Յանկարծակի մէկ մի տեսայ,
Որ կու ցողայր գունն լերկսէն,
Թալցայ անկայ ի տեսլենէն,
Շողայր կաժէր լուսն ի վզէն։

5 Աչերն է ծով, ունքն թուխ ամպ,
Մազն է դեղձան ոսկի թելէն,
Ինքրն ճռճար դէտ դուռի ճեղ,
Հևրով այրէր գերկեր ամէն։

Ճոխապնաց, մանրաքայլոդ,
10 Հոգի ի մարմնէ քակող,
Լութֆէն է ծածկեր դամէն աշխարհս,
Շաքար կաժէր իւր քարամէն։

Երբ իմ աչերս ի քեզ դիպաւ,
Նա՛յ վառեցայ դէտ մոմեղէն,
15 Խելապնաց ի վայր մնացի,
Զարհուրեցայ ի տեսլենէն։

Եւ Յովհաննէս Թուլկուրանցի,
Խիստ մի հաներ դոսքդ ի ծրէն՝
Աղէկ սուրաթն երբ մեռանի,
20 Յամքի դնայ գունն երեկէն։

ԺԲ

Աչերդ է թասն ու պետա, դու խորոտիկ ես,
Թաֆուր վարդի ներման անուշհոտիկ ես.
Դու փունջած մանուշակ, վարդ ու ծաղիկ ես,
Տարեն ելուկ ներման կանանչ ուռիկ ես։

5 Դու սպիտակ ու կարմիր խատիչ խնծոր ես,
Անուշ հոտով դու զիս աppենցուցեր ես.
Դու մեղրով շաղրղած նուշ ու շաքար ես,
Կ'թուի բրբի լուսին, դեռ աբեզակն ես.
Դու հալած ու թափած ոսկի արծաթ ես,

10 Զումաշ ես խաղրնի, քանի' գովեմ զքեզ։
Քո սերդ ի զիս դիպաւ՝ ստոյգ կայրիմ ես,
Արե'կ ինձ դեղ արալ, իմ ճարըն դու ես.
Կրտրեր քունն այչեըրուս՝ դու ֆարապաթ ես,
Քո սերդ զիս մոմ արար, դու ինձ պղպաատ ու քար ես.

15 Դու գիշեր ու ցերեկ մեչ իմ սրտին ես,
Անմահ ու անգրող գշոցիս հաներ եա։
Դու ինձ սիրելի ե' ինձ բարեկամ ես.
Զարկաննն գայլ չեր աներ, գինև որ դուն կանեա,
Անfourը ե' անդաnակ գարիւնա հեդեր ես,

20 Դնաց իմաատութիւնս՝ գմիտքս տարեր ես։
Ես եմ ափ մի հողէ, դուն հրեղէն ես՝
Քանի' զիմ այըեցել սիրաա արյունեա.
Յորտեղ որ կա նաթիմ զիս կմոռանամ ես՝
Միթէ զիս դեղեցի'ր, կամ դու կախա'րդ ես։

25 Զայղ քո ծով ծով աչերդ դեղող լյեր ես,
Ունեըդ կամապարական ի վեր քաշեր ես.
Դու ես կանանչ աղբեըը, ի ծով ներմանեա,
Քանի' մեկ լայղ ծովեղ ծարաւ կենամ ես։
Զկայ քեզ ներման, դու աննման ես,

30 Աատամունքդ մարգարին, շաքարբերան ես.
Յաշխարնս խորոտիկ գեմ դու մինակ չե°ս,
Աատըուրս շատ եկեր ե' այլի գայ քան զքեզ։
Ասա' գրանդ, Յովհաննես, չէ°ր կու խնայես,
Դու սուրբ Կարապետի ճորան ու ծառան ես.

35 Սուրբ Կարապետ շատ կու խնդրեմ ըդքեզ՝
Զասողքս և զլասողքս ի չարէն փրկես։

ԺԴ

Դու ես գարնանային վարդ ու բուրաստան,
Աչերդ է ծովեր, խաւմար ու մշատան,
Քո ծոցդ է դրախտ, մրրգաց անդաստան,
Դու ինձ դատաւոր, արա՛ դատաստան։

5   Սիրով մի՛ սպանաներ, ճելլատ էփէնտի։

Սիասաթ ունիս քան զօրաւոր խաչ,
Հբեղէ՞ն ես, հողեղէ՞ն, թէ մարդպադէմ քաշ․
Հիւանդ եմ՝ ողջանամ, երբ ինձ նրատիս յաչ․
Է՛ վիզ շողկտան, է՛ այտեր կակաչ,
10 Թող անփորձ մընաս քան զնշդար կանանչ։
     Սիրով մի՛ սպանաներ, ճելլատ էփէնտի։

Սիրուն չղխմանալ նախահայրն Ադամ,
Վանց սիրոյ եղաւ յեղեմ դրախտէն համ։
Չ'Դաւթայ գործքն լիշեմ և քան զուռ դողամ,
15 Սողոմոն ի սուզ ւ՛ ես այլ ի ճետո լամ։
  Չ'Վահրատ Շիրինէն գլխապարն ես ո՞նց տամ։
     Սիրով մի՛ սպանաներ, ճելլատ էփէնտի։

Աէրըն կու տանի գամօֆն յերեսէն
Ի հաբեղայէն ւ՛ ի վարդապետէն,
20 Երեց, սարկաւագ կու ձգէ ի կարգէն,
Տանի գլխլքն ի գլխուն, գամօֆն յերեսէն,
Շինէ մալամաթ, հանէ յարեէն։
     Սիրով մի՛ սպանաներ, ճելլատ էփէնտի։

Է՛ շահրի սիվաթ և աշխարհի զարդ,
25 Յովսէփ Դեղեցիկ ւ՛ անօրինակ մարդ,
Չինչ ձուկն ի սիրոյ յանկարձ ընկնի կարթ։
Ի՞նչ խըրատ կու տաս, է՛ անժառամ վարդ։
Չի մընաց քեզ ի վրաս այլ գովելու պարտք։
     Սիրով մի՛ սպանաներ, ճելլատ էփէնտի։

30 Է՛ մեղր ու կարագ և կեղևմծ նուշ,
Քո նենգ հայոցին յայՔըն հաջար փուշ,
Է՛ սալվի չինար և բապխտակ թուշ,
Է՛ կամար ուներ և աղեզան կուշ։
     Սիրով մի՛ սպանաներ, ճեLլատ էփէնտի։

:35 Է աղվոր քաղաք, բարձր ու ամուր բերդ,
Է փունջ մանուշակ, կարմիր վարդի թերթ,
Շատոց ես լափեր դու աղմորդու լերդ.
Քանի գովեմ զքեզ՝ կու զօրանաս, բերդ։
    Սիրով մի՛ սպանաներ, ձէլլատ էֆէնտի։

40 Քան գթիթելն ի հուրն որ է ի վառման,
Եկալ որ ալրիմ և մոժիր դառնամ,
Յորժամ տեսալ զքեզ, է՛ արևերման,
Անձրս սարասփեց ու դեռ կու դողամ։
    Սիրով մի՛ սպանաներ, ձէլլատ էֆէնտի։

45 Ո՞վ զքեզ ռամմից ՛ ի լերես ենան,
Ակն սարդեհոն, եաղութ, կարկեհան.
Ինձ մի մեղադրեր, է՛ շան, է՛ սուլժման,
Թէ սիրեմ զքեզ, է՛ կուլի տատման։
    Սիրով մի՛ սպանաներ, ձէլլատ էֆէնտի։

50 Երեսդ է արև, ճակատդ է Զօհրան,
Կրլափդ է ինձնր, ծրծերդ է շամամ,
Չինչ լեղեմ դղրախտի՛ ի քո ծոցդ կան.
Երբ շաքարն ի մոստ՝ ինձ ի Մլար ի՞նչ բան։
    Սիրով մի՛ սպանաներ, ձէլլատ էֆէնտի։

55 Պագ մի լերեսէդ ամէ զենքկան,
Զհապաշ ու զնամման, զՏիլ ու զՀնդուստան.
Երկու վարագ է գին, է՛ Չին ու Խութան,
Պուլդար ու զՃատմբոլ ու շահրի Ճապատն։
    Սիրով մի՛ սպանաներ, ձէլլատ էֆէնտի։

60 Ի՞նչ ընդ ալլ կու տաս, Թլկուրանցի խև,
Խելացդ ես թեթև քան զնրդղրիկու թև։
Ալլ քո աստլուղ կանկնած հագար դե,
Որ չթողու ի մարդ ալլ սրբութեան ձե։
Կարես սիրով շիներ հագար երես սե,
65 Ի՞նչ ընդ ալլ կու տաս, Թլկուրանցի խև։

ԺԴ

Գեղալ բանա՛ր ս ալլ՛ի բանա՛ր,
Ալլ՛ի կստան սիրոյ խարար.
Ծով ծով աչեր ու լուս քընար,
Ունքն է կեռեր քան ըզկամար։

5 Ճակատող է լոյս ու լոյս կուտալ,
Բոլոր լուսին, շամս ու դամար.
Վարսերդ ոսկի թելով քաշած՝
Վերալ անձինդ իշեր հաւսար։

Երեսրդ վառ է ծիրանի,
10 Վարդ, բղեման ու նունուֆար.
Ծոցդ է բաղչալ վարդով ի լի,
Մարգարիտ ատամունքդ շարեշար։

Քո ճայնդ անուշ քաղցրեդանակ,
Բերնեդ ի վալր թափի չուսար.
15 Ալդ քո մատունքն է լուսեղէն,
Ալլ արեդակն լուս չի տար։

Անձդ քո ճոխ բուսեր չինար,
Կու ճռճռալ քան զուր դալար.
Ալդ անստատ ծովուդ նման,
20 Որ դիս ի քեզ արբիր դապար։

Հանցեդ ներսով դիս խացեցիր,
Որ ալլ չունիմ բժշկարար.
Է՛ գեղեցիկ կերպիւ սւրաթ,
Որ է ստեղծած նախշ ու նիգար։

25 Նշաբենի ծառ ես ծաղկեալ,
Պոււղ կուսաս մուշկ ու ամպար,
Բենեց հագնիս ու ծիրանի,
Ծրբերդ ամէն մարգարտաշար։

Քաղաք Խաթալ, Չքն ու մաչին
30 Ու Բուրասյու բերած պաշար,
Ալդ ճանապարհդ, որ կու քալես,
Բուսեր շուշան ու նունուֆար։
Կարմունջ կապած ես ապիկի,
Եւ դետա՛ դինե որախսարար,
35 Ով որ խումէ ի քեզանէ՝
Ուրախանալ սրտով յօմար։

Ար՛եկ իշոււմք ի բադչենին
Եւ բըբուլին անենք նադար,
Որ ի քաֆոււր վարդի սիրան
40 Ի շատ կուպալ քան դդեււնար։

Դարնանալին ամիսն երբ գալ,
Հաւսար ծաղկի չոր ու դալար,
Չքեդ լորդոր գրնացք առնուն,
Ի լեւեևրուն թափին ի վալր։

45 Մարդ որ սիրու կու ճանդիպի,
Նալ քան ըզկրակ կու լինի վառ,

Այլ ոչ ապոթք միտքն կու գալ,
Ոչ լալմաւուր կարդալ և ճառ։

Շրթունքդ շող է լուսեղէն,
50 Պռակեցդ ի վայր թափի չնհար,
Ով որ գմեղաց ճաշակն առնու,
Այլ աստուծոյ չի տայ խապար։

Սէրն գԱղամ դրախտէն եհան,
Ցերկիր ձրգեց ե՛ արար շիւար,
55 Եւ ստուանի ըդնա մատնեաց,
Որ չարչարեաց ամ վից հազար։

Սեթալ որդիքըն խանապկեցան,
Որ ճրգնաւորք էին յոժար՝
Չփողն ու գյնծրդպրյան լսեցին,
60 Ամէնն եկին լսնէն ի վար։

Կինն գԹովհաննէէան գլխատեաց·
Հերովդիաս պղծոյն համար,
Որ նա վառեալ էր ցանկութեամբ,
Փութով տարաւ գկմք քն ի կատար։

65 Սէրն ճանէ գմարդն ի խելաց,
Որ այլ իսկի չրկալ խապար,
Իմաստութիւնըն խափանի
Եւ հէնց գառնալ քան գզիւահար։

Կինն քաղցրիկ գերուց ունի,
70 Բան գոձ քալլէ ե՛ առնու գալար,
Չթիւնքն թափէ լանկարձակի,
Որպէս գակնատ ըռնէ անճար։

Չունքըն քաղդ, դաչքն դեղէ,
Չինք գարդարէ դեռ նշի ծառ,
75 Մէշքն ու պակունքն ծրումէ,
Չմարդիկ ձգէ ի սար ե՛ ի քար։

Դու ստեղծեր գկինն ի կողէն,
Վասն Ադամայ սիրոյն համար՝
Թէ անէցք և բազմացէք
80 Եւ շրշեցէք լերունք ե՛ ի չար։

Դեռ այն սիրոմւ բորբոքին
Այս հողածին մարդիքս շար,
Որ ճանապաց կու պառնկին,
Երթան ի կեր որդանցն յոժար։

85 Թուրկուրանցին գձեգ կապաչէ,
Թէ՛ կնոչ սիրոյն մի՛ տիրանալք,
Որ չգրկէք անճառ լուսին
Ի՛ այլ լատուծոյ չլինի ձեգ ճառ։

ԺԵ

Աստուած անսկիզբն և անսահման,
Անտանելի և անթարգման՝
Զգարունն արար հանց պատուական,
Նրման դրախտին եղեմական:
5 Ծառք և դրախտք կանաչեցան,
Մրգապայծառ զարդարեցան,
Ազդիլականք յորդորեցան,
Մոլ և գնահք ի գնացք եղան:
Զորքոտանիք որ արդիեան
10 Ի գոմերուն՝ զարկին ւ՛ եղան.
Կոզեռ տղայքն կու խաղան,
Զխաղլու տեդաքըն ի շուրջ կու գան:
Սիրոյ տեղենին կու հոխանան,
Վերայ թևին հալին ւ՛ երթան:
15 Աղշկունք գվարսըն կու գիզեն,
Ծեմին, քալեն ւ՛ի հետ ցընծան:
Հաւերտ ամէն ուրախացան
Եւ ի ւրեանց դադարքն եկան.
Մեծունուըն եկին և բուն դըրին,
20 Սադմոս ասցին գտուն ի լըման:
Ունանաչաւն ու բռղնան,
Զումբին ունին լույ քաղցր ձայն,
Գիտեն քարող, գանձեր և տաղ,
Մեղեղեք ու շատ շարական:
25 Արագիլն ու սագն ու բաթն
Եւ շնորորն ուրախացան,
Թլբուլքն եկին փափապանօք
Ի վարդենին Թաւալեցան:
Եոաց երկիր և կակղացաւ,
30 Բիւրք ի բիւրոց ծաղկունք բուսան,
Դաշտունք ամէն ծաղկօք լցան,
Որ ի հոտոյն մարդիկ ցընծան:
Շուշան, կանաչ մուրտ ու մարախն
Եւ մանուշակն ի մի դարձան,
35 Դնացին վարդին երկրպագին՝
Զտեզան ունէին ւրանցին ալամ՝
Այն նարկըզգին հոտըն բուրեաց,
Խաշխաշըն Թագ պաճունեց,
Նաւսաւֆարն ի չըրէն ի դուրս
40 Դեղին կանաչ երևեցաւ
Համտսիւն ի մէջ ծաղկանց,
Որ մայր ասի իմաստութեան,
Եւ բժշկէ գլուրուկ բորոտն,
Եւ երկի յոր համբարձման:
45 Ըզգալականք և բուսականք
Եւ ամենայն որդիք մարդկան՝
Ամենեքան ի մի բերան
Օրհնեն զանեղ բանն էական:

Կակզացան ծառոց ոստունքն,
50 Մէկ ճեղ մէկի մրգունք հասան.
Թութն լառածեաց քան ըզՀալլան,
Կեռասն ադեղ էր ի նման:
Միշմիշն ի ծառն դեղնեցան
Ի՝ այր խնձորբիղ կարմրեցան:
55 Մրգունքն ըզգանձն խոտեցին՝
Մ՜ինչ հասանէ կայր անսասան:
Ընկոզն, լունապն ու կատանան,
Նուշն ու ֆընտուխն քաղցրացան:
Նուսն այլ երաց Հազար ակասն,
60 Ապրասն ի ծառն կախիցյաս,
Սերկևիլն դեղնեցաս,
Խոխն ի կապէն թուլցյաս անխաս:
Նարինջն, թուրինչ, լեմոնքն գալ
ԵՆ զարդմորբուն բուքըն բանալ:
65 Թէ այլ ճեծելտ էր որ անցաս,
Կու գալ խաղողըռն գովական,
Չի սալ ենան գմեզ ի գրախտոէն,.
Յորժամ եներ ըզնալ Ադամ:
Չփակեալ զուղուբն գրախտոին
70 Կրկին խաղողն երաց մարդկան:
Տէր մեր Յիսուս Քրիստոս զգենին,
Առաքելոցըն վերնատան,
Ասէ առէք արբէք լուսով՝
Սա է արիւն իմ փրկական:
75 Ով արբէ զզալ սրբութեամբ,
Ո՜չ ճաշակէ զմաՀ լաւիտեան.
Նա ի լիս ըրնակեացէ
 Եւ եւ ի նման անզրաւեական:
Հոսկ երեկ աւուբք աշնան,
80 Որ է անցուին ամէն սերման,
Դաշոք ի բուսուց զատարկանան,.
Ծաղկունք անցնին ՝ այլ չերեան,
Ծառք ի պաղդղ զատարկանան,
Տերեաթմի լուսող եղան:
85 Հաւերն երամ կապեն ու լան՝
Թէ այլ ո՞վ լինի զարնան արժան:
Թէ շատ ուտեն, թէ շատ խմեն,
Նալ ցանկանան աւոր զարնան.
Աշան նրման է ծերութեան,
90 Մերբք մեռանեն ՝ անցնին զնան:
Պարտ է մեզ սպասել անանգն,
Որ լաւիտեան է անվախճան,
Ու հանապազ օրն է զարնան,.
Փառք ու պատիւ է անխափան:
95 Ով զերախտիքտ զալա չիշէ
Եւ փառա տալ աստուածութեան,.
Ես զիւանաբ ասեմ նման,
Կամ ստանալ անբրատաւան:
Ով զալա պարգես մեզ երես,
100 Դարձեալ խնդրէ այսր փոխան,
Եղպալրասէր, աղօթասէր,
Սուբբ և խոնարն և զգզական:
Թէ զալա պանես՝ նալ աստէն քեզ,
՝Ի անդենին քեզ այլ սեկրական:
105 Եւ. թէ անդարծ մնաս դու մեղող.
Մատնիս հրոյն զինենական:
Ահե Յովնաննէս Թուլզորբնցի,
Լցեալ մեղող թշուառական,
Խնդրէ ի ձենջ սրտի մոզք
110 Հոգոյն ասել զատեր ողորմալ:

ԺՉ

Է՛ մահ, քանի դքեզ լիշեմ,
Կու դողամ ու սարսափիմ ես.
Չրկալ քան ըզքեզ լեղի,
Ի՞ ամենայն լեղոյ լեղի ես.

5 Լեղի ամենայն լեղոյ,
Մի՞թէ դու ի քեզ նմման ե՞ս.
Դրժոխք քան ըզքեզ լեղի,
Եւ լսալ դաՌ ալ դու թերես։

ՍողոմՈՆ լիշեաց դքեզ
10 Եւ ասաց՝ եղո՞ւկ, վայ եմ ես,
Նախատեաց գիմաստութիւն,
Ինքն ի լինքն ասաց՝ փո՛ւ ի քեզ.

Ինչ շահ է իմաստութիւն,
Քան դանգետ աղքատ մեռալ ես։
15 Անմեղք ի լաշխարհս եկի
Ու մեղօք գրնամ սեներես.

ՍողոմՈՆ արքայն ասաց.
Մի՛ ասեր թէ արքայ եմ ես,
Ունիմ շատ դրամ, շատ գանձ.
20 Շատ դարպաս և ոսկի ի ներս։

Ի դուր խրոովեալ գանձես,
Ոչ գիտես թէ ում ժողովես.
Զաշխարհս ես ի գերկդ առեր,
Քեզ ի խոր դժոխք կու փորես։

25 Է՛ մահ, թէ դու քէն ունիս,
Ի՞ Ադամալ որդին կու հանիս.
Կամ մեղաց հարուած ես դու
Ի մահու պլտողէն ծրնեալ ես.

Մովսէս մարգարէ չասես,
30 Ի՞ ի Դավթալ իսկի չամաչես,
ԶԱբրահամ հայրըն տանիս,
Զիսահակ ի հողն աճռնս.

ԶՏրդատ լաթռողն ձգես,
ԶԿոստանդին ի լաշք չբերես։
35 Թէ կանգնէր հազար հեծել
Եւ ժողովք իսկի չի վախսս.

Թէ հագեր է վեց գրեն,
Նետ նետես ի՛ ի թնախն անցրնես.
Տանիս դնալ ի քանտ աճես,
40 Դէմ դրռանն քար մի ձգես։

Արծիւ ես, լերագ թռոշես,
Լաշնաձիգ զիթեղս սարածես,
Զինչ աշխարհս հրգոր մանուկ,
Ի թեիդ ծալըն ծրաճես։

45 Հազար երանի՛ նորա,
Զոր բարի գործով գրտանես.
Հեղեղ բոցեղէն տարեր՝
Ի մեղաց մէջըն դով բռնես։

Յովհաննէս Թուլկուրանցի,
50 Զոր կասես, դալ ոչ խըրատես,
Եօթանասուն ամ լրցեր,
Ի՛ ի մահուն դուռն հասեալ ես։

Ֆէ

Քանի՞ դատիս ի հետ մեղաց,
Է՞ անըզգամ մարդ կատաղած.
Զանչափի չարիքդ որ գործեցիր,
Հերիք արալ, դարձիր մեղաց:

5 Ի լԱղամալ մինչև ի քեզ
Շունչ կենդանի գոք չէ թողած.
Գիտեմ չլսես խրատու գերող`
Մեղաւորաց թ'ինչ կա պահած:

Ալ որ ունէր բերդ ու քաղաք,
10 Դարպասրընի ոսկով ծեփած`
Ցեստոլ եթող դամէնն անտէր,
Ներքև հողուն են պառըկած:

Ալ որ խըմէր գանուչ գինին,
Զինքըրն բրտէր քան դլոզ ուռած`
15 Ցեստալ ըզնալ խիստ ատելի,
Զանուշահոտ դէշ մի ճրգած:

Ալ որ հեձնոլր ձի թարգրավկիգ
Ու թուր քաշէր ամէն դինաց`
Ցեստալ ըզնալ խիստ փոշիման,
20 Երկու փալտի մէջ պառըկած:

Շատ աղջրկունք, կին դեղեցիկ
Մամն ու վարսերն էր լօրինած.
Նոքալ ունին պալժառ հանդերձ,
Չէտ դարեգակն են բոլորած:

25 Ճօճին չ'ոլոր առնին կամաց,
Լինին ամէն մարդոլ սիրած,
Ի մահուն օրն են ատելի,
Գէշ ու դագիր են տեսողաց:

Քրիստոս նստի լաթոռ փառատս,
30 Հատուցանէ վարձ սիրողաց`
Արդարոցըն տալ պրաւակ,
Ի պապշխարող մեղաւորաց:

Ասե Յովհաննէս Թուլկուրանցի`
Սրտի մրտոք զականչրդ բաց.
35 Ասետէս արալ քեզ ճար շուտով,
Անտէս աննուս պասկ փառաց:

ԺԷ

Թէ ըսկի շրկալ սուրբ վարդապետա,
մեզ սուրբ գլրօք խրատ տուէր,
Մանն հերիք է մեզ խրատ,
որ կենդանի զոք չէ թողեր։

5 Ո՛չ թագաւոր և ո՛չ իշխան,
թ'ունին հարիւր հազար հեճճել,
Ո՛չ քահանայ ՝ո՛չ եգնաւոր,
ո՛չ մեծատուն ՝ո՛չ տառապել։

Տեսալ հզօր մեծ թագաւորքն
10 լերկու կանկուն տեղ պատիկել,
Այն աշխարհիւանցում լեգուն
ո՛չ նրշմարանքնրն չէ մնացել։
Այն փափիկասնունդ մարմինն
նրման գիշոյ մրխագալ հոտել,

15 Քակեր զօղուածըն մարմնոյն,
մնացեր փտած կողն ի փայտեր։
Տեսալ գիշխանքն և գմեծատունքն,
որ ահագին քան դշատին ի վեր,
Նա տեր չէին երկու փողու,

20 իւրենքն երկու փող չէն արժել։
Որ ասեր՝ Ես եմ Սողոմոն,
նայ մրշման էր հնագանդել,
Նայ ոտանցըն լուանին,
՛ աչքըն հողով էր լցցուեր։

25 Տեսալ գՀզօր քաջ մանկտրնին,
որ զգագանքն ին սարընցուցեր,
Նայ չունին ճանճի մի ուժ,
ո՛չ առտտուր ՝ո՛չ ալ խոսիլ։
Տեսալ գՀարսունքն և գփեսանին,

30 գեղեցկութիւնն գնացեր,
Եւ ի վերալ գերեզմանին
սարդին իւրեն ոստէն հիներ։
Մայըն որ տքնէր ի նեա տղային՝
վմէ, իմ որդեակս է շատ լացեր,

35 Ի մէկ տատպանին պատիկեր,
այլ տղային գիրկ չէր աձեր։
Եւ յԱդամալ մինչե ի քեզ
գինչ որ ծրներ՝ ամէն մեռեր,
Թէ կալ ի քեզ իմաստութին,

40 դալլ ի մտացդ մի հանես։
Չալս էր տտեսալ սուրբն Գրիգոր,
անձամբ ըզանձն ի խաչ հանես։
Սուրբն Յակոբ դալս իմացալ,
շատ հզնութեանց դանձն տուեր։

45 Գխտաց և դալս Անտոնիոս,
որ ի լերինքն գփաշն առնէր,
Մանեաւ և դալս Պող եգնաւորն,
գկին և դտունն ի բաց թողեր։
Եւ յամննալն սուրբք կշռեցին,

50 և ի լուշինչ են համարեր։
Եւ ամննալն ոք դալս գիտէ,
վալ լիմարին որ չի գիտես։
Ախ Յովհաննէս Թլղուրանցի
հատտտատ ցուցեր օրինակներ,

55 Չանալ փախլեր ի լաշխարհէս,
օրինակացդ լեր ընկեր։

ՓԹ

Քեզ հոգևոր խրատ մի տամ,
Է՞ անպիտան անձն իմ, լլսէ։
Չերդ պաղաքեր ծառ ի արմատ
Ի սրբութդ մէջն պատորուէ։

5 Թէ սէր ունիս հետ աստուծոյ,
Դու զգինին ու գրողն ատէ։
Գինին է մայր ամէն մեղաց,
Որ ամէնայն գիրբք վրկայէ։

Գինին շնութեան է օգնական,
10 Սողոմական ախտրն շարժէ։
Գինին սպանումն գրգռէ,
Թող թէ հոգոյն բանի չար է։

Գինախումն է մաղասկաթ,
Բան զգիւահր ու այլ չար է։
15 Դասուց մի գլուխս ի վայր բերէ,
Չէս մի ցաւօբ վիրաւորէ։

Ու հետ փրնշալ քան զգայլ գազան,
Չկշտանայու չափրն չրգիտէ,
Փախէ զերեսն ի վրայ դնէ,
20 Շունն գրերանն գայ լիզէ։

Ընդ ճամփուն լանքրն քալէ,
Դէշ հեծկլտայ և ծրոկտէ,
Չրագուկն ատի շ՚անդի ձգէ,
Ով հանդիպի նայ հարկանէ։

25 Բարձր պատեր ի վեր հանէ,
Յարշե աշից զարձուցանէ,
Անկից ի վայր գլխիվարէ
Ի՞ ի լարեւն շուտ մի հանէ։

Պողոս առ մեզ կու հրամայէ,
30 Թ՚արբեցութիւնրն խիստ չար է։
Ով գխարբեկնայրն հալալ ատէ,
Չերդ շունն ի տերրն կու հաչէ։

Գինին մարդոյ ամօթ բերէ
Եւ ի լեզոս չար արկանէ։
35 Քան զգինին լեռ հացին.
Երկու է՚իրեբն՝ այլն չան չէ։

Եւ Յովճաննէս կարճապան է,
Ով որ լլսէ նալ շատ շահէ.
Ով զայս խրատիս համֆրն ճաշէ,
40 Չարբքալութիւնրն ժառանգէ։

Ա

Օրհնեալ անուն անմահ բանին,
Որ ի կողէն ստեղծեալ է կին։
Ո՛չ կողն ծուծ ունի, եղբայրք,
Ո՛չ կինն ուղեղ, որ խելք բերէ։

5 Կինն ի լայլոց քաղցրախոս է
ՉԱդամ դրախտէն շուտ արտաքս.
Կինըն ստանին ընկեր է,
Աստուած փրկէ կնկան շառէ։

Կինն ըզԴաւիթ արքայն պղծէ,
10 Ու զՍողոմոն ապականէ,
Զաւրբ Յովհաննէս ա գլխատէ,
Աստուած փրկէ կնկան շառէ։

Կինն չգանի և ո՛չ ոքէ,
Ո՛չ ի շնատ, ո՛չ ի թուրքէ,
15 Զով որ սիրէ՝ հաւատն այն է,
Աստուած փրկէ կնկան շառէ։

Կինն զեղբայրքն խանասկէ,
Զվէճ ու կռուն ի մէջ ձգէ,
Զիւրն կասէ, զալլոց չլսէ,
20 Աստուած փրկէ կնկան շառէ։

Կինն զգեղեցկատիան Յովսէփ
Առնէ իւրեանն որդի անէ,
Յետոյ գսիրան չար սերմանէ,
Աստուած փրկէ կնկան շառէ։

25 Կինն զմանուկն ապականէ,
Ալլվի դառնալ «եղբայրը» ձևէ.
Սիրոն երբ սիրէ՝ զհաւատն ատէ,
Աստուած փրկէ կնկան շառէ։

Կինն դաշք ու դունքն դեղէ,
30 Ու զերեսին կարմիր քսէ,
Զոր հալ ազգիս ընկէ պարտ չէ.
Աստուած փրկէ կնկան շառէ։

Կինն օրհնաց հակառակ է,
Յեկեղեցին երբ որ մտնէ՝
35 Աւետարան մտիկ չլնէ,
Աստուած փրկէ կնկան շառէ։

Կինն աղօթից փափագել չէ,
Զազգականքն կարօտէր է,
Կուզէ գնալ և տեսանէ,
40 Աստուած փրկէ կնկան շառէ։

Կինն թ՝այսօր ապաշխարէ,
Վաղն քանց դե ու այլ գէշ է.
Աչքն արտասուէ, սիրտն արատ է,
Աստուած փրկէ կնկան շառէ։

45 Կինն երգնու, երդմամբ հայթէ՝
«Քեզի համար ինձ մահ տիրէ»,
Մի հաւատար թ՝ի կողուն է,
Աստուած փրկէ կնկան շառէ։

Կին որ գիշած է և բարի,
50 Ի սուրբը կուսանքըն նմանի,
Ապա թէ չար և անդարձ է,
Դիւաց լինի ինքն տեղի։

Յուհաննէսն ի կրնկանէ
Շատ է խմեր տատոռքանէ,
55 Անչափ սրտովս յետ գրգէ,
Աստուած փրկէ կնկան շառէ։

ԻԸ

Իմ սիրտ լաւ չ՚ականչ արա՛,
Որ սիրելի իսկի չկայ՝
Ոչ դրացին և ոչ եղբայր,
Ոչ միակեց, ոչ քանանայ։

5 Այս ժամանակս հանց եթեր—
Ով որ չգիտէ թող գիտենայ—
Չով որ գիտես խիստ սիրելի՝
Հուրն ի ընկենէն ի դուրս կու գայ։

Թէպէտ շինես շատ սիրելի՝
10 Մի՛ հաւատար սրտովդ ի նա.
Ամէն դինաց փորձէ և տես,
Ապա գխորհուրդ աստ նորա։

Շատ մարդ լերեստ է քաղցրախոս,
Ի սիրան հուր կու բորբոքայ.
15 Սեղնի լինի սուտ սիրելի
Ի՛ ի փորձութեանց ժամն ուրանայ։

Քանի ողջ ես գքեզ պահէ,
Դլուխս և անձինդ պէտ արայ.
Եթէ հաքիմ կարի լինիս՝
20 Կևանքդ քան գհով անցնիի՛ ՛ երեքայ։

Ի հետ անգետ սուտ սիրելուն
Ով երկու խօսք առնու և տայ,
Նա ականչուիս հանց քան լէ,
Որ միտ դրնէ և գարմանայ։

25 Ցիշխանաց քաշ և գինաւորն
Ցերակ որ տեղն տրտում կենայ՝
Գայ մօտ ի քեզ նատի հրեշտակ,
Եղէ գնա քան գատանայ։

Դու պահէ գսէրն կանգուն,
30 Սիրտդ սիրով թող լիենայ.
Ատելութեան տեղիք մի տար,
Որ բարութիւն երթայ մնայ։

Ես Ցովհաննէս Թուլկուրանցի
Ազատ պահէ գմիտքն ի վերայ.
35 Մարդասէրն է աստուածատէր,
Եղբայրատեացն է սատանայ։

ԻԲ

Հիմիկ ճարտար բժշկես դու
որմն... քան գմա... բարակ.
Ամէն մարդոյ մարմին է խոց,
բայց քո հոգիդ է խոց առակ։

5 Զբեղ ոչխարաց հովիւ ճանես,
ասես՝ չկայ ինձ նմանակ,
Երբ քան գաշխարՆս ես շա... անմիտ,
է՞ր պարծենաս, է՛ չար մշակ։

Իսկի լինի՞ ճանց խրատտու,
10 որ խրատէ գաշխարՆս երեսակ,
Ինքն ի լամէն խրատէ ի դլրս,
ամէն մարդոյ խախք ու կատակ։

Որ ասես՝ մի սպանանես,
մի՛ գողանար և մի՛ շնար,
15 Նայ սպանանես, շնաս գրկիս,
և միացիր չարեաց զլւակ։

Դու այն կորաց առաջնորդ ես,
մարդկան կապես բեռ ու շալակ,
Դու մատնեմք ի նետ չաւգնիս,
20 բայց թէ խապող ես ն՛ անառակ։

Զամենայն մարդ խրատիս,
քո հոգւդ երես փախերակ,
Զանայ ու գործէ բարի
ու չարին կացիր հակառակ։

25 Փորեցիր քեզ գուբ ու խոր,
որ կու եռալ լորդն ի լատակն,
Վառեցիր ճանց հուր ու բոց,
որ չունենաս իսկի ճարակ։

Մարմին արալ չարեաց հերիք,
30 մի կալ բարոյն այլ ճակառակ.
Աստուած գթած և ողորմած,
Թէ արատսւաց ճեղեր վատկ

...իտ գի լււժ ինիմ (!) մեղաւոր,
ճանց որ չունիս քեզ աւբինակ.
35 ի ճգնութիւնն քեզ մաշէ,
կամ լեր մարմնով նախատակ։

Մի՞ թէ մեղաւք հիւանդացար՝
լապաշխարհիւն առ քեզ ճարակ-
Փորձեցիր գմեղքն ու տեսեր,
40 այլ մի կոխեր այնպես կրակ։

Մի պարծենար իսկ Յովճաննէս
Թլգուրանցի լեգուով արագ,
Ապաեցեր գՆողիս մեղաւք,
միացիր խաւար քան գսե Ճրագ։

ԻԳ

ՏԱՂ ՔԱՋԻ ԼԻՊԱՐՏԻՆ

Հոգևովրդ սուրբ ես և ամբիծ,
Չքեզ էր ընտրեալ տէրն ի երկնից,
Պարծանք եղեր քրիստոնէից.
Ո՛վ մեծ հրդոր քաջ Լիպարիտ:

5 Անձամբրդ քաջ Սամփսոն էիր,
Յորժամ ճօշանրդ հագնէիր՝
Թուրքն ի լանէդ դառնար մոխիր.
Ո՛վ մեծ հրդոր քաջ Լիպարիտ:

Արեգական նրման պայծառ,
10 Երեսրդ լոյս էր կամար,
Բարքրդ բարի, խօսքրդ շաքար.
Ո՛վ մեծ հրդոր քաջ Լիպարիտ:

Բնութեամրդ բարի դէմ աղքատաց,
Լսող էիր վարդապետաց,
15 Քո բանդ լամէն երկիր գոված,
Ո՛վ մեծ հրդոր քաջ Լիպարիտ:

Չանձնրդ տուիր վան օրինաց,
Մէն կանգնելով հագրի դիմաց,
Քո սւրրդ շատ սրտեր երած.
20 Ո՛վ մեծ հրդոր քաջ Լիպարիտ:

Դու հագարաց դէմ պանապան,
Մարդ չէ տեսեր քեզիկ նրման
Ապս հոդածինքս որ լերկրի կան.
Ո՛վ մեծ հրդոր քաջ Լիպարիտ:

25 Սրասլ երկրիս աստղ լուսատու,
Կանգնող էիր լամէն ժամու,
Թուրքն ի լանէդ սարասէր մահու.
Ո՛վ մեծ հրդոր քաջ Լիպարիտ:

Այս չար պանիկն որ քեզ հասաւ՝
30 Քեզի օգնող չրկայր բրնաւ,
Անձնրդ կարմիր գոյն ներկեցաւ,
Ո՛վ մեծ հրդոր քաջ Լիպարիտ:

Չայն չրրաչար մահն որ տեսար,
Կսկիծ է մօրն որ դուն ծրնար.
35 Ալադ ուզքեզ բերան հագար,
Ո՛վ մեծ հրդոր քաջ Լիպարիտ:

Սրասլ երկրին պաղչա ու ձառ,
Դոնք ի դունաց ծադկունք որ կայր՝

Հառաչանօք առին գերար.
40 Ո՛վ մեծ Հրդոր քաշ Լիպարիտ:

Կաթողիկոս և վարդապետ,
Սուրբ քահանայք ամէնն ի Հետ՝
Շատ արտասուօք սրտերն երեր,
Ո՛վ մեծ Հրդոր քաշ Լիպարիտ:

45 Հիւսիսային Հոդմըն Հիմիկ՝
Սարգիս լիշող եղաւ քեզիկ,
Դուն սիւն էիր Հայոց՝ մեզիկ,
Ո՛վ մեծ Հրդոր քաշ Լիպարիտ:

* * *

Է՛ աստուծոյ անունըն օրՀնեալ,
50 Որ անըսկիզբն և անվախճան,
Որ ուժ երեա քաշ Լիպարատին
Եւ զօրացոյց զիւր սուրբ ծառայն:

Ի սուրբ Սարգիս քաջն ի նըման,
Ի սուրբ Թորոս, ի սուրբ Վարդան,
55 Քան ըզՄուշեղ այլ խիստ լաղթող,
Քան ըզՏրդատ Հայոց արքային:

Յորժամ Հեծնւր գիւր ձին վազան,
Ի ձեան առնոլը զրրում ՀօՃան,
Սասանէր ազգըն Թուրքմանաց,
60 Դողալը ամէն Թուրքմանստան:

Պատերազմին չըկայր խափան,
Ամէն տարի տատ և քրասն.
Մ՚ինն ըզԹումանըն Հալածէր,
Արիւն Հանէր դէտ դեա Ջինան:

65 Ապա այլազգն այն աննաեան...
Օձ և կարիճ ի լիծ նըման.

Զերթ քացխով տրիկ չարեօք լըցան,
Ժողովք առին ու ի Սիա եկան,
Մանչալ անուն չարեաց մառան.
70 Մօտ ի քաղաքն եկան Հասան:

Վախսուն Հազար մալդ միրան
ԶրէՃն Հագան ու ի ձին Հեծան,
Զեսուին առին զրրում ՀօՃան,
Թուր և ատար, ու կանգնեցան:

75 Վախսուն Հազար Թուրքմանք եկան,
Զայն ձրգեցին և կատողման,
Հարին ըզփող պատերազմին,
Ըդպուկն ու զնափիրն զդաւ Հարկան:

 Այն անօրէն չար կենդանիքն,
80 Որ են նոքա այլանըրման,

Եւ ի լանէն քաջ Լիպարտին
Զինչ զւռ դողան, առաջ չի գան։

Յայնժամ ասէ սուրբ Թագաւորն.
«Քաջ Լիպարիտ, մեծ գօրական,
85 Հեծելս քեզ համար եկան
Մինչ լայս տեղիս, որ կանգնեցան։

Վաթսուն հազար մարդ կոտրեցիր,
Որ զՄանչակին գռված տղան առիր.
Զթախոքն սուլթանայ բերիր,
90 Զիանունն շատ թախտան (արիր)»։

Քաղցրիկ եւււր պատասխանի,
Թէ «Ես՝ քաղքիս չարբին փոխան.
Բայց չէ պատեհ գլբոց առնել,
Թէպէտ հասաւ ինձ օր մահուան»։

95 Էշ եւ թամբեաց զիւր ձին վազան,
Հազաւ գրէ է՛ ի վերայ ճօշան,
Ի գլուխն եդիր լաղթող վահան,
Ի ձեռն էառ զզռում ճօճան։

Երկրպագեաց սուրբ աթոռին,
100 Եւ ծունր եդիր ամէն խորան,
Փառաւորեաց զեբրողդութին,
Գովեաց զեշխանսրն միաբան։

Հառչեաց, գօրղեակըն համբուրեաց,
Հանց, որ գճեծեն ի լաց եկան։
105 Ասաց. «Որդեա՛կ իմ Յովհաննէս,
Վասի՛լ, եղբայր իմ սիրական։

Փառոք տիկին դու Մանանայ,
Իշխանութին արեներման
Հայեա՛ց պատկերս ի մանկութեան,
110 Որ մի մնում ի հող տապան։

Քաջ Լիպարիտն ասաց զարքայն.
«Հայոց Թագւոր ազնուական,
Հաստատ ի՛ ամուր պահէ զկարմունեն,
Որ ես մնում ի մէջս ու գամ»։

115 Յիշեաց զՔրիստոս անեղաձայն,
Կտրեց ի՛ անգաւ առիւծման,
Զհեծելն արաբ փախրստական,
Ի՛ ի հետ եդիր ընծանմամ։

Լաշկարն արար դիզան դիգան,
120 Հանց որ արիւն գետեբ եղան.
Նա՛ Թագւորբն չարացաւ,
Զհեծելն առաւ ու հետ դարձաւ։

Թուրքաց հեծելն առաջ եկան,
Զկարմունեն տռին ու կանգնեցյան,
125 Երբ Լիպարիտն ի լետ դարձաւ,
Նա չար հեծելն ի դէմ եղան։

Բումբ դբրին ամէն դինագն,
Շատ խոցեցին զլաղթող վըկյան։

Հայեր ողորմ լաչ և ի ձախ,
130 Զոչ ոք գրտաւ իւր օգնական։

Գապանադէմ անօրէնին
Սրբոյն արեան ծարաւէին,
Զիւր սուրբ մարմինն ի հօն թողին,
Զգլուխն առին ի հետ տարին։

135 Նրբ որ հնձեւքն ի լետ գնացին,
Ի՞ապա սրացէքն ի դուրս ելան.
Կրկին առին է՝ի Սիս մտան,
Փաղքին կրրակ գարկին է՝ելան։

Շատ դարպասնին աւեր աձին,
140 Ի՞եկեղեցիքն գանապան,
Երէցկնին գերի տարան,
Սարկաւագունքն մրաբան։

Ձառագայթեց լուլսն ի վեռան
Սուրբ մարմնույն ի հանգրստեան.
145 Քաշ Լիպարիտն ու սիր Յոհան
Քրիստոնէից համար մեռան։

Յորտեղ նստին հաց է՝ի սեղան,
Ժողովք բագում և շատ իշխան,
Յիշեն զնա սուրբ քանանալք,
150 Տէր ողորմի, ասեն նրմա։

Այժ Յովհաննէս Թուլկուրանցին
Կարճ և ողորմ ասաց զայս բան.
Դուք լիշեցէք զինքն հանապագ,
Ցառակ աւէք ի մի բերան։

ԻԴ

Գեղ մի կալր՝ Նարեկ անևն,
Որ լաթոռն էր վարդապետին.
Անզբր տանուտէր մի կալր,
Իւր անունըն Գորգիկ ձայնէն:
5 Ապրեր էր հարիւր տարի,
Չէր եկեր ի ժամատեղին:
Վարդապետն ի վեր եկաւ
Ու խնդիր լողորկեաց Գորգին.
Թէ Գորգ, տանուտէր ես դու,
10 Յէ՞ր չես գար ի ժամատեղին:
Նայ հանց պատասխան ետեւ.
Շատ մշակ ունիմ՝ չըրանեն:
Վարդապետն անեձք էած՝
Զի հանցչի մարմինդ ի հողին:
15 Երեկ բոլորից տարին,
Գորգ մեռաւ ի մէջ գիշերին.
Չորս մարդ ի լուսին առին
Ու տարան եղեն ի հողին.
Ելթըն դերեզման բացին,
20 Հողըն մուտ չերեա Գորգիկին.
Երկաթէ օղեր արին,
Իւր ոտից կռնեն անցացին,
Երեք օր երեք գիշեր
Կախեցին ի պատն արեգին:
25 Անսալ հոտեցաւ մարմին,
Գորգ անկաւ ի մէջ փողոցին.
Ոչ շուն իւր մեձն ուտէր,
Ոչ թռչունք վերոքն անցնէին:
Շատ մարդ, շատ ազգունք ուներ,
30 Նոքա ալլ թէպատիր արարին,
Ելան միարան գնացին.
Յոտն անկան սուրբ վարդապետին:
Վարդապետն լառաչ եկաւ
Ու լիշեց պատառած կենդանին,
35 Ի գաւազանին անկաւ
Ու հարցուՑՖ եւուր մեռելին,
Թէ՛ ոնց ժընեցար ով Գորգ,
Որ եկիր ի լեզեր հողին:
Գորգ ըզգլուխն ի վեր վերուց,
40 Յոտն անկաւ սուրբ վարդապետին.
Տէ՛ր, ինձ թողութիւն արալ,
Զիս մոլար ճանեփով կու տանէն:
Նայ դաշն ի վեր եևան՝
Գո՛րգ, հանդի՛ր ի մէջն ի հողին.
45 Զաւրէնս քեզ համարով տալ,
Որ դատեա ի լաւր կիրակին.
Համբաւն ալլ ի Սիս հասաւ
Սքանչելիք սուրբ վարդապետին:

Նարեկ վարդապետ մի կալ,
50 Որ կուտայ հոգի մեռածին.
Երեք վարդապետ սրացի,
Երեքեան ի Սիս քաղաքին,
Ելան Հանապարհ անկան,
Վարդապետն ի տես կու գային.
55 Եկին դեմ լիրբար առին՝
Կարածէր գոչխարն ի սարին.
Քիչ մի գիշատես էր նա,
Մէկ մէկի հալին ծիծաղին.
Հոգով սուրբ էր Նարեկացին,
60 Իմացաւ զխորհուրդն ի սրտին.
Իմ տէ՛ր, թողութիւն արէք,
Աշակերտ եմ վարդապետին.
Ենթն դալ սարին նստէր
Ու ալյա կենին ուշաբին.
65 Նայ դղալլերն ի վայր ձեներ
Ու հովիւ եղիր ուշաբին.
Չերիքրց գաւադան էառ,
Դեմ լիրբէն խուցրն գնացին.
Երեք աղաւնի քրոնեց—
70 Օրրն պաք էր՝ չորեքքապթին—
Խորրից ու խորվից ադաւր
Ձ եղիր լռոշկ հիւբերբին.
Հրամեցէք բարի հիւբեք,
Ձաշակիմէք ի լյա սեղանին.
75 Նոքալ ձեռք լիրար գարկին,
Դրին գմատն ի վերալ պլռկին.
Անեն. Տէ՛ր, դալլա ինչ արիր,
Օրս պաք է չորեքշապթին.
Կամ կերէք, բարի հիւբեք,
80 Կամ հրաման տուէք որ թոչին.
Երեք վարդապետ սրացի
Ալն խոսիցն ի վայր մացին.
Իմ տէ՛ր, ամ ընց տամք հրաման,
է խորված դլրած սեղանին.
85 Վարդապետն, լառաշ եկաւ
Ու լիշից ըդտէր կենդանին.

Նայ դաշն ի վեր եհան,
Թեաթափի եռուր թեւերբին.
Թե առին եւԹնապատիկ
90 Վերայ գլուխս սուրբ վարդապետին.
Վարդապետն օրհնեց զնայ,
Ու Թրռան հասան երամին։
Երեք վարդապետ սրացի
Յուռն անկան սուրբ վարդապետին.
95 Ասեն. Կաժենաս դու տեր,
Որ հագարբք ըցքեց գովէին։
ԵրԹամք ու խապար տանիմք
Առ Սրասլ ԿաԹուղիկոսին՝
Ծրշմարիտս եւ ըղորդ կասեն,
100 Որ կուտաս հոգի մեռածին։
Բանիբս Յովհաննեան ասաց,
Յովհաննեան այն Թուրկուրանցին.
Ով բանիս իմ ականչ դրնէ՝
Աստուած իւր մեղացն առնէ ԹողուԹիւն։

Ա

ՏԱՂ ՅՈՎԱՆԷՍԻ ՎԱՍՆ ՍԻՐՈՅ

Ես քո սիրուն չեմ դիմանար, հալալ արա, հանսր մեռալ,
Առ ի հետս այլ գոսկի փետտատ, ւ՚եկո՚ փորբէ ինձի թութպալ։

Թող զիս երեն տառայպուլով, որ իմ սիրբատիս բոցրն գոռալ,
Շատ մարդ ի յայս կրրակն րնկնի, չորն երի դալարն ի վրրալ։

Թող լրվանան՚ ըզիս գինով, մորուպ բերեն ինձ քանանայ,
Կանանչ տերերն թող պատանեն՝ տանին թաղեն ի նոր պաղչայ։

Հա՛յ հարամի ու մարդրսպան, հալատն ի քուվզ աշկերտա կու գայ,
Շատ դըրեր ես սիրու զըննտան, դուող ու դըրունքդ է դանարայ։

Զսիրու երեցիր ու սդկեցիր ու քաշեցիր յաչքրդ սուրմայ,
Դարձար դարիւնըս վաթեցիր ւ՚ի ոտվընիդ դըրիր ճինայ։

Քարկոծեցէք զիս խնձորով, քաղցրը լեզւով խոցոտեցայ.
Անուշ գինով զիս խե արիր՝ որ ի ծոցրդ զնտանեցայ։

Այս գիշեր ի յերագիս կրաորրատեցին տիքայ տիքայ,
Գագանք արիւնս կրշտական ու թոչունք ի լաշիս վրրայ։

Վրրաս բերան է առւծու, արիւնըս գետ չուր կը բխայ,
Ով արիւնէս է ծարաւէր՝ թող գայ խրմէ որ լիանայ։

Կրտորրծվորացն լուտիցն ի հող, մէկ հողեկ մի ունիմ ֆետայ,
Իմ ճիկարրս քապաղ հերիք, արիւնս թող գինի լինայ։

Գրլուխս ամպերն ի վեր իշեր ի սիրբատիս լեռներուն վրրայ,
Մաղձրն սիրբատիս մրշուչ կապեր, արեան արցունքս կու ցոշայ։

Կերակրեցաք ի մի սեղան, ու խրմեցաք ի մի կրթխալ,
Մէկտեղ եղաք մէկտեղ նրստաք, ան ժամանակն ո՞ր է ճիմալ,

Մ՞ւր է դավլըղ, ո՞ւր է երգումն, որ րունեցաք գաստուած վրկալ,
ի դատ րնկաք օտարացաք, չարկամն եղե մեզ մաճանայ։

Աստատած մեր չարկըմին չար տայ, որ իւր չարովրն լիանայ,
Թարեկամացըն տայ բարի, մեր բանն ալվալ բարի լինայ։

Աստուած ճամբայ տայ իմ սրտիս, ծառըն ծաղկի ու կանչանայ,
Կամ իմ սրտիս ծառրն րունենի, ճազրն խոսի ու ճրվըլլայ։

Համբերելով գործք կատարի. խե Յովանես, դու համբերէ,
Աստեն լինի գայ իւր կամաւ զինչ ճեռաւոր գինք համբուրէ։

ₚ

ՏԱՂ ՍԻՐՈՅ

Ալսաւր էի խխատ տրբրտում,
Էնկիւենտի էսկի տեբրտիմ. (Նորազվեզաւ հին ցավս)
Կատարեցաւ ընծի խնդում,
Քի խարի սելրանէ կաւլրտում: (Որ յարին զրոսնելիս տեսա)

Ուներ ունէր ունքն կամար,
Զարատիր դաշլարի խումար. (Սև են խումար հոնքերը)
Իսկ եղալ ես նորալ համար,
ԻՀու կուլյուստանլու դէմէր: (Դեմքը լուսին է պայծառ)

Անչապ սէր տվիր ընծի,
Ալ դաւնծա կուլլերինկ կենծի. (Ո՜վ կոկոն վարգերի լավը)
Ալվալ հագար նարընծի,
Էլլէտունկ պենի զարընծի: (Ինձ դարձրիր քնահատ)

Վալրի եղնեու նման,
Տուշուրատունկ կոնկլումէ կու մէն. (Սիրոս կասկած ձգեցիր)
Ակռատ մարգարիտ շարման,
Սէն էլլէ տերտիմէ տերման: (Դու իմ ցավին դեղ արա)

Նման է ծոցդ ի դրախտին,
Կէլ ըջմա՛ կոնկլումունկ թահոր. (Արի սիրաս մի կոտրիր)
Աչացս լյս և իմ հոգի,
Սորբելում ավմբումուղ վախոր: (Թող վայելենք պահն կյանքի)

Նռան հատին ես դու նման,
Զարանֆիլիլէ ըռահ«աճ. (Մեխակ ես ու ռեհան)
Աղվոր ծաղկունքն ի քեղ նման,
Քիմէ պենկզեր նազլու զուգան: (Ում է նման նազլու զուգաս)

Երբ տեսանեմ զքեզ, աննմա՛ն,
Արթըք դալմաղ պենտէ ֆերման, (էլ չմնաց ինձ ճրտմաս)
Աղվոր աչերտ ի ծով նման,
Սէն էլլէ տերտիմէ տերման: (Դարդիս արա դու դեղ դարմաս).

Սուրաթտ է քո բոլոր լուսին,
Զոլ տարտիմէ ղոնծա կուլսինկ (Կոկոն ժպտա թող իմ դարդին).
Եկ մաւտեցիր քո ծառային,
Է՛ գալմ նագիք ու շիրին: (Ով զալում անուշ ու ևբբին)

Ի լայսմ աշխարիա միջին,
Սէնսիկ շեհրի Չին ու մէչին. (Դու ես քաղաք Չին ու մաչին)
Երգողիս Յովանիսին
Ըռահմ էլլէ պաշրնկ իչուն: (Գութ ունեցիր գլխիդ ճամար).

Գ

ՀԱՅՐԵՆԻԿ ԱՍԱՑԵԱԼ Է ԹՈՒՐՔՈՒՐԱՆՑՈՒ
Ի ՎԵՐԱՅ ՍԻՐՈՅ

Ա

Ծառայ այն ճակտին լինիմ՝ մարգարտէ քըլըտինք կու ցողայ․
Անցի թէ պագիկ մ՛առնում, նա տեղիկն է խիստ դալապայ։

Բ

Իմ եարն երկու դուռ ունէր՝ մէկըն դադտ ու մէկն ալանի․
Նըստէր ի դադտուկ դըռնակն, կու կանչէր հալերէն դագալի։

Գ

Ով սպիտակ ծոց ունի, թող լըրջուկ շապիկ չի հագնի․
Երթանք անիծենք քաղաքն որ լեղակն ի մէջն կու բունի․
Պոյաճուն կարասն ալիրի, իւր սիրտոըն թող հալի պատռի․
Պոյաճին ալլ ինչ անէ, իր տարտերն քանց ձերն աւելի․
Երթամ աղաչեմ գասատուած, որ լեղկան ընտիկն անցանի,
Ո՛չ սպիտակ ծոց լուրջ հագնի, ո՛չ մանկան սիրտոըն նըւաղի։

Դ

Կասեմ թէ՝ Աղկեկ ես դուն, նա կասէ թէ՝ Տէրն է սըրեր,
Անցի թէ՝ պագիկ մի տուր, ինքն ասաց՝ պագըս գին ունի․
Անցի թէ՝ պագիղ գին ի՞նչ, նա ասաց՝ պագիս գին՝ հոգիդ․
Հոգեկս ալ հոգիդ ուզե, չէ չասեմ, հանեմ տամ ի քեզ,
Վախեմ թ՛աչերըս ուզես, հապ՝ ինչո՞վ հալիմ դեպ ի քեզ։
Աչեր եօթն ու վեց պիտեր, եօթն ու վեց կամ քառսուն ու վեց․
Մէկունս ալլ աշխարհ հալիմ, ալլն ամէնն ալլ դեպ ի քեզ։

Ե

Երեսղ է սերով մածուն, պագդ անուշ եր քանց ամենուն․
Թեր պագնեմ լայս երեսղդ, որ չերթաս գանգատիս քո նեըուն․
Քո նեըղ ալ շատ վարձք արեր ու կապեր կարմունç գետաերուն․
Դուն ալլ ալդ վարձկունք արա՛, քո մէկիկ աղբոր արկուն։

Դ

Ալբէն մինչև ի քեն գանկատ անեմ եu,
Բարև լէ՞ր չես ի տար, սուտ խոոսվեր եu.
Դիտես որ քո վերալ չար քաշեր եմ եu.
Դու ինձ ոնց կու ենեգես, դէմ անօրեն չեu:

5 Ես ո՞ւմ երթամ գանկտմ, իմ ճարբս դու եu.
Չալդ արեգակ երեսդ լինել կու պանես.
Երբ դաս առաւտուն լուսոյ նրման եu.
Ընդ ալս կու գարմանամ, թէ ինձ լէ՞ր կու խնալես:

Թողի դքեղ ի բաց՝ դու զիս թողել չեu.
10 Ժամ է ինձ ճար արա՛, թէ չէ կորալ եu.
Իմ տունն ալդ չէ ճափալ գոր դու կու քաշեu.
Լաւ քո մխտքն լիմանաս որ սուտրն դու եu:

Ասել ու երդումդ ուր է, որ ինձ արևեր եu.
Ծոար դու դ դալլտա, թեթնեհաւատ եu.
15 Կապուտն է մեզ վկալ, որ կու սիրեմ գքեղ.
Հոդ եմ եu քո ոտիցդ լորտեղ կու կոխեu:

Չաննիկլղ լնեցի՛ ուրախացալ եu.
Դալլիկ նետ ինձ արևր ու մոռացեալ եu.
Ծարտի քար չեմ ՛ երկաթ, որ դիմանամ եu,
20 Միս եմ, կաշի ՛ ոսկոր, զիս լէ՞ր կու հալեu:

Յառաջ զիս խաբեցիր, թէ կու սիրեմ գքեղ,
Նա՛լ լետոլ սուտ ելար, դավլի հալան գքեղ.
Շատոռք են զիս խաբեր, դեմ դու մինակ չեu,
Ողորմած է աստուած, զիս չառնէ անտու:

25 Զարեր շատ եմ քաշեր, դոր քաշ վիտոակ եu,
Պատճաոըն դու եղար, անճապատիկ գքեղ.
Չանսա գարիննա խրմեu՛ բալց կարենալ չեu.
Ռատի լէ՞ր չեu կենար որ կու սիրեմ գքեղ:

Սիրամարգի նման նաշխաճ-փետուր եu,
30 Վարդի նրման գունով աշխաս հալել եu.
Tես քեղ եմ Հնապանդ՝ թէ գինչ որ սաես,
Բամեալ լադդրա մարդկան սարթանըs դու եu.

Ցրնծամ ուրախանամ երբ տեսանեմ գքեղ,
Ի՛ իւծեալ ի սեր քոլին կամ լանդիման քեղ.
35 Փաոս տամ արարողին, որ նորոգեաց գքեղ.
Քարոզս ու շարականս ՛ ուստւլրա դու եu:

Ե

Ախ ինչ կրակ էր դիս այրից,
Կամ ինչ խաւար՝ որ դիս պատից,
Ես վեմ անխախտ էի՛ խախից,
Պողպատ ամուր՝ գէտ չուր հալից։

5 Եկաւ անցաւ ու ճոև քայլից,
ձոճաց ու դմէչքըն կոտրից,
Դարձու ի լետ խոշոր նալից,
Անձըս տեսաւ ու գաճընդից։

Օրն էր շաբաթ լոյս կիրակի,
10 Վերի վանիցն ի վայր կուգի,
Բուրվառն ի ձեռս ու խունկն ի լի,
Սագմոսարանն յանդս ունէի։

Հետ կու գայի, հետ կարդայի,
Թ՛ երթամ հանիմ ճաշու ժամի.

15 Եկի առ հանց կրակի՝
Ո՛չ գրէի, ո՛չ կարդայի։

Մէկ մի հեձեր պոզ պետաւլի,
Եկաւ անցաւ քաջ մուճալի,
Աչեր ունէր Թաւրէգ տանի,
20 Ունեըն գխեըքըս կու տանի։

Խնձոր ձգից, մտիկ չարի,
Մէկ մ՛ալլ ձգից՝ ցաձցաց առի.
—Սէն միսիւրըման, մոլլա դղդի,
Պէն Յովաննէս, քեշիշ օղլի։

25 Խնձորդ ի լիս ի՞նչ բան ունի։

Նորա, նորա, կեաւուր օղլի,
Կնոժուր պիցտոէն մուճալ սօղի,
Պէն միսիւրըման, մոլլալ դղդի,
Սէն Յովաննէս, քեշիշ օղլի
30 Չիբար սիրեԽք խոշ կու լինի։

Յովաննէսին մալըն է տղայ,
Հագեր վալլայ, վրան չուպայ,
Չորն ի վաներն ի ժոռ կու գայ,
Ու խունկ ու մոմ կու խոստանայ։

35 —Սարկաւագի՛, ասէք «մեղա՛յ,
Հաբեղանի՛ Հտէս ողորմեա՛յ,
Միժէ իւր խեըջն ի վերան գայ,
Թ՛ իմ Յովաննէսն ի տուն դառնայ։

Մէկ մի չսաց թէ՛ Հտէ՛ր, մեղա՛յ,
40 Ամէնն «ալլահ» ու «շեկոււլայ».
Յետոյ վայս ճուդական ասացին.
—Այլ Յովաննէսին ճար չկայ։

—Մո Յովաննէ՛ս, ձո ի՛մ տղայ,
Դարձիր ի տուն, ասա «մեղա՛յ,
45 Հոն քո տերտերն կու ճորալ,
Թէ Աշան ընկեր ի ճետ նորա։

—Ա՛լ իմ մարիկ, ես քեզ ծառալ,
Թէ իմ ութատերն զիս ճորալ,
Նալ ես զԱշան ցցնեմ նորա,
50 Քան զիս ու ալլ ընկ կու լինալ։

—Մո Յովաննէ՛ս, ծո ի՛մ տղալ,
Դարձիր ի տուն, աստ ւմեղա՛լթ,
Դու մէկիկ ես, ալլ ճար չըկալ,
Ալլ լինալու ճարակ չըկալ։

55 —Ա՛լ իմ մարիկ, ես քեզ ծառալ,
Զկաթդ որ կերալ, հալալ արալ,
Զխելքս աւին ու խև եղալ,
Յիսնէ ի քեզ ալլ ճար չըկալ։

—Մո Յովաննէ՛ս, ծո ի՛մ տղալ,
60 Դարձիր ի տուն, աստ ւմեղա՛լթ,
Քեզի բերեմ հայու դրստրիկ,
Ըզքեզ օրհնել տամ քանանալ։

—Մո Յովաննէ՛ս, ծո ի՛մ տղալ,
Դարձիր ի տունն, աստ ւմեղա՛լթ.
65 Աշան տաճիկ է անօրէն,
Ա՛ին քո հաւատուն նետ կու շանալ։

Հալ իմ մարիկ, մի՛ տրխմարնար,
Զրկալ նրման գէմ Աշալին,
Լեգուն պիլապիլ, ծայնն դումրրի,
70 Մէշքըն քարալ գէտ ֆռունկի։

Աշան նստեր փանճարալին
Ու խախտ տրատում, ափն երեսին,
Թ՛ այսօր ծեծեց իմ հալր դատին—
Է՛ր կու սիրես գէաչուն որդին,
75 Տես թէ կելնէ մէկ մի կու գա՛լ։—
Ականշըն խո՛ւլ Յովաննէսին։

Խև Յովաննէսն երբ զայն լսեց,
Բռնեց զճանփան ի լուսֆին
Ու գլխիբրաց, գտակն լափին,
80 Գնաց կանգնեց լարշ խանիին։

Բարև երետ Թագաւորին.
Նոքա շուտով գրաբէն առին.

Բանեց ըպոզ ձիւն ագին,
Կաֆալ ասաց ամէն ձարին:

85 Աշան կանգներ ի վերալ թերգին,
Մրտիկ կանէր Յովաննէսին.
Քոփե է կանգներ դեղին հագնողն,
Ինքն՝ զկանանչն ու գծիրանին:

—Մո Յովաննէ՛ս, մտիկ արա,
90 Ի վերալ թերդին ինչ կո խաղալ,
'Եեղնրվո՛ր, ես քեզ ձառալ,
Կանաչվորբին գանուն ասա.
Թէ չէ լինիմ շանհն բագալ,
Թուչիմ նոտիմ Թեիդ վերալ:

95 Պապուս անուհն տահն մօլլա,
Աղբորս տահն քաղբքի շանհալ,
Եւ գիմ անունն տահն Աշալ,
Մէկ ալ քրոչըս՝ Չուլութալ,
Չիմ մօրս անունն տահն Ֆափմալ,
100 Ու հորս տահն դատի մօլլալ:

Ալ Յովաննէսան է քո ձառալ,
'Իու իմ խոցոյս ճար մի արալ,
Թէ չէ խեցալ լեոներն ընկալ,
Չետ մով ի տեղրա հալեցալ:

105 —Մո Յովաննէ՛ս, մզկիթ մանուլ պիտիս,
Մատնիկդ ի վեր կանուլ պիտիս,
Հետ մօլլանուն ժոտ գալ պիտիս,
Ապա ծոցուս տեր կու լինիս:

—Աշա՛լ, սերա ինձ հարամ լինալ,
110 Թէ ալդ բանիրդ հանց կու լինալ.
Աշա՛լ, գտնուս լորդ ի մահուն,
Չինչ շանացիր հետա իմ հալտուն:

Ուլբլ կանոն սադոս ուսալ,
Չան ալ ի քո սիրուտ մոոցալ,
115 Օր մի չասի թէ «տէ՛ր, մեղա՛լ»
Ամէնն՝ «ալլահ» ու «շեյտուլբալ»:

—Մո Յովաննէ՛ս, փոքր ի պոլաց,
Փոքր ի պոլաց, ձանր խիլալ.
Չես տրանար դքո ատոտած,
120 Ու չես լւեր դո մէկ խոսալ:

Գնա շինէ եկեղեցի,
Որ դամ մանում կոշկովա ի նեսա,
Պասկ դնես, զմեզ օրհնես,
Թող քո սրտին կամ քն լինալ:

Բ. ԳԱՆՁԵՐ

= 1 =

ԳԱՆՁ ՎԵՑ ԱԻՈՒԲ ԾՆՆԴԵԱՆ

Ա.

Ցանեղական լուսոյն խոնարհեալ,
յերկնից իջեալ եւ առ մեզ եկեալ,
բանդ որ ընդ Հաւր յերկրի երեւեալ,
եւ ի Կուսէն մարմին զգզեցեալ,
Աստուած եւ մարդ նոր միաւորեալ,
մարդ եւ Աստուած անշփոթ միացեալ,
ի բեթղդահէմ ի յայրին ծընեալ,
խանձարրապատ ի մրսուր եդեալ,
յարեւելեան մոգուցըն պատուեալ,
ոսկի, կընդրուկ եւ զըմուռ բերեալ.
Բարեխաւսութեամբ մաւր քո եւ Կուսի,
զմերս ընկալցիս պատարագ բանի.
Աղաչեմք :

Բ.

Ողորմեցար ծեռաց քոց ստեղծեալ,
ազգի մարդկան, մեղաւք վարատեալ,
զճաւտ քո յերկինս անմօլար թողեալ,
մոլորելոցս ի խընդիր եկեալ,
զոր եւ զըտեալ եւ ի յուս բարձեալ,
եւ յերկնային փարախըն մուծեալ,
ըզճրագ մարմնոյդ լուսով քո վառեալ,
եւ անմաքուր•տանս աւել աձեալ.
Դրըտեր զպատակեր քո նորացուցեալ,
եւ երկնայնոցըն ճաղորդս արարեալ :
Բար.

Գ.

Վերապատուեալդ ի հրաբուն զաւրաց,
անլրելի ձայնիւ սրբասաց.
ի սկըզբանէ Բանդ Հաւր առ Աստուած,
եղեր լըրումըն տեսանողաց.
զգեցար ըզկերպա հողեղինաց ,=

Նրկարագիր Հաւրըդ եւ լոյս փառաց.
զոր աւրհնութիւն բատ կարի մըրաց,
քեզ մատուցուք Տէր բատ արժանեաց.
Փառք եւ պատիւ ՚ւ երկրպագութիւն,
ճացիդ կեևաց եւ մեր փրրկանաց :
Բար.

Դ.

Այսաւր երկինք ի վերուստ ցրնծան,
եւ լուսաւորբըն պայծառացան.
այսաւր երկիրըս նորոգեցան,
քանզի որոմըն չարին բարծան.
այսաւր խաւարըն կռապաշտութեան,
ճայածեցան եւ անճետ կորեան.
ցաւք եւ անէծք, ՚ւ երկունք ծնրնդեան,
այսաւր բարծան ծնրնդեամբ կուսական.
այսաւր ճրբեշտակք ընդ որդւոց մարդկան,
փառաւորեն զԱստուած յաւիտեան :
Բար.

Ե.

Նոր աւրհնութիւն նորոգ բազմացաւ,
նոր արքային որ այսաւր ծրնաւ.
անտանելին ի մարմնի տարաւ,
եւ անսահմանրն սահմանեցաւ՝.
անժամանակն ընդ ժամանակալ,
եւ ճինաւուրցն Աստուած մանկացաւ.
ճուրն ի խրռւ եղեալ ոչ կիզաւ,
եւ մորենի կոյսն անուանեցաւ.
զի ի սկրզբան մարդըն ցանկացաւ
աստուածանալ, եւ անդ ոչ ճասաւ.
իսկ արարիչն եկեալ մարդացաւ,
վասն այնորիկ մարդն աստուածացաւ :
Բար.

Զ.

Էն միշտ յէէն, միշտ Հաւրէն ծրնեալ,
կերպիւ մարդկան յերկրի երեւեալ.
որպէս զանձրեւ ի գեղման իջեալ,
քանզի Դաւիթ այսպէս վրկայեալ.
Կոյսրն լրղացեալ, զՄանուկլ ծրնեալ,
եւ ի յերկրի ընդ մարդկան շրրջեալ.
վէմն ի լեռնէն անձեռին ճատեալ,
եւ Բելիար եղեւ խորտակեալ.

զմարգարէիցն կանխաւ ճառեալ,
այսաւր զթղլորն եկեալ կատարեալ.
որ էր ընդ Հաւր ի յաթոռ բազմեալ,
եւ ընդ Հոգւոյն յախտեանս աւրհնեալ։
Թիշ.։ Եւ եւս.։ Ջանձ.։

Է.

Սուրբ սրբունի մայրդ անհարսնացեալ,
ի հրակերպից դասուցն երանեալ.
սափոր ոսկի, զաւազան ծաղկեալ,
տախտակ բանին, մատամբ ծեռագրեալ.
լեառն խրնկեալ, եւ հովիտ ծաղկեալ,
դուռն փակեալ, եւ աղբիւր կընքեալ.
աթոռ կազմեալ, ուր արքայն բազմեալ,
ամպ լուսափայլ, ցող քաղցրածաւալ.
զերգրս մատոյ, զնրւէրս աղերսեալ,
առ Բանն Աստուած ի քէն մարմնացեալ.
լեր բարեխաւս բանիդ մարդացեալ,
տեսլեան իւրոյ մեզ արժանանալ.(*)
եւ ի գալուստան իւր սուրբ հանդերծեալ,
ի յանդրանկաց դասըն միանալ։
Ոդ.։

C Ganj 2

ԳԱՆՁ ՀԻՆԳ ԱՌՈԻՐ ՀՈԳՈՅ ԳԱԼՍՏԵԱՆ

Ա.

Ցաւէտ իսկապէս, ընդ Հաւր միապէս, եւ աստուածապէս.
եյումն էսապէս, անրսպառապէս, եւ անհատապէս.
ինքնիշխանապէս, հրզոբեղապէս, եւ նոյն միրապէս.
Որդոյ նմանապէս, փառաւորապէս, եւ արարչապէս.
ինքնագաւրապէս, կատարելապէս, բանաւորապէս.
որոշելապէս, անբաժանապէս, միասուտուծապէս.
անորոշապէս, անգիտելապէս, եւ անյեղապէս.
առ հա կեցո զմեզ, Տէր, եւ արդարացո, Հոգի Աստուծոյ։
Ա. . . .։

Բ.

Որ ի չուրս գոլով, ստեղծագործելով, ըզքեզ յայտնելով.
զհրեշտական առնելով, դասիւ եւ կարգով, շնորհիւս բաշխելով.
զերկիր ստեղծուածով, բուսով եւ տրնկով, խոտով բանջարով.
զերկինս երկնային, զարդարեալ զեզով, լուսնով ւ աբելով.
ըզծովըս լրելով, լողական զեռնով, մեծամեծ կիտով.
զաւդս օղակնով, զարդարեալ շրքով, թռուչուն հաւերով.
զագանս անասնով, եւ յորքոտանով, սողունս առնելով.
զԱդամ ստեղծելով, ի տիպ առնելով, քեզ նրման գոլով.
յԱդամ փրչելով, զոր ստեղծեալ ծեռով, հոգով կենդանով.
պարգեւըս տալով, նոխս ցուցանելով, երկրի տիրելով։
Անա . . .։

Գ.

Վեն երեւելով, Ադամ իւր պատուով, զերագանց գոլով.
իմաստ շնորհելով, քանանայելով, թագաւորելով.
ի դրախտին դնելով, բաղմախիտ ծառով, կանաչ տերեւով.
զանագան պրդովով, անթառամ գունով, եւ անուշ հոտով.
պատուիրան տալով, բազմացն ուտելով, միոյն յուտելով.
զոր ոչ պահելով, մերկացաւ փուքով, ծածկեալ Թրգենով.
զնոյն այսաւր գոլով, քո պայծառ լուսով, նոր զարդարելով։
Անա . . .։

Դ.

Աղբեւր գիտութեան, պարգեւ բարութեան, տուրք ողորմութեան.
Հոգիդ զաւրութեան, եւ իմաստութեան, հոգի գիտութեան.
հոգի խորհրդեան, հանձար իմացման, առաջնորդական.
երկիւղածութեան, աստուածպաշտութեան, եւ յաջողութեան.
Քոյին զաւրութեամբ զուրք բաժանեցան, ճանապարքք բացան.
մատրն հայրական, աստուածայնրման, ստանսա զամենայն.
յորժամ եւ յորքան ախորժես զարժանն տաս անհատական.
քանանայական, եաւթըն խորհրդեան, եկեղեցական։
Անա . . .։

Ե.

Նոր ծայնիւ գոչեալ, նոր երգս յաւրինեալ, նուագիւ պար առեալ.
Հոգւոյդ պարգեւեալ, որ այսաւր իջեալ, յառաքեալս հանգեալ.
զնոսա մրկրբտեալ, մարմնով հրայցինեալ, եւ հոգով մաքրեալ.
զորդոյ խոստացեալ, եւ զնաւր պարգեւեալ, քո տեր կատարեալ.
ծիր առատ հեղեալ, պարգեւըս բաշխեալ, լեզուս բաժանեալ։
Անա . . .։

Զ.

Նոքա որբ տեսեալ, որբ անդ պատուրաստեալ, յաշխարհաց եկեալ.
Պարթեւքըն սարսեալ, Մարքն զարմացեալ, Գամիրք հիացեալ.

Կրետացիք լլւեալ, Արաբիք սաքրեալ, է այլք պարաւանդեալ.
զոր Պետրոս ելեալ, զճովիէէլ բերեալ, զգիրն յայտ արարեալ.
որում ճաւանեալ, եւ ճաւատացեալ, երեք ճազար լեալ.
եւս առաւելեալ, թիւ քան զթիւ անցեալ, անսաս երեւեալ:
Աճա ...:

է.

Նոր նորոգաւղին, Հոգւոյ ճշմարտին, փառս տացուք նրմին,
որ ընդ ճրեշտակին, յաւետիս կուսին, լիշանեէ բանին.
կազմող տաճարին, լինէր էակցին, ստեղծանէր մարմին.
առ Թորդանանին, աղաւնայկերպին, ճանգչէր առ Որդին.
վասն որոյ տանջին, որք ճայճոյեցին, զԱստուած սուրբ Հոգին.
եւ ոչ ունիցին նորայ թողութիւն աստ է յաւիտենին:
Աճա ...:

ը.

Եիդ երգեցուք, զեզ փառատրեցուք, լեէդ խնդրեցուք.
ճոգւով մաքրեցուք, մարմնով սրբեցուք, զի արժանասցուք.
ըզմեղբս թողցուք, եւ անարգեցուք, երես դարձուցուք.
յԱստուած դիմեցուք, բարիս գործեցուք, աղօթս արասցուք.
զտեարբս պաշտեցուք, զգծընդս պատուեցուք, զիրեար սիրեցուք.
քեզ ծառայեցուք, սպասաւորեցուք, երկրպագեցուք.
զքեզ դաւանեցուք, խոստովանեցուք, եւ ճաւատասցուք.
շնորճիէ բո լցցուք, զմեզ կանոնեցուք, զայլբս խրատեցուք:
Թիշ.: եւ եւս.: Ջան.:

թ.

Սուրբ կոյս Մարիամ, վարդատիպ փայլմամբ, ծաղիկ անթառամ.
ի քէն ալերսամ, փափաքեալ ցանկամ, բաղձանաւբ տռւիամ.
ճոգովբս տենչամ, սասւսէմ եւ դողամ, զի արժանանամ.
ճոգով ժբրանամ, մարմնով զգաստանամ, եւ կարողանամ.
ի մեղաց դառնամ, արտասուեմ եւ լամ, զի արդարանամ.
սրբոիւ ճաւատամ, առ քեզ դիմեմ գամ, մայրըղ բարեխնամ.
զի ի միւսանգամ, զայլրստեանն յայնժամ, նորոգեալ ցընծամ:
Աղ. ...:

ԳԱՆՁ ԽԱԶՎԵՐԱՑԻ ԵՐԿՐՈՐԴ ԱԿՈՒՐ

Ա.

Ցայն եղեմական, դրախտին փափկութեան, ծառոյն գիտութեան․
տրընկոյն աւրհնութեան, նախնոյն նորոգման, դու փայտ փրրկութեան․
եղեր զենարան, եւ մեծ նեմաշար բանին հայրական․

աղբերաց նոսման, ի կողէն արեան, որ ի քեզ նեղան․
դրժոխք պարտուցան, նիմանց քակտեցան, եւ դրախտին բացան․
խաւարրն լուծան, լուսով նաստեցան, եւ պայծառացան․
մարդիկ զալբացան, եւ արժանացան դրախտին փափկութեան․
երգեմք ընդ նոցայն, նոգւոց փրկութեան, նոր երգս աւրնունւթեան։
Ընկալ զերկրրպագութիւն խայիդ փրկական․ աղայեմք։

Բ.

Որ բարձրանալով, ի քեզ Հաւր կամով, անեղըն մարմնով․
արբեալ րսպունդով, զլեղին բացախնով, դառըն զրմրռով․
զի քաղցր առնելով, իւր ճաշակելով, զայՆմ որ խաբելով․
տիգին խոցուածով, զկողածնին թողլով, զյանցանս քաբելով․
սուրբ պատուիրանով, եւ քարի գործով, զմեզ ազատելով։
Ընկալ ․․․։

Գ.

Վենին գալագան, փայտ կենդանութեան, սուրբ խաչ զաւրութեան․
Դու ցուպ յաղթութեան, եւ Նոյեան տապան, առիթ փրկութեան․
ով ծառ սաբեկայն, խոյին կախարան, Սանակայն փոխան․
սանդունւբք Յակոբայն, էջ նրբշտակական, ելք ազգի մարդկան․
աղիւսանըման, ակըն պատուական, եւ զէն ամրութեան․
որով փրրկեցան, ազգն իսրայելեան, եւ ազատեցան։
Ընկալ ․․․։

Դ.

Անարկու նրշան, դրոշմն ուզգայութեան, Մովսեսի մանկան․
քանին պատուանդան, զառին զենարան, պարծանք պալղոսեան․
զալբեղ պանապան, դու որդւոց մարդկան, որ ի քեզ յուսան․
երգաւք ծայնական, ծունր աղաւթական, երկրրպագական․
սուր անքրթական, եւ մեծ ակողեան, անծանց պանապան․
սուրբ նացին սեղան, որ կեանս տայ մարդկան, մեղաց քաւարան։
Ընկալ ․․․։

Ա.

Ներբողից յարմար, վրշտաց մրխիթար, սուրբ խաչ կենարար.
դիւաց մահարար, վանող զպատահար, եւ ուխտակատար,
աշտանակ զաւճար, աշխարհիս խաւար, լոյս եւ լուսարար.
սեղան սրբարար, ճաջին կենարար, միջնորդ ճաշտարար.
կուրաց լուսարար, կաղաց զնացարար, ախտից սրբարար.
մեղաց քաւարար, մահու կենարար, մեզ ազատարար:
  Ընկալ...:

Բ.

Նախ Մովսէս տեսեալ, զՏէրն ի քեզ կախեալ, եւ կեանք անուանեալ.
զգաւազանն արկեալ, վիշապացուցեալ, զղիւթացըն կրլեալ.
գաւազան ծրգեալ, զծովըն պատառեալ, յերկուս բաժանեալ.
եւ ըզփայտն աւրճնեալ, ի ջուրն ընկեցեալ, եւ քաղցրացուցեալ.
նրպատակ ցրցեալ. եւ գաւձըն կախեալ, զքեզ աւրինակեալ.
Դաւիթ նրշանեալ, եւ լոյս անուանեալ, ՞յաղեղանց փրրկեալ.
Սողոմն երգեալ, փայտ կենաց կոչեալ, եւ արդարացեալ.
Եսայի տեսեալ, աթոռ բարձրացեալ, ըզքեզ վերացեալ.
Սուրբ խաչ դու աւրճնեալ, գովեալ ւ երանեալ, եւ փառաւորեալ:
  Ընկալ...:

Գ.

Երեւիս նրշան, լուսով աննըման, գուշակ գալրստեան.
լուսով քո ցրնծան, եւ ուրախանան, բոլորս եղական.
եւ յամաւէ մրնան, ազգըն ճրէական, լուրթ ոչ ճաւատան.
տաճնիկք մրսրյման, եւ որբ ուրանան, զլապչըն փրրկական.
զաւրբըն վերնական, գունդք ճրաթունական, ճոյլըն անմարմնական.
զքեզ պատոունեալ ցրնծան, պարեալ զուարճանան, եւ ուրախանան.
Սուրբ խաչ յաղթական, նրշան պատոունական, լեր մեզ պաճապան.
արա զմեզ արժան, բոյին աւրճնութեան, եւ ողորմութեան:
  Ցիրեա...: Եւ եւս...: Ջանձինս...:

Դ.

Սրբուճոյ կուսին, Մաւր անեղ բանին, սուրբ Աստուածածնին.
Ծովաննու մեծին, սուրբ Կարապետին, եւ Ստեփաննոսին.
Սրբոյն Գրիգորին, մեր Լուսաւորչին, ընդ Սրբոյ Խաչին.
մաղթանք ճիւսեցին, քեզ աղերս լիցին, ւ առ քեզ ինկեցին.
բարեխաւս լիցին, քեզ ճաճոյացին, որդիդ մշածին.
քաղցրն Թրւեցին, աղայանք սցին, ընդ մերս ճաւատին.
բանդ եղեալ մարմին, որդի Սուրբ Կուսին, խաչեալդ ի փայտին.
տալով մարդկային, ըզխաղաղութիւն եւ զողորմութին.
սրբոյ տաճարին քում ճաստատութիւն եւ անդորրութին.
Սուրբ Հայրապետին եւ քաջ արքային Հայոց աւգնութիւն.
մեր ժողովրդին, ճամայն ճասակին, մեղաց Թողութին.
ծերի եւ տղայի, եւ ամենայնի, տալով սրբութին.
գանձիս ասողին, Տէր Ծովաննիսին, ի Թրլղուրանին.
եւ ստացողին, Տէր Մարտիրոսին, եւ ծնաւղաց նորին.
եւ սրբագրողին, եւ փոխարկողին, մեղաց Թողութիւն:
  Ողորմեաց...:

Vasn steł‑cman ašxarhi (VSA)

«Ումանաւր պատմու(թի(ւն) Յոչանիսի վ(ա)ս(ն) ըսահգձման (աշխարհ(ս)».
Եւ Յովաննէս Երևատ ոգի, որ մակահու Թուրքովրանցի.
Կ(ա)մաւ իմով է ՝ոգ մահ. քանս ժողովեալ ինձ սեշեելի
Ասա կարձաք(ա)ն ՝սասափցցէ. Ցարարածոցն Սովսեսի.
Սեկնեալ (վարգան) վարգապալետ. ք(ա)ղեալ է ՝սարցէն ՝սոգեւլէ։

(Այս ՝ներաձականին տակ, լուսանցքին վրայ վեր‑‑ին գր‑է մը
աւելցած է « վ(ա)ս(ն) ստեղձձ(ա)են ար(ա)ր(ա)ծ(ոց) »):

Սկսասցն է սկեղցն ընկենեալ ըղբան. արասրեք ա(ստու)ա)ծ յաւիաան,
Զոր եւ Սովսէսի սայանեաց, ի ՝ծորեք սինան աււբեւական՝,
Գէ‑ի ՝ որ այլանդագ ձա(ստուա)ծս. բարբանէձմունք որ բարբաւռել‑եան,
Սոլսելք ի բագում ա(ստուա)ծս, ան‑ենա(ա) ՝ ասենեք իոսեցան,
Զոր ինքեն աւեն գեղեսլքս‑, գերկինե եւ գերկեր սաու ելան,
Վ(ա)ս(ն) այն որ մարգարէին. յամա‑ ձանյց նայ գայ ասենային,
Ի ՝սկեղրան՝ արսար ա(ստուա)ծ, ‑են ասերեը եւ ան‑թվակա‑‑,
Ա(ստու)ա)ծ սիայն ասեսակեղրն, ան‑րակ եւ ան‑ասասան,
Երկիեր եր ասենեսյթ, ‑ել եր սեէ. ‑ել եր սեսասան,
Եւ ‑ութրն ձաձ‑եր գ(ասխարի)ս, ‑ել եր սար՝ ստեղձեալ ՝երեեսն,
Եւ որ ասեսասատ սաէ. ‑եէեր գարգ ‑ել եր ‑ոսասան,
Ո‑ ձսաք ո‑ ‑երրեք ո‑ գաս‑եք. ո‑ գեսասնք եւ սյ ‑ոգսկան,
Իսասրն՝ ան‑գ‑ող վ(ե)րայ), սարեսալ ‑ոսք‑ն ‑ոս‑‑ լեսրական՝,
Ան‑ս‑‑գը են ‑րըրի ասենն. եւ ‑որայ որ ան‑ս‑սասան,
Հոգի ա(ստուա)ծս‑յ ‑ր‑ը‑‑ր. ‑ս‑սր‑‑ե‑սվ ‑ս‑րգն ագգ‑ողական,
Զի ‑երալ‑ցեք եւ Յոⅱ‑ե, ‑ոգ‑ սասն ‑ե պա‑ա‑ա‑ական,
Ի ‑կեղրան՝ ‑րսար ‑ս‑ստ‑ա)ծ, ‑այա‑‑ե(թ(ե)‑ է ‑որ‑ ‑եա‑ան,
Եւ ‑(ո(ր))ք ‑ո‑‑ ‑յն ‑ս‑‑՝. ‑ա‑ս‑. ‑րսարեե եւ ‑որ ‑ասսական՝,
Ցեսս‑գ‑րան‑ ‑րս‑տ‑ս‑(թ(ան). ‑են ‑ա‑ս‑ն ‑եգ ‑‑գ‑ ‑ր‑գ‑ան,
‑ս‑‑ ‑ս ‑ր ‑ր‑ր, ‑եսք. ‑է ‑րեր ‑ելեն ‑սս ‑եեր ‑ր‑ր‑ն՝,
Եւ ‑սս ‑(ստ‑‑)ծ ‑եղ‑եէ ‑սս‑, եւ ‑ս‑ր‑ս‑ան,
Եւ ‑ես ‑ե‑ս‑գ‑ն ‑սս‑ն, ‑ս‑ս‑ես ‑ս‑ն ‑ս‑ս‑ս‑(‑սս)‑,
‑ս‑ս‑ ‑ս‑ս‑ս‑ա‑ ‑րե‑ս‑. ‑ս‑ս‑ս‑ս‑‑ եւ ‑ս‑ս‑ս‑ն,
‑ս‑‑ ‑ս‑‑ս ‑ր‑ս‑ ‑ս(‑)‑‑ր‑ն, ‑ ‑ս‑ս‑ յ եւ ‑եգ‑ ‑ս‑‑ս‑՝,
Թե ‑սյս ‑ես ‑ս‑ս‑. ‑ս‑սս. ‑ս‑ս‑ե‑ ‑ ‑ս‑ս‑ս‑ասան,
‑սս‑ ‑ս‑ս‑ե ‑ս‑ս‑ն՝ ‑ս‑ս‑ս. ‑ս‑ս‑ս ‑ս‑ս‑ս‑ս‑ս‑ն,
Զ‑ս‑ս‑ն ‑ ‑ս‑ս‑ ‑ս‑ս. ‑ս‑ս‑ս‑ն ‑ե ‑ս‑ս‑ ‑ս‑ս‑ն,
Ե‑ս‑ս‑ եւ ‑ս‑ս‑ս‑ս‑ն. եւ ‑ս‑ս է ‑ս‑ ‑ ‑ս‑ս‑ն,
Ասա Ք(ր)ր‑յ‑ [7] ‑ս‑ս‑ս‑ե‑. եւ ‑ս‑ս‑ս‑ս‑ս‑ ‑ս‑ս‑ն,
‑ս‑ս ‑ս‑ս‑ս‑ս‑ս‑ս ‑ս‑ս‑ս‑ե ‑ս‑ս‑ս‑ս‑ ‑ս‑ս‑ս‑ս‑ ‑ս‑ս‑ս‑ն [8]՝,
‑ս‑ ‑ս‑ս‑ս‑ս‑ս‑(‑)‑ է ‑ս‑ր ‑ս‑ս‑ս‑ր ‑ս‑ս‑ր ‑ս‑ս‑ս‑ն [9]՝,
‑ս‑ ‑ս‑ս եւ ‑ս ‑ս‑ս‑ս‑ ‑ս‑ս‑ս ‑ս‑ս‑ս‑ս եւ ‑ս‑ս‑ս ‑ս‑ս‑ն,
Ասար ‑ս‑ս‑ս‑ս‑ս‑ս‑(‑‑)‑ս. ‑ եգ ‑ս‑ս ‑ս‑ս‑ս‑ս‑ս‑ս‑ան.
‑ս‑ս‑ս‑ն եւ ‑ս‑ս‑ն ‑ս‑ս‑ս‑ն ‑ս‑ս ‑ս‑ս [10] ‑ե ‑ս ‑ս‑ս‑ս‑ան,
Ասար ‑ ‑ս‑ս‑ս [11] ‑ս‑ս‑ն. ‑ս‑ս‑ս‑ս‑ս‑ծ եւ ‑ս‑ս‑ս‑ս‑ան,
Ե‑ ‑ս‑ս‑ս‑ս‑ս‑ս ‑ս‑ս‑ս‑ս‑թ [12]. ‑ս‑ս‑ս‑սր եւ ‑ս‑(թ)‑ս‑ս‑ան [13]՝,
Եւ ‑ս‑ս‑ս‑ս [14] ‑ս‑ս‑ս‑ն ‑ս‑ս‑ս‑ս‑ն ‑ս‑ս‑ս‑ս‑ս‑ս ‑ս‑ս‑ս‑ ‑ս‑ս‑ս‑ս‑ան.
‑ս‑ս(ս)‑ս‑)‑ս‑ս‑ս‑ս‑ե ‑ս‑ս‑ս‑ս‑. ‑ս‑ս‑ս‑ ‑ս‑ս‑ եւ ‑ս‑ս‑ ‑ս‑ս‑ս‑ս‑ն [15]՝,
‑ս‑ս‑ս‑ս‑ե եւ ‑ս‑ս‑ս‑ս‑ս‑ս‑ս‑ս‑ե. ‑ս‑ս‑ս‑(թ(ի‑ն)‑ն), ‑են ‑ել ‑ս‑ս‑ս‑ան.
‑ս‑ս‑ս‑ս‑(թ(ի‑ն)‑ք), ‑ս‑ս‑ս‑(թ(ի‑ն)‑ք). ‑ս‑ս‑ս‑(թ(ի‑ն)‑ք). ‑ս‑ս‑ս‑ս‑ ‑ս‑ս‑ս‑ս‑ն,
Ս‑ս‑ս‑ս‑ք եւ ‑ս‑ս‑ս‑ք, եւ ‑ս‑ս‑ ‑ս‑ս ‑ս‑ս‑ս‑ս‑ս‑ական,
Զ‑ս‑ս‑ս‑ս‑(‑ս)‑ [16], ‑ս‑ս‑ս ‑ս‑ս‑ս‑(թ(ի‑ն)‑ք), ‑ս‑ս‑ս‑ս‑ս‑ [17] ‑ս(‑ս)‑ք ‑ս‑ս‑ս‑ս‑ս‑(թ(ա)‑ն)՝,
Ն‑ս‑ս‑ս‑ ‑ս‑ս‑ս‑ ‑ս‑ս‑ս‑ս‑ս. ‑ս‑ ‑ս‑ ‑ս(‑ս)‑ն ‑ս(ստ‑‑)ծ ‑ս‑ս‑ս‑ան,
Զ‑ս Պ‑ս‑ս‑ ‑ս‑ս‑ս‑ եւ ‑ս‑ս‑ս. ‑ս‑ս‑ս‑ս‑ս‑ եւ ‑ս‑ս‑ս‑ս‑ան,
‑ս‑ս‑ս‑ս‑ե եւ [18] ‑ս‑ս‑ս‑ ե‑ ‑ս‑ս‑. ‑ս‑ս‑ս‑ս‑ծ ‑ս Բ (2) ‑ս‑ս‑ս‑ս‑ն,
Օ‑ս‑ս‑ն եւ ‑ս‑ս‑ս‑ս [19]. ‑ս‑ս‑ս‑ս‑ս‑ եւ ‑ս‑ս‑ս‑ս‑ակ‑ս‑ն,
Եւ ‑ս‑ս‑ս‑ս‑ ‑ս‑ս‑ս‑. ‑ս‑ս‑(թ(ի‑ն)‑ս) ‑ս‑ս‑ս ‑ս‑ս‑ս‑(թ(ա)‑ն).
Ասա ‑ս‑ս‑ս‑ [20] ‑ս‑ս‑ս. ‑ս‑ս [21] եւ ‑ս‑ս‑ս ‑ս‑ս‑ս‑ս‑ ‑ս‑ս‑ս‑ան,
‑ս‑ս‑ս ‑ս‑ս‑ս‑ն ‑ս‑ս‑ս‑ս‑ք. եւ ‑ս‑ս‑ս‑ս‑ք ‑ ‑ս‑ս‑ս‑ս [22] ‑ս‑ս‑ս‑ան,
‑ս‑ս‑ս‑յ ‑ ‑ս‑ս‑ս‑ս‑յ. ‑ ‑ս‑ս‑ս‑ ‑ս‑ս ‑ս‑ս‑ս‑ս‑ս‑ն [23]՝,
Եւ ‑ ‑ս‑ս‑ս‑ս‑ս‑ս‑ ‑ս‑ս‑ր. ‑ս‑ս‑ս‑ [24] ‑ս‑ս‑ս եւ ‑ս‑ս‑ս‑ս‑ան,
Ասար ‑ս‑ս‑ս‑ն ‑ս‑ս‑թ. ‑ս‑ս‑ս‑ս‑ս ‑ս‑ս‑ս‑ն ‑ ‑ս‑ս‑ն [25]՝,
Զ‑ս‑ս‑ս‑ն եւ ‑ս‑ս‑ս‑ս‑ն‑. եւ ‑ս‑ս‑ս‑ն ‑ս‑ս‑ս‑ ‑ս‑ս‑ս‑ն [26]՝,
Զ‑ս‑ Թ‑ս‑ս‑ն ‑ս‑ս‑ս‑ս ‑ս‑ս‑ս. ‑ս‑ս‑ս‑ս‑ եւ ‑ս‑ս‑ս‑ս‑ան,
Ց‑ս‑ս‑ս‑ եւ ‑ս‑ս‑ս. ‑ս‑ս‑ս‑ն է ‑ս‑ս‑ս‑ս‑ան,
Ե‑ս ‑ս‑ս [27] ‑ս‑ս‑ս ‑ս‑ս‑ս. ‑ս‑ս ‑ս‑ս‑ ‑ս‑ ‑ս‑ս ‑ս‑ս‑ս‑ս‑ն [28]՝,

Խաւարքն չէ դոյու թի(ւն). լոյան է դոյ եւ յոյժ պիտեւան [1].
ի պակասու թե(ան) լուսոյն, տարբերացն ընտուերք զօրանան։
Արեւն ի Հօրով դնա [2]. եւ լուսինն ի սառ սողըման.
Անմոյար մոյորականք, աստեղունք ուստ ուստ ընծանան.
Արեզակն է լուսոյ ակն. եւ լուսին է Բ (2) [3] քերան,
Զլոյան արեզակէն [4] առնու. կամ ծածկոյթ է բացիբբկական։
Սոբա են քանն [5] եւ Հակք. տարբերց [6] եւ աս\ող դուզական,
ժամնուց եւ ժամանակաց. շրջանից կետից Հանգրաստան.
Արեւն յայծեղչիբըն իջևալ. մեզ Հմհռն եւ կեա սուզական.
ի Հարաւ ամտանանայ. ժամանակ պաղոդ Հարըման.
ի Հինգերորդուռ [7] ալուրն. արարէչ ստեղծօղն եական.
Առաջ ծնանիբլ Քրոյն. մեծամեծ կետոք եւ լողական։
Նափ եւ առաքին եկաւ. ծովայնոց վիճրաց լեւաթան.
Օրինակ ստանանայի. ստակէ է օր դաղրատան [8]։
Անթիւ անչամար կետունք, եւ դեռունք ի Քուրա յորոնան.
Ցելնղոցըն ինոմ չունին. ի ծնանեկլրն միչտ մոռանան.
Նղնեկա ե օդային Թաչունք. որ ի Քուրս ունին ընակարան.
ի ծոմե Թոդուն զծնունդս. անինամ ճադն դոյանան [9].
Երկեր Հանեն անասունք. դադանք եւ Թաչունք Թեւական.
Կերպարանք զարմանալիք [10]. զի տեսևալ մարդքէ Հիանան.
Շադիկ եւ արմանք դեղոց. ցանեկլով զապոդչու թի(ւն) տան.
Բայց թէ կերեալ ուտեչով. նայ լինէ տաւթ մահչըան.
Նղնեկա դադանացըն Հոքք. ոչ թէ մարդակերք սռռռան.
ինկլղրանն Հանաջիք է թ. ընդ մ(ա)րդոյ են ըչխանութեան.
Մէնչ չէր մեղդւեցեալ [11] Ադամ. չունեկին որի Թշամակա.
ին\նատւեցես եւ դաչն [12] եւ առֆն. ընդ ոչխարս էին մխարա.
ի պաղող ծտեաց կերեալ. անասունու եւ երէքք ամ(ենայն).
Դադանք սղունք եւ Թաչունք. Հաչա. էին սերով սեռական.
Երեւք [14] են զարդեբք լերանց. եւ Քրոց դետունք ամ(ենայն).
Նաւուրդւոց ե անդատարաց. միբնթո եւ ընտոֆարան.
Ցարւալեղ ե եզնեբւաղան. յուչկավապըն պեղդաոբեւան.
Ի մանք մանն թէ [15] է եւ չէ. ոչ դիտանն թէ կան թէ չկան։
Են ի ստորոտ (ա)խարչ\ին. մաչաչանեղ դապոնք դիւական [16].
Երբ ա(է)ըն ըզմեղ իբրատէ [17]. Ն(ո)ց(ա) ծոռն է դիդ մաչըռան.
է ծով բոլոր (ա)խարչ)ին. եւ անուն է անդընդական.
Եւ ամբք [18] անդի Քուր Հանեն. եւ ոչ ոք ոչ [19] Նաւդ ընծանան.
Զբոլորս որ արար ա(ստուա)ծ .ի պատրհ. մարդոյն ընտոդան [20].
Զէ ի ստեղծանել մարդոյն պատրասեւլ դոցե դամեան\ց.
Ո(ր)դ(եա)ն ոք դ(թ\ա)դ(աւռ)ք. որ սերով առնե մեծարան.
Նախ ըզոունն դարդարէ. պիտոյիւք բարեւաք դամադան.
ի վեզերորդուռ ալուրն. Հարդասէր ՀայբրԼ դղթական.
Առաջ ընդ բնու\թեան որդին. արարացուք զԱդամ մեղ նբման։
Պատկեր ա(ստուծո)յ տասեք. երրակէ Թրչոյն միու(թե)ան).

Զի ենք միար եւ բան չոգի. անձն երրեակ եւ մարդ միական։
Ի՛ նման որ[ ] ն(ո)ր(ա) որ եսամ ք հանձապեկա (թ)ե(ա)ն.
Գիտուն . իմաստուն հոր չար, եւ չոգով անմա( ) բանական,
Թէ անձն չարն[ ] եր միայն. որապ որ ք շեր պատահանական,
Այլ կանլըն միայն րան եր. եղանել դոյցս ամենայն.
Ոչ էր անեղեակ որդին. իորչրդոյն[ ] քո չորն լական,
Զի քանե մերայ քող մեգ, զի դեռաց ք եկղու ք գամ(ենայ)ն.
Քան գրորեր դզից սակզոււածա. Մ(ա)րդզց է, շ ս որ շ ք յա ւել ան,
Զի զե(ո)ւ(ա) րանեւ որար, եւ գաս պատուով մբրական.
Պատեկեր որառց ք նեան[ ]. զզայական դզից ք ե ի ան.
Զի չոգ է յերկրեն առ ս եւ. եւ ֆ ոււ մ րն շ ս ր ք չոգեկան.
Բանա ս ր եւ մս ս ոււ. եւ չոգե ան մ Ju(եի)(ս)(եա)ն,
Շ նող վս ս ոց [ ]. եւ ձ ս ս ս s մեզ ս (ս ս ս)ն(ւ]ս)ն.
Արար ս (ս)ծ դ(ս)դ զ Ա դ ս ս, է պս եկ ս ս ս ւ ս (ս)ք ս ս ս ս.
Զ ս ս է Զ (6) դ ս ս դ ս ս ս. ի ս ս ն ս դ ս ս ս ս եւ ս ս.
Ն ս ս ս ս ս չ ս դ ս, մս դ չ ս է ս ս ս ս.
Հ ս ս ս (ս)ք ս ս ս ս ս [ ]. Ն ս ս ս ս ս ս չ ս է Մ(ս)ս դ ս ս [ ].
Լս ս դ ս ս ս ս ս ս ս. եւ ս ս դ ս ս ս ս.
Զ ս ս ս ս ս ս ս ս ս, ս ս ս ս ս ս ս ս ս.
Զ ս ս ս ս ս ս ս ս ս [ ]. եւ ս ս ս ս ս ս ս ս.
Ս ս ս [ ] է ս ս ս ս ս. եւ ս ս ս ս ս ս ս.
Ի ս ս ս ս ս ս ս ս ս [ ]. ս ս ս ս ս ս ս ս ս.
Զ ս ս (ս)ս ս ս ս ս ս. ս ս ս ս ս ս ս ս ս [10].
Ք ս ս ս ս (ս)ս ս ս ս. ս ս ս ս ս ս ս ս ս,
Ս ս ս ս ս ս ս ս, ֆ(ս)ս ս ս ս ս ս եւ ս(ս)ս ս ս ս.
Ն ս ս (ս)ս ս ս ս ս. ս ս ս ս ս ս եւ ս ս ս ս ս [11].
Ս ս ս ս ս ս (ս)ս. եւ ս ս ս ս ս ս ս ս ս.
Ս ս ս ս ս ս ս ս ս. եւ ս ս ս ս ս ս ս ս ս,
Զ ս ս [12] ս ս ս ս ս ս. ս ս ս ս ս ս ս ս ս.
Ս ս ս ս ս ս ս. ս(ս)ս ս ս (ս ս)ս ս ս ս ս,
Ն ս ս ս ս (ս)ս ս ս ս ս, ս ս ս ս ս ս ս ս ս [13].
Ք ս ս ս ս ս ս ս ս [14], ս ս ս ս ս ս ս ս ս [15],
Ս ս Ju ս(ս)ս ս է ս ս ս ս [16] ս ս ս ս ս ս ս.
Ն ս ս ս ս ս ս ս, եւ (ս)ս ս ս ս ս ս ս ս,
Թ ս ս ս ս ս ս ս ս ս, ս ս ս ս ս ս ս Ju(ս)ս ս.
Ս ս ս ս է ս ս ս ս ս. ս ս ս ս ս ս ս ս ս,
Ք ս ս է ի ս ս ս ս ս. ս ս ս ս Զ (6) ս ս ս ս,
Ս ս ս ս ս ս ս(ս)ս ս ս, ս ս ս ս ս ս ս ս ս [17],
Ի ս ս ս ս ս [18] Մ(ս)ս ս ս, եւ ի ս ս ս ս ս(ս)ս ս ս ս,
Զ ս ս ս ս ս ս ս ս [19]. ս ս ս ս ս ս ս ս ս [20],
Ֆ ս ս եւ Ք ս ս ս Ս ս ս ս [21], Ն ս ս ս ս ս ս ս ս,
Ս ս ս(ս)ս ս ս ս ս [22], ս ս ս ս ս ս ս ս ս,
Պ ս ս [23] ս ս ս ս ս ս ս. ս ս ս ս ս ս ս ս ս.

Իշանեն [1] Քուրթն ի ելանեն, եւ հարթեն հոբ եւ պատուճան,
Մաանեն ի ծոց յերկիր․․ ի ներբոյ երանց ընժման։
Փիսոն Յեննաւոն ելանե, ի յաբելելից հեսփասեան,
Գոյ ի հապերշահ Հնդկաց․ որ ոսկին է ոգերստական։
Զոր ձերԺնաւեձք պայհեն․ եւ ոսկին է այն բուստական,
Զկողչեն հարաւոյ պատ, և ի կարմիր ծովն առնե զդպրան։
Իսկ ոնեն որ ոստոսկ ոստ․ կայծ կարմիր նա է կարկեհան։
Նոյ ի դեշեբի պտանեն․ զե վառե եւ է [4] անշիջան։
Զկապե ոբ թագուցանել [5]․ կամ ծամծկմն [6] առնել դոստան [7],
Դաշանակբն ծիրանեն․ զեզինանե այն է շափերայն։
Գեհոն ի լուսին ելանե․ որ բին․ կողթն հարաւան,
Հաստանեն զինֆովախա․․ Նզիստոս [8] նռվա օրանմն [10]։
Հահշեն գատա է Տերեիս [11]․ ելանե զեգշեն ողորեան,
Հաստանեն բգՄիշամգ Աստքոսանեն [12] ացհգինան։
Ի ներբոյ ներեկոնեն․ ատ ե Նֆրատ յերբար ժմանեն։
Ոլորասոմ աք գեսջի ք․ մաստեն ժոֆյն Պարակական։
Նֆրատ ի Կարնոյ եննե․ եւ Ոսիմանին [13] ի յերկոսական,
Շատ գեսը մասնեն ի նա․ բագոմ Քոբք յերբար ժմանեն,
Նզ ասոսամծ զբ(ա)բզն [14] ի զգրասնն․ զե զգրասնկն ի զորս արոսան,
Գործեբ եւ պահել բզֆն [15]․ յարասբշեն աստֆն հրամծեն [16]։
Գործեբն է ինամ մանեն, ի յեկոսզ մոֆից [17] պասշոսան։
Կամ թէ երկերգած եննեբ, արսբենն [18] զգսոսեբն [19] բնկոսան։
Պասոսբեբոսզ ասոսա)ծ մ(ա)զգբն․ բսոզգբն թ(եսմ)ք գեծզ յայբական։
Բոլոս զգբբսեբոսֆն սպասզն [20] ոսեբոսզ է բզգ բասսական։
Գֆսոս թե(ան) սպասզգզն [21] ֆսֆ․ Հեզ լեցգե [22] սպասծսս ի բնզ [23] ժմնեն։
Մեբգ եֆն Ազգսմ է Նֆայ․ անստասստ եւ անզզոսզական։
Յեոս մեզանեզոյս ասստ, զմեֆֆ)են[24] բզբ(ս)ոսզգ գբոսզան,
Զ ի մեզգֆն զգգՀսզ [24] բֆբֆ, թէ ֆստոսզմանֆ գֆսեննեն։
Նսեն ստոսանս [25] զՍզզ(ա)ֆ զսբզգսբեբ ֆսսոֆ մեբսան,
Նզ Հեզֆսմֆբգֆսֆ եֆնսզ․ զսsֆնֆ [26] յյֆ Թզոսսոսքսն [27]։
ՅսյֆսֆսՖ նս զոֆբֆ ֆսսբեսզ․ եւ սսս բֆսֆն[28] բնսսսան,
Պսսզֆ ֆսոսսբֆս նֆս [29]․ թէ ստնֆմ զգֆգ բֆֆ զոսսսան։
Նսֆս նս զֆֆսս սսզֆսզ․ ՍզֆսսՖ զսս նֆ ֆֆսսսսան։
Ասֆն թէ ոֆֆֆ սսսսզ․ նս ֆզֆ սզգոսֆֆ սս Նֆսս։
Կսս թէ սսսզսսֆֆն սսֆֆ․ ո(ս)ս(ֆֆ) զֆֆ բսզսմ բՀսսսֆս [30],
Կսս զֆֆ բֆֆ(սս)զ [31] սսշսսֆսսս։ ի ֆֆֆ [32] բսզ ֆսսֆսսս։
Ասսզ թէ ֆսզֆս զֆսֆֆ․ ֆ սսս զսսֆՖս [33] սս(նֆս)։
Զֆ Հֆս ֆսսֆֆ [34] սֆֆսս, սսսզֆս [35] ս(սսս)ֆ է սֆսֆ։
Ասսզ զսֆ(նֆ) ոսֆֆ․ բսզ ֆ ի ֆսֆֆֆ զֆսս թֆ(սՖ)։
Նֆսսզ յֆսֆ ոս․ թէ սֆ է ստֆ մսֆ։
Կսսնֆս սս ֆֆս զյֆսյ [36]․ զֆսսսսսս սս ֆսսս։

Այլ ա(ստուա)ծն[1] անափ եկեր. և եղև ա(ստուա)ծ պետական։
Ի որ[2] հաճոյ թուեցաւ սուտ. մեղքն է միշտ աչաց հաճական.
Զի սուտ խորամ պարծեցի. զփառս և զպատիւ մեծութե(ա)ն։
Եւայ ի անդեառ եկեր[3]. և Ադամ ի սերն ի կնկան[4].
Մերկացան անձ(ա)ռ[5] լուսոյն, և մնացին յոյժ թըշուառ(ա)կ(ա)ն։
Եօթըն չարիք[6] գործեցին, և յա(ստուծո)յ այնով հեռացան,
Զխորհուրդ տ(եա)ռ(ն)ըն ցրուեցին[7]. բանսարկուին դրին[8] յանդիման։
Զբան տեառըն սուտ գիտացին. և օձին բանին հաճեցան.
Զբարոյ բարին չյիշեցին. և օձին[9] հաւանեցան։
Կերեալ զպատուիրանն անցան. գող ա(ստուա)ծանալ կամեցան.
Ի հարցանելըն ա(ստուծո)յ. լիրբ և անպատշաճ խօսեցան։
Զոր պարտ էր արհայմարհել. հայհոյել և ատել նախատան,
Նա զկինըն լաւ հաշուեցաւ. քան ըզդրախտն և զփառսն տէր(ա)կ(ա)ն։

Տունք. Ճարխր[10]։

Խընդիր մին գողի արար. նա Գ (3) յառաջ մատուցան.
Հանին զպատճառն յա(ստուա)ծ. և եղեն որդիք կորստեան[11],
Եւթըն պատիժ պատժեցան. ըստ եւթից[12] մեղացն յանցըման.
Վ(ա)ս(ն) այն քրտունք և վաստակք. գործ և երկիր անէծ[13] կոչեցան։
Տրտմութ(եամ)բ երկունք ծնընդեան[14]. յա(ստուծո)յ նզովս ընկալան,
Մերկացան զշնորհս և փառս[15]. և ի դրախտէն. արտաքս ընկեցան[16]։
Ա(ստուա)ծանալ ոչ հասին, ընդ մահու մահուամբ դրեցան[17],
Երկինք էին կաւեղէն, լոյս էին խաւար դարձան։
Անմահ մնալոյ[18] էին. ի կենաց ի մահ փոխեցան,
Ի փառս[19] ի պատիւ էին. անասնոց անբան նմանեցան։
Դրախտ անժառանգ մնաց[20]. զի չունէր զայլ ոք մնացական,
Ո՜հ[21] թէ զինչ պատահեց(ա)ւ, վայ մ(ա)րդկ(ա)ն մեծի կորըստեան։
Թէ անմեղ կերեալ էին. և անպատճառ վ(ա)ս(ն) ա(ստուա)ծութե(ան),
Կամ թէ ուր մեղայն լինէր. չլինէին յոյժ մեղադրական։
Զըղջմամբ սուգ էառ ա(ստուա)ծ. զի ա(է)ր էր և հայր գթական[22].
Սուք[23] առին զօրքըն հրաբուն. ամ(ենայն) դասք հրեշտակական։
Սուք[23] առին գազանք սողունք. և անասունք թռչունք[24] ամ(ենայն),
Զի տեսին զարքայն իւրեանց. վայ և եղուկ և յոյժ լալական։
Թէ անմեղք մնացեալ[25] էին. աճէին ի դրախտն[26] եդեմեան,
Լցուէր դրախտն[26] և երկիր, և փոխումն իբրև զենովքեան։
Զի թէ ընդ մեղօք անկան, աճեցին դեռևս յուռացան[27].
Որչափ և եդէմ դրախտին, որ անանց և անապառական։
Զպատճառ աճմանըն գիտէ. որ բանիւ արար զամ(ենայն).
Ո(ր)պ(էս) կոչն Ադամա[28]. էր ծընունդ անաշխ(ա)տակ(ա)ն։
Հեռացաւ մ(ա)րդն ի յա(ստուծո)յ, և ա(ստուա)ծ դեռ հայր գթական[22],
Արար հանդերձ մաշկեղէն. և զգեցոյց զԱդ(ամ և զԵւայն։
Իբրև զմի ի մէնջ[29] առեալ, չէ հեղնել և ոչ ոխ մախնական[30],

Այլ մ(ա)րդ էինելզյ խոստումնին. առ յապա բանին կատարման։
Հան զն(ո)ս(ա)՚ արշակելաց. եւ հանզլզ զրախտին բնակելգան,
Զի մինս հայլոյին է նա², է պապՃատա պապշխարբո(թ)ե(ա)ն։
Ա.հին անեձբ թե.ամթամփ. հղակլբ առզայր մահիման.
Զի զմ(ա)րզն՚ նա ՀՈզ արբաջ. եւ է՚ լանՀբն ունելբ զաստուծան³։
Յետ ելիզն Լ (30) ամեան. Հրբաման առին ձՀբնզեան,
Ոեան՚ նախ զբբզ(ց)է՚ Կայեն. զմ(ա)բզապան որզին կբբբամեան։
Ապա եւ զարզգբն ՄԱբԵլ՚. եւ եղե նա Լ (30) ամեան։
Զոբ եւ ք(ա)Հ(ամ)յ կաբզեաց.. եւ պատեւ առաՃնորգու[[ե](ա)ն։
Աեեբ թե բաբբ էինեբ. եւ գաբձոզ միՀտ արբաբոբ[ան։
Կբբկին մատեեբ է զբախան. եւ անանՀ միացբ⁹ յ(ա)ւ(ի)տ(ա)ն(եա)ն։
Խբբամեբ Աչ(ա)մ զորբեան. կեալ պատբատա ա(ատու)ա)ծ սբբու[թ](ե)(ա)ն,
Հանել պատարագ բաժին. ա(ատա ծ)յ տաւաբին բաբու[ե(ա)ն։
Մատոզ պատարատ ԱբԵլ. եւ եղե ա(լ)ա)ն բնզունելկան,
Մատոզ եւ Կայեն ոչ լաւ. եւ չեղե այն Հաճզական։
ԱբԵլ զատանղ զբնսբն¹⁰. եւ յոմ(ա)բ Հաօբ¹¹ կամական։
Իսկ Կայեն զանաբզն յոբզեաղ. անսպաս¹² անսպատյաՃական։
Ցոբեաթ չբբկալատ ա(ատա ծ)ծ. Հեաղատ եզբայբբբո[թ](ան)¹³։
Ասեբ սա է զբախան եբ[եազ.. եւ եա լինեմ արբաբտ միաՃական։
Ե:[թ]²³ մեղբ առաբ Կայեն. եւ պատփբբ bԸ [[թ](ա)(ե)կան։
Զբնձայն որ անաբզ մատոզ. եւ նախան Ը՚Ղ եզբայբին(թ)ե(ա)ն)։
ԱբԵուն որ անապատ Հեզեաղ. մեզբբն նոբ ան(ատա ծ)ն ՚ա)ե(ա)ն։
Ի աբԵաԵբ Հարախեաղ զեբկեբ. աութ¹⁴ ձեզ(ա)յն ե[թ]զ տրատական¹⁵։
Լբբբո[(կա)ո]բ պատատականԵն. մի [թ]է. ե՚ն էզեմ պատՀայ[ան։
Զի մ(ե)բ տաբգանեբ զ[ոմ[. է պատ Ճատա պապՀխարբո[ե(ա)ն։
Առատ ա(ատա ա)ծ բՈզ Կայեն. թԵ անՀզr ՄատԸ¹⁶ կայական,
Չեձատ եՒ եբեբատ զոբատ. զատբԵեբեն¹⁷ ապզԵ մ(ա)բզզ(ար)ն։
Բոբոբ մարմնոզ բոբատբո. եւ Հեբեն բեզ տեզ Հանզ[բատմean։
ԵզԵբբբ¹⁸ բուսաեեբ է զլոխտ. զզ Կայեն լինեբ Հայոհեկան:
Եւ որ սպանանեբ զԿայեն Ե (7). եւ[թ]Հաոռ¹⁹ պատտմ[ի կբԵ ²⁰ այն,
Զոբ Քբ՚Եզեզ²¹ կրբեան. Կայեն ապԵբբԸ ²² ամ(Ենա)զn).
Եւ Կայեն ²³ զնZ[վոմ]բ ձ[ատ ²⁴. եւ որզԵբ մ(ա)բզգան կոշեղան։
Ննոմբ բզգայեո է զատ. Նա բզ[Մաբպ[տեԵ[Հարո [(ե(ա)ն.
ՄազատեԵ[զԾատ[ատ. ապզ եւ[[²⁵ ապԵբբ Կա[թ[նեՆ։
Գամեբ Բ (2) կԵն ունեբ. ան(ուz)ե ²⁶ մերզ Հարո[[ե(a)ն։
Գամեբ ԸՂ կանայb տատեբ. խաբխոԵԵ[բ զ ոբ[ատ ա(ատ]բ ձու[(ե(ա)ն:
ՇեազԵb Ը[բ ապզԵb ԱԵ[ ]ay. որ որզՒբ ա(կան)[ն ան[ան]ե[ban.
Ի ԱԵlա ծ[ա] ²⁷ զ[ա]չ[բ. եբբա[[բbzra[եզե [ա] զ[ւա]։
Ի է Ա[զ[ ][թ]ծ[²⁸ թbbէ[, որ աբա[բ [[p]ov ᴮ զ]ab[]ruṇ[[ան),
ԱԵֆն ա[բ]][[br եւ[ʣա[bo[[. ունա[z] կ]ab]ay] [Հaro[(ān),
ԱՒ[ba]]] Ը[[բ]ap[z]Ե[Ա[b[a]y. եւ[եզ[e]զ[ն]b. եւ ²⁹ կam[zan।
Ի[k]Կa[yen]la[l]oz[ ]tate[b. ara[bz[ ]a(ata)ծ [p]la[zak]an.
Ա[ta]za[la]na[z][n]ko[z]z[e]mazen]b[n]ṇ̌]ir]or]ma[Հ[ean։

Այր Կամաւք եսպան զկայեն. ոչ թէ սա է թունն ներովբեան.
Եւ խոստովանէք կանանցն. որ շկրբէք զպատոիծ[1] Կայինեան
Դարձյոյց մեզ յաղգէն Սեթայ. եւ յԱգ(ա)մ ի նախինին էւայն.
Կ(60) ուսաք եւ զուսաք ուեեէք. որ անուանեցն չեն երևեան[2].
Իսկ Ագամ զԱԼԹ ծնաւ[3]. որ ձնզգացն եղեւ սիրման[4].
Ի ի ԱԼԹա ծնաւ[5] Ներովս մարդ բարի արման բարութ(եան);
Ներովս[6] յուսապայ յա(ստուա)ծ. թէ իննումով է եւ չայր գլմակաան[7].
Եա ոչ ժոսանաս զմէզ[ ] այս տաս, յաուուրն յարութ(եան).
Փկչումիս[ ] որ մերկեաց Ագ(ա)մ. զնգն Ներովս . Ներովբ ընկալան.
Սորա տրարեին բզգերս. եական զայիզ յուցական;
Հոգւոց[10] եւ Տասգ է ճաշ. իսմասանգն է գործբական.
Իրրեւ զա(ստուա)ծ է տեակղ. բարճրուբեան խորագ զիսական.
Իան զոսկի ընեեք է սա. իան զարճմաբ եւ այլ պետեւեա.
Իան զականա է պատուեկան. եւ ապբիբ[11] սա անմասէուբան;
Ցինչն չարբիբ եւ երեսուն աս են[12]. Ագամայ օր մնեելուբան.
Ի եղիս եւ ի ժ. (10) ամին. եւ ԱԼԹայ էըաս վազբնան[13];
Հայբիբ եւ իննսուն ամագ. զՆերովս ծնաւ զԿայնամայն[14].
Ներովս եեա ՆովԲն Բբւով[15]. ժամանեագ օբն մաբգ(ան).
Կայնան[16] զՄապաբեէլ ծնաւ[17]. եա զԲաբէգ բզչայբն ներովբեան[18]
Իսկ Ցաբէգ ծնաւ[17] զեեովբ. պաբգամիա եւ ա(ստուա)ծագան;
Ներովբ Ագամայ լբուա. Թէ մեգբն է պատոտա մաչըան.
ՄՆաւ[17] զՄաԹուսաղայ. ակեղբ արաբ ապաչբաբու(թ)(ա)ն;
Ոչ մեա ա ոչ պատոլ[19] եկեբ. բայց մեայն գիտա ու բուսական.
Եա չաբ ի գլուեին[20] եգ աստ շիմ արբման երկեեղ աեսու(թ)(ա)ն;
Սա ատագ գոբծ յաբու(թ)եան. զոստեակբ ատեկան գպբատան.
Կայգէ աեբ բեբբող զաբբող. բասնեաբբբն չբեւասնական;
Փոբեւաց աեբ ա(ստուա)ծ բգեա. ի գբաբետն որ անմասական.
Ջի մի սպանանէ Կամաւք. յաբագսբծ մաբբիմով ապատան[21];
Ջէ[22] Լ (7) օբ ճանգեաա ա(ստուա)ծ. սա եղեւ ճանգեիսա ա օԹեան[23].
ԹԷպետա մեզբն յաղԹեաց կեեագ. սա[24] բաբիսբ յաղԹեաց մաչըան;
Եղբա եեա ընգ եմա[25]. փոբստական եբկեացն օբ եղաս;
Ի յամօԹ չեբմուածոբգացն. որ անմաս մնաբլոյն չ.աատան;
Ցեա փոբեէլոյն Ներովբայ. եբկեբիբ անճիբզ[26] ճաանզկան.
Ի շեսաան Աչեբման[27] եղաս. Ճզեբին[28] ված անմասէուբան;
Ի ձայբ Ճզեռու(Թ)(ան) չեբին. այլ ԻՋին եւ ագուկպգան.
Անկան ընգ զասեբս[29] մաբգկան վավաշոուՈ(թ)(ամ)ր շբՋեան;
Եբեեբ էբ սպանանեաց. եւ չՀաաց ոք աղբբական.
Ի (20) այբ ընգ մի կին շբայբ[30]. եւ շլբեեբ շեգեգ սեբբնան;
Այլ ծնանեբ բաբջբ[31] ճատավ. չեգճնզբ ճայն ի օբ ծնընգնան[32].
Լբեեբին չբեկաց ապապբ. Խ (40) կանկան եբբեայն;
Գբեաչուեշբ ա(ստուա)ծամաբսբ. մաբգակեբբ ա աեծնոաիբկ[33] գագան.

Զինաց [1] սուրբ եւ ոչ արդար. բայց մխայն Նոյ ազնուական.
Մանթուսապա պարգամիտա էր. անիշէ եւ աներեւական.
Սայ [2] է որ զՂամէ.ր ծնաւ [3], Ղամէ.ր զՆոյ թռայն արբունական.
Նոյ՛ էր կատարեալ արդար. քան զնախինչն իւր ազգն ամ(էնայն).
Են (500) ամաք եւ սա. ձգնաղղեաց մէրպ կասու(թե)ամբ.
Ի լերին ա՛ եւ յանապատա, ի մարմնի վարք շրեշտակական.
Հասնչայ եղեւ ա(ստուծոյ). քան զրոլոր որդիս Աղամեան.
ԻՆղ Նոյ խոսեցաւ ա(ստուա)ծ. եւ ասաց թէ դործէ. սապան.
Կին արա ե [6] որդի սապէր. Նոր երկիր պատճա ծռչղեան [7].
Ծնաւ [3] Նոյ երեք որդիս. զՍեմ զՔամ զՅեԼեթ սերական.
Աբին եւ նոքա կանայս. բայց եւ Քամ ազգէն Կանենան [9].
Աշխէս բարեգործ էր Նոյ. զի Ջ-Ճ 600 ամն ի լրման [10].
Երեք ութսուն [10] մխայն ծնաւ [3]. զի դարչէ.ր ի խատանախս ԹՎ(ա)ն.
Երեք Ճ (100) կանկան երկայն. Ծ (50) լայն գործեաց Նոյ [11] սապան.
Եւ Լ (30) բարձրութիւն. փայտ անփուտ իւրչ հատատական.
Հշէչէս ի գործոյն չիսասաց. յամէն ակամճ մեծասախ.
ԻՆե պատուրատ լերամբ մարգերկ. Քրշեղեղ [12] յասեալ կան եւ զան [13].
Ասե մեր ա(ստուա)ծ րՆղ Նոյ. ցնախասայրն իմ ազնուական.
Մաստ զու եւ որդիերդ քո. եւ կինք [14] չարասնքե ամէնայն.
Մանեալ ի սապանն ամողղ [15]. սբբու(թե)ամբ է այս չրաման [16].
Յեղանեն ապակես չոսաց. այլ բնդ կին խաջղն կոչիցայն.
Յանասնոց սրբոց [17] Է (7). ե ի խասնջղա Նոյն Թվական [17],
Ընդ քեզ ի սապանն առցես. յանարբոցս [19] Բ (2) բաւական.
Ջանասբբաբն [20] առս ասաց. զի մեր է յասուռ զխասան.
Զի մի զաղբաբն եներցեն. մի եներ լիցին մարդրկան.
Յորժամ կատարեալ եղեւ. սապանն չնասածրն ամ(էնայն).
Գ,ոլթս եւ կարասնեԹով [21]. արտաքա [22] եւ Նեբքարն ծեճիցեան.
Կաս ան ի կողմանեն [23] Թողեալ. զիւրաբանում սենից գգայական.
ԻՆզ մարութ [24] ի մխեասատն. կերակուբ եւ պեաք [25] կանագայ.
Վերատացուն եւ մխեասատուն Նեբբիստուն յոդ իւրչշբբրական.
Վերատատուն երեսից Նման [26]. ասմարսինաց զորաց բնակբրան.
Միջնատուն եղեմ զբիստն, արդարադ զսատաց կայսսան.
Նեբբստատուն երեսս Նման [26]. որ անս(ուր)թք եւ ս(ուր)թք օրանան [27].
Յետ պյարբ ի [28] սապանէն. չոտ անսւչ խնկոց [29] բուբեզան,
Գ (3) [30] զիմեցէն առ Նոյ. մարբեր չարջ զգջ ոչ յխնացան [31].
Երեք զոր եւ մեր ասաց. եւ կատարեցաւ չրասան [32].
Փակեզ [33] ա(է)բ ա(ստուա)ծ զզևան [34] արտաքոյ չնաբեւք պետական [35].
Հինկ Ճ (100) աման էր Նոյ. յորժամ են չրասան զաարբանն [36].
Ի Ջ-Ճ(600)ն աման չեղեն, եւ ութ [37] ապաշխարու(թե)ան.
Բացան յորչ ասչասեչ երկնից, յանդղձնողդ ապեղէ.ք բբելեան [38].
Վերեն եւ Ներքին Քրոյն [39]. յորչատ(խ:)ե չերաբ մխացան.
Քան զլերինս բարձ ակլ [4] ե վեր. Ժե (15) կանկան զեղգեան,
Գրասան մխայն մնաց [2]. ոչ եշա [3] Քուբբն կորբռստան.
Աղղ էր սեստանեզ զազգան, անասնոց զմայ [3] բասստան.
Ի(ա)զլ(ու)նք չզբան [5] առ սապանն. եւ չեղեն զինչ որ կամեզան.
Լայն չայբչ եւ մայբչ որղզեք. եւ լայրնե օշեզս չաշեցան.
Խ (40) տիե եւ Խ (40) զեշեբ [6], ամ(էնայն) չասսաբ [7] Քշէցեան.
Ոչ ադորռական անեժես, այլ յերկնից չեղէ.ղ տոսեզան.
Հեղելան ի գործ մեզաց, չեղեղ(ա)զ Քբբով սուշեզան.
Ծեշեաց ա(է)բ ա(ստուա)ծ զՆոյ. զմո.զբու(Թ)ա[9] եւ զիւբն [10] ամ(էնայն).
Որ ոչ Տոսան [11] երբեք. զծասայա իւր ազեսական [12].
Հբասայեցո չոբմով չոզեցին. աղբիւբք եւ սաչասկ բցեզան,
Ճ-է-ի ԾՋ (156) [13] աւերն յեսաց. զազանմունչք լեբանց բացբւան.